SolidWorks® for AutoCAD® Users

Greg Jankowski

SolidWorks® for AutoCAD® Users

By Greg Jankowski

Published by:
OnWord Press
2530 Camino Entrada
Santa Fe, NM 87505-4835 USA

Carol Leyba, Publisher
David Talbott, Acquisitions Editor
Barbara Kohl, Associate Editor
Daril Bentley, Senior Editor
Jean Cooksey, Development Editor
Cynthia Welch, Production Manager
Michael Button, Production Editor
Beverly Nabours, Production Editor
Liz Bennie, Director of Marketing
Lauri Hogan, Marketing Services Manager
Lynne Egensteiner, Cover designer, Illustrator
Michael Kline, Indexer

Copyright © 1998 Greg Jankowski

SAN 694-0269

First Edition, 1998

10 9 8 7 6 5 4 3 2

Printed in the United States of America

Library of Congress Cataloging-in-Publication Data

Jankowski, Greg, 1959–
    Solidworks for AutoCAD users / Greg Jankowski.
        p.   cm.
    Includes index.
    ISBN 1-56690-156-1
    1. Computer graphics. 2. SolidWorks. 3. Engineering models. 4. Computer-aided design.
    5. AutoCAD (Computer file) I. Title.
    T385.J37   1998
    604.2'0285'5369—DC21   98-10871
                                                          CIP

Trademarks

OnWord Press is a trademark of High Mountain Press, Inc. SolidWorks is a registered trademark of SolidWorks Corporation. AutoCAD is a registered trademark of AutoDesk Corporation. Windows, Windows 95, and Windows NT are registered trademarrks of Microsoft Corporation. Other products and services mentioned in this book are either trademarks or registered trademarks of their respective companies. OnWord Press and the author make no claim to these marks.

Warning and Disclaimer

This book is designed to provide information about Solid-Works. Every effort has been made to make this book complete, and as accurate as possible; however, no warranty of fitness is implied.

The information is provided on an "as-is" basis. The author, SolidWorks Corporation, and OnWord Press shall have neither liability nor responsibility to any person or entity with respect to any loss or damages in connection with or arising from the information contained in this book.

About the Author

Greg Jankowski is president of CIMCo, a company that develops training materials for the CAD industry, and that provides application development and consulting. Greg has been a mechanical designer and application engineer within the field of computer-aided design for 15 years, and has experience with SolidWorks, Pro/ENGINEER, and ComputerVision CAD systems. He is also the author of the computer-based training product *Exploring Solid-Works 97Plus*, also distributed by OnWord Press.

Acknowledgments

I would like to express my gratitude for the support shown by my wife, Sandy, and my daughter, Alexis. Without their patience and understanding, this work would not have been possible. I would also like to thank everyone at SolidWorks. They have been very supportive of all of my efforts since SolidWorks 95.

Thanks also go to Jeff Nauman, Roger Killian, Gopal Shenoy, and Mark Gibson for reviewing the text. Finally, my thanks to editors Scott Brassart and Daril Bentley at High Mountain Press.

The editors would especially like to thank Dave Murray of CADimensions, Inc., for technical review and content support throughout the project.

Contents

Introduction

This book was developed to aid users in their transition from a 2D or 3D AutoCAD environment to a 3D solid modeling system. AutoCAD users who have worked in a 3D wireframe environment will find that solid feature-based modeling requires a different mind-set than they are used to. SolidWorks is a native Windows application that takes full advantage of the standards (e.g., user interface, use of right mouse button) and technology (e.g., Object Linking and Embedding) that have made Microsoft Windows and Windows-based products such a success.

Audience, Structure, and Content

This book deals with the processes involved in using the SolidWorks product. It also addresses the problems a 2D CAD user faces when moving to a parametric, solid modeling CAD system. The methodology and ways of thinking used to produce designs change when you move to SolidWorks. You will find yourself focusing more on design intent rather than spending a lot of time and effort on maintaining 2D or 3D geometry throughout a drawing. You may also find that with SolidWorks, more time can be devoted to design work rather than trying to learn the software or carrying out involved commands.

SolidWorks for AutoCAD Users is also meant to guide a new user, or AutoCAD user making a transition, through the phases of implementing SolidWorks. Also covered are topics related to—and issues that arise before, during, and after—the installation of a new CAD system. Many of the chapters in this book include step-by-step processes on how to carry out a SolidWorks command or function. It is an excellent reference guide for anyone who wants to learn the SolidWorks program, or for current users who need a reference source. This book can also be used by those wanting to make an informed and intelligent decision on whether or not SolidWorks is the CAD program for them.

Chapters can be, for the most part, covered in any order for those using this book as a reference guide. However, those individuals attempting to learn the SolidWorks software should work from Chapter 1 and proceed sequentially through the rest of the chapters. The chapters in this book are functionally grouped based on topic and are presented in logical order from first to last.

Chapters get increasingly more involved as you move from one to the next. Therefore, you can make a decision as to "how far" you should continue, based on your needs. The most rudimentary basics of SolidWorks are covered up front so that even the newest of users can start from the beginning and work their way up the scale of difficulty. Chapters contain the following standard sections:

Introduction	Each chapter has an introductory section that discusses the main theme of the chapter, as well as prerequisites, content, and chapter objectives.
Prerequisite	If applicable, chapter introductions contain a prerequisite section that details what you should be familiar with before attempting to read the chapter.
Content	This subheading to introductory sections discusses the main topics covered within the chapter.
Objectives	This subheading to introductory sections discusses the objectives for the chapter topics. These objectives consist of the information, skills, or procedures you should walk away with after reading the chapter.
Summary	Summary sections draw general conclusions about the content of a chapter as a whole, and briefly reinforce chapter objectives.

AutoCAD/ SolidWorks Comparative Discussion

Each chapter contains notes scattered throughout denoting important differences between the philosophy, procedures, and techniques between AutoCAD and SolidWorks. These sections are denoted by the AutoCAD/SolidWorks comparative discussion text icon, shown at left. In many cases, direct comparisons cannot be made due to the inherent differences between the programs. These differences are also pointed out in the text.

Text Conventions and Book Features

The following text conventions are intended to present material in a consistent and readable form. Formatting conventions such as the previously mentioned AutoCAD/SolidWorks comparative discussion icon, the **NOTE** feature described here, lists and tables, and numbered steps—along with the illustrated glossary, appendix, and index—are intended to aid you in finding what you are looking for efficiently.

Names of menus, dialog boxes, commands, and similar items appear with initial capital letters. Where names of such items, in keeping with the software's convention, combine initial capitals and lowercase, quote marks (" ") enclose the name. For example, the "Name feature on creation" field. Colons that appear with names in the software are dropped when such names are referred to in the text. For example, "Line Count:" would appear as Line Count.

File names, Web site names, words used as words, and emphasized terms and phrases appear in italics.

Special notes appear periodically throughout the text that contain information that makes using SolidWorks easier, more efficient, and more productive. An example of these notes follows.

➩ **NOTE:** *When reporting problems to a vendor, customer, or SolidWorks, include a copy of this report file for reference. This can help pinpoint problems.*

Overview and the SolidWorks Interface

Introduction

In this chapter, you will explore the basic look and feel of the SolidWorks user interface and how it compares to AutoCAD. Some of the terminology used in this book will be explained, so that the program will feel more comfortable to you. There are many aspects of the SolidWorks user interface that are similar to AutoCAD, but many that are not. In many cases, it is difficult to unlearn old habits; therefore, the primary focus of this chapter is on helping you establish the correct mindset for working with SolidWorks.

Prerequisite

At this point, it should be safe to assume that you have a good working knowledge of the Windows 95 or Windows NT 4.0 mechanics. If not, it would be to your benefit to run through a Windows tutorial of some sort so that you will feel more comfortable. Also, some familiarity with drafting would help, although this becomes much more important when discussing drawings in an upcoming chapter.

Content

This chapter consists of the following major topics. The "Objectives" section that follows informs you, in general terms, of what you should expect to gain as a result of reading and studying them.

- Starting a SolidWorks editing session
- Opening an existing document
- Types of documents
- Creating a new document
- Saving and closing documents
- The SolidWorks user interface
- Context-sensitive help

Objectives

At the end of this chapter, you should be able to successfully start a new SolidWorks session, save your work, and work with both left and right mouse buttons to select entities and open menus. Many of the terms used by Solid-Works and solid modelers in general will be familiar to you, as will the SolidWorks interface. You should also have a good feel for what the SolidWorks program in general is meant to accomplish, and how it can make the engineer's or designer's desktop a friendlier place from which to work.

Starting a SolidWorks Editing Session

If you own a copy of SolidWorks, you will be able to follow along with the examples presented in this chapter and elsewhere. If not, the screen shots included in this book will help you along for the time being. Those of you who can follow along, can go ahead and fire up the Solid-Works program by double clicking on the appropriate icon. Before you explore the SolidWorks interface in depth, a note on "Tip of the Day."

Tip of the Day

This is a new feature, incorporated into SolidWorks 97Plus. It does not require much explanation. This is a feature that displays a tip that may be beneficial to new users. It can be turned off by unchecking the "Show tips at startup" option, located in the Tip of the Day dialog box.. If you do turn off tool tips, you can turn it back on later by clicking on the Help pull-down menu and selecting Tip of the Day.

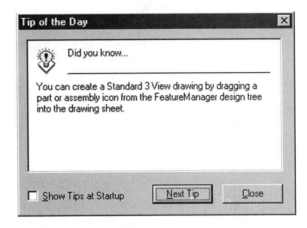

*The Tip of the Day
dialog box.*

Windows Standardization

There is a certain amount of standardization that many Windows programs possess. SolidWorks is no exception to this. For example, the pull-down menu structure follows a basic pattern, with File being the first menu selection, and Help being the last. This is no different from AutoCAD, and the options contained within some of the menus are also similar.

Take, for example, the File pull-down menu. There are the standard options File/New and File/Open, to name just a couple. Before a new file is actually started, or before an existing file is opened, you will notice that the pull-down menus are greatly simplified. This follows a common theme that SolidWorks uses to full effect. For instance, if a particular command is inaccessible at a particular moment, it may be grayed out in the menu, or not present at all. This makes selecting the appropriate command all that much easier because there is less clutter.

AutoCAD achieves this to some extent, but not nearly to the extent that SolidWorks does. The AutoCAD menu may have options that are grayed out from time to time, but most of the time the menu choices are simply there, and there is nothing stopping the inexperienced user from selecting incorrect or inappropriate commands.

Another good example would be the AutoCAD screen menu. When a command is initiated, the screen menu often updates to show you a number of related options for that command. Once the command is completed, the screen menu remains, even if the options for the completed command are no longer valid. Of course, the reasoning behind this is that if you want to repeat the command, it is easily accessed. However, this is not really necessary, considering a command can be repeated by clicking the right mouse button anyway (to name one option).

A word or two should be said about the standard toolbar icons at this point. Once again, many native Windows programs have adopted a standard set of icons for such basic tasks as saving or opening files. SolidWorks is no exception. Specifically, the first three icons on the toolbar are counterparts to the pull-down menu commands File/ New, File/Open, and File/Save, respectively. Whether you use the pull-down menus or the icons is up to you. Generally speaking, it is better to get familiar with the pull-downs first. If you later want to start using the icons, go ahead; they will usually save you at least one mouse click.

A SolidWorks Overview

Before moving to an in-depth discussion of the mechanics of the SolidWorks program, it is important to understand the philosophy behind the software and what its programmers are striving to achieve. If SolidWorks could be summed up in one phrase, it would best be described as a *feature based, parametric, solid modeling design tool.* Parse this statement one segment at a time and you will better understand the nature of the SolidWorks program. The following sections explain the ideas contained in the phrase.

Feature based

This is a term used to describe the elements that constitute a part. Just as an assembly consists of individual parts, a part consists of individual features. There are two types of SolidWorks features: sketched features and applied features. The differences between them are as follows.

Sketched features: These are based on 2D sketch geometry. Creating a sketch is covered at length in this book. It is the basis of much that is done in the SolidWorks program, and therefore requires some elaboration. Certain steps should be followed when creating sketch geometry, but once those steps are understood, most everything else will begin to fall in place. Sketched features can be extrusions, rotations, sweeps, or lofts.

Applied features: Features that are applied do not require a sketch. They are applied directly to a model. Examples of this type of feature are chamfers, fillets, and shells, to name a few.

Parametric

With respect to dimensions, the term *parametric* refers to the ability to make changes to dimensions and drive the shape of a part with those changes. In AutoCAD, changing a dimension would result in breaking the associativity with the model. Anything other than the default value for the dimension would keep the dimension from updating if the model were scaled or stretched. In SolidWorks, changing the dimension changes the part. That is what parametrics is all about.

Solid model

There are 2D drawings, there are wireframe models, there are surface models, and there are solid models. Solid modeling packages are the most complete, but are also the most system intensive. This is why when an upgrade to a solid modeling program is made from a 2D drafting tool, the hardware must also usually get upgraded (because the system requirements are more demanding). It is the nature of the beast, and not the program itself, that requires the upgrades to the hardware.

The downstream benefits are very much worth the investment in almost all cases. Surface modeling can be very system intensive also, but is better suited to a different range of disciplines than solid modelers. For instance, mechanical elements are better suited to solid modelers. Anything from minuscule springs and gears to tractor trailers can be easily modeled in SolidWorks, but organic shapes such as the dinosaurs in the Jurassic Park movie would be better suited to surface modelers.

To be fair, surface modelers can be much more demanding than solid modelers in such a situation, because real-time animation of organic shapes with natural textures applied to them is far beyond the scope of any solid modeler. For applications such as that, high-powered multi-processor computers are run in parallel in order to achieve the high degree of computations involved. The number of processors involved are in the hundreds, and the necessary memory is measured in gigabytes.

Opening an Existing Document

An existing document can be opened by clicking on File/ Open. This will give you a familiar-looking dialog box, shown in the following illustration, that will allow you to browse your directories, or "folders" as Windows likes to call them. Navigate to the desired folder by double clicking on the folder, or move out to the parent folder by clicking on the Up One Level icon. If you are not sure what icons are what, hold the cursor over the icon in question, and a yellow pop-up "tip" will appear to tell you what the icon is for. SolidWorks conforms to this standard as well, so the cursor can always be held over an icon if you need to see what the icon's function is.

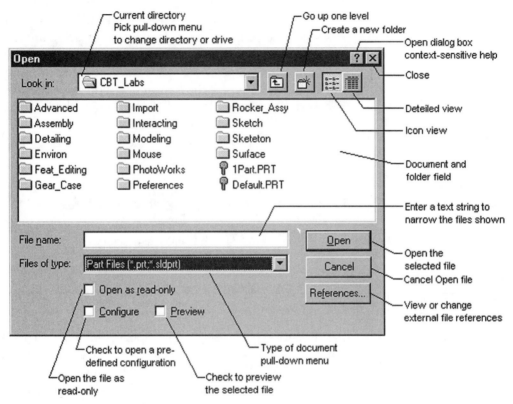

The Open dialog box.

When the File/Open dialog box is first opened, it looks for part files. This is fine if you are looking to open a part file. If you are looking for something else, however, you must tell SolidWorks what type of file you are looking for. Hence, the "Files of type" section of this dialog box. Notice that SolidWorks is looking for files with a .prt or .sldprt extension. These are the extensions for SolidWorks part files. Changing "Files of type" allows you to open assemblies or drawings, or to import other file types. Note that extensions were modified in SolidWorks 97Plus to eliminate confusion with other programs. Specifically, Cadkey users were having a problem due to the fact that Cadkey also used a .prt extension for its part files.

Take a look at the following table to see what the actual file extensions are for various SolidWorks file types. What these file types are and what functions they serve are discussed later in this chapter. Pay attention to the first three, as Library Feature parts are not considered one of Solid-Works' main file types; they are really more of a function of a part file. This is expanded on later in the chapter. Also, you will see other file types not listed in this chart. These are file types SolidWorks can translate into its program. These are covered in Chapter 11.

Document Type	SolidWorks 95-97 Extensions	SolidWorks 97Plus Extensions
Part	<filename>.prt	<filename>.sldprt
Assembly	<filename>.asm	<filename>.sldasm
Drawing	<filename>.drw	<filename>.slddrw
Library Feature Part	<filename>.lfp	<filename>.sldlfp

Use "Files of type" to browse for specific file types. This is how you would open an assembly or drawing. However, an in-depth explanation of these file types is given in Chapter 11. What is important at present is a general knowledge of the purpose they serve.

The following illustration shows the Windows Explorer. A SolidWorks document can be opened by double clicking on the desired icon.

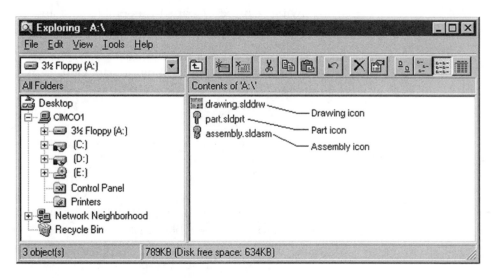

Windows Explorer.

Types of Documents

The following sections explain the three major types of SolidWorks documents (file types). These are part, drawing, and assembly documents.

Part Documents

As touched on in previous paragraphs, SolidWorks has multiple file types. AutoCAD uses a .dwg extension whether you are creating a 2D engineering layout, an assembly, or a solid model. SolidWorks has a separate file format for each of these. A part file is a collection of features (see Chapter 1) that are added to shape a model. Normally, this is the first file created. More than one solid model cannot coexist in the same part file.

Drawing Documents

After a part is created, typically an engineering layout is generated. This generally consists of top, front, and right-side views. It may also consist of section or detailed views, notes and dimensions, a bill of materials, and other items generally found in a typical drawing layout. Drawings can be of one or more parts and can contain multiple sheets, which are the paper pages used for each drawing.

Drawings can be of parts or assemblies, in any combination.

A drawing sheet is a function that allows for the creation of a drawing containing multiple drawing formats. Each drawing format resides on a different sheet.

Assembly Documents

Assemblies are, in their most basic form, collections of part files. An assembly can consist of two parts or two hundred parts. Actually, an assembly can consist of just one part, but that sort of defeats the purpose. An assembly can also contain other assemblies, which are generally considered subassemblies in that type of situation. It is possible to have assemblies that contain other assemblies, which in themselves contain assemblies, and on and on. The only limiting factor on the size of an assembly (or a part, for that matter) is the physical hardware in your computer, such as the amount of hard drive space and the amount of memory.

With that aside, there are some other important things you should know. A common annoyance to AutoCAD users is the fact that only one document can be opened at a time. This continues to be the case with AutoCAD release 14. In order to open up two documents at once, you must actually open up two AutoCAD editing sessions. This obviously is a greater drain on system resources. This is not the case with SolidWorks. It is possible to open up multiple parts, drawings, and assemblies—all within the same session and in any combination.

All documents related to a design task can be opened at the same time. When changes are made, the related documents can be activated to view the changes immediately. Multiple windows also allow you to cut, paste, drag, and drop objects from one window to another.

Another important topic is the term *bidirectional associativity*. This is an impressive term to describe a basic principle, which is: the three basic SolidWorks file types (parts, drawings, and assemblies) are dependent on one another. For example, say you have just finished creating your latest solid part, the infamous widget. It is then time to create your layout, which is literally a drag-and-drop operation, which will be explored later.

The head honcho on the dreaded widget project decides some serious design changes need to be made. Therefore, you open the part file and make the changes. Now what happens to the drawing? SolidWorks takes care of it, because the very next time you open up the layout (probably appropriately named widget.drw), SolidWorks automatically updates the drawing to match the part. Any dimensions will change to match the true values, views will get updated to reflect design changes made to the part, and features that have been removed or added will show up correctly.

Now say that Mr. Honcho is looking over your shoulder as this is going on. He decides that maybe the dimension changes to the overall length of the widget should not have been altered so drastically, and he recommends a change. You alter the dimension on the drawing, and the part automatically updates to reflect the change. Furthermore, if said widget is being used in an assembly, the assembly will update the first time you open it. And again, the assembly can be edited and the change will reflect back to the part. This is where the "bidirectional" of the term *bidirectional associativity* originates.

What does all of this mean? Well, it will cut down on your editing time, because it is all being done for you. That much is obvious, but this topic raises some other issues. For instance, maybe you do not want the assembly to update because an earlier revision of the widget is being used in it, and the changes being made to the new widget are only going to affect future assemblies. If the new assembly used a different version of widget, the file used in the assembly could be easily changed by selecting the assembly component using FeatureManager. You would press the right mouse button, and select Component

Properties. The referenced part file can be changed by selecting Browse in the Model Document Path field and selecting the new widget version.

Creating a New Document

This is where a new SolidWorks document is born. You are almost ready to start some serious solid modeling. However, there are a few things to get out of the way first. There are two ways to start a new SolidWorks document: click on the appropriate icon or use the pull-down menus. You should be noticing a common theme here (toolbars or pull-downs); therefore, icons will from now on be mentioned less and less, except to tell you what they look like. Use of icons is up to you.

Getting back to the process of creating a new document, the New icon looks like a white sheet of paper with it's top right corner folded over. This, once again, adheres to the Windows convention. Clicking on File/New will accomplish the same thing, which is to open the New dialog box. The following illustration shows what the New dialog box looks like.

The New dialog box.

As you can see, it is possible to start any one of the three document types from this point, whether it be part, drawing, or assembly. As is typical of working in SolidWorks, your choice will be the Part option, followed by clicking on OK. This option is typical because drawings are normally generated from parts, and assemblies consist of parts. Therefore, a part is normally the first document you would create on a typical project. This would not matter in AutoCAD, or at least not to the same extent. The closest analogy would probably be to create a solid (or wireframe) in tiled model space, then create your layout in paper space. Again, however, in AutoCAD's case, this would all be done in the same file.

As soon as the new or existing file is opened, the first thing you notice is the addition of some new toolbars and that the pull-down menus increase in number. This goes along with SolidWorks' idea that fewer choices make the program easier to learn and use.

Some would argue that "ease of use" would translate to "not as powerful" or "less functionality." This is not necessarily the case. SolidWorks' use of the Parasolids kernel combined with Windows programming techniques and in-depth use of functions such as object linking and embedding (OLE) makes for a feature-rich and well-rounded software package. In the case of SolidWorks, "ease of use" translates directly to "getting the job done." Getting started building a solid model is discussed in an upcoming section, but first, you need to know how to save that solid model.

Saving and Closing Documents

It really does not matter if you save your model right now, before anything has really been created, or if you save it in five minutes, or ten. What does matter is that you save your work on a regular basis. For those of you who have been working computers for some time, you realize this. However, it is surprising how often even a seasoned veteran forgets to save. *The point is to save your work, and save it often.* To save your work, perform the following steps:

1. Click on the File pull-down menu.

2. Click on Save.

Use the icon that looks like the floppy disk, if you want. It does the exact same thing. The first time a file is saved, the Save As dialog box appears. This is because the file has not been named yet.

When you first save a file in SolidWorks, and accept the file name it assigns on its own, the name of the file (assume a part file here) will be Part1.sldprt. If you started another new part and saved it, it would be Part2.sldprt, and so on. The next time you start a SolidWorks session, meaning when you next start the SolidWorks program, the naming convention starts all over again. This means that if you do not give the file a new name, it gets saved as Part1.sldprt again, and you will be prompted to see if you really want to overwrite the file of the same name left on your hard drive during the previous session.

This is no big deal. Normally, you would go ahead and type in a unique name for the file anyway, just like you would in any program. What is convenient about this is that if you are doing some experimenting and saving your work, but do not really care about permanently saving the file, you do not have to type in a file name. This also cuts down on clutter, because, for example, half a dozen files titled Part1, Part2, Part3, and so on simply keep getting overwritten. If at some point you decide you want to keep one of these generically named part files, just use the Save As option.

Saving Documents with Save As

You will find the Save As option under the File pull-down menu. It is a very simple procedure. After clicking on File/Save As, a dialog box opens that lets you name your current file with a new name or location. This is no different than any other software program, including AutoCAD. What actually happens is that the file you were working on is saved to the hard drive under its original name, and the newly named file becomes the file you are currently editing.

Saving Documents with Save As/Save As Copy Toggle

This is identical to Save As, with one minor difference. When you check the Save As Copy check box, the newly named file is the one that gets saved to the hard drive, not your current file. In other words, your current file remains your current file, and the copy goes to the hard drive.

Closing Documents

Now that you have learned how to save, it is time to learn how to shut down and pack it in for the day. Closing your documents is as easy as clicking on File/Close. Whatever document is active will be closed. If you do not save it first, SolidWorks will ask you if you want to save it before it shuts the file down. The following illustration shows the SolidWorks prompt when closing a document with unfiled changes.

Result of the File/Close command.

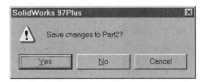

Keep in mind that the program will not ask you if you have already saved a file. Occasionally, a new user will shut down a file and think to themselves that they forgot to save their work. Have no fear. One of two things happened. Either no changes were made to the file, in which case there is nothing to save, or the work was indeed saved. It is actually difficult to lose your work. You have to try pretty hard. Rest assured that as long as you are reading the warnings SolidWorks is giving you on the screen, your hard work is successfully saved on the hard drive.

Exit Windows shortcut.

Exiting out of the program will give you the same warnings if you have not saved your documents. It does not matter if you have opened and edited two dozen documents, you will get prompted for each of them. To exit out of SolidWorks, either click on the "X" button to the right of the title bar or use the pull-down menus and click on File/Exit. The illustration at left shows the Exit Windows shortcut.

The SolidWorks User Interface

Most of the SolidWorks interface should be Windows components somewhat familiar to you—at least from a terminology standpoint, if not in practice. For instance, there are the toolbars, whose icons you will get more accustomed to as time goes by. Likewise, there are the pull-down menus, which are referred to throughout this book. There is also the title bar, which resides at the top of every Windows application, whether it be Windows 95, Windows NT, or even Windows 3.1. However, there are other components of the SolidWorks interface that are more alien. These elements are discussed in the upcoming sections.

If you are sitting in front of a computer and have Solid-Works running, open a new part file using the methods described earlier in this chapter. If not, refer to the following illustration, which shows a new part file.

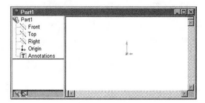

New part file.

FeatureManager

What is displayed along the left-hand side of the screen is known as the SolidWorks FeatureManager. This is a trade-marked name, and as its name implies, allows you to track and manage the creation of features. The features are displayed chronologically from top to bottom. FeatureManager requires elaboration because AutoCAD does not have a counterpart to a SolidWorks feature. A feature can be thought of as a component to a part. It might be what is known as a boss, such as when material is being added to a part, or it might be a cut, when material is being removed from the part. As features are being added, the part is built up and gains complexity until the final model is complete.

SolidWorks features contain intelligence. This does not mean that a feature can beat you at a game of chess. It means that the part file database contains information that makes the feature more than just a set of spatial coordinates connected by lines and arcs. A solid model contains much more information in its database than a wireframe model does. There is the parametric aspect of the model, along with topologic information.

Boolean Versus Parametric Modelers

Another important difference should be drawn between Boolean modelers such as AutoCAD and parametric modelers such as SolidWorks. Consider what you would have to go through in order to create a simple rectangular block with a hole in it in AutoCAD. First you would create a rectangle of the proper size. Then you would have to turn the rectangle into a region, which is a prerequisite to turning AutoCAD profiles into a solid. The region could then be extruded into a solid object. The alternative would be to create a solid by specifying the appropriate primitive command, which would allow you to create basic solid building blocks.

Once the block had been created, you would then use approximately the same process to create a cylinder. The easiest method would be to create a cylindrical primitive, located in the correct position relative to the block. If it were not already properly located, that task would also have to be completed. This scenario might exist because it is sometimes more simple to create an object off to the side and then move it to the proper location.

Once the location is right, a Boolean operation must be performed. A Boolean operation can be thought of as a logical operation between solids, at least in solid modeling terms. This might be adding two solids together, such as a union, or subtracting one or more solids from an existing solid. It might also mean the intersection of two solids to form a separate solid piece of geometry, such as an interference section.

Assume for a minute that the block has now been built and has the hole cut out of it. In other words, the cylinder has been subtracted from the block. If the hole is in the wrong spot, what do you do? This goes to the heart of the matter. First, you would have to create another solid to fill the hole. Then you would have to recreate another cylinder of the correct size in the new location. Last, you would perform another Boolean operation. Just hope that the hole is in the right spot this time. Needless to say, this greatly impedes the design process.

The SolidWorks Alternative to Boolean Operations

Now look at this operation from a SolidWorks standpoint. It starts out much the same way, by creating a rectangle. Instead of worrying about accuracy, however, the rectangle is "sketched," and then dimensions are added that drive the shape of the rectangle. It is like adding dimensions in AutoCAD, only easier, and the dimensions literally control the shape of the sketch. This is what the term *parametric* means. AutoCAD's dimensions will change if certain editing tasks are performed, such as stretching or scaling a model, but that is as good as it gets. With a parametric modeler such as SolidWorks, you can change a model by modifying its dimensions.

Next, the rectangle is extruded, much the same way you would in AutoCAD. Specify an extrusion height and you are done with the block. Now, sketch a circle, dimension it, and cut it through the part. The ability to "cut" the circle through the part reduces the two steps performed in AutoCAD to one in SolidWorks because there are no Boolean operations.

This reduces the design process in itself, but it is only the beginning. Where the real fun starts is when a design change needs to be accomplished. Take, for example, the task of moving the hole in the block. In SolidWorks, the dimensions placed on the hole can be edited to move the hole. (The mechanics are explored later, but the process is basically nothing more than a dimension change and a click on the Rebuild icon, with the part editing then completed.)

Graphics Window

To the right of FeatureManager, and taking up most of the screen, is the area in which you will see most of your work come together. If you are used to AutoCAD's typical black background, try to adjust to the white background of SolidWorks. It is possible to change it to black (or pink, for that matter), but it is not recommended.

Consider this: in AutoCAD, most of what you are probably used to creating are 2D layouts. Light lines show up nicely on a black background. AutoCAD's wireframe representations of its solid models normally take this form. However, in SolidWorks, you will be creating solid models that can be dynamically rotated in shaded mode; therefore, you do not need that black background.

There are other technical reasons you will not want to alter the white background, which have to do with the way certain entity types are displayed and the color cues SolidWorks gives you. Give it a chance, and you will probably grow to like it.

Between FeatureManager and the graphics window is a vertical bar that acts as a separator. This vertical bar can be adjusted. If the cursor is moved over this bar, it will change into a double arrow shape that allows the vertical bar to be adjusted. This allows you to either move the bar to the right, which lets you see all of the names in FeatureManager, or to the left to increase the size of the sketch area.

Origin Point

In AutoCAD, there is the User Coordinate System, or UCS. SolidWorks has the Origin Point. They are used very differently. Gone are the days when the UCS is always down there in the left-hand corner. The origin point (referred to hereafter as the "origin") still represents your x-y axis, and it still relates to 0,0 Cartesian coordinates, but that is where the similarity ends. The origin is never moved (as the UCS was) in order to specify planes that will be worked on. In SolidWorks, a plane or planar face is selected, and then the sketch is started.

Another important aspect of the origin is that it acts as an anchor. In other words, a sketch can be anchored to the origin so that it will not float around in space. Think of the origin as a clamp used to hold a sketch in place so it can be worked on. Whenever a new sketch is started, another origin is created for that sketch. In contrast, there is never more than one UCS. When a part is first begun, the origin will appear gray in the sketch area, as shown in the illustration at left.

Once a sketch is begun, the origin appears red to let you know that you are in an active sketch. It also helps to orient your perspective with regard to where the x and y axes are, as well as the positioning of the current sketch plane. The UCS in AutoCAD behaves much the same way when it appears at different angles on the screen. (More on origins is discussed in Chapter 5.)

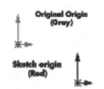

Sketch area showing origin in gray.

Pull-down Menus – A Quick Comparison

If you are used to using the DOS version of AutoCAD, you will be accustomed to the pull-down menus remembering the last command selected in that particular menu. AutoCAD is among a few programs that offers this function. Windows programs do not work that way, including SolidWorks.

Customizing SolidWorks pull-down menus cannot be done as easily as editing a text file, as is possible in AutoCAD. Third-party programmers that integrate their menus directly into the SolidWorks menu are usually known as Gold Solution partners by SolidWorks Corporation. There are many of these Gold Solution partners that have brought higher and specialized functionality to the SolidWorks program by seamlessly integrating their software directly into SolidWorks, almost as if it were part of the same program.

These third-party programs range from CAD/CAM tool path software, to photorendering (for example, Photo-

Works, shown in the following illustration), to Finite Element Analysis (see FEM in the following illustration), to many others. In fact, SolidWorks is likely to rival AutoCAD in the sheer number of third-party developers creating software for the SolidWorks program. The number is already quite high.

Whether you are working on a part, drawing, or assembly, the titles of the pull-down menus will not change. However, what is underneath the menus will change, depending on what document type is being currently worked on. This is referred to as a context-sensitive command and menu structure. If all three document types are open at the same time, it depends on which document is active at the time that determines what the pull-down menus will contain. For example, the Insert pull-down menu will allow you to insert features if editing a part, but will allow you to insert only mating relationships if working on an assembly.

Toolbars

AutoCAD release 13 had over 50 toolbars. You would never want to have them all open at once, or it would be unmanageable. SolidWorks has a total of 12 toolbars. They can be turned on by clicking on View/Toolbars… and checking the appropriate check box, which is shown in the following illustration.

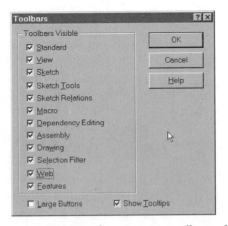

Result of the View/
Toolbars... command.

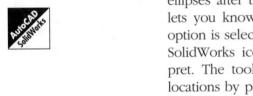

Typically, you will have four to six toolbars displayed at any given time. Incidentally, you may have noticed the ellipses after the word *Toolbars* in the View menu. This lets you know that a dialog box will be opened if this option is selected, which follows suit with AutoCAD. The SolidWorks icons are straightforward and easy to interpret. The toolbars can be dragged to different floating locations by placing the cursor over the edge of the toolbar and dragging it while holding down the left mouse button, which is the same functionality as AutoCAD. They can also be docked to various sides of the screen, as in AutoCAD. This is standard Windows functionality. Most Windows programs that implement toolbars operate the same way.

Toolbars are also context sensitive. By leaving only standard, sketch and view toolbars checked, the other major toolbars (Sketch tools, Features, Drawings, and Assemblies) will appear when the appropriate document type is activated. The default state of the toolbars is determined by the toolbars active at the end of the last SolidWorks session.

SolidWorks toolbars also have small yellow tool tips that pop up if the cursor is placed over them. To try this, hold the mouse cursor over an icon without moving or clicking the mouse. After a second, the box will appear. A more lengthy description usually appears in the status bar at the bottom left-hand corner of the screen. This may vary slightly, depending on the version of Windows being used, but the implementation is always the same.

Toolbars can also be customized, but you will have to try that at your own risk. It is not recommended that you try this at this point. Wait until you are much more comfortable with the program. The following illustrations show the various SolidWorks toolbars. Their functions are discussed through the course of this book.

Macro toolbar.

Standard toolbar.

Sketch toolbar.

View toolbar.

Sketch Relations toolbar.

Sketch Tools toolbar.

Dependency Editing toolbar.

Web toolbar.

Assembly toolbar.

Drawing toolbar.

Selection Filter toolbar.   *Features toolbar.*

Status Bar – A Quick Comparison

The AutoCAD status bar has a couple of functions (at least in release 13), but mostly it is there to display information. Granted, one could use it to toggle some user preferences, but those functions could be easily accessed by other means. The status bar is really just that: a bar to display the status of one function or another that might be going on at any one time.

SolidWorks does not make much use of the status bar. It displays things such as the current x-y coordinates of the cursor during the sketch process (like AutoCAD), whether or not the current sketch is fully defined, and other tidbits of information. The status bar also displays a more complete description of the tooltips. If you would like to turn it off, click on View/Status Bar. It is a toggle switch, so this method can also be used to turn the status bar back on.

Context-sensitive Help

If you have used Windows help before, you know how to use SolidWorks help. If the Help menu is accessed, there is an option for SolidWorks 97Plus Help Topics. This will open the dialog box shown in the following illustration.

The Help Topics dialog box.

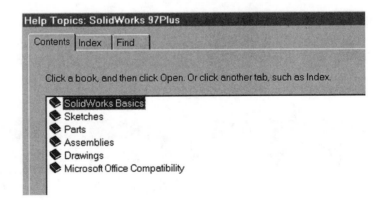

Help is there for a reason. Use it if you need it. It contains step-by-step examples of how to carry out specific functions. Accessing context-sensitive help in AutoCAD is easy, because all one has to do is punch the F1 function key (or F2, depending on the version) during a command and the help dialog box for that command pops up on the screen. This is what is meant by the term *context sensitive*. Depending on what is being done at any given time determines what is displayed on the help menu.

SolidWorks Help Functionality

SolidWorks performs the same function, but in a slightly different manner. If you find yourself in need of assistance during a SolidWorks command, click on the help button on whatever dialog box happens to be open at the time. This will bring up a step-by-step explanation of how to carry out the command in question, along with the options available.

SolidWorks makes very good use of dialog boxes. Unlike AutoCAD, there are no commands to type in at the command line, or C prompt. Everything is a user-friendly dialog box and visually interactive. There are not half a dozen command line options you have to know in order to complete a simple command, and most commands are laid out logically and intuitively.

Also, in contrast the AutoCAD, commands in SolidWorks do not vary depending on the approach to entering a command. This is because in SolidWorks there are logical courses of action you must follow in order to implement the commands, as opposed to many ways in which to complete any one task.

About SolidWorks 97Plus

This is actually a menu pick that resides under the Help menu. It gets mention here because it allows you to determine the date code of the SolidWorks version being run. The year is stated first, followed by the numerical day of the year. This can be helpful for technical support reasons. SolidWorks Corporation currently provides updates to maintenance subscribers on the Internet so that they can receive enhancements and patches to the software. It also allows for accurate tracking of software glitches that may arise. The following illustration shows the 97Plus menu pick.

SolidWorks 97Plus menu pick in the Help menu.

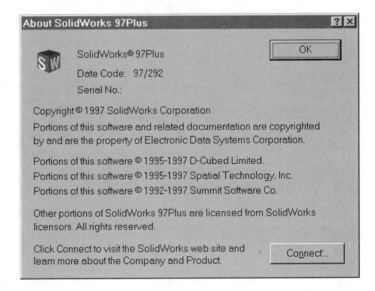

The same dialog box contains a button for connecting to the SolidWorks web site. Clicking on the button will attempt to connect to the SolidWorks web site automatically. However, there are too many configurations possible to guess how this will react on your machine. Clicking on Connect… certainly will not hurt anything, but if you do not have a modem, do not expect miracles.

Summary

As similar as AutoCAD and SolidWorks seem in some respects, they are fundamentally different. There is a different mind set involved in creating parametric solid models. Think in terms of adding features when using SolidWorks. A feature can be a sketched feature, such as an extrusion or revolved feature, or it may be an applied feature, such as a fillet or chamfer. But they are always features, and they are always being added, as opposed to carving pieces of material from a block of wood. Because of this parametric feature geometry, elements in the model can be easily edited and manipulated. Many documents can be opened at one time, which might be parts, assemblies, or drawings, in any combination.

Chapter 2, Implementation, deals with the requirements needed to physically get the SolidWorks program up and running in your company. The chapter also deals with many of the hardware questions you might have. If there is a system administrator in your company that takes care of such things, he or she may want to read this. Chapter 3 discusses more about actually using the program, including navigation and selection techniques, and how to begin creating your first solid model.

Implementation

Introduction

This chapter discusses issues that arise when implementing a new CAD system. It reviews the concepts behind planning, preparation, training, and management issues you need to address to ensure the maximum return on investment for a new SolidWorks installation. A good understanding of implementation issues will facilitate a smoother transition and help ensure the success of a new system. Two important objectives during the implementation phase are to minimize the time required to become effective with SolidWorks and to develop those skills that will allow you to reduce time to market and produce better-quality designs.

Developing an implementation plan can provide a company with a clear idea of how the system will be installed, how the transition process will be handled, how existing legacy data will be handled, and what hardware is required for the new system. An implementation plan describes the issues a new SolidWorks installation should address. The term *legacy data* refers to existing documents from older software programs. "Legacy" may also refer to hardware that is obsolete, or that is being replaced by new and improved technology.

Prerequisite You should know how to open files in SolidWorks, so that existing AutoCAD or other files can be brought into the program (see "Opening an Existing Document" in Chapter 1). This chapter deals with networking and hardware issues as well; therefore, a basic understanding of these topics is required.

Content This chapter contains the following major topics:

- Implementation plan
- Training plan
- Translating legacy data
- Hardware considerations
- Determining a reasonable pilot project

Two key sections in this chapter concern legacy data and hardware considerations. The section on legacy data describes methods for handling the legacy data of an existing CAD system. There are a number of approaches that can be applied. This section describes these options so that you can make informed decisions concerning legacy data. This section also explores techniques that make the reuse of legacy data possible. The "Hardware Considerations" section reviews the items that need to be considered when purchasing a system capable of efficiently running SolidWorks.

Objectives With the completion of the section that discusses an implementation plan, you should be able to successfully implement SolidWorks on a project level. When you have finished the section on maintaining and reusing legacy data, you should understand the options available to handle existing CAD data, be able to arrive at an informed opinion as to how the existing data will be handled, and understand how existing 2D legacy data can be used to produce 3D models. You will also understand the requirements for a SolidWorks computer system and how these requirements can affect the productivity and performance of your system. The possibility of a pilot project will be presented to you, including whether or not such a project would be feasible for your company.

Implementation Plan

When implementing a new CAD system, a plan should be developed to determine the requirements and implementation schedule. Goals of the implementation plan should be a smooth transition from the existing system, development of a method for handling existing legacy data, training of new users, and piloting and full implementation of the new system. The following are issues you should address in an implementation plan.

- Development of a training plan
- How to translate legacy data, if needed
- Upgrading hardware to accommodate new software
- Identification of a pilot project

Training Plan

A training plan should provide complete, consistent training for all users. Providing training for users helps ensure that new concepts associated with a new implementation are understood. Even though SolidWorks is easy to use, training helps to ensure that new concepts and principles are applied correctly and effectively. Additionally, ideal training addresses old habits and methods of operation carried over from a previous CAD system.

Training is most effective just prior to a user's hands-on use of SolidWorks on the job. If the user does not have a chance to use the CAD system immediately after training, thereby reinforcing the learning, much of the material and information will be forgotten. Training should be coordinated with the timetable of employees' use of the software.

Benefits of Training

The following are benefits you should derive from a successful training plan:

- Better-trained users will use available tools more efficiently and effectively than users who are not trained or who are undertrained. Effective training can also help ensure that users understand solid modeling technology and apply it effectively.

- An effective training program produces users who require less internal and external support. This helps reduce the burden on your support personnel, or cost associated with external support.

- Solid modeling systems can provide more complete information more quickly when applied properly. Training provides the knowledge of available tools and how to apply these tools efficiently.

- A user can become frustrated with trying to implement new technology if he or she is still bound by old habits. Attention should be given by the instructor to mold old habits into a pattern of new habits that will better suit the new software.

Elements of Effective Training

Complete, effective training is important to your company's long-term success. Training needs to be viewed as an ongoing process to ensure that available tools and technology are fully applied. Effective training requires a broad, long-term vision. There are several elements that can be combined to provide a comprehensive training solution. Developing a training plan can help identify the tools, personnel, timetable, and budget required to train existing and new users. The following are elements of an effective training plan.

Training Schedule

A schedule for training users should be based on a few criteria. Try to schedule training so that, upon completion, students will be able to go back to the work place and begin using the program. It does no good if Solid-Works is taught, only to have the students go back to the office and not touch the software for two months. As of this writing, a SolidWorks training course is five days long. This includes probably 90 percent of all features and capabilities found in the program.

Tutorials

Computer-based tutorials can be used as a prerequisite for classroom training. Many of the basic SolidWorks skills can be reviewed and practices introduced using this type of training tool. SolidWorks 97Plus (along with previous versions) has included tutorials to get the new user warmed up to the software. CIMCo's *Exploring Solid-Works 97Plus* computer-based training CD-ROM also provides an excellent introduction to training.

Classroom Training

Classroom courses provide valuable interaction with an instructor. Having an instructor well versed in the program and understanding of a new user's common mistakes can greatly increase the level of productivity for students. It is very important that each student have his or her own machine with which to explore the program and to complete exercises.

Management should take responsibility for ensuring that the maximum benefits are derived from classroom training before it happens. Having a chance to get oriented within SolidWorks before instruction, using the tutorial included with SolidWorks or using computer-based training tools or books, can help ensure that the user has a general idea of the principles and terms used during the class.

Consulting

Consulting can be used to show a customer how to apply new technology to specific needs, and how to develop implementation and training plans. A customer can also be assisted in an actual project. Use case studies and customer references that are fact and figure based (i.e., time to market savings, cost reduction, measurable quality improvement, and so on).

Mentoring

Customer use of internal one-on-one mentoring can be an effective training mechanism. These internal resources understand the company's application and help reduce external support requirements. Power or super users of a technology exist within every organization, and a company can benefit by recognizing and encouraging the effective use of this type of user for training and support. Medium to large sized companies may want to employ one user that is very well versed with the software and can answer questions the other employees might have.

Internet Support

Using a company intranet is a very effective mechanism for providing and disseminating useful information. The Internet, or World Wide Web, is another excellent way to keep up with changes or obtain information and tips on how to use software. Discussion groups and user groups can provide an outstanding source of knowledge and diverse ways of doing things.

Translating Legacy Data

One question that arises when a new CAD system is installed is what should be done with existing (legacy) CAD data. The ability to effectively handle existing CAD data can be a key factor in determining the success of a new system. It is rarely practical to take all existing drawings and designs and immediately turn them into solid models and assemblies. The ability to integrate existing data cooperatively with a new system and to reuse existing data can help minimize the impact of the new system and maximize the utility of existing information in producing new designs.

SolidWorks offers features that provide an alternative to redrawing or converting legacy data by allowing the import of existing 2D or 3D geometry. The actual techniques involved will be covered in future chapters. If you have a project that needs to get done right away, turn to Chapter 11 for specific instructions on importing files.

Strategy Determined by Application

Address the issue of legacy data management early to determine the strategy that should be used for your application. The various methods used will be determined by the existing CAD program. In the case of AutoCAD, .dwg and .dxf files can be directly imported by clicking on File/ Open, and specifying the appropriate extension in "Files of type."

It is rare that when a new CAD system is installed the old system is removed and all existing data is converted to or redrawn on the new CAD system. This would not be a productive use of personnel time. An alternative to this is to maintain two systems. Maintaining two systems allows for more gradual transition to the new CAD system. The existing legacy data can be modified on the old system and new designs can be made on the new system. If needed, existing data can be imported into SolidWorks and edited from there.

The advantage of this method is that transfer work is minimized because files do not have to be saved within the new system. The disadvantage is that the existing CAD system might be incompatible with a new computer system. For example, users converting from a DOS-based system may not be able to run the old CAD system on a Windows-based computer. This issue should be recognized and addressed from the onset. It will play an important role in determining which operating system is used.

Legacy Data Maintenance Considerations

The following sections discuss considerations to think about at the implementation planning stage, and then to follow through on as the process continues. A key issue to be weighed is the time required to reuse and complete a design with SolidWorks. Simple changes to an existing product that does not require the advantages of a solid modeling system would not be as good of a candidate as a design that has more changes or requires more analysis of the fit or function of the design.

Minimal Changes Required for Existing Drawings

If a couple of 2D drafting changes are all that is needed, it may very well be easier to open the drawing in AutoCAD and make the changes. Print the drawing out if necessary. This requires little time and effort, and no translation is needed.

Major Changes Required for Existing Drawings

This is a different story. It should be considered that more time spent on the AutoCAD system means less time spent on SolidWorks. If many design changes are needed, there are a few options, depending on whether the existing data is 2D or 3D.

Two-dimensional Layouts

A 2D drawing layout can be imported and edited as a SolidWorks drawing. In SolidWorks, it can be edited in the usual fashion as a typical 2D layout. However, this does not take full advantage of the most powerful Solid-Works tools, and has no downstream benefits to speak of.

The preferred method would be to import the 2D data, and then use that data to build a solid model. Once this is done, any design changes that need to be made can be performed efficiently and quickly. The time spent creating the model is well spent in the long run because of the time saved when making future design changes and in creating the new 2D layout.

Three-dimensional Wireframe

This poses a bit of a dilemma. It is impossible to import 3D wireframe geometry into SolidWorks. Even if you could, there is no way to transform the wireframe geometry into a solid model. It has to be recreated either from scratch or by building the solid up from 2D geometry. This is due to the nature of solid modelers, not the Solid-Works program itself. It would be possible to build up the solid within AutoCAD, little by little, using the existing wireframe, but it would have no intelligence. You are better off recreating the model in SolidWorks. Not only will it be much easier, you will also reap all the rewards of having a parametric solid model when you are done.

One method of reusing 3D wireframe geometry is to break up individual features into separate 2D sketches. These individual sketches can be used to create sketches within SolidWorks using the "Sketch from drawing" function.

Three-dimensional Solids

Three-dimensional solid geometry can be exported from AutoCAD as what is known as an ACIS solid. AutoCAD uses the ACIS kernel, whereas SolidWorks uses the Parasolids kernel. It is believed by SolidWorks and other high-performance CAD system programmers that the Parasolids kernel is superior. Take for example that as of this writing ACIS versions of the kernel number no fewer than six (1.5, 1.6, 1.7, 2.0, 2.1, and 3.0). The kernel keeps changing, because ACIS keeps trying to improve it. Also take for example that each one of these variations *are not intercompatible.* A built-in translator is needed to move between programs using different versions of the same ACIS kernel.

Another way of exporting solids from AutoCAD is through the IGES format. If you have AutoCAD release 13, you will have had to purchase the IGES translator separately because it was no longer included with the main program. IGES translators can usually export geometry as wireframe, typically known as 3D curves, or as trimmed surfaces.

A solid model contains topology information, as discussed in Chapter 1. Think of a simple cube with six sides. Each side can be thought of as a surface. Additionally, each surface has an outside and an inside. Last, each surface is "trimmed" to its adjacent sides. The cube has a complete boundary that can be read by SolidWorks and "knitted" together to create the solid model. The SolidWorks IGES translator is included with the program.

When a solid or surface model is imported and knitted into a solid model, the imported geometry is displayed as a single feature within SolidWorks. Features can be added to modify the original feature, but the imported geometry cannot be redefined.

New Designs

This is a no-brainer. There is absolutely no reason you would want to create a new part in AutoCAD and translate it over to SolidWorks. The benefits of creating the part in SolidWorks far outweigh any reasons one might have for creating it in AutoCAD. Parametric design, component assembly, real-time rotation of shaded parts, and exploded assembly drawings are just a few of the features available to a SolidWorks part as opposed to an AutoCAD model.

Hardware Considerations

The computer requirements of a solid modeling system differ from those of a 2D CAD system. Solid modeling is more computationally intensive due to the calculations required to build and display geometry. This type of system can benefit from a fast CPU (central processing unit), memory, video cards, and hard drives. The trade-off between saving money and improving a system's performance can make for difficult decisions. There are some system components that can provide more "bang for the buck." This section describes these components but does not recommend a specific brand or manufacturer.

One difficulty when considering hardware is determining how to measure the effective increase in productivity of one system over another. The most effective methods of sorting out the possibilities in hardware are based on a macro file that runs programs that represent the type of work your company performs on a regular basis. However, most people do not have access to the types of machines they might consider buying for running these types of tests.

Consider a part typical of the parts designed by your company, and use it in profiling various systems to see how the systems will handle the part. For instance, test a part with many complicated features, or a large assembly, which can be used to judge how various machines will dynamically shade or rebuild the part during demo sessions.

Operating Systems and Network Software

SolidWorks uses Microsoft's Windows 95 or Windows NT operating systems, either on the Intel or Alpha platforms. The choice of operating systems could be based on company standards, support requirements, or availability of operating systems from your hardware vendor. The Windows NT operating system provides a more robust, stable platform. Windows NT provides a multitasking system that handles engineering applications better in terms of memory usage, security, networking, multiple CPUs, and misbehaving applications. Windows 95 better supports old 16-bit (i.e., DOS-based programs) applications better than Windows NT.

The general rule of thumb here is that if your company is running older software or DOS programs, go with Windows 95. If networking security is of primary concern and you are looking to squeeze every last ounce of performance out of your hardware, go with Windows NT 4.0. This rule of thumb will still apply when Windows 98 and NT 5.0 are released. NT runs faster because it does not use any of the old 16-bit code, but this is also the reason it lacks backward compatibility. NT is a more stable and robust operating system for full-time CAD use.

Networking software is also an issue, but the out-of-the-box performance of Windows networking is very easy to set up and administer. Also, networking is included with the operating system software, so why buy something extra that will not add functionality? Microsoft's networking software does the job, and does it well.

Processors

With the advent of Intel Pentium Pro and Pentium II processors and the DEC (Digital Equipment Corporation)

Alpha chip, CPUs are processing faster than ever before. The days when an expensive Unix workstation was required to effectively run a solid modeling CAD system are gone. Many NT workstations rival the performance of a Unix workstation for a fraction of the price.

The latest CPUs are typically priced at a premium when they first arrive on the market. The trade-off between additional performance and the added cost must be weighed to determine the value of the faster processor. Do not choose a slow processor to save a small amount of money. The increase in productivity over the course of six months to a year using a faster processor will probably far outweigh such savings.

Windows NT also supports multiple CPUs. SolidWorks supports multithreading for some (e.g., display) functions. A multithreaded application means that the tasks for a process can be split up so that two or more processors can handle the task. An additional CPU might add to the system performance, but not all functions within your applications, or within SolidWorks, can take advantage of the multiple CPUs. This is why servers benefit the most from having more than one CPU. Many applications are being run at any given time, and the applications can share the CPUs present in the server.

It should be noted that Pentium Pro processors can be run with up to four processors in the same machine, and are very well equipped to handle heavy server loads due to the second-level cache (or L2 cache), which runs at the same speed as the CPU. Pentium II processors have an advanced floating point unit, but the L2 cache works at half the speed of the CPU, like all other Pentium processors, and a maximum of two processors can be implemented at one time. Nevertheless, the Pentium II can currently run at 300 MHz and has a built-in MMX instruction set, along with some other technological advancements that make it a chip worthy of SolidWorks.

Intel's next-generation chip, code named Deschutes, will have an L2 cache that will run at the same speed as the processor and will support 100-MHz bus speeds. Current bus speeds are 60 or 66 MHz for Intel chips.

Memory

Memory or RAM (Read Access Memory) is used by a system to place data in a temporary, quick-access area for operating system or application use. Memory prices have dropped significantly over the past couple of years, making the addition of sufficient memory a cheap option for improving system performance. Even though SolidWorks can run on a system with 32 Mb of RAM, a full-time Solid-Works design system should be configured with a minimum of 64 Mb of RAM.

To determine the amount of memory required for a system, consider how many applications will be running at the same time and the size of the files. To run Microsoft Word, Excel, and SolidWorks at the same time, a system with 64 Mb of RAM would be acceptable, but the common catch phrase in the industry is "you can never have too much memory."

If the system runs out of RAM, the hard disk will be used to cache the application. This is considerably slower than using RAM and should be avoided. Consider that memory access time is measured in nanoseconds (billionths of a second) and that hard drive access is measured in milliseconds (thousandths of a second). This should give you some idea of the speed difference.

You may need more memory, depending on the sort of parts or assemblies you are creating in SolidWorks. Sixty-four Mb of RAM is acceptable for average parts with dozens of features, and for assemblies with one or two dozen parts. If you are going to be creating parts with many complex features—such as complex spline-type waveforms, swept or lofted features, variable radius fillets, or large patterns (known to AutoCAD users as arrays)—128 Mb or more may be required.

Large assemblies with hundreds of components may require 256-512 Mb or more. With extremely large parts, containing in excess of 1,000 features, or assemblies with more than 500 parts, consider the DEC Alpha machines with very large memory capacities. SolidWorks will do the job, but the only limitation is the hardware.

Hard Drives

Hard disks come in a variety of bus styles, such as IDE, SCSI, and Ultra Wide SCSI. The access time (milliseconds) and the transfer rate (megabytes per second) measure the speed of a hard disk. The quicker the access time and greater the transfer rate, the faster a hard disk will perform. The fastest types of hard disks are the Ultra Wide SCSI types. These disks are more expensive than the IDE variety, but offer increased performance.

The latest standard emerging is the Ultra IDE standard, which supports throughput rates of 33 Mb/sec. Standard IDE is 16.6 Mb/sec. There is some question as to whether a rate of 33 Mb/sec on the Ultra IDE drives can be achieved with the slower disk rotation of those drive types. That is beyond the scope of this book.

The SCSI drives offer a greater degree of performance for more than one reason. The disk rotations on these drive types are faster, which accelerates seek times when searching for data. Second, data throughput is higher when using Ultra Wide SCSI drives (40 Mb/sec). And most importantly, SCSI drives contain their own processor, which makes for less draw on the main CPU, but more importantly, allows for multitasking on the hard drive.

SCSI drives can process more than one command at a time, but an IDE drive must finish the first command before processing the next one. This makes SCSI drives an ideal solution for applications such as video editing and animations, and for file servers.

Video Cards and Monitors

Video cards and drivers are a key factor when determining the performance of a system. There are graphic cards that work well in a 2D wireframe environment, but do not perform as well in a 3D solid modeling system. A good video card will have an OpenGL-compatible graphics card with sufficient memory for running at a resolution acceptable for your monitor size. Resolution is measured in pixels, and is typically anywhere from 640 x 480 (width by height) to 1,280 x 1,024. Even higher resolutions are being reached now, but not all monitors will be able to view the higher resolutions. Generally speaking, more memory on a video card does not increase its speed, but increases the color depth.

Color depth can be anywhere from 256 to 16.8 million colors. For everyday applications, such as word processing or spreadsheets, 256 colors is fine. If you are working with graphic images or CAD software with shaded parts or renderings, a step up from 256 is the least you will want to go. Intermediate settings are typically 32 or 64 thousand colors. Sometimes the color depth is referred to as "high" color (64 thousand) or "true" color (16.8 million). If you are a power user, once you get used to true color, you will never want to go back to anything else. True color makes for very smooth and nicely shaded parts.

Most CAD operators will have at least a 17-inch monitor. Larger (19-, 20-, and 21-inch) models are available today in a wide range of capabilities and prices. With respect to resolution, the larger the monitor, the higher you can go with the resolution settings, assuming the graphics card can support them. At higher resolutions, text and icons (and everything else) get smaller if they have to fit into the same screen space. On a 21-inch monitor, a setting of 1,280 x 1,024 would not be uncommon because there is enough screen space to see everything. If the same resolution were squashed into a 14-inch monitor, everything would be too small to see.

Another thing to consider when purchasing a graphics card is texture memory and 3D accelerator chips. Some cards contain both, and these cards contain varying amounts of texture memory, some as high as 32 Mb. Without going into too much detail, SolidWorks has no use for texture memory. Neither does AutoCAD. Texture memory is important in applications where texture-mapped surfaces are being rotated or animated on your screen.

Three-dimensional accelerator chips, however, play a big role in graphics performance with respect to SolidWorks. A good $300 3D accelerator card can outperform a "high end" card costing more than $2,000. The high-end card is more expensive due to the level of texture memory you may never use. Three-dimensional accelerator graphics cards come in two basic varieties: integrated 2D/3D cards, and dedicated 3D-only accelerator cards. If you already have a good 2D Windows graphics accelerator, the dedicated 3D card is the choice for you. If you are shopping for a new system, go with the integrated 2D/3D card.

A new type of technology on the market is the Accelerated Graphics Port (AGP). This new technology shows much promise, but it will be awhile before it reaches its full potential. AGP allows the graphics card access to system memory via the PCI bus, thereby giving the graphics card a much larger memory pool from which to draw. Yet there are many other aspects of this technology that must be considered. For example, the PCI bus is still only 32 bits wide. Some graphics cards use a 128-bit-wide path to graphics card memory.

Also consider the PCI bus speed of 66 MHz. AGP 1x will run at this same bus speed, but AGP 2x will essentially double this rate to 133 MHZ. When Intel's new 440BX chipset hits the street, system bus speeds will jump to 100 MHz, and AGP 4x should be emerging. Many excellent AGP cards are emerging on the market now, but research them well to be sure you know what you are getting.

There are a number of medium and high-end graphics cards on the market. Many of the larger PC manufacturers now have a line of cards they refer to as a workstation-caliber system. Keep in mind the main reason you are buying the card and what you want to do with it, and remember that more expensive does not always mean faster graphics processing. Talk to your hardware vendor or VAR to discuss the applications that will be used and to determine which graphics card would be best suited for running your SolidWorks application.

Determining a Reasonable Pilot Project

Instead of rushing into a complete conversion upon development of an implementation plan, you should consider a pilot implementation project. This allows you to work through known and unforeseen implementation issues on a small scale before you undertake a large-scale project. However, at times a small-scale preview is not possible, probably because a critical project has come up that needs to be undertaken right away.

If this is the case, which is very common, the critical project can serve as your pilot project. Most companies do not have the luxury of picking and choosing a pilot project. If it is feasible, take some of the following thoughts into consideration for your first SolidWorks project.

A pilot project should be limited, if possible, in terms of amount of work and complexity so that new users can focus on the techniques and principles required when developing good SolidWorks work skills. The ultimate goal of a pilot project should be to learn how to apply effective solid modeling skills. A pilot project helps to determine how solid modeling technology can be best applied to your company's products, and to identify additional training that may be required to reach this goal. The following are items to address within a pilot project.

Setting SolidWorks Preferences

SolidWorks contains a number of preference settings that can change the way the program operates, many of which are similar to AutoCAD. Most of the customization options should not be used at all until you get more adept with the program. Unlike AutoCAD, there are no alias files to modify, pull-down menus cannot be edited, and the function of toolbar icons cannot be changed or created from scratch.

The ability to customize AutoCAD is one of its strengths, but it can also be a weakness. For example, it might be difficult or impossible to use someone else's AutoCAD interface if they have modified it completely differently than yours. Another example is conflicts with menus because the menu on the machine that created the drawing is different than the one on the machine currently viewing the drawing. AutoCAD layer names have always been an issue when trying to standardize throughout a company.

Most of these problems do not exist in SolidWorks. However, there are a few settings that should be agreed upon, such as the size and type of note and dimension fonts, use of ANSI or ISO, the form of drawing templates, and so on. These are essentially topics that would need to be standardized no matter what software were being used. A meeting among appropriate personnel and departments for resolving these issues is recommended.

Directory Structure and Naming Conventions

This is another issue that exists no matter what program a company is using. As far as SolidWorks is concerned, it is best to set up specific directories for individual projects. Because of the associativity between parts, drawings, and assemblies, it is necessary to keep track of what parts are being used in which assemblies, and what revisions of what parts are being used in those same assemblies.

Depending on the circumstances, this can turn out to be quite a headache. Rest assured that if your company requires it, there are program applications specifically designed for your needs—everything from workflow management to project tracking to automated revision incrementing. Talk to your vendor or VAR for recommendations.

If you do not require anything quite as extravagant as the aforementioned strategies, it is still necessary to keep files organized by creating logically established directories for storing files. This holds true for any software that generates large amounts of data. Also, now that file names no longer have to be a measly eight characters in length, naming conventions can be much more descriptive. What your company decides on is a matter of internal policy.

Employee Management

When planning a pilot project, identify users who have strong CAD skills and who are receptive to new technology. Selecting users for a pilot project who are motivated to achieve the goal without bias as to how it is achieved can help ensure that the maximum benefit will be derived from the pilot project. This type of user is also useful when the full implementation occurs, serving as an internal resource for other users. The benefit to an internal resource of this type is that the person is familiar with your company's organization and products. Many companies identify and nurture this type of user within their organization.

Lessons Learned from a Pilot Project

When the pilot project is complete, a full implementation can proceed. Lessons learned from the pilot project can be applied to ensure a smooth transition for all users. A training plan should address the training of new users at the transition stage, as well as ongoing training and support.

Summary

Proper planning and training helps ensure a smooth transition to a new software product. This up-front planning can save work in the long run and reduce the time required to get users up to speed using SolidWorks. Any successful project, including the implementation of a new CAD system, will benefit from a well-conceived project plan.

The ability to maintain and reuse legacy data is a strong feature of SolidWorks. SolidWorks effectively handles legacy data and does not necessarily require that this information be recreated. When selecting a new CAD system, the ability to maintain and reuse existing data should be a key consideration.

The type of hardware, network, and operating system that incorporates an effective SolidWorks document and project management system will be based on the size and complexity of your designs and the overall size of your company. Small gains due to a faster system can add up to larger savings when looked at long-term. There are always newer, faster, and cheaper computer systems coming out on the market. Select a system that is adequate for your needs, does not limit your productivity, and allows for room to grow and expand.

Getting Started

Introduction

This chapter is concerned with the concepts you will need when considering how a model will be created in a SolidWorks session. Topics covered in the following sections examine basic information required to begin a SolidWorks session and the thought processes involved. Differences regarding basic philosophy of starting a model with AutoCAD and with SolidWorks are addressed.

Prerequisite

At this point, you should have a good working knowledge of the Windows operating system; specifically, how to open and close windows, how to minimize and resize windows, and related functions considered standard to most Windows users. Along with opening, closing, and starting a new SolidWorks document, basic terms used by the SolidWorks program should be familiar to you. If it has been awhile since you opened this book, it would be beneficial to review Chapter 1.

Content

The main goal of this chapter is to convey the fundamental thought process behind starting a part in SolidWorks, as well as how this differs from the same functionality in the AutoCAD environment. Additional terms used by SolidWorks are introduced. This chapter contains the following major topics:

- Getting started
- Sketch planes
- Sketch profiles
- Design intent
- Preference settings

The section on preference settings describes methods used to define and change a few of the more common SolidWorks preferences. These user-definable properties are used to set attributes and characteristics used to create a document and define interaction properties for Solid-Works.

Objectives

With completion of this chapter, you should be able to start a SolidWorks editing session preliminary to actually sketching entities. Completion of the section on preference settings should give you an understanding of how to define and change some of the more common Solid-Works settings. You should know how to distinguish proper sketch profiles to start a part, and be able to determine the best plane to sketch on. You should also understand the concept of design intent.

Getting Started

SolidWorks can be started using the Windows Start menu, or by double clicking on its shortcut. With a default Solid-Works installation, a program group is created in the Start menu, but no icons are placed on the Windows desktop. The steps in the following section show you how to create a shortcut.

> ↝ **NOTE:** *Whenever the word* click *is used in this book, it refers to clicking once with the left mouse button. With regard to Windows and SolidWorks, this usually selects what is clicked on.*

Creating a SolidWorks Shortcut Icon

To create a shortcut icon in SolidWorks, perform the following steps:

1. Click on the Start button in the lower left corner of your desktop.

2. Click on Settings.

3. Click on Taskbar... to open the Taskbar Properties dialog box.

4. Click on the Start Menu Programs tab at the top of the dialog box.

5. Click on the Advanced... button.

6. What you should now be looking at is Windows Explorer. It is opened to a section of your hard drive that contains all shortcuts to your programs. It contains an exact copy of the programs listed in the Program list of your Start menu. Directly below the pull-down menus, you will see a folder called Start Menu, and below that, Programs. Click on the plus sign to the left of Programs to expand it.

7. Click on the SolidWorks folder.

8. All shortcuts for the SolidWorks folder should be visible at the right of the screen. Select the SolidWorks icon with your right mouse button and, holding the mouse button down, drag the icon over to your desktop and let go.

9. When you let go of the right mouse button, a menu will appear. Select Copy Here. Keep in mind that you do not want to select Create Shortcut Here because the item you are dragging is already a shortcut. That would create a shortcut to the shortcut! It would work, but it is better to just copy the shortcut.

This method will work for anything else in your Program group you would like to create a shortcut for. When you are done, click on File, Close, and then OK.

⊶ **NOTE:** *The properties (e.g., icon graphics, name, default startup location) can be customized by selecting the icon, pressing the right mouse button, and selecting Properties. The shortcut attributes can be modified for the user's needs. Selecting a new default startup location can be used the start SolidWorks in the directory used to store your parts.*

Starting a SolidWorks Session

Start the program by double clicking on the SolidWorks icon. Your icon probably says SolidWorks 97Plus, or maybe SolidWorks 98, but for the sake of simplicity, herein it will simply be called SolidWorks. Close the Tip of the Day screen (see Chapter 1), and begin a new part by clicking on File/New and selecting Part. The following illustration shows the New dialog box, used for starting a session.

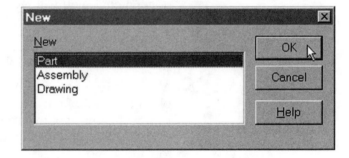

Starting a SolidWorks session in the New dialog box.

Drawings and assemblies are discussed in upcoming chapters. For the time being, parts will be the focus, because that is where the basics of SolidWorks should be developed. The Cancel button should be self-explanatory. It simply cancels you out of the command. The Cancel button's function is the same in any SolidWorks dialog box, and is standard throughout all Windows programs.

The same Windows standardization holds true for the Help button. In SolidWorks, the Help button is context sensitive, and will give you help for whatever dialog box you happen to be in at the time. As is par for the course with SolidWorks, a step-by-step description is usually given, which describes how to carry out the command. To begin, click on OK.

Saving a New Part

When a new part is started, there are always certain components that will appear in the SolidWorks interface. Along the left-hand side of the screen and to the right of the document area—which takes up most of the screen and in which you will be doing all sketching and editing—is FeatureManager, as discussed in Chapter 1. In the middle of the sketch area is the origin point, which should be grayed out at this time. If you have been tweaking settings or experimenting prior to this stage, some aspects of your screen may be slightly different. Do not worry about this. Everything should become clear as you proceed. In FeatureManager you should see a few items listed, as shown in the following illustration.

FeatureManager.

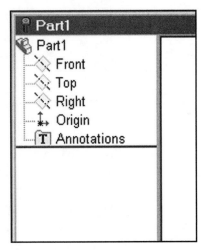

You will start at the top and work your way down. First, there is the name of the file itself. This should be Part1 on your screen. After saving the file, the name at the top of FeatureManager changes to reflect the new file name. Save the part with the name Widget by performing the following steps. The illustration that follows shows the result of this name change.

1. Click on File/Save.

2. Where Part1.SLDPRT is highlighted, type in the name of the part (use *widget*).

3. Click on the Save button.

Name change result in the FeatureManager design tree.

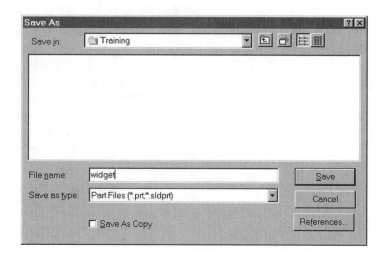

Notice that the name of the part has changed in FeatureManager. Immediately below the part name there are three planes listed, followed by the origin point. Everything listed in FeatureManager will have an icon associated with it. Different features have different icons. This makes finding what you are looking for a lot easier, especially when the feature list begins growing.

At the bottom of FeatureManager are two small icons, as shown in the following illustration. They allow you to go from FeatureManager to ConfigurationManager and back again. If you purchase third-party programs, they may be represented here as well. (ConfigurationManager is discussed in Chapter 6.

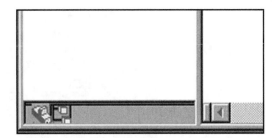

FeatureManager and ConfigurationManager icons.

Sketch Planes

Just like a piece of paper is needed before a pencil drawing can be started, so must a sketch plane be selected before a SolidWorks sketch can begin. The sketch plane can be a plane feature or a part face. For this reason, SolidWorks gives you three planes to start with. After a first-time installation, the planes will automatically be named Plane1, Plane2, and Plane3. This is not very descriptive, so give them new names.

Many options and parameters can be set from the Options dialog box, which can be very intimidating to new users. Therefore, the entire dialog box will not be discussed here. What works best is to modify a setting here and there as needed, so as not to overwhelm first-time Solid-Works users. To see what this means, click on Tools/ Options.... The following is a step-by-step procedure for opening the Options dialog box and renaming planes. The illustration that follows shows the Options dialog box.

1. Click on the Tools pull-down menu; then click on Options....

2. Click on the Planes tab.

3. Rename Plane1, Plane2, and Plane3 to Front, Top, and Right, respectively.

4. Click on OK.

The Options dialog box.

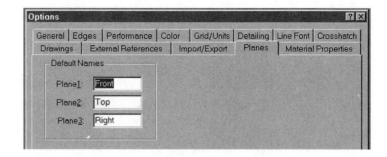

You will expect to see the new plane names in Feature-Manager, but that will not happen. This is because the default names were changed, which means that the next time you start a new part, you will see the change.

Renaming Features

Perhaps you would like to rename the names of the planes in the current part. No problem. If you are familiar with renaming files in Windows 95 or NT, this will be easy for you. Do what is referred to as a "slow double click" on the plane you would like to rename. This can be accomplished by clicking on an item in FeatureManager, waiting a second, and clicking a second time. A cursor will be displayed at the end of the object being renamed, and the name will be outlined with a rectangle. For practice, go ahead and type in the new names for each of the planes. Remember, Plane1 is Front, Plane2 is Top, and Plane3 is Right.

A feature can also be renamed by selecting the feature in the FeatureManager design tree. Press the right mouse button, select Properties, change the Name field, and select OK to close the dialog box.

Keep in mind that this can be accomplished for almost anything listed in FeatureManager. During the creation process, it usually helps to name features as you go. This makes it very easy to find features later if they need editing.

Viewing Versus Selecting Planes

New users have a tendency to think that viewing a plane and selecting a plane are one in the same. This is not the case. SolidWorks will give you visual cues for many things done within the program. This is especially true when selecting objects or sketching. Explore this a little further, with regard to planes.

First, click on one of the planes in FeatureManager. If the front plane is selected, it will appear as a rectangle on the screen. The other two will appear as lines, because they are being viewed from the side. The point, however, is that the plane is green. Anytime something is selected, it turns green (with few exceptions). File this bit of information away for future reference: if something is selected, it turns green.

Now try this: click anywhere in the sketch area. The plane disappears, right? This is because it is being deselected. The Escape button on your computer keyboard will accomplish the same thing. Give it a try. The planes have not actually been turned on. One of them, depending on the one you selected, was merely temporarily selected. To turn on the planes, or Show them, a different tact is required.

Introduction to the Right Mouse Button

The right mouse button performs many tasks in Windows 95. It also plays a big role in SolidWorks. At the moment, you will use it to show the three default planes, which should be named Front, Top, and Right. Use your right mouse button to click on the Front plane in FeatureManager and you should see what is known as a context-sensitive menu. This means that what is in the menu is dependent on what you right click on. To show a plane, you would perform the following steps. The illustration that follows shows a Front plane display.

1. Right click on the Front plane in FeatureManager.

2. Select Show.

Front plane display.

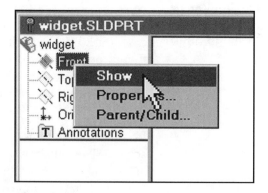

That is all there is to it. Notice that the plane is still selected. Deselect the plane by using either of the two methods previously described. It is usually easiest to press the Escape key on the keyboard, but do whatever is easiest for you. The plane should still be visible, even though it has been deselected. This is because it has been shown. Now repeat this process for the other two planes.

Before manipulating the view orientation is discussed, some basic differences between AutoCAD and Solid-Works should be pointed out. What SolidWorks refers to as a sketch plane is similar to what a user would have if he or she manipulated the User Coordinate System (UCS) to a specific orientation. The UCS must be changed every time a new surface needs to be drawn upon. Constantly having to modify the UCS from place to place can get tedious.

Also, it is not necessarily a surface the UCS is placed on, but a theoretical plane extending in all directions and defined by the user in some fashion, such as with three points. SolidWorks allows you to draw on a plane or a planar face of existing geometry simply by selecting it and clicking on the Sketch icon. Planes can be created for a wide range of functions in SolidWorks, but AutoCAD does not have anything analogous to this, as "plane" entity types do not exist.

Introduction to View Orientation

AutoCAD has its View toolbar, and SolidWorks has the View Orientation dialog box. They are very similar in what they achieve, but different in appearance and operation. Access the View Orientation dialog box by performing the following steps:

1. Click on the View pull-down menu.

2. Click on Orientation....

3. Click on the "pushpin" icon in the top left-hand corner of the View Orientation dialog box.

The pushpin keeps the window on top of your desktop. Otherwise, the dialog box would disappear as soon as the next mouse click was performed outside the View Orientation box. The thought behind this is that you could change a view and be happily on your way, with the View Orientation window automatically going back into hiding. The following illustration shows the View Orientation window.

The View Orientation window.

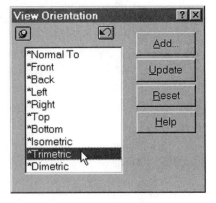

AutoCAD's View icons allow you to change views to top, bottom, right, left, and so on. There are also four isometric views: southeast, southwest, and so on. SolidWorks approaches this slightly differently. There are the views Top, Bottom, Right, Left, and so on, like AutoCAD. However, SolidWorks also offers Isometric, Trimetric, and

Dimetric views. All system views are preceded by an asterisk, and cannot be deleted. Other views can be added and deleted as desired.

Double click the desired view in order to activate it (using your left mouse button). There is one other system view SolidWorks offers, and that is the Normal To view. Before Normal To is selected, a plane or planar face must be chosen, unless you are in a sketch.

Without going into too much detail regarding what "normals" are at this point, suffice it to say that it gives you a plan view. A plan view is a plan view no matter what software program you are using, and Normal To accomplishes the same thing as AutoCAD's Plan command, which is to place the view parallel to the screen. In other words, your line of sight is perpendicular to the view plane.

Some people do not like the size of the View Orientation dialog box and would like to resize it. That is not possible, but it is possible to drag it over to a corner where it is out of the way. What works well is to drag it over to the bottom right-hand corner so that only the view names are showing. If you would rather remove it from the desktop, deselect the pushpin icon and it will hide itself the next time you click outside the View Orientation window. The following illustrations show what the three default planes would look like if you double clicked on Trimetric.

Another option is to define a function key to activate the View Orientation dialog box. The function keys can be assigned a SolidWorks function using the Tools/Customize menu. The keyboard tab is used to define a function to a keyboard key. See Chapter 12 for a complete description.

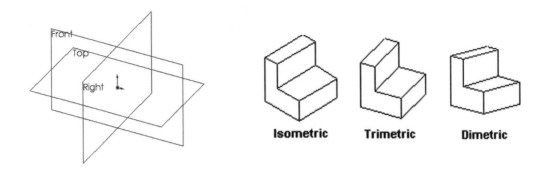

Isometric   Trimetric   Dimetric

Example of a simple L-shaped part using the Isometric, Trimetric, and Dimetric system views.

If you have not saved your work in awhile, you may want to do so now. Click on File/Save, or just use the icon that looks like a floppy disk. Recall from Chapter 1 that you do not want to use Save As, because that will allow you to rename the file. For now, stick with the name Widget.

Sketch Profiles

An important aspect of creating a solid model is to first mentally visualize how the model should be built. Solid-Works parts are built up from features, and the order in which those features are created is important. Sometimes, feature order can be determined by how it would be easiest to build the part. Other times the features must be created in such a fashion because they cannot physically be created any other way. An example of the latter would be a simple block with fillets and a hole. The fillets and hole cannot be created before the block because they are dependent on the block for their existence.

All parts, whether working in AutoCAD or SolidWorks, require some sort of base feature. AutoCAD allows the creation of multiple solids without regard to where those solid components exist in space. Solid shapes and primitives are moved to desired locations and then added or subtracted from the base component in order to achieve a desired shape. Because a SolidWorks part file is a contiguous solid model, only one solid can exist at one time within a single part file. This is not a limitation, however, because in assemblies many parts can coexist in any configuration.

Because of SolidWorks' feature-based parametric nature, it is desirable to select a profile that best describes the part when the first feature is created. For instance, if you were creating a new keyboard for a computer company, it would be possible to create a rectangle on the top plane and extrude the shape downward, or sketch a cross-sectional shape on the right plane and extrude it to the left. The second scenario would result in a shape that would more fully represent the actual shape of the part, and would be the preferred way to create the keyboard's initial base feature.

AutoCAD's ability to create numerous shapes in multiple locations is not necessarily a strength. Initially, Solid-Works may seem more rigid in comparison to AutoCAD, but in practice it is actually extremely flexible. In Solid-Works, you decide what would be the best profile to start with, then select a plane with which to begin.

Design Intent

Design intent is a topic more important when working with a parametric modeler than with a Boolean modeler. The term *design intent* is defined as how a part will change if a dimension or constraint is modified. Constraints, a bit more complicated than dimensions, are discussed in depth in Chapter 5. Dimensions, however, are easy enough to understand.

AutoCAD certainly has dimensions, but they do not alter the model when changed. AutoCAD dimensions will actually lose their associativity if they are modified to be anything other than their default value. SolidWorks, on the other hand, will rebuild the model for you after changing a dimension. This is one reason SolidWorks is considered a design tool. Likewise, it involves a slightly different way of thinking.

Because AutoCAD does not use parametric dimensions, a great deal of care must go into creating a drawing. When a line is drawn from point A to point B, it must be accurate. With SolidWorks, if it is in the ballpark, that is good enough. When the dimension is added and a value is put on the dimension, it will modify the line to match the dimension value. This holds true for sketch or feature dimensions, and the dimensions can be modified at any stage in the design process. Just keep in mind your design intent.

For example, picture in your mind a simple block with a hole in it. Ask yourself what's more important. Should the hole start on the front plane, or the back? Should it be dimensioned to the upper left corner of the block or the lower right? If the overall dimensions of the block are changed, should the hole remain in the middle of the block? The answers to these questions depend on your design intent.

Preference Settings

User preferences define standard default values and system settings, such as how the system interacts with the user (i.e., single pick per command, naming features or dimensions upon creation, and so on). They also set default attributes and values, such as units of measure or number of decimal places. These preferences are used to define default properties and characteristics for sketches, parts, assemblies, and drawings.

Default values should be defined prior to starting your first design project. Setting consistent, standard configuration values for multiple-seat sites will make sharing documents easier. Carefully reviewing and setting default user preferences can help eliminate the need to redefine properties after documents have been created. Standard configuration values will make it easier to produce documents that look consistent and do not require users to change standard values when working on a document created by someone else. The mechanics involved in getting to the Options dialog box are easy. To do this, perform the following steps:

1. Click on the Tools pull-down menu.

2. Click on Options....

3. Make the desired changes.

But wait! You should read on before proceeding.

What Is Affected by Option Settings

Most option settings will affect the part that is open. However, some tabs have an option box that changes this condition. There are a few tabs that allow you to select whether the changes made will affect the current document, future documents, or both. What you select depends on whether the changes made should become the system defaults or not. The following is a list of the three option setting types and their individual scope.

System Defaults	Settings will affect all new documents.
Active Document	Settings will affect only the document being edited.
All Possible	Settings will affect the current document and all new documents.

To date, the tabs that have the Apply To drop-down dialog box (see the following illustration) are as follows:

- Color
- Grid/Units
- Detailing
- Line Font
- Crosshatch
- Material Properties

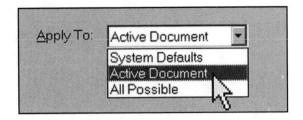

The Apply To dialog box.

In the previous illustration, only the current drawing will be affected. It should be noted that even if option settings are made to affect All Possible, they will not retroactively affect previously made documents, whether they are parts, assemblies, or drawings. Previous documents already created in SolidWorks have had their individual settings established and must be changed independently. For this reason, it is all the more important to decide on company-wide standards before embarking on a large, company-wide project.

Realistically speaking, there just are not that many settings that need to be decided upon when attempting to implement standards. Decide on ANSI or ISO, for example, and on other options, such as English or Metric, tolerance types, and maybe plane names. That pretty much covers it. Templates and title blocks are defined elsewhere and are covered under a separate topic.

One more word on setting options: if any options are set before a document is actually begun, all changes will automatically affect only future documents. This is why the Apply To drop-down box is grayed out. When you think about it, the reason is fairly obvious.

Quick Reference for Options

The Options dialog box is divided into functionally grouped tabbed sections. Each tab covers a different group of option settings, as shown in the following illustration. Changes to preference settings can be made to as many of the categories as you desire. Click on a tab to view the settings for that section.

Options dialog box tabs.

NOTE: *The following section is for reference only. It is not intended that new users begin tweaking all of the options available in the Options dialog box. It is highly recommended that settings be changed on an as-needed basis. SolidWorks is a very easy program to learn, but attempting to customize the interface at this point could result in making your interface different than that used in this book. Use caution when changing settings you are not familiar with.*

General Options Tab

This tab defines default settings for various commands, and for sketching, document backup, FeatureManager, and rotational behavior. The following characteristics can be defined within this tab:

Model	Defines model commands and input defaults.
Sketch	Defines sketching preference values for constraining sketches, model reference properties, and default settings when adding over defining dimensions.
FeatureManager Design Tree	Defines the default characteristics of FeatureManager.
View Rotation	Defines the increment/decrement values for view rotation when using keyboard shortcuts. Defines the speed for rotation using a mouse.
General	Defines whether to use the last open document when starting a SolidWorks session, to maximize documents by default, and whether to create a backup copy when a document is saved.
Use English Language	Select to use English as the default language for multilingual systems. Grayed out if no other languages are available.

Edges Options Tab

Edges preferences define the default display mode for edges within documents. The following characteristics can be defined within this tab:

Hidden Edges	Defines the display method for hidden lines and the ability to select hidden objects.
Part/Assembly Tangent Edge Display	Defines the display method for tangent lines.

Performance Options Tab

The Performance tab defines the default display quality for documents. The following characteristics can be defined within this tab:

Shaded Display Quality	Defines the smoothness for shaded display. A smaller deviation will produce smoother cylindrical surfaces.
Wireframe Display Quality	Defines the display quality for wireframe display.
Rebuild	Check this option to provide a higher level of error checking when creating or modifying features. Slower model rebuilds will occur with this option checked, because all surfaces will be verified. If you encounter problems rebuilding a model, check this option.
Windows 95 Zooming	This allows zooming in on small features or parts very closely, but may slow down the display. Not active in Windows NT.
Transparency Quality	Defines the level of transparency quality. If your computer has a graphics card that can perform alpha blending in hardware, this option works very well.

Color Options Tab

Color defines the default color for parts displayed in shaded, wireframe, and hidden modes. The following characteristics can be defined within this tab:

System	Different color attributes can be assigned to the items listed. Double click with the left mouse button on the item to be changed. Select or redefine the desired color.
Features	Different types of features can have different color attributes assigned to them. Double click with the left mouse button on the feature type to change it. Select or redefine the desired color.
Reset All	Restores the default system colors.
Edit	Edits the color of the selected object type. A preview of the color is shown below the Edit button.
Advanced	Used to set shading characteristics. Shading must be selected from the System field for this button to be active.

Grid/Units Options Tab

Grid/Units defines the default unit of measure, angular units, and grid characteristics. The following characteristics can be defined within this tab:

Grid Properties	Defines the default grid characteristics. These include grid display, snap, and major and minor grid spacing.
Snap Behavior	Defines snap-to-grid characteristics.
Units (Length)	Defines the default linear unit of measure (inch, mm, cm, feet, or feet/inches) and decimal precision used for linear dimensions.
Units (Angular)	Defines the default unit of measure (degrees, degrees/minutes, degrees/minutes/seconds, or radians) and decimal precision used for angular dimension.
Spin Box Increment	Defines the increment/decrement values used for length and angular spin boxes.

Detailing Options Tab

The Detailing tab defines default dimension characteristics for documents. The following characteristics can be defined within this tab:

Dimensioning Standard	Select ANSI, ISO, JIS, DIN, or BSI drafting standards. Dual dimensions and datum display are also defined within this field.
Arrows	Defines the default characteristics for dimension and leader arrowheads.
Break Lines	Defines the default value for the distance between break lines on broken views.
Center Marks	Sets the default size and display for center marks.
Witness Lines	Defines the default value from the object to the start of the extension line, and the default value from the dimension line to the end of the extension line.
Datum Feature Symbols	Enters the letter or number for the next datum label.
Notes	Defines the font, balloon, and leader properties for notes.
Dimensions	Defines the font, tolerance, and precision for dimensions.

Line Font Options Tab

The Line Font tab defines the default line font display for drawings. The following characteristics can be defined within this tab:

Type of Edge	Selects the line style to be modified.
Line Style	Selects various styles of lines.
Line Weight	Selects various line weights.
Preview	Previews image of the selected line font.

Crosshatch Options Tab

The Crosshatch tab defines the default display characteristics for crosshatch entities. Crosshatching is used to
denote the cutaway area of a section view. The following
characteristics can be defined within this tab:

Type	Defines the currently selected crosshatch pattern.
Length Unit	Defines the default crosshatch pattern, angle, and spacing.

Drawings Options Tab

Drawing options are used to define the default sheet
characteristics for drawings, such as the default view
scale, method of projecting views (first or third), display
characteristics, and others.

Default Sheet	Defines the default sheet scale.
Type of Projection	Sets whether first- or third-angle projection is used for typical engineering layouts.
Default Display for New Drawing Views	Defines the default display mode for new views and how tangent lines are displayed. Typically, hidden lines are shown in gray.
Detail Item Snapping	Allows for inferencing when dragging dimensions.

External References Options Tab

The External References tab defines default read-write
access and file locations. This option's setting can be used
to define documents that are read-only or to create a
search list for files not within the same directory. A read-
only file allows access to a document (part, assembly, or
drawing) for which changes cannot be saved.

You can also use External References to create a list of
search directories. In this way, if a file referenced by an
assembly is moved, SolidWorks will search the Folder list
before asking you if you would like to browse for the file
yourself.

Import/Export Options Tab

Export preferences are used to define the default characteristics for exporting documents. These settings can be changed or modified depending on where the information is going, where the information has come from, and how the information is going to be used. They can also be changed to fix problems that occurred during data exchange. The following characteristics can be defined within this tab:

IGES	Defines the default characteristics for IGES output and specifies IGES flavors when exporting to particular applications.
Parasolid	Defines assembly and version properties for Parasolid output.
DXF/DWG Output	Defines the version level and font characteristics for DXF/DWG output.
ACIS	Defines the version for ACIS output.
STL	Defines the quality of STL output files and whether a preview will be displayed.

Planes Options and Material Properties Options Tabs

The Default Names area is used to define default plane names that will appear on all future parts and assemblies. The Material Properties tab defines the density of the current part.

Summary

An important aspect of SolidWorks is selecting the appropriate sketch plane. Consider what the best profile should be when creating the base feature of the part, then take into consideration what plane the profile should be placed on. That plane should be your initial sketch plane.

Use the right mouse button to your advantage. It serves many functions in Windows 95 and Windows NT, and SolidWorks follows this principle. The right mouse button opens what is known as a context-sensitive menu, providing options relevant to what was selected with the right mouse button.

Design intent refers to how the solid model will change if dimensions or constraints are modified. Consider design intent before applying dimensions or constraints, as this will affect your model if design changes are made at a later time.

Defining consistent preference settings within your company will produce consistent patterns between Solid-Works documents that are easier to share and understand. These values should be carefully reviewed during the implementation process to determine which settings should be defined.

Interacting
with SolidWorks

Introduction

This chapter is an interactive introduction to the concepts you will need when beginning a SolidWorks session. The topics covered in the following sections examine the skills and information required to become familiar with the rudimentary and general operating techniques of SolidWorks. Similarities and differences will be addressed along the way regarding some habits that may have been carried over from working with AutoCAD.

Prerequisite

The SolidWorks interface should be familiar, as well as most of the basic terms used by the SolidWorks program. Concepts such as design intent and using planes to sketch on should also be understood. Being able to select an appropriate profile and plane prior to beginning a part should also be understood.

Content

The majority of this chapter will deal with how to select objects, using the right mouse button, using the zoom and view commands, and comparing SolidWorks grid and snap features to AutoCAD. The following major topics are covered in this chapter:

- Selecting objects
- An introduction to system feedback
- The right mouse button
- Display functions
- Setting grid and snap properties

The section on preference settings describes the methods used to define and change certain SolidWorks preferences. These user-definable properties are used to set the attributes and characteristics that create a document and define the interaction properties for SolidWorks.

Objectives

With completion of this chapter, you will be able to begin a SolidWorks editing session preliminary to actually sketching entities. You will also understand how to navigate using the zoom and pan commands, and the differences between AutoCAD's grid and snap settings and how these settings will affect your work in SolidWorks.

Selecting Objects

Before you begin, you should understand the word *objects*. Objects are just what they sound like. Anything created by the user in SolidWorks is considered an object. These can be sketched entities, dimensions, features, assembly components, planes, views, and anything else you might place into a drawing, part, or assembly. The word *entities* is also a common term used to describe objects. Generally speaking, entities may often describe sketched objects, such as in the phrase "Select entities by placing a window around them." However, the two words, *objects* and *entities*, may be used interchangeably.

The reason something is selected depends entirely on what is being accomplished at the time. In AutoCAD, you may select entities in order to erase them, move, copy, stretch, array, or any number of other operations. It is much the same in SolidWorks. The left mouse button is always used to select objects. That is the left mouse button's primary function, and this holds true throughout almost all Windows programs.

There are a couple of default selection methods used by AutoCAD. Clicking on an entity would select it, with AutoCAD highlighting the entity to look like a dashed line. In SolidWorks, selecting is done the same way, with the exception that if you are selecting more than one entity, the control key must be depressed. When objects are selected in SolidWorks, they turn green. Solid model edges and faces are the exception to this rule, and turn into blue dashed lines when selected.

Deselecting objects works the same way in SolidWorks as it does in AutoCAD. Click on an object a second time and it will become deselected and lose its green highlight. Just remember to hold that Control key down if there is more than one entity selected already!

Another default selection method used by AutoCAD is the window or crossing box method. This is handy for selecting many objects at once. SolidWorks allows you to use the window method as well. To implement this, click a blank area on the screen, hold down the left mouse button, and drag the opposite corner to create a "window." It does not make a difference if you drag from right to left, or from left to right. There is no crossing box in Solid-Works; therefore, entities need to be completely enclosed in the window before they are selected.

An Introduction to System Feedback

SolidWorks is always giving you visual cues as to what is going on in the program. The chapter on sketching explores this topic much more fully, but for now, discussion will be limited to system feedback as it pertains to the realm of selecting objects.

By placing the tip of the cursor over certain components of a part, you are given feedback by SolidWorks that confirms what type of entity the cursor is actually over. At that precise moment, if the left mouse button is clicked, that entity will be selected. This can be very important when trying to select specific entity types, such as edges, faces, vertex points, or dimensions. The cursor is constantly changing to let you know what the cursor is over. These changes take place dynamically as the mouse is moved over the part.

Remember the Widget part? Go ahead and open it now if you have not done so already. You should still have the three default planes turned on and the view set to Trimetric. Now move the cursor slowly over the planes and the origin point. The cursor should change as it encounters the various objects. This is the system feedback just discussed, and it plays a major role in how you interact with SolidWorks.

If you have the sample parts loaded on your system, you can open a sample part to test this system feedback functionality and get a better feel for what is happening. If you are not sure if the sample parts were loaded, use the Windows Explorer to check the SolidWorks directory and look for the *Samples* directory. There will be quite a few directories under *Sample*. The one you want is the *examples* subdirectory. You will find some sample part files there. Open up *Sump.sldprt*, the content of which is shown in the following illustration, and use it to view the system feedback under discussion.

The Sump example part.

Just move the cursor over the part and you will see the cursor change, depending on what the cursor is currently positioned over. Experiment with selecting various entities. If the samples were not loaded on your machine, or you do not have SolidWorks, refer to the previous illustration. The illustration at left shows examples of system feedback.

Examples of system feedback.

Later, when there are more objects on the screen to work with, you will see firsthand how the cursor changes depending on what it is over. A vertex point is either an endpoint of a line or arc segment, or it can be a junction of two or more lines or arcs. When the cursor is placed over a vertex, a small square representing a point is displayed. If the cursor is placed over an edge on the solid model, a line will be displayed. Faces can be either planar or nonplanar surfaces. If the cursor is over a face, it will change to show you the third example on the right in the first illustration of this chapter.

There are other examples of system feedback, such as with dimensions, that will change the cursor to have a small representation of a dimension attached to it. You will be spending a good deal of time on system feedback in upcoming chapters, particularly in Chapter 5.

↩ **NOTE:** *It is very important to pay close attention to cursor feedback. It cannot be stressed enough that you must be aware of the changes taking place with the cursor and be able to correctly interpret this information.*

The Right Mouse Button

The SolidWorks right mouse button is not used at all the same way that AutoCAD's right mouse button is. For this reason, new SolidWorks users will find it annoying when they right click, expecting to reinstate their last command or enter a return, only to get a pop-up menu.

The general rule of thumb is that the left mouse button is for selecting objects, and the right mouse button opens a context-sensitive menu. You saw an example of a context-sensitive menu in Chapter 3 when turning on the planes in the Widget part. There are many other tasks that can be accomplished with the right mouse button in addition to just turning planes on and off.

The point to remember is the term *context sensitive*. Depending on what the cursor is positioned over at the time the right mouse button is clicked will make a difference between what is actually displayed in the menu. The menu is *in context* to what is being selected with the right mouse button. Often, the cursor does not have to be positioned over anything, in which case many of the items in the menu will be nothing more than shortcuts to commonly used functions. The following illustration shows an example of this.

Notice there are sketching shortcuts, dimensioning and relation (constraint) shortcuts, and zoom shortcuts. Of course, it is not much of a shortcut when the respective icons are only an icon away. In terms of mouse clicks, clicking an icon is only one, but using the right mouse button and selecting from that menu can be as many as two. This is because it is possible to access and select from the right mouse button with only one click. To do this, right click to bring up the menu, continue to hold down the right mouse button, then position the cursor over the item you want to select. When the right mouse button is released, the desired selection will be made.

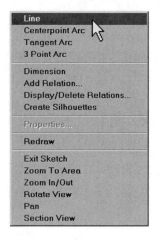

Typical context sensitive menu.

With this selection capability, what is the sense in using the context-sensitive menu? If your screen is large and it is more of a chore to slide the mouse over to the toolbar, it may be easier to right mouse click and bring up the menu. The second reason is that sometimes the right mouse menu contains options that cannot be found quite as easily in other areas, such as the pull-down menus. The right mouse button menu is an easy place to find commands that relate to the particular item over which you are right clicking. It can save you a lot of time and effort in the long run. Do not forget that this function is available.

~ **NOTE:** *If you cannot remember where a specific command is located, try the right mouse button method of locating options.*

Display Functions

When it comes to ease of use and functionality, Solid-Works is much more convenient than AutoCAD in the area of display functions. For example, take the simple task of manipulating a shaded part. SolidWorks can easily pan, zoom, and rotate the shaded part in real time. AutoCAD comes close to this functionality with RTPAN and RTZOOM in release 13c4 and release 14, as long as you have the WHIP drivers loaded.

However, what if you want to perform these maneuvers with hidden lines removed, or when the part is shaded? It is just not going to happen in the AutoCAD environment. As a matter of fact, once you get accustomed to Solid-Works' ability to perform these functions, going back to maneuvering in AutoCAD seems extremely constricting. Take another look at the View toolbar, which is shown in the following illustration.

The View toolbar.

The View toolbar shown in this illustration will look a little different than yours if you are comparing this to what is on your SolidWorks screen. That is because the toolbar shown here has been customized to show all available icons. The last two icons are for section views and perspective views. These are not used much and their icons are not placed on the toolbar by default.

~ **NOTE:** *It is highly recommended that new users to the SolidWorks program do not attempt any customizing of the SolidWorks interface. Doing so can result in the program not working as it was intended to in its* *default configuration, and your version of Solid-Works may not match the configuration used by this book. Also, it is best that new users learn the program in its "natural" state.*

Do you still have the Sump part open? If not, open it up. You are now going to explore some of the view and display commands.

Zoom and Pan Commands

Start at the left of the toolbar and work your way to the right. The first five icons are the zoom and pan icons, which can also be found under View/Modify in the pull-down menus.

Zoom To Fit

The magnifying glass with the red rectangle is the Zoom To Fit icon. Its function most closely resembles AutoCAD's Zoom/All command. Clicking on it zooms the model to fill the screen, leaving some space around the edges. Only the model is taken into consideration when Zoom To Fit is used. Planes or dimensions may not be shown in their entirety if they are larger than or are at some distance from the model.

Zoom To Area

This is represented by the magnifying glass with the red plus sign. It most closely resembles AutoCAD's Zoom/Window operation and is implemented exactly the same way. After clicking on the Zoom To Area icon, select a point to start a window and drag the mouse to establish the opposite corner of the window. This window will be the area zoomed to. Smaller windows will zoom in more quickly.

AutoCAD's zoom function is very powerful in the respect that it can zoom in or out great distances. This is because AutoCAD was created primarily as a 2D architectural drafting tool. SolidWorks is primarily a 3D mechanical design tool. With AutoCAD, you could theoretically write a book on the head of a pin, or draw the solar system at full scale. The solar system example has actually been done, but AutoCAD has stopped including it in their sample files.

SolidWorks can be used to create trains, boats, or tractor-trailers, or it can be used to create tiny gears and springs. However, if you are looking to design a new solar system or write your next novel on the head of a pin, maybe the SolidWorks program is not for you.

Zoom In/Out

To implement this command, click on the Zoom In/Out icon, then hold the left mouse button down and move the mouse either toward you to zoom out or away from you to zoom in. The RTZOOM command in AutoCAD release 13c4 or release 14 is closely analogous to this function.

Rotate View

New users sometimes find this to be a little on the tricky side. Click on the Rotate View icon, which looks like the two clockwise-pointing circular arrows. Hold the left mouse button down and move the mouse cursor left and right or up and down to obtain the desired view. It may seem tricky at first, but with a little practice, you will master it.

There is no counterpart in AutoCAD for this command. You might argue that the Dynamic View command can be used to dynamically rotate an AutoCAD model, but it does not come close. AutoCAD's most recent release of version 14 still does not have any capabilities that match SolidWorks on this level.

Rotate About Screen Center

This is an option that slightly changes the way the Rotate View function works. It is a toggle found under View/

Modify/Rotate About Screen Center. When not checked, parts rotate about their center of mass (centroid). When checked, parts rotate about the center of the screen. This is most easily demonstrated if a part is close to the edge of the screen. Try it with the Sump model to see if you can notice a difference.

Pan

This icon has the four arrows, which point north, south, east, and west. It functions similar to the AutoCAD RTPAN command, but not like the generic PAN command. AutoCAD users will generally try to pick two points that define the pan vector, but SolidWorks does not require this. In SolidWorks, you simply hold the left mouse button down and drag the model in the direction you want it to go. As a quick reference, use the following table to compare SolidWorks view commands to their respective AutoCAD counterparts.

SolidWorks Command	Similar AutoCAD Command
Zoom To Fit	Zoom/All
Zoom To Area	Zoom/Window
Zoom In/Out	RTZOOM
Rotate View	None
Pan	RTPAN

Keyboard Shortcuts

In addition to the icons and pull-down menus, there are some keyboard shortcuts that can be used. In some cases, the keyboard shortcuts do not actually have counterpart icons that perform the same function. These are pointed out in the following list with the use of italics. Use the following keyboard shortcuts for panning and zooming if you find it works easier for you:

Command	Keyboard Shortcut
Rotate the model incrementally	Arrow keys
Rotate the model 90 degrees	Shift + Arrow keys
Rotate clockwise/counterclockwise	Alt + left/right arrow keys
Scroll the model	Ctrl + Arrow keys
Zoom in	Shift + Z
Zoom out	Z

Rotating the model clockwise or counterclockwise using Alt + left or right arrow keys has a setting that changes the increment value at which the part is rotated when these keys are pressed. The following steps are how you would change this incremental value. The illustration that follows shows this operation.

1. Click on Tools/Options....

2. In the View Rotation section of the General tab, specify the number of degrees in the Arrow Keys box.

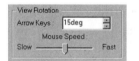

Adjusting the rotation increment.

The default value for this setting is 15 degrees, and that works out quite well. The Mouse Speed slider bar determines the mouse sensitivity when rotating the part using Rotate View. Moving the slider to the right increases sensitivity, and decreases sensitivity if moved to the left. Do not turn up the sensitivity too high until you get the hang of using the Rotate View command.

Display Options

Here is another area where SolidWorks excels over AutoCAD. The next grouping of icons on the right-hand side of the View toolbar are the Display icons. They can also be found in the pull-down menus under View/Display. Some of the Option settings that affect display quality are also explored in this section.

Wireframe

This option will display a simple wireframe view of a part. There is nothing fancy going on here. What is displayed will be very similar to a typical AutoCAD part in its natural display state, which is also wireframe. There is an option that allows you to set the wireframe display quality. The following steps adjust this setting. The illustration that follows shows this operation.

1. Click on Tools/Options in the pull-down menus.

2. Select the Performance tab.

3. In the Wireframe section, select Custom.

4. Adjust the slider bar as desired.

Adjusting wireframe display settings.

What determines where this setting should be set is dependent on the hardware in your computer. Graphics card and processor speed will make a big difference as to how high this setting can be adjusted. If you have a fast machine, crank the slider bar all the way to the right. If you start to see that the computer is slowing down, it might be necessary to move the slider bar to the left. Make small adjustments at a time until a good "middle of the road" setting is found. The goal is to establish the highest display quality with the best performance. This is especially true with regard to shaded display quality. The wireframe display quality also affects the next two display types, discussed in material that follows.

One final note: AutoCAD has a setting called VIEWRES and FACETRES. Basically speaking, VIEWRES sets a system variable that allows you to zoom in and still have arcs and circles look like arcs and circles, instead of looking like various sided polygons. Set the VIEWRES to low, and your circles look like octagons. Set VIEWRES too high, and there may be a performance penalty. If working with solids, FACETRES controls how many facets the model will have when hidden lines are removed. The wireframe performance setting is similar to VIEWRES.

Hidden In Gray

This option could actually be expanded to say "Hidden In Gray" or "Hidden In Dashed." It all depends on another Options setting, which is discussed in upcoming material. The Hidden In Gray icon will calculate where hidden lines are, depending on the current view, and display those hidden lines in a light gray color.

If the model is rotated, hidden lines are recalculated and redisplayed as required for the new view. If the model has many free-form faces, such as lofted or swept geometry, calculating hidden lines may take more time. This holds true for the next display option, which is Hidden Lines Removed. To adjust whether or not hidden lines are displayed as gray or as dashed lines, you would perform the following steps. The illustration that follows shows this operation.

1. Click on Tools/Options....

2. Select the Edges tab.

3. Select the desired option.

Selecting line display for hidden edges.

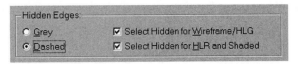

The other two check box options in the Hidden Edges section of the Edges tab are Select Hidden for Wireframe/ HLG and Select Hidden for HLR and Shaded. Select Hidden for Wireframe/HLG allows you to select edges during the editing or design process that would normally be hidden lines if displayed as Hidden In Gray or during Wireframe display. Checking Select Hidden for HLR and

Shaded allows the selection of lines that would be considered hidden while the model is displayed with Hidden Lines Removed or Shaded.

Hidden Lines Removed

This option does not need much explaining. However, you can draw a comparison with AutoCAD here. AutoCAD's hidden line algorithm has been improving through every major release, but it is still archaic when compared to SolidWorks. AutoCAD's hidden line command will remove hidden lines, but there is no way to display those hidden lines as dashed. In AutoCAD, Hidden lines are invisible, and that is that.

Furthermore, if the model is zoomed, panned, or regenerated for any reason, the hidden line display is lost. Hidden line removal will only work with certain AutoCAD entity types. A simple wireframe cannot be displayed with its hidden lines removed; therefore, care must be taken in the creation process to ensure that entities are used that will allow for the hidden line process to be implemented. For SolidWorks, editing a part while its hidden lines are removed is just an icon click away.

Shaded

As previously mentioned, AutoCAD has no capabilities that compare to SolidWorks when dynamically rotating a shaded solid model. The best that AutoCAD can do is render the part, but as soon as the next regeneration takes place, the image reverts back to wireframe, just as with the "hidden lines removed" function. Be it said that AutoCAD is an excellent product, and many of its functional strengths are still superior to SolidWorks. However, in its display capabilities, SolidWorks is superior to AutoCAD.

As with wireframe, shaded display quality can also be adjusted in SolidWorks. Follow these simple steps to change the display quality of the shaded display mode:

1. Click on Tools/Options....

2. Select the Performance tab.

3. In the Shaded Display Quality section, select either Coarse/Fine or Custom.

4. If Custom is selected, adjust the slider bar as necessary.

When adjusting the shaded display quality, as shown in the following illustration, a preview is given that illustrates the "choppiness" of the display. No preview is given for the shading itself. Setting the preview to look like a circle by moving the slider bar from left to right usually makes for a good setting. This gives the best performance while retaining a good shaded display quality. If you will be doing a lot of zooming, it may be necessary to move the slider farther to the right.

The Shaded Display Quality dialog box.

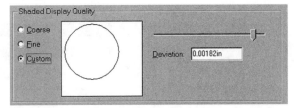

As with adjusting the wireframe display quality, a good middle ground needs to be reached. The more powerful your machine is, the farther to the right you will be able to place the slider bar. Check the hardware section of Chapter 2 for more information regarding this matter.

Other Display Options

The last two display options are Perspective and Section views. The icons on the View toolbar shown in the fourth illustration of this chapter may not be present on your toolbar, but this does not mean that their functions are not present. Do not worry about customizing toolbars at this stage. Just use the View pull-down menu.

Perspective View

To show a model with Perspective mode enabled, click on View/Display/Perspective. There probably will not be a big difference, because this is much more noticeable with long parts. However, the intensity of the perspective can be adjusted. Make sure you are working in shaded mode, then perform the following steps to adjust the degree of perspective. The illustration that follows shows this function.

1. Click on the View pull-down menu.

2. Click on Modify.

3. Click on Perspective.

4. Modify the value in the Perspective Information dialog box.

5. Click on OK.

Modifying perspective settings.

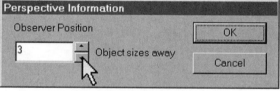

The default value for perspective is 3. A lower value will increase the perspective. The spin box arrows can be used to increment the perspective value up or down. Try setting this to a value of 1 to see if you can perceive a difference. You may need to dynamically rotate the Sump model in order to realize the changes. Then modify the perspective setting a second time and decrease the value even more by typing in a value of .25. With a value of .25, there should definitely be a noticeable difference.

AutoCAD's version of a perspective view is enabled through the use of the DVIEW command. This has always been a chore. For those of you who have worked with DVIEW, you know that some nice results can be achieved, but obtaining the correct Target and Camera angle is cumbersome, to put it mildly. Perspective is enabled through the Distance option, and the UCS changes to remind you that you are in Perspective mode. SolidWorks does not have the limitations AutoCAD does when enabling perspective. All of the Zoom and Display options are still available, and there are no handicaps imposed on the selection methods used.

When you are all done playing with SolidWorks perspective command, you may want to reset the perspective setting to 3. Make sure you turn off Perspective mode when finished. If you do not, you will find the planes and dimensions look particularly weird. Perspective mode makes for a nice effect, but it is not a mode that should be used when designing or editing parts. To turn off Perspective mode, click on View/Display/Perspective. It is a toggle switch; therefore, the check will simply be removed from in front of the Perspective menu option and Perspective mode will be turned off.

Section View

An excellent way to check the design of a model, especially with increasingly complex parts, is to use the Section View function. This allows you to "look inside" the model and check various aspects of the design. It is very useful with parts that have a high degree if inner detail that might otherwise be obscured by other lines and edges of the part. The following are the steps you would use to activate a section view. The illustration that follows shows what the Section View dialog box looks like.

1. Click on View/Display/Section View.

2. Click in the Section Plane(s)/Face(s) list box area of the dialog box.

3. Select the Right plane from FeatureManager.

4. The Right plane should be listed in the Section Plane(s)/Face(s) list box. If another plane is also listed, select that plane from the list box and press the Delete key on your keyboard.

5. Click on Display.

6. If the wrong side is being displayed, click on Flip the Side to View.

7. Click on OK.

Setting up a section view.

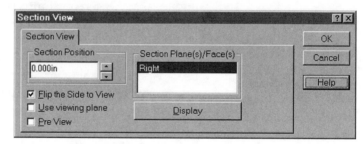

The Pre View check box will automatically update the display every time an option or setting is changed in the Section View dialog box. It is usually easier to make whatever setting changes are necessary, then click on Display to see the effects. The "Use viewing plane" option will use a plane parallel to the current view. No selection of a plane is necessary because the plane used by Solid-Works is dependent on whatever view you happen to be using at the moment.

Section Position will offset the section plane selected in the Section Plane(s)/Face(s) list box. If adjusting this setting, look at the screen to see a preview of where the section view plane will be positioned. Click on Display or OK when the desired offset value is achieved.

Section views can be created in AutoCAD through the use of a workaround method. There is no user-friendly, straightforward way to create one. Sections can be created for drawing layouts, but that is a different topic. See Chapter 8 for comparisons regarding 2D section views.

↝ **NOTE:** *Section views are used for viewing purposes only. The geometry that results from creating a section view does not actually exist in a model and cannot be selected or used in any way to edit or build on the model. Section views can only be used for verification purposes. For this reason, it is best to turn off the section view before continuing the editing or design phase of a model.*

To turn off a section view, click on View/Display/Section View. You should notice that the check mark is then removed from the menu item and the original model view is restored. Section Views and Perspective mode can be used in combination. See the following illustration for an example of this. The lighting has been modified to accent the sectioned faces. (Lighting characteristics are covered in Chapter 9.

Sump part with Section View and Perspective mode enabled.

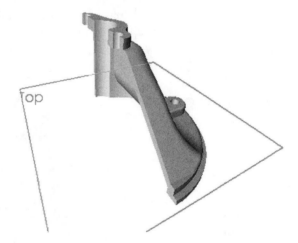

Drawing Layout Section Views

Two-dimensional section views can be created for layouts as well, but this procedure is much different and is covered in Chapter 8. Drawing-section layout views include Curvature and Redraw. The following sections explain these two functions.

Curvature

Curvature is a function that does not get used every day. For this reason, Curvature does not have its own icon in SolidWorks. In AutoCAD, there is no command that performs this function. What does the SolidWorks Curvature command accomplish? It shows where the radius of curvature is smallest on a part. The Sump part is a perfect example to use for this command because it has varying degrees of curvature. If you are running on a slower computer (Pentium 100 or less), you may want to think twice about attempting this.

To perform this command, click on View/Display/Curvature. The model will be shown using shades of green, yellow, orange, and red. Green represents slight curvature, with red representing the highest degree of curvature (smallest radius). It may surprise AutoCAD users that the part can be freely rotated and zoomed without causing a regeneration. To toggle the Curvature display off, click on View/Display/Curvature. The model will return to its normal state. The following illustration shows an example of the Curvature display.

Example of the Curvature display.

Redraw

This icon is not on the View toolbar, but this chapter is a good place to introduce the Redraw command. Redraw functions much the same way as AutoCAD's Redraw command. The screen is repainted, or refreshed. It is nothing more than a refresher for the graphics display. Nothing in the part or model database is recalculated; no regenerations are performed. To complete a Redraw, use any one of the following options:

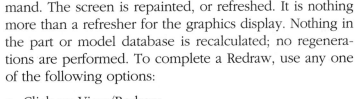

- Click on View/Redraw.
- Click on the Redraw icon located on the Standard toolbar (see the illustration at left).
- use the Ctrl + R hot key combination.

The Redraw icon.

If at any time you notice dots or lines on the graphics display you do not think should be there, perform a redraw to see if the images in question go away. If the images remain, keep reading!

Setting Grid and Snap Properties

The following sections discuss grid and snap settings. These settings establish characteristics of grid and snap behavior that determine how a part is sketched or drawn.

Grid Settings

Grid properties can be set to define the characteristics of the grid and snap behavior. The grid can be applied when creating part sketches or drawings. The grid can be used as a visual aid and to set the snap grid characteristics. This can make creating a sketch easier, but also has some drawbacks, which are explored in this section.

The Grid Function

The grid can be left visible without the grid snap active, and vice versa. The grid can be defined with system default values and changed as required during sketching. Aligning the grid to a model edge can make the spacing easier to work with if the model edges do not necessarily conform to the horizontal and vertical nature of the grid. Accessing the grid can be done in two ways. The easiest method is to click on the Grid icon on the Sketch toolbar, as shown in the following illustration.

Accessing the Grid/Units tab from the Grid icon.

The second method is to perform the following steps:

1. Click on Tools/Options....

2. Select the Grid/Units tab.

The following list is a quick rundown of what the various settings will accomplish in the Grid Properties section of the Grid/Units tab, which is shown in the illustration that follows.

Display Grid	Toggles the grid display on and off.
Dash	Displays the grid as dashed lines as opposed to light gray.
Automatic Scaling	Redefines grid parameters if zooming in close or far away in order to achieve a more reasonable grid spacing. Otherwise, zooming out too far would result in the grid being too dense and therefore not displayed at all.
Major Grid Spacing	Sets the spacing for major grid lines.
Minor Lines Per Major	Specifies how many divisions the major grid spacing will have.

Grid Properties section of the Grid/Units tab.

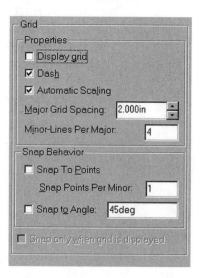

Most CAD programs have some sort of grid function. They are implemented differently, and look slightly different, but the functionality remains basically the same. Using a grid for creating a mechanical part is usually not necessary. However, sometimes a grid has a tendency to help new users get their bearing on what plane they are sketching on. The grid will not be visible unless sketching; therefore, in order to see the grid, you have to enter sketch mode. Without worrying about the mechanics involved with entering a sketch, discussed in Chapter 5, follow these steps so that you can experiment with the grid settings:

1. Make sure you have the Sump.sldprt model open.

2. Select the Top plane from FeatureManager (this may be called Plane2 on your system). This will be your sketch plane.

3. Click on Insert/Sketch.

If the grid is not visible, complete the process previously mentioned in order to turn it on. Feel free to rotate the part and make some modifications to the grid settings to get a feel for how they operate.

Aligning a Grid to a Model Edge

If it is your preference to use the grid, there may be an occasion when the horizontal alignment of the grid does not lend itself very well to the current situation. Take for example a typical AutoCAD drawing in which most of the lines are orthogonal, but at an angle other than horizontal.

In this scenario, the AutoCAD operator would typically enter the Drawing Aids dialog box and set the snap angle to the desired value. This rotates the grid and crosshairs so that entities can be created with minimal effort. Aligning the grid to a model edge in SolidWorks has much the same effect. Align a grid to a model edge using the following procedure. The illustration that follows shows the Align Grid dialog box.

1. Select the model edge (must be in sketch mode, but the font edge can be selected before or after activating the dialog box).

2. Click on Tools/Sketch Tools/Align Grid.

3. Select Apply.

4. If the alignment is not satisfactory, select a different edge and reapply.

5. Click on OK when done.

The Align Grid dialog box.

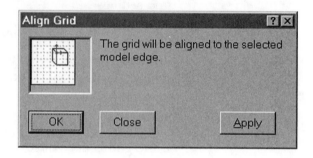

Snap Settings

SolidWorks' snap settings functionality is similar to AutoCAD's. However, as with grid settings, snap setting implementation is different between the two environments. For those not familiar with what a snap grid is, the snap grid can be thought of as an invisible grid that controls where the cursor can draw. Endpoints of lines and arcs will always "snap" to the closest node on the snap grid.

The Snap Function

If the snap grid is set to the same size as the display grid, all snap points will appear to be on the visible display grid. An example of setting snap behavior is shown in the following illustration. The list that follows describes the various SolidWorks snap settings and the functions they perform.

Setting snap behavior.

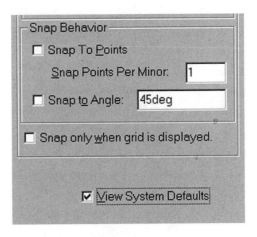

Snap To Points	Toggles the snap grid on and off.
Snap Points Per Minor	Sets the number of snap points per minor grid line.
Snap To Angle	Toggles angle snap on and off and sets the value of the angle snap.
Snap Only When Grid Is Displayed	Enables snapping when grid is on only. If the grid is off, snap mode is disabled. View System Defaults must be checked in order to activate this option.
View System Defaults	Enables you to see what the current system defaults are. These may be different from settings for the current document.

AutoCAD does not have a Snap To Angle function. Snapping to an angle is convenient if all or most of the angled lines in a sketch have the same angle. For instance, a setting of 45 degrees would make drawing an octagon much easier because all of the angled lines would be at 45 degrees.

Using a snap grid and snapping to geometric points are two completely different things. SolidWorks contains the capabilities that allow you to create a snap grid, much like AutoCAD. AutoCAD also has Object Snaps and Running

Object Snaps. SolidWorks has a version of these geometric snap functions, which are discussed in Chapter 5.

A Final Word on Using Snap

Whether or not you use snap is ultimately up to you. If it works for you, and you find it a useful and convenient tool, use it to your advantage. It should be noted, however, that implementing the snap function is something normally just not needed in SolidWorks. This goes back to the basic underlying differences between AutoCAD and SolidWorks.

When creating wireframe or solid geometry in a nonparametric program such as AutoCAD, accuracy is the name of the game. If lines are not of precise length, the model is no good and will have to be edited or rebuilt. In SolidWorks, lines are roughly sketched in, then driven by dimension values. It is not necessary to be 100 percent accurate when drawing the sketch, because SolidWorks takes care of the accuracy when the dimensions are added. For this reason, and this reason alone, a snap grid is just not needed.

Summary

Selecting objects in SolidWorks is done with the left mouse button. Clicking on an entity will select it. If selecting more than one item, hold down the Control key. When selecting sketch geometry, use the window method to select more than one entity at a time. The window drag direction makes no difference in SolidWorks, as it does in AutoCAD.

Always pay attention to the cursor! It changes to let you know what is going to be selected. This may be a vertex point, edge, face or plane, dimension, or some other type of entity such as a line or arc. The right mouse button displays a context-sensitive menu. What is displayed in the menu that pops up as a result of a mouse click depends on what the cursor is placed over when the right mouse button is clicked.

Display functions in SolidWorks are much more user friendly and powerful than AutoCAD's display functions. The ability to dynamically rotate a shaded part aids in editing a part and finding any aspects of the part that may need correcting. Most of SolidWorks' zooming and panning commands are similar to commands found in AutoCAD.

Use the grid and snap functions if they will offer some benefit to the design process of the part being created, but keep in mind that SolidWorks parametric capabilities render the snap function superfluous. When creating a sketch, dimension values shape the model. This is opposite to an AutoCAD user's way of thinking.

In Chapter 5 you will get down to business with creating sketch geometry. All of the sketch entity types will be covered, from lines and arcs to elliptical arcs and splines. System feedback will be explored in much greater depth, and you will also get into feature geometry and how to create your first base feature.

5 Sketching

Introduction

Sketches are a collection of 2D entities (e.g., lines, arcs, circles, and splines) used to define a profile of a solid feature. These 2D sketches are the foundation of the solid modeling process. Planes and model faces are used to define sketching planes. A sketch profile is created on a 2D plane and then used to define a solid feature (e.g., an extrusion or cut).

Mastering sketching skills is fundamental to becoming a proficient solid modeler. Sketches are the building blocks of solid features. Much of the parametric intelligence and flexibility of a model is defined during this stage of the design process.

Content

Because sketch geometry is so fundamental to the Solid-Works design process, much importance needs to be placed on the techniques used when creating a sketch. The "Sketch Basics" section describes some of the basic sketching concepts and fundamental principles used in creating a sketch. The "Sketch Entities" section discusses how individual SolidWorks sketch entities are created, with steps to guide you through the process. The section "Sketch Tools" introduces other tools used to draw various sketch entities and shows you how to extract existing sketch geometry from features.

The "Sketch Dimensions and Constraints" section shows you how to create sketch dimensions and add intelligent relationships between sketch entities. The "Modifying a Sketch" section discusses various aspects of how an existing sketch can be edited. SolidWorks allows for an existing sketch feature to be redefined, thereby modifying the shape of the part. The sketch can be redefined to add or delete sketch entities, dimensions, or constraints. The sketch plane for the sketch can also be redefined, and this section contains process steps that show you how this is accomplished.

The chapter ends with an example sketch that guides you through an actual design of a part. This example demonstrates how a part is created using sketch geometry to create solid features.

Objectives   With completion of the "Sketch Basics" section, you should understand how to select a sketch plane and how the complexity of a sketch affects a part. You should also be able to create dimensions and add geometric constraints. Completion of the "Sketch Entities" section will enable you to create all of the various sketch entities. You should also be able to modify an existing sketch, dimension, or constraint, or change the sketch plane itself. In addition, you should also understand how to reuse an existing sketch to create a new feature.

Sketch Basics

The skills required for sketching include the ability to identify features and sketch planes, as well as the methods necessary for constraining sketch entities geometrically and dimensionally. The methods used to define these features determine how a part will behave when edited. There are some basic steps that need to be performed repeatedly in order to build a new solid model. There are also some basic rules that need to be followed. These rules and steps will be examined first. The following illustration is an example of a very simple sketch. It contains simple line segments and dimensions. Also notice the origin point in the center of the sketch.

Sample sketch.

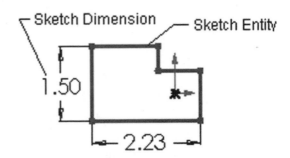

Feature-based Modeling

Feature-based modeling is a term used to describe the various functional components of a part. The ability to identify features is key to intelligently creating parts and assemblies. For example, a sketch might contain a single circle to define a cut, or a group of holes that define a hole pattern. If a group of sketch entities are related to one another, and they perform a common function (e.g., mount hole pattern), they can be created within the same sketch.

The following illustration shows an example of feature-based modeling. Take a moment to look at all of the various feature types that were actually used to create this solid model. Pay more attention to the actual feature type and not the names of the specific features.

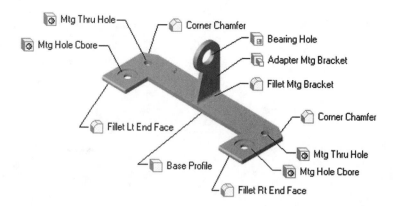

Many separate features constitute a complete model.

This sample part consists of a series of boss and cut extrusions, fillets, and chamfers. The holes can be added by performing a cut and extrusion, or by using the hole wizard. You will learn both of these methods in Chapter 6.

Sketched Features Versus Applied Features

Features can be divided into two groups. These are sketched features and applied features. The main difference between these two feature types is that a sketched feature requires a sketch, and an applied feature does not. Examples of sketched features are extrusions, revolved features, or swept or lofted features. Applied features are applied directly to the part and do not require sketch geometry. For this reason, they are easier to create. Examples of applied features are fillets, chamfers, domes, and shells. (All of these types of features are explored in depth in Chapter 6.)

An important distinction that should be made between AutoCAD and SolidWorks is that SolidWorks uses feature-based modeling techniques, whereas AutoCAD does not. AutoCAD's equivalent, Boolean operations, requires adding and subtracting of solid geometry to shape a part. In SolidWorks, features are always added. Also, SolidWorks features can be changed later, whereas Boolean features cannot. Even though a cut feature will remove material, you are still adding a feature. Try to think in these terms, as it will help you to understand the different mindset needed to work well in SolidWorks.

Sketch Guidelines

There are a few simple rules that should be followed when sketching. There are always exceptions to rules, but generally speaking, a sketch should be a *closed non-self-intersecting profile*. Take a look at the following example to see what a sketch should *not* look like. The following illustration shows a self-intersecting profile, an open profile, and a profile with intersecting islands. Islands can be defined as independent profiles.

Examples of what a sketch should not look like.

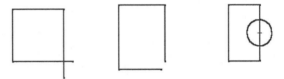

The process of creating a sketch can be broken down into five steps that are repeated numerous times to create a solid model. It would be to your advantage to memorize these five steps. They are as follows:

1. Select a sketch plane.

2. Enter sketch mode.

3. Create the sketch.

4. Add dimensions and constraints.

5. Create the feature.

File these steps away somewhere in the back of your mind for later use. Every sketched feature created will be based on them. The exception is applied features that do not require sketch geometry. (Sketched and applied features are explored in Chapter 6.)

Sketch Complexity

Another good rule of thumb is that *it is better to have less complicated sketch geometry and more features than complicated sketch geometry and fewer features.* Sketches that are overly complex can be difficult to create, dimension, and maintain. Making many overly simplistic sketches can create too many features in a part, which makes the part difficult to understand and modify. A good rule of thumb is to create sketches with logically grouped sets of features. The following illustration shows an example of a sketch with more geometry than a single sketch should have.

Too much sketch geometry for one feature.

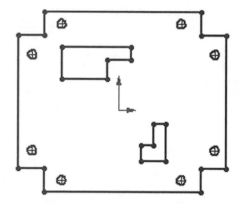

If this sketch were extruded, it would probably create a set of features you do not want. Because of the islands (separate profiles) within the larger main profile, Solid-Works would interpret the smaller islands as cuts.

Creating complex sketches can make feature editing more difficult. Combining too many features into a single sketch can make the part less flexible, and in some cases unusable. It is easier to modify, suppress, reorder, or delete the features of a sketch when the features are contained in a separate sketch. The following illustrations show how the features could have been created by separating the sketch geometry into logical groups.

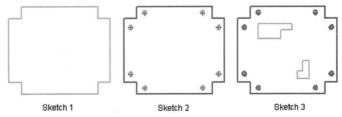

Sketch 1   Sketch 2   Sketch 3

Same sketch divided into separate features.

The first sketch shows a good sketch for the main feature, otherwise known as the base feature. Sketch 2 illustrates a typical sketch for cutting the eight holes out of the base feature. Sketch 3 contains two shapes used to create bosses on the base feature. The sketch geometry is grouped logically and performs independent functions.

Constraining Sketch Geometry

A constraint is a method used to define the position or size of a sketch entity. A constraint can be either geometric or dimensional. A geometric constraint is a relation added to the sketch to control an attribute (i.e., horizontal, vertical, tangent, and so on) of a sketch entity or between two or more sketch entities. The number and type of dimensions and constraints added to a sketch depend on the design intent of the model. Some constraints are added automatically by SolidWorks during the sketch process, with other constraints added using the Add Relation function.

A dimensional constraint is a sketch dimension used to define the size or angle of a sketch entity. A sketch dimension can be modified to change the size or shape of the dimensioned sketch entity. SolidWorks does not require that dimensions be added to a sketch. For instance, if a dimension value is not known, the dimension does not have to be added. Be aware, though, that in order to modify a dimension, one must be present.

It is good practice and common sense to place dimensions in the sketch. This way, the dimensions can be accessed at a later time and the values of those dimensions can be changed as needed. Additionally, dimensions placed in the sketch will carry over to the drawing layout when that drawing is created. If there are no dimensions in the sketch, there will be no dimensions brought over from the part file into the drawing. As a result, reference dimensions will have to be added.

You should dimension a sketch in a manner that defines the design intent. By dimensioning the sketch in this manner, the sketch and model can be changed to tweak the design and achieve the desired shape. References to existing feature geometry can be made, resulting in a part that will change shape predictably when modifications are made.

The following illustration shows how a hole pattern was dimensioned to impart the design intent for the feature. The spacing between the holes and the distances from the top left corner of the base feature define the locations for the holes. Additional geometric relations (i.e., horizontal, vertical, and equal radii) were also defined to reduce the number of dimensions required to both produce the sketch and maintain the ability to change one value and have both circles update together. The various constraints available are discussed later in this chapter.

Sketch dimensions placed to create design intent.

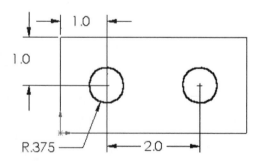

Take a closer look at the options available when placing dimensions in the previous example. If the horizontal dimension of 1 inch were modified, the two circles would move left or right. This is because a horizontal dimension from center to center between the circles has been included. In this model, it was more important to directly control the distance between the centerpoints of the circles. Alternatively, the circle on the right could have been dimensioned to the upper right corner of the rectangular base feature. It all depends on design intent, which is what must be considered during the design process and when placing dimensions and constraints.

Constraints

You need to understand what *constraint* (called "relation" in SolidWorks) means in the SolidWorks environment. If two line segments are drawn in SolidWorks, and one line is constrained parallel to the other, moving either line will result in the other line moving to maintain the parallel relationship. If the same two lines were drawn in AutoCAD, they may very well be parallel to start with, but moving the end of one line will not effect the other line whatsoever. This is a fundamental difference between the two programs.

Constraints are added in one of two ways. They can be added by SolidWorks automatically while sketching, or they can be added by the user afterward. When constraints are added by SolidWorks during a sketch, the cursor changes to let you know exactly what constraints are being added at that time. Just as it is very important for a new AutoCAD user to read the command prompt, it is very important for a new SolidWorks user to watch the cursor.

When SolidWorks changes the cursor to let you know what is going on, it is known as *cursor inferencing.* (This concept is covered in detail later in this chapter, and you will have a chance to see inferencing in practice.) The following are the SolidWorks constraints available to you.

- Horizontal
- Vertical
- Perpendicular
- Parallel

- Concentric
- At Intersection
- Tangent
- Symmetric

- Midpoint
- Coincident
- Collinear
- Coradial

- Equal Length/Radii
- Merge Points
- Pierce
- Fix

Many of these constraints are self-explanatory. Some should look similar to AutoCAD snap options, and others may be completely new terms. (The section "Modifying a Sketch" later in this chapter discusses exactly what all of these constraints do and how you can add and delete them.)

Sketch Planes

When you create a sketch, you must define a sketch plane on which to place the new 2D sketch. This is step 1 of the five-step process previously mentioned. If you were a drafter working on a wooden drawing board, you would need a sheet of paper before you could start drawing.

Likewise, in SolidWorks you must have a plane before you can start sketching. This is the plane that will be used to define the location of the sketch. The sketch plane can be a planar model face or a plane entity. If the plane does not exist, the plane must be created prior to creating the sketch. This can be accomplished in one of seven ways, which are explained in material that follows.

AutoCAD does not require a sketch plane. A 3D line can be created by just typing in its x-y-z coordinates. This is possible in SolidWorks, but it is not important to this discussion. What is important is to realize the similarities and differences between the UCS and a SolidWorks sketch plane. The UCS can be moved by defining its geometric location through a variety of options, such as AutoCAD's 3Point option.

SolidWorks allows the creation of a plane through a similar option. AutoCAD can create wireframe 3D geometry without the need of a plane, but SolidWorks does not need or use wireframe geometry. When creating an extrusion in AutoCAD, the extrusion direction is perpendicular to the UCS (using default options). In SolidWorks, the extrusion direction is perpendicular to the sketch plane.

SolidWorks planes are represented by a rectangular box, but theoretically extend infinitely in all directions. The direction the solid feature should go, such as for an extrusion, determines the desirable orientation for the sketch plane. The example shown in the following illustration shows how a plane or a part face can be used to create a sketch. The sketch can then be used to create a cut (material removed) or boss (material added).

Selecting sketch planes.

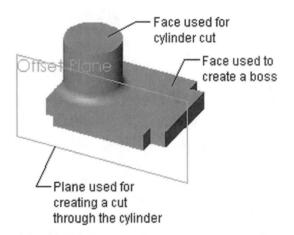

Face used for cylinder cut

Face used to create a boss

Offset Plane

Plane used for creating a cut through the cylinder

Compare the previous illustration to the following to better understand what features were being added and why the sketch planes were chosen the way they were. A plane can be used when a sketch plane does not exist on a part, such as with the cut through the side of the cylindrical boss. There is no flat face that can be used to create the 2D sketch. A plane (Offset Plane) was defined to create the sketch. The solid cut was then defined to cut through the cylinder.

Resulting features are perpendicular to their respective sketch planes.

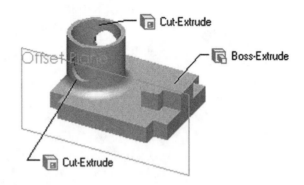

➥ **NOTE:** *It is usually a good idea to rename a new plane using a meaningful name. This helps document the design, and makes understanding and modifying the design easier. Remember the slow double click technique of Chapter 3. This renaming function works for features and sketch names as well.*

Creating a Sketch

Sketches are used to define 2D geometry, which in turn is used to define features in a solid model. Starting a sketch is a very simple procedure. It involves selecting a plane and clicking on an icon. Do you remember the Widget part started earlier? If you would like to follow along at this point, open up *Widget.sldprt*. If you did not save your work, start a new part. Right click on the front plane to show it and turn off (hide) any other planes that might be on. If the view needs to be changed, remember to click on View/Orientation and change to the Front view by double clicking on Front. You may want to click on the View Orientation pushpin to keep this dialog box on top.

Entering Sketch Mode

Perform the following steps to enter sketch mode:

1. Click on the Front plane to select it—either from the FeatureManager or in the sketch area, it does not matter. It should be green when selected.

2. Click on the Sketch icon.

You should now be in sketch mode. You can verify this a number of ways. The first tell-tale sign is the origin point. It should be red instead of gray. This represents the x-y axis. Another sign is the sketch icon. It will appear depressed, as though it is pushed in. Take a look at the title bar. It should now read *Sketch1 of Widget.sldprt*, or something similar. The title bar lets you know what sketch is currently active and the part being edited.

Also, FeatureManager will have a new item in it. At the bottom of the FeatureManager list should be the name of the new sketch just started. SolidWorks starts out naming sketches as Sketch1, then increments the number as more are created. If Sketch1 were deleted, SolidWorks would still name the next sketch Sketch2, even though Sketch1 no longer existed.

Sketch Orientation

Sketching can be done in any view orientation. There are times when an orientation normal to the sketch plane may make sketching, constraining, and dimensioning sketch entities easier. Sometimes sketching in a plane view may be more difficult because it is difficult to see certain aspects of the existing solid geometry. The view orientation will not affect the sketch geometry; therefore, use any view that makes your job easier.

In the previous example, step 1 asks you to click on the Front plane. Bear in mind that this can be any plane or planar face. A very common error is for a new user to select the plane they would like to sketch on, and then instead of clicking on the sketch icon, doing something else first. It may be changing a view, changing a setting in their options, turning the grid on, or any number of things. When this happens, the selected plane normally becomes deselected. The user then clicks the sketch icon sometime later, whereupon SolidWorks puts the user on a plane other than the one originally intended.

➣ **NOTE:** *The easiest way to eliminate this common error is to follow one simple rule: After selecting your sketch* *plane, immediately click on the sketch icon. Following this very simple rule will keep you out of trouble later on, and will probably eliminate a good deal of frustration.*

Cursor Inferencing

The cursor can offer many visual clues for two main reasons. The first reason for the cursor changing is to provide you with a symbol showing what entity will be selected if the left mouse button is clicked. As previously stated, this entity might be a vertex point, plane, face, edge, and so on. A second reason for providing visual feedback through the cursor is to allow constraints to be added during the sketch process and to aid in sketching.

Cursor inferencing is a function that displays the cursor in a different manner when creating a sketch entity, depending on the object being created and the placement of the cursor with respect to other entities in the sketch. Understanding the meaning of the cursor icons can save time and effort, while producing better sketches and models.

The inferencing cursor graphically shows the geometric sketching relationships added automatically during sketching. Inferencing can be used to automatically define geometric relationships. SolidWorks will tell you exactly what constraints are being added as you sketch. It is up to you to recognize them and use these intelligent cursor symbols to your advantage.

➠ **NOTE:** *Good sketching techniques will define the quality and robustness of a solid model.*

The importance of carefully choosing geometric constraints is that the choices made during sketch creation will determine how the model can be modified. Always try to choose meaningful geometric constraints. Adding unnecessary constraints can prove inconvenient when modifying the model and may have to be removed at a later time. They may even overdefine the model to the point that the model is unsolvable. The following illustration shows an example of cursor inferencing.

Cursor inferencing while sketching a line.

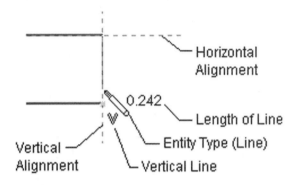

Inferencing Cursor Symbols

The cursor shape will change when creating a sketch entity. The cursor will also display additional information (e.g., length or radius) based on the type of entity being created. If the cursor is placed over an entity, the symbol will be displayed for that entity. The following is a list of the various sketched entity symbols you might see:

- Arc
- Centerline
- Centerpoint Ellipse (SolidWorks term for an elliptical arc)
- Circle
- Ellipse
- Line
- Point
- Rectangle
- Spline
- Text (listed as sketch geometry here, not as a note)

Other Sketch Symbols

In addition to symbols that tell you what type of entity the cursor is over, SolidWorks will also display many other symbols to help while sketching. With AutoCAD, you would use object snaps to control the geometric placement of entities. In SolidWorks, the "snapping" happens on the fly. There is no middle mouse button pop-up menu to access, because it is not needed. The following list contains a good majority of SolidWorks symbols you might see while actually sketching geometry. The symbols that will result in an actual constraint being added by SolidWorks appear in *italics*.

- 0° quadrant point
- 90° quadrant point
- 180° quadrant point
- 270° quadrant point
- Arc included angle = 90°
- Arc included angle = 180°
- Arc included angle = 270°
- Coincident
- Endpoint

- Horizontal
- Horizontal alignment
- *Intersection*
- *Midpoint*
- *Parallel*
- *Perpendicular*
- *Tangent*
- *Vertical*
- Vertical alignment

In the next section, "Sketch Entities," you should try to follow along with the book. It is also urged that you pay close attention to the cursor and watch for the various inferencing symbols that might appear.

Sketch Entities

In this section, which explains the various types of sketch entities, a step-by-step process is provided so that you can follow along or refer back to this book at a later time. Open the Widget part or start a new part if you will be following along in SolidWorks. Before you start, review the following points.

- Prior to sketching, a plane or planar face must be selected.
- The sketch icon should be clicked on immediately following plane selection.
- As you sketch, the cursor will display symbols that aid in the sketch process.
- Some constraints will be added automatically by SolidWorks as you sketch.
- Always keep an eye on the cursor while sketching or selecting entities.

- Use View/Orientation or the arrow keys to change views.
- A slow double click on an item in FeatureManager allows you to rename the item.

In AutoCAD, setting the grid and snap grid would probably take place at this point. If you would like to set up the grid, which might help keep you oriented as to what plane you are sketching on, turn the grid on at this point. It is strongly recommended that the snap grid be left off. The reasons for this were explained in Chapter 4.

Right click on the Front plane and show it. Remember, it usually helps to show the plane being sketched on. This serves as a visual guide, but is not required. Next, make sure the Front plane is selected (entities are green when selected), then click on the Sketch icon. This is the icon that looks like a pencil on the Sketch toolbar, as shown in the following illustration.

If you have successfully entered sketch mode, you will notice that a new sketch has been started in FeatureManager and that the origin has turned red to indicate an active sketch. In addition, the Sketch Tools toolbar should now be active. You will initially be dealing with the first nine icons on this toolbar.

Clicking on the Sketch icon.

During this section, hold the cursor over an icon if you need to see the yellow tool tip that will tell you what the icon's name is. This information will be displayed at the bottom left-hand corner of your SolidWorks screen as well. You can also reference the following illustration to see what the names of the first nine Sketch Tool icons are.

The sketch entity icons.

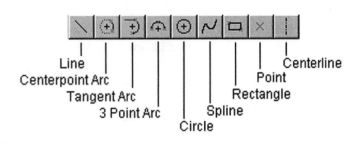

•➤ **NOTE:** *In the following examples, the terms* pick *and* drag *will be used. When an item is picked, it is being clicked on by the left mouse button. If the term* drag *is used, the left mouse button should be held down and the mouse moved at the same time. In other words, the common phrase "pick and drag" means to select something and move the mouse while keeping the left mouse button depressed.*

In order to begin sketching an entity, you must click on the appropriate icon. To draw a line, you must click the line icon. Simple enough, right? Check one optional setting before you begin. Click on Tools/Options... and look in the top left corner of the General tab. There will be a check box option "Single command per pick." Make sure it is *not* selected. The reason for this is because if this option is selected, a command (i.e., line or circle command) will exit after using the command. This is inconvenient when you want to draw more than one line or circle, or whatever you happen to be sketching.

Leaving "Single command per pick" unchecked allows you to continue using the selected command until that command is no longer needed. In this case, the command must be exited manually. This can be done in a number of ways. In order to exit out of a command, you can perform any one of the following:

• Click on the command's icon again to deselect it.
• Click on the Select icon (this looks like a cursor) on the Sketch toolbar.
• Press the Escape key on your keyboard.

In the steps contained in the sections that follow, which describe entity types, it is assumed you know enough to click the appropriate icon in order to start the command. Reference the sketch entity icons in the previous illustration if you need to. Also, some of the entities in the examples are green and some are blue. Realize that green simply means that an entity has been selected. It should also be noted that when an entity is drawn, it is selected by default. You will notice this if you are working along with this book. It is standard operating procedure for SolidWorks.

Line

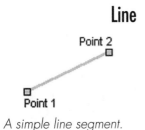

A simple line segment.

A line is defined as a straight line segment between two points, as shown in the illustration at left. To sketch a line, perform the following steps:

1. Pick a point to start the line.

2. Drag the second endpoint.

Centerpoint Arc

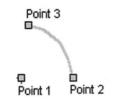

A completed arc using Centerpoint Arc.

A centerpoint arc, shown in the illustration at left, is defined by its centerpoint, radius, start point, and endpoint. There are three ways to define arcs, and Centerpoint Arc is the trickiest. Give it a few tries for practice by performing the following steps:

1. Pick a point to define the centerpoint.

2. Drag the radius. Where you release the left mouse button determines the radius and the arc start point.

3. Pick a second time to drop the first point. Drag the arc's endpoint. Release the button to drop point 3.

Tangent Arc

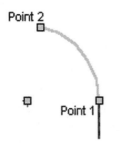

Creating a tangent arc from a small line segment.

A tangent arc, shown in the illustration at left, is defined by selecting a sketch entity endpoint and dragging the arc to the desired location. The arc will remain tangent to the selected sketch entity. This arc option is very user friendly, but it is important to remember to select an existing entity endpoint. Whether it is the endpoint of an arc or line makes no difference. To sketch an arc tangent to an existing sketch entity, perform the following steps:

1. Pick an endpoint to draw the arc tangent to.

2. Drag the arc length and radius. Where you let go determines the endpoint of the tangent arc.

3 Point Arc

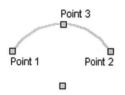

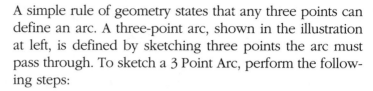

A typical three-point arc.

A simple rule of geometry states that any three points can define an arc. A three-point arc, shown in the illustration at left, is defined by sketching three points the arc must pass through. To sketch a 3 Point Arc, perform the following steps:

1. Select the start point for the arc.

2. Drag the endpoint for the arc.

3. Pick and drag the arc midpoint (the green dot, or point 3 in the previous illustration) to define the radius.

Circle

Picking and dragging a circle.

A circle does not need much of an introduction. It is one of the most user-friendly of all sketch entities, and is similar to AutoCAD's Circle command with the Radius option. To sketch a circle, perform the following steps. Picking and dragging a circle is shown in the illustration at left.

1. Pick to place the center of the circle.

2. Drag the radius.

Ellipse

Do not spend too much time looking for the Ellipse icon. There is one, but it is not on the Sketch Tools toolbar by default. Use the pull-down menu for this one. The ellipse function defines an ellipse, shown in the illustration at left, by specifying major and minor axes. To sketch an ellipse, complete the following steps:

1. Select Ellipse from the Tools/Sketch Entity pull-down menu.

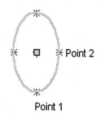

Pick and drag twice to create an ellipse.

2. Pick the center of the ellipse and drag the first axis length. Where you let go of the mouse button will also determine rotation of the ellipse (see point 1 in the illustration at left).

3. Pick and drag the second axis length (usually at a point 90 degrees from the first axis, such as with point 2 in the illustration at left).

The order in which the major or minor axes are created does not matter. If the first axis is longer, it would be considered the major axis, and vice versa.

Centerpoint Ellipse

A centerpoint ellipse, shown in the illustration at left, defines an elliptical arc with a major and minor diameter and a start and endpoint. Do not let the name throw you off, as this command could very well have been called Elliptical Arc instead. The centerpoint ellipse is a partial ellipse. The start and endpoints are defined after an elliptical outline is created.

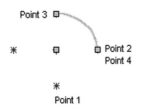

The steps to create this entity start out exactly the same as those for Ellipse, but have one more step added. If you were having trouble with Ellipse, go back and practice before you attempt this one. To sketch a centerpoint ellipse, perform the following steps:

To complete a centerpoint ellipse, you must pick and drag three times.

1. Select Centerpoint Ellipse from the Tools/Sketch Entity pull-down menu.

2. Pick the center of the ellipse and drag the first axis length. Where you let go of the mouse button will also determine rotation of the ellipse (see point 1 in the illustration at left).

3. Pick and drag the second axis length (usually at a point 90 degrees from the first axis).

4. Pick the start point of the elliptical arc (usually somewhere on the blue dashed outline of the ellipse, such as with point 3) and drag the endpoint (point 4).

Spline

A spline is a curve defined by a set of control points. These control points define locations the curve will pass through. An alternate spline creation method can be selected from the General tab in the Tools/Options menu and selecting the Alternate spline creation check box (see the following illustration).

The Alternate spline creation check box.

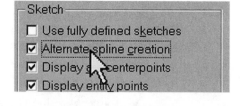

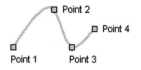

A simple spline with four control points.

Both spline creation methods will be covered so that you can see how each one functions. If Alternate spline creation is *not* checked, perform the following steps. The illustration at left shows a simple spline.

1. Pick the start point of the spline and drag the second control point.

2. Pick the second control point and drag the third control point.

3. Repeat as necessary for all of the control points.

4. To complete the spline, double click on the final control point, or click once anywhere but on the last control point.

If Alternate spline creation *is* checked, perform these steps:

1. Pick wherever a control point is needed (no dragging is necessary).

2. Double click on the final control point to complete the spline.

As you can see, the alternate method for creating splines is much easier. The method used in creating the spline will make no difference to the physical qualities of the spline. Use whichever method is easiest for you.

Rectangle

A rectangle, shown in the illustration that follows, is a set of two vertical and two horizontal lines joined at the ends. This function is quicker and easier than sketching four

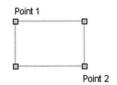

Rectangle created with the Rectangle command.

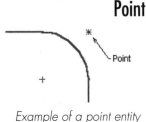

Example of a point entity constrained to an intersection of two lines.

A simple centerline entity.

Point

Centerline

Text

separate lines, and SolidWorks will add the horizontal and vertical constraints automatically. To create a rectangle, perform the following steps:

1. Pick to place the first corner of the rectangle.

2. Drag to place the opposite corner of the rectangle.

A point is a reference entity only. Points are useful for referencing theoretical intersections, such as in the illustration at left, and sometimes for constraining purposes. Another good example is the use of points to define a plane. Dimensions can also be attached to sketch points. Unlike AutoCAD, SolidWorks points cannot have their appearance changed. A SolidWorks point will look like an asterisk, or a green dot if selected. To create a point, all you need to do is select a location with the left mouse button.

A centerline, shown in the illustration that follows, is created similar to a line and is used for mirroring, revolving, dimensioning references, and establishing geometric relationships. Even though it has all of these functions, it is still considered a reference entity only. Points and centerlines are unique entity types because they do not contribute to the geometry of a solid model. To create a centerline, perform the following steps:

1. Pick to place the centerline start point.

2. Drag the second endpoint.

Sketch text can be used to create text on a part face or plane and then used to create a feature. This feature can be a cut, extrusion, or other feature type. Common uses are for raised lettering and sunken text. When using text in a sketch, the text must be the only entity in the sketch. For instance, if the word *Text* is inserted into the sketch, all of the Sketch Entity icons will become disabled and appear grayed out. Likewise, if any entity is drawn in a sketch, the Text option will no longer be available.

Adding text to a sketch in this fashion is not the same as adding a note. Sketch text has one function, and that is to create a solid feature for your solid model. (Adding text as a note is covered in Chapter 8.)

You may want to open another part before attempting this. Sketch text cannot be created as a base feature (the first feature in your part) because it would create islands of geometry. As you might recall from Chapter 1, a part must be one contiguous solid. If you feel confident enough to create a basic block shape to use for this example, go ahead. You might also try sketching text on the Oil Screen part, located in the SolidWorks\Samples\examples directory. To create a text sketch entity, perform the following steps:

1. Pick a point where you would like the text to begin. SolidWorks uses bottom left justification.

2. Select Text from the Tools/Sketch Entity menu. This will open the Text dialog box (see the following illustration).

3. Type in the text you would like to use for this sketch.

4. If you would like to specify a different font, uncheck Use Document's Font and select a new font. You will have access to all Windows fonts on your computer.

5. If you would like to see a preview of what the text will look like, click on the Preview button.

6. To change the size of the text, change the value in the Scale box and click on Preview again.

7. Click on OK when you are satisfied with the results.

*The Text
dialog box.*

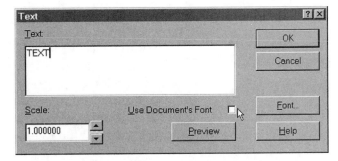

When you are finished, you should see text on the part that looks similar to that in the following illustration. Of course, yours will probably be different if you typed in something besides the word *Text*, and if you used a different font.

Sample of sketch text.

A couple of final words on sketch text. SolidWorks has to perform some technical wizardry on the Windows fonts in order to be able to do this. To be precise, the text has to be "vectorized." This means that the text winds up being made of lines, arcs, and splines. More often than not, the text is usually splines, which are computationally intensive. To make a long story short, it will make your computer chug. Turning text into solid geometry is not something that generally needs to be done on a regular basis, but when it does need to get done, it is recommended that it be one of the final operations in the design process.

Construction Entities

Construction entities are not actually sketched. However, any sketched entity can be turned into a construction entity. The construction entity is a reference entity used to create or constrain other sketch entities. Construction lines are not all that useful in SolidWorks, but they do have their time and place.

AutoCAD has a large need for construction lines, and even created an actual entity type devoted to construction lines in release 13. Do not think of SolidWorks construction lines in the same light. They are used as reference entities only. To make a sketch entity a construction entity, perform the following steps:

1. Right mouse click over the entity (or entities) you would like to convert.

2. Select Properties from the context-sensitive menu. This opens the Properties dialog box for the specific entity selected.

3. Check the Construction check box. The dialog box shown in the following illustration is for a line entity.

4. Click on OK to accept the change.

Changing a line to a construction entity in the Line Properties dialog box.

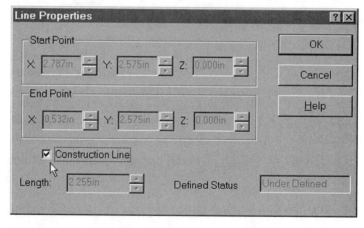

It should be noted that construction lines can also be changed into regular sketch entities by using this same procedure. There really is no difference between a centerline and a construction line. Both perform the same tasks. They are reference entities.

Sketch Tools and Mirroring

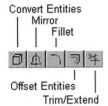

Convert Entities
| Mirror
| | Fillet
| | |

|
Offset Entities |
Trim/Extend

Last five icons in the Sketch Tools toolbar.

Sketch tools are used to manipulate 2D sketch geometry and to create sketch geometry from model geometry. These are accessed from the last five icons on the Sketch Tools toolbar, shown in the following illustration.

Not all of these tools can be demonstrated at this time, although the commands can all be explained. This is due to the fact that solid geometry needs to exist before some of the tools can be used. Specifically, Convert Entities and Offset Entities require solid geometry. These will be covered last.

Mirror is used to create a symmetrical (mirrored) copy of selected sketch entities around a centerline. Only one centerline can be selected for mirroring, even though there can be more than one centerline in a sketch. Once the new geometry has been created, it is associated with the parent geometry and the mirror line, but not dependent on it. In other words, the original geometry could be deleted after mirroring the geometry without removing copies. Deleting the mirror line or the original entities, however, would delete the symmetrical relationship.

Mirroring can be done one of two ways while working with sketch geometry. You will examine both of them. First, assume you have already created some sketch geometry you would like to mirror. Make sure there is a centerline in the sketch that will serve as a mirror line. To mirror selected sketch features around a centerline, perform the following steps. The illustration that follows shows the selection of entities for the mirror operation.

1. Select the entities to be mirrored. Make sure the Control key is depressed if selecting more than one, or use the window method to select entities.

2. Select the centerline to use as a mirror line while holding down the Control key.

3. Click on the Mirror icon or select Mirror from the Tools/Sketch Tools menu.

Selecting entities for the mirror operation.

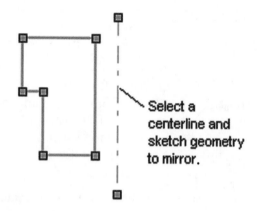

Select a centerline and sketch geometry to mirror.

Example of a dynamic mirror line.

There is another way in which objects can be dynamically mirrored as they are created. Once again, a centerline is needed. Therefore, in order to attempt this operation, draw a centerline down the middle of the screen. Complete the following steps to dynamically mirror sketch geometry:

1. Select the centerline to be used as a dynamic mirror line.

2. Click on the Mirror icon. The centerline should look like the one in the illustration at left.

3. Create sketch geometry as needed. It will be mirrored as you sketch.

4. Click on the Mirror icon a second time to turn off dynamic mirroring.

If you have successfully created some mirrored geometry, leave it up on the screen for the next discussion on dragging geometry.

An Introduction to Dragging Geometry

This is the perfect opportunity to introduce you to dragging geometry and why it can be beneficial. Now that you have an idea of what the term *dragging* means with regard to sketching, you can apply the same phrase to geometry that has already been sketched. Hopefully there are sketch entities on your screen at this time. If not, it

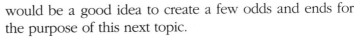

would be a good idea to create a few odds and ends for the purpose of this next topic.

In SolidWorks, it is possible to move sketch geometry around the screen, much like AutoCAD's use of grips. Clicking on a grip allows AutoCAD users to move endpoints, lines, centerpoints, and so on. This same type of "pick and drag" functionality can also be accomplished in SolidWorks. There are no grips, just endpoints, and all you have to do is select a point and drag the mouse while holding down the left mouse button. Try this on the mirrored geometry from the last exercise.

Depending on what portion of specific sketch geometry is selected makes a difference as to how it is dragged. Dragging an endpoint moves just the endpoint. Picking and dragging a line moves the line. Dragging a circle by the edge resizes the circle. Get the idea?

There are a few reasons why this is especially important. First of all, dragging geometry can tell you a lot about a sketch you may not have realized. For instance, dragging might tell you that the line you thought was attached to the other three sides of a rectangle was not attached. Dragging will show you your mistakes and it will show you if the correct constraints have been added to the sketch. It is a very good idea to drag sketch geometry for the feedback it will give you. Use this technique often.

Entity Functions

The following sections describe the process for using various entity functions. These include Fillet, Trim/Extend, Trim, Extend, Convert Entities, and Offset Entities.

Fillet

A fillet, shown in the following illustration, is a tangent arc entity attached to two line segments, a line and an arc, or an arc and an arc. A fillet can actually be a round or a fillet. SolidWorks does not differentiate between the two, and it does not really matter. Typically, cosmetic fillets are not included within a sketch unless they are a design element. Inserting a sketch fillet is an easy way to place a tangent arc between two existing lines. Keep in mind that this is a sketch tool only. Adding fillets to feature geometry (applying the fillets as features) is a different procedure and should not be confused with sketch fillets.

Before creating a fillet, make sure the corner to be filleted forms a perfect intersection. Unlike AutoCAD, SolidWorks will not automatically trim or extend lines as needed. This goes along with the need to pay attention to the cursor during the sketch process. Creating clean corners is very easy if you are paying attention. Remember, these are not wireframe parts that are being created, but solid parametric models. Draw yourself a rectangle and try stepping through the fillet process with this book. The Sketch Fillet dialog box is shown in the following illustration.

The Sketch Fillet dialog box for sketch geometry.

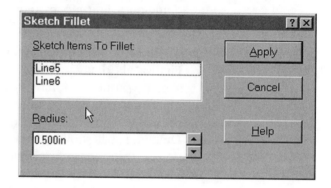

Walk through the following steps to complete a fillet. The illustrations that follow show lines selected in this process and the outcome.

1. Click on the Fillet icon, or select Tools/Sketch Tools/ Fillet... from the menu.

2. Type in a value for the radius.

3. Click in the Sketch Items to Fillet area and select two entities to fillet.

4. Click on Apply.

5. Repeat as necessary, changing the radius if needed.

6. Click on Cancel when you are finished.

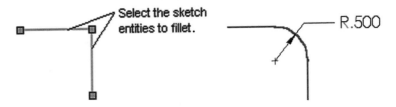

Selecting lines to fillet, and the result of filleting.

When certain dialog boxes are opened, it is not always necessary to hold down the Control key when selecting more than one entity. This should become standardized in the future. If you notice that the selection of entities is proving difficult, the reason is probably because you need to hold down the Control key for multiple selections.

Trim/Extend

The Trim/Extend function is used to lengthen or shorten sketch entities. This command performs both functions, depending on entities selected and where they are selected. The Trim/Extend command is intelligent and infers the function based on your input. This eliminates the need for separate trim and extend commands. This is different from AutoCAD's separate Trim and Extend commands, and works much differently. There is no selection of cutting or boundary edges, and there are no command line options to go along with the Trim/Extend command.

Trim

As previously discovered in the section on dragging geometry, it is possible to lengthen or shorten lines and arcs by simply dragging their endpoints. However, there will be times when you will need something a little more powerful than this. SolidWorks' Trim command is much more user friendly than AutoCAD's. As with AutoCAD, you will be clicking on the portion of the entity to be discarded. To trim (shorten) a sketch entity, perform the following steps. The illustration that follows shows implementation of this command.

1. Click on the Trim/Extend icon or select Trim/Extend from the Tools/Sketch Tools menu.

2. Select the portion of the entity to be removed.

Implementing the Trim command.

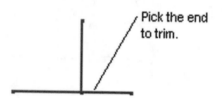

Pick the end to trim.

This procedure represents the Trim command in its most generic state. SolidWorks trims the entity selected back to the next intersection it encounters. Similar to AutoCAD, SolidWorks currently will not totally eliminate an entity, but probably will in future releases of the software. If the trim would result in the complete deletion of the entity, SolidWorks will refuse to do it. If this is the case, delete the entity.

➤ NOTE: *To delete objects in SolidWorks, make sure the object is selected and press the Delete key. This holds true for all SolidWorks objects.*

What if the entity to be trimmed needs to trim back to an entity other than the first one it encounters? The answer is "dragging." Drag the entity to be trimmed to the entity you would like to trim it to so that the trimming entity (or "cutting edge") is highlighted. When the mouse button is released, the entity will be trimmed. If you are able to implement this function, you already know how to Extend.

Extend

As with the Trim function, SolidWorks is much more user friendly than AutoCAD and requires no preparation.

Because the Trim/Extend commands are one in the same, just clicking on an entity implies to SolidWorks that it should be trimmed. To extend, the entity must be dragged. The illustration that follows shows the Extend function. To extend (lengthen) a sketch entity, perform the following steps:

1. Select the Trim/Extend icon or select Trim/Extend from the Tools/Sketch Tools menu.

2. Select the end of the entity to be extended and drag to the entity to be extended to.

3. When the proper entity (or "boundary edge") is highlighted, release the mouse button.

Implementing the Extend command.

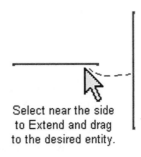

Select near the side
to Extend and drag
to the desired entity.

Convert Entities

The Convert Entities function is used to create sketch entities based on model edges. The key word here is *convert*. What is happening is that edges of existing geometry are being converted to sketch geometry. Think back to one of the primary five steps needed to create a feature. They are the following:

1. Select a plane or planar face to sketch on.

2. Enter Sketch mode.

3. Create the sketch.

4. Add dimensions and constraints.

5. Create the feature.

The step you should be most concerned with at this point is step 3: Create a sketch. A sketch must be created before a feature can be created when trying to create a sketched feature. What Convert Entities does for you is to convert *existing sketch entities* into sketch geometry for the current sketch. This sketch geometry can then be turned into a feature.

Why are Convert Entities and Offset Entities important? Convert Entities and Offset Entities add external references from sketch geometry to existing feature geometry. Any changes made to existing geometry will be reflected in the sketch entity made using Convert Entities or Offset Entities. Single edges can be converted or offset. By selecting a face, all edges that define the face are converted or offset.

There is a prerequisite for implementing either of these two sketch tools, and that is to select model edges, a model face, or geometry from another sketch prior to initiating either command. If the Convert Entities or Offset Entities icon is selected without any model geometry selected, the system will display an error message.

Another important aspect of these two commands is the projection of the entities selected. To put this quite simply, any edge selected for conversion or offset will be projected perpendicular to the sketch plane. The illustration that follows shows the conversion of edges. To convert model edges into sketch geometry, perform the following steps:

1. Select the edges or model face to be converted.

2. Click on the Convert Entities icon or select Tools/ Sketch Tools/Convert Entities from the menu. The selected edges or model face edges will be projected to the current sketch plane and converted to sketch geometry.

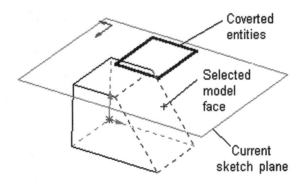

Converting feature edges into sketch geometry.

Offset Entities

The Offset Entities function is used to create sketch entities based on model edges offset to a specified distance, as shown in the following illustration. It is very similar to Convert Entities and is different in only one aspect, and that is that offset is added to the converted entities.

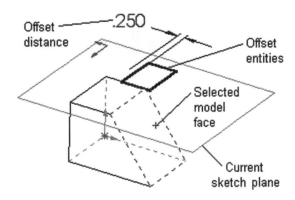

Using the Offset Entities command.

All of the rules that govern Convert Entities apply to Offset Entities. All you need to do is supply an offset and an offset direction. This is easily accomplished through the use of a user-friendly dialog box, shown in the following illustration.

*The Offset Entities
dialog box.*

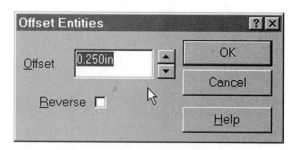

After selecting the appropriate edges to be offset, click on the Offset Entities icon and fill in the information in the dialog box. Offset distance is required, and a side to offset is also needed. This is very similar to AutoCAD's Offset command in the respect that you must select the entity to be offset first and then specify the "side to offset." The obvious difference with SolidWorks is the references established to existing feature edges, which make for an intelligent model.

As with converted entities, anything offset using the Offset Entities command results in a link back to the original feature edges. If the original feature is modified, the dependent sketch will also update. To offset selected model edges or faces, perform the following steps:

1. Select the edges or model face to be offset.

2. Click on the Offset Entities icon or select Tools/Sketch Tools/Offset Entities from the menu. The selected edges or model face edges will be projected to the current sketch plane, offset the specified distance, and converted to sketch geometry.

Sketch Dimensions

Dimensions are used to display distances. This is nothing new to anybody reading this book, and is a simple concept. Dimensions in SolidWorks are used for the same reason, but have additional functions. Dimensions are placed on 2D sketch geometry so that the geometry can be shaped and driven with these dimensions. This allows you to edit the values of these dimensions and have the software update the geometry.

The dimensions add intelligence to the part, and dimension placement determines how the part can be modified. This is related to the concept of design intent, previously discussed. It is possible to create a complete model without dimensions, but this is not practical. Again, the two main reasons for putting dimensions on your SolidWorks part are:

1. Dimensions allow you to parametrically control a model.

2. Dimensions added to a part can be automatically transferred to a 2D layout.

That is the nuts and bolts of it. Now all that is left is the mechanics of adding dimensions. The following section discusses how this is accomplished.

A Universal Dimensioning Tool

Starting the Dimension command.

The Dimension command can be used to place a dimension between two vertices (endpoints), a single sketch entity, a line and a point, two arcs, radial or diametric dimensions, and so on. All of this can be done with SolidWorks' easily used dimensioning sketch tool.

The following examples assume that you have already selected the Dimension icon and are ready to apply dimensions. The Dimension icon, shown in the illustration at left, can be found on the Sketch Relations toolbar. This toolbar consists of three icons, one of which looks like a dimension. This is the icon you want.

To insert a point-to-point sketch dimension, perform the following steps. The illustration that follows shows this function.

1. Select the first point to dimension to.

2. Select the second point to dimension to.

3. Select a location to place the dimension lines. This will determine the distance the dimension lines are from the items being dimensioned.

Placing a point-to-point dimension.

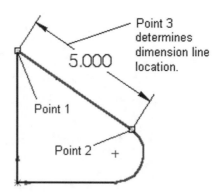

Point 3
determines
dimension line
location.

5.000

Point 1

Point 2   +

There are a couple of optional settings that should be addressed at this point. What is onscreen may differ from what is being displayed in this book; therefore, you need to make sure you are working with the same set of rules. The following are a few optional settings that can be found under Tools/Options..., along with what these options do and the recommended settings for each.

Input dimension value. This is found under the General tab. When checked, this option, shown in the following illustration, allows you to supply a value for the dimension as soon as it is placed on the sketch. Leave this one on so that you can plug in values on the fly.

Leave "Input dimension value" checked.

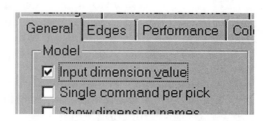

General | Edges | Performance | Col

Model

☑ Input dimension value

☐ Single command per pick

☐ Show dimension names

Center text. This is found under the Detailing tab. When this option is checked, SolidWorks automatically centers dimension values. This is sometimes desirable, but when adding radial or diameter dimensions, the dimension values are placed over the centers of the arcs or circles. The dimensions must then be dragged out of the way to access centerpoints. Leave this option off for now, as shown in the following illustration.

Leave "Center text" off.

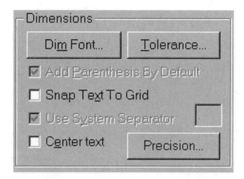

Dim Font.... In the same area as "Center text," this button allows for changing the size and font of dimensions. Usually a setting of .125 to .25 works well, but the exact setting is up to you.

Always display text at the same size. To find this option, click on the Annotations button, which is found under the Detailing tab, all the way over to the right from the Dim Font... button. Click Annotations to open the Annotation Properties dialog box. If "Always display text at the same size" is checked, text will stay the same size if you zoom in or out. Otherwise, text may get extremely small or extremely large. This is a nice feature. Make sure it is checked.

That takes care of optional settings for now. The following are other dimension types to be considered.

A point-to-point dimension is really the same as a parallel dimension. In AutoCAD, this dimension type would be considered an Aligned dimension. Also in AutoCAD, it is possible to select an entity and pick a location to place a dimension. This can be done in SolidWorks the same way. The results are the same. To place a parallel (or "aligned") dimension, perform the following steps. The illustration that follows shows this function.

1. Select the line to be dimensioned.

2. Select a location to place the dimension lines.

Placing a parallel dimension.

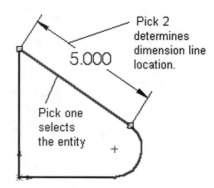

You can see from the previous illustration that there is no difference in the aesthetic value of the dimensions. The next thing to consider is diametric dimensions.

Diametric Dimensions

Basic diametric dimensions, such as when dimensioning a circle, are very easy to create. Use the same universal dimensioning tool you would use for any other dimension. To place radial or diametric dimensions, perform the following steps. The illustration that follows shows both of these types of dimensions.

1. Select the arc or circle to be dimensioned (point 1, following illustration).

2. Select the location for the dimension values (point 2, following illustration).

Create diameter or radial dimensions the same way.

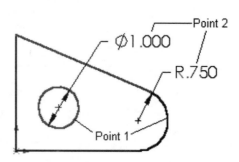

There is another type of diametric dimension that can be created for revolved parts, which is shown in the illustration that follows (revolved features and features in general are covered in Chapter 6). The need for this results from bringing dimensions into a drawing from part files that have been revolved and contain only linear-style dimensions in the sketch.

In the following example, it would be standard procedure to place a dimension between the centerline and the right-hand edge of the part. When a dimension of this type is seen from a top view of the revolved cylindrical part, it does not look right. To remedy this, perform the following steps to create a diametric dimension from a linear dimension:

1. Add a dimension from the centerline to the desired point or line.

2. Select the dimension with the right mouse button.

3. Select Properties…. This will open the Dimension Properties dialog box.

4. Check the Diameter dimension box.

This will turn the dimension into a diametric dimension. However, a diametric symbol needs to be supplied because this is still not actually an arc or circle being dimensioned, and you must force SolidWorks to display the appropriate symbol. Add a symbol by performing the following steps:

1. Select the Modify Text… button. This opens the Modify Text dialog box, where text or symbols can be prefixed or appended to an existing dimension.

2. Select the Diameter symbol with the cursor positioned in front of the <DIM> symbol. This is the default position for the cursor.

3. Select OK on the Modify Text menu to go back to the Dimension Properties menu.

4. Select OK to accept the changes. Your dimension should look similar to that shown in the following illustration.

A diametric dimension for revolved parts.

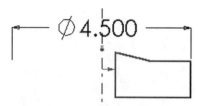

This trick only works if there is a centerline in your sketch. This is because SolidWorks assumes a revolved feature will be created because you are using a centerline to create revolved features. However, simply including a centerline in the sketch is not enough. You must actually dimension to it or the Diameter dimension check box will not be available.

Angular Dimensions

Angular dimensions are used to show the angle between two lines, as shown in the illustration that follows. To create and angular dimension, perform the following steps:

1. Select the first line to dimension (point 1, following illustration).

2. Select the second line to dimension (point 2, following illustration).

3. Click to locate the dimension value (point 3, following illustration).

Creating a 68-degree angular dimension.

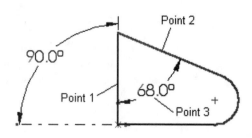

Horizontal Dimensions

Horizontal and vertical dimensions, shown in the illustration that follows, can be placed between a line and a point automatically without any extra user intervention, or between two points if you force them. For example, if a dimension is placed between a vertical line and a point, it will be horizontal by default because the line is already vertical. There is no other possible solution; therefore, SolidWorks acts accordingly.

The same holds true if a dimension is placed between a horizontal line and a point. However, if a dimension is placed between two points, SolidWorks needs to be told that the dimension should be horizontal or vertical. Otherwise, SolidWorks assumes it should be a parallel dimension. The key to performing this task is the right mouse button. To insert a horizontal or vertical dimension, perform the following steps:

1. Click on the Dimension icon.

2. Right mouse click in any blank area. SolidWorks understands that the dimensioning tool has been activated and alters the context-sensitive menu accordingly.

3. Select either Horizontal Dimension or Vertical Dimension.

4. Select the first vertex point to dimension (point 1, following illustration).

5. Select the second vertex point (point 2, following illustration).

6. Click to place the dimension line (point 3, following illustration).

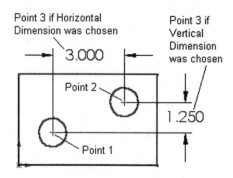

Forcing a dimension to be either horizontal or vertical.

Driven Dimensions

Driven dimensions are usually created by accident by new users to the SolidWorks program. When there are too many dimensions or constraints on a sketch, the sketch becomes overdefined. What this means is that there are too many rules applied to the sketch for Solid-Works to interpret, and something has to give way in order that all criteria can be met. This usually results in a dimension being driven.

Keep in mind that dimensions control the shape of sketch geometry in SolidWorks, which is very different from AutoCAD's way of doing things. If there are too many driving dimensions, SolidWorks' solution to this dilemma is to make the last one added a "driven" dimension. Driven dimensions do not control the shape of geometry.

Driven dimensions are actually much closer in nature to the type of dimensions AutoCAD uses. These dimensions will update accordingly, just like AutoCAD dimensions, if a part changes size or shape. If an overdefining dimension is added, you will see the dialog box shown in the following illustration.

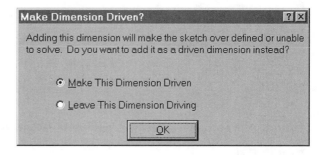

What you see if you have added too many dimensions.

The default is to make the troublemaking dimension driven, but you are not obligated to do so. If this situation is encountered by accident, it is recommended that the reason for the overdefinition be determined. Methods for making this determination are discussed later in this chapter.

Adding a few driven dimensions as reference should not cause any problems in the sketch because driven dimensions cannot overdefine a sketch. Overdefining dimensions causes problems only if you leave them overdefining. Driven dimensions will appear gray and surrounded by parentheses. A driven dimension is shown in the following illustration.

A driven dimension.

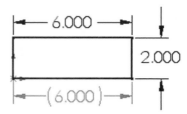

The default operation used when adding overdefining dimensions can be controlled with settings in the Options dialog box. Click on Tools/Options... and under the General tab look for the section shown in the following illustration. Make adjustments as needed, but for new users still getting accustomed to the software, leaving both boxes checked is a good idea.

> ┌─ Overdefining Dimensions ──────┐
> │ ☑ Pro**m**pt to set driven state │
> │ ☑ Set **d**riven by default   │
> └────────────────────────────────┘

An Introduction to Sketch Color Codes

There are a number of problems that can be encountered when creating a sketch. SolidWorks supplies color codes to aid you in recognizing these problem areas. The following is a list of the various color codes and what they mean.

- *Blue.* Sketch geometry is underdefined. Entities may move about if dragged, and may change position unexpectedly.

- *Black.* Geometry is fully defined. You have full control over sketch geometry.

- *Red.* Geometry is overdefined. There are too many constraints or dimensions.

- *Brown.* Usually means a dimension is referencing an entity that no longer exists. Hence the term *dangling*.

- *Pink.* The geometry's position cannot be determined using current constraints.

- *Yellow.* Sketch would result in invalid geometry if solved.

The last two color codes are not very common. If you are a new user, the first three are the color codes you should concentrate on. As a rule of thumb, blue is okay, black is best, and red is a no-no.

Editing a Sketch

An existing sketch can be modified at any time. This allows you to change, add, or delete geometry, dimensions, and geometric constraints after the initial sketch has been exited. It is easy and quite common for a new user to accidentally exit out of a sketch. You can modify a sketch by clicking on the sketch icon or by rebuilding the part. The Rebuild icon is found on the Standard toolbar and looks like a street light with the green light lit.

The key to editing a sketch is by right clicking on it in FeatureManager. A very common mistake is to click on the Sketch icon to enter back into an existing sketch, but this is not correct! By clicking on the Sketch icon Solid-Works thinks you are attempting to begin a new sketch. If you want to edit an existing sketch, perform the following steps:

1. Right mouse click on the sketch in FeatureManager to activate the context-sensitive menu.

2. Select Edit Sketch.

3. Edit the sketch geometry as needed.

4. Click on the Rebuild icon (or Sketch button to turn it off) when done to accept the changes made to the sketch.

Editing Sketch Entities and Dimensions

Existing sketch entities can be manipulated by dragging them. Dragging sketch entities, as shown in the following illustration, will maintain geometric constraints. These constraints cannot be violated; therefore, these relationships will be maintained as the geometry is dragged and reshaped.

Dragging sketch geometry.

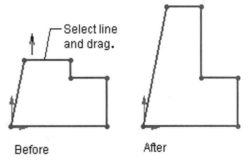

Before   After

If there are too many dimensions on a sketch, dragging will not be possible. In this case, dimension values must be modified in order to resize and reshape the sketch as needed. To modify a dimension value, double click on the dimension value with the left mouse button. The following illustration shows this function.

Modifying a dimension.

When modifying a dimension, either type in a new value or use the spin box arrows to increment the dimension value up or down, as shown in the illustration that follows. When the desired value is obtained, click on the green check to accept it or the red X to exit the box without accepting the change. The spin box increment amount can be adjusted to better suit your particular needs. If the spin box increment is too coarse or too fine for your application, follow these steps to adjust it:

1. Click on Tools/Options....

2. In the Grid/Units tab, specify the desired spin box increments for Length and Angle.

3. Click on OK.

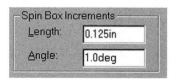

Setting spin box increments.

An Introduction to the Undo Command

Sometimes after modifying a dimension or dragging sketch geometry, the results may be far from what you were expecting. Enter the Undo command. The Undo icon will undo the last command performed, just like AutoCAD's Undo command. AutoCAD's Undo function is one of the best around, and has gotten quite a few AutoCAD users out of many a sticky situation.

SolidWorks' undo function is not quite as extravagant as AutoCAD's, but it gets the job done. The Undo icon in SolidWorks is found just to the left of the Rebuild icon and looks like an arrow. This follows standard Windows icon conventions.

It is generally recommended to not rely too heavily on the Undo command. This will help to develop good skills. If the Undo command is used too often, there will come a time when it will not be there when needed. This is because SolidWorks will not allow an unlimited number of undo commands to be carried out. After a rebuild or after exiting a sketch (which actually forces a rebuild), the Undo command list is cleared and is not available.

This is not at bad as you might think. AutoCAD needs a powerful undo option because its editing capabilities are not as powerful as SolidWorks. When it is possible, as in SolidWorks, to edit any aspect of a solid model at any time in the design process, an undo feature is less important.

Even with SolidWorks' power and flexibility, the fact remains that it is nice to be able to undo a command or two once in a while. If modifying a sketch gives you unexpected results, click on the Undo icon and try again. The drop-down list box attached to the Undo icon will display a list of commands that can be undone. Selecting a command from this list will undo that command, as well as every command above the selected command in the list. Use it if required, but be cautious. SolidWorks does not have a Redo command.

Sketch and Relations Functions

The following sections describe various sketch and relations functions. These include modifying a sketch, adding relations, displaying and deleting relations, the Scan Equal function, the Constrain All function, and deriving a sketch.

Modify Sketch

The Modify Sketch function allows for translating, scaling, and rotating an existing sketch. Existing dimensional or geometric sketch constraints cannot be overridden. Therefore, fully defined sketch geometry is not a good candidate for the Modify function. If a sketch is anchored to the origin point, it cannot be translated because of the fact that it is anchored. Use common sense before implementing the Modify command.

If sketch geometry is unconstrained, the sketch can be translated, scaled, or rotated. The sketch can be modified from inside or outside sketch mode. If a sketch is currently being edited, meaning that you are in an active sketch, click on Tools/Sketch Tools.../Modify....

If you are not currently in a sketch, make sure the sketch to be modified is selected first. Select the sketch from FeatureManager before clicking on Tools/Sketch Tools.../Modify.... This will open the Modify Sketch dialog box, which is shown in the following illustration.

The Modify Sketch dialog box.

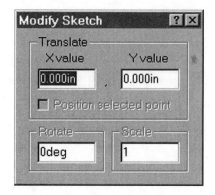

The following are some of the functions that can be performed with the Modify Sketch dialog box.

- To translate (move) a sketch, perform the following steps:

    1. Specify an X and/or Y value in the dialog box and press the Return key, or

2. Hold the left mouse button down and drag the sketch by moving the mouse.

- To rotate a sketch, perform the following steps:

  1. Specify a rotation angle in the dialog box and press the return key, or

  2. Hold the right mouse button down and dynamically rotate the sketch by moving the mouse.

- To scale a sketch, type a value into the dialog box and press Return. Note that the sketch will be scaled using the origin point as a base point.

- To relocate the sketch origin with relation to the sketch geometry, place the cursor over the black square at the origin point, where the X and Y axes meet, and drag the origin to the desired location.

- To mirror the sketch geometry across the X or Y axis, right click over the black square on the tip of the X or Y axis on the sketch origin.

- Exit out of the Modify Sketch dialog box when finished, or just press the Escape key. Do not forget to rebuild your part when finished.

Adding Relations

Geometric relationships are used to define a geometric association between sketch entities, as shown in the following illustration. These relationships can be as powerful as dimension sketches in defining design intent for a part. Properly determining and defining geometric relationships will produce a part that will more significantly incorporate the design intent you require.

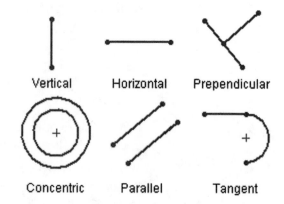

*Six examples
of geometric constraints.*

Vertical   Horizontal   Prependicular

Concentric   Parallel   Tangent

➤ **NOTE:** *The terms* constraint *and* relation *mean the
same thing. They are used interchangeably throughout this text. The icon used for adding constraints is
named the Add Relations icon.*

As this book has previously explained, AutoCAD does not
use intelligent relationships between sketch entities. Take
a look at another example and this fact should become
quite clear. Assume you have a circle drawn in AutoCAD.
The drawing requires that another circle be drawn concentric to the first, meaning they have the same centerpoint. This task is easy enough to accomplish by
snapping the centerpoint of the second circle to the center point of the first. Now the two circles are concentric.

Now say that the second circle's grips are enabled. If the
center grip is selected, the circle can be moved to any
position on the screen and the first circle remains where it
was. Remember, this is a fundamental difference between
AutoCAD and SolidWorks. If the second circle were
moved in SolidWorks, the first circle would move with it
to maintain the relationships you set.

More than one relationship may be defined for a sketch
entity. The system only displays relationships that are
applicable to selected geometry. SolidWorks is intuitive
enough to know what constraints can be added for

selected entities. If the constraints you expected to see are not active, it means one or more entities were not selected correctly. Just exit out and try again.

Conflicting or invalid constraints can be added that over-define a sketch. It is up to you to incorporate the proper relationships to achieve the desired design intent. What constraints have already been added will determine how the geometry will change when constraints are added. The following is a list of geometric relationships you can add, and a description of each.

Horizontal	Constrains a line, centerline, or two points horizontally.
Vertical	Constrains a line, centerline, or two points vertically.
Collinear	Constrains two lines, line and face, planes, or axes so that they are aligned linearly.
Perpendicular	Constrains two lines, or a line and an edge, to be 90 degrees.
Tangent	Constrains an arc, spline, or circle tangent to another entity.
Midpoint	Constrains a point to the center of a line, centerline, or edge.
Coincident	Constrains a point on a line, arc, circle, or nearly any other entity type.
Symmetrical	Constrains two entities to be symmetric about a centerline.
Coradial	Constrains two circles or arcs to have the same radius and centerpoint.
Parallel	Constrains two lines, or one line and an edge, to be parallel to each other.
Concentric	Constrains two circles and arcs to have the same centerpoint with relation to each other or a vertex point.
At Intersection	Constrains a point to the intersection of two lines.
Equal Length/Radii	Constrains two lines, arcs, or circles to be of equal length or radius.

Fix	Constrains an entity to the current location. This acts as an anchor.
Pierce	Constrains an entity to pass through, or pierce, a point at the position the point resides on its sketch plane.
Merge Points	Similar to Coincident, constrains two sketch endpoints to become one point.

Many geometric relationships are added automatically when you sketch, as discussed earlier in this chapter. This function can be disabled, but it is not recommended. If you would like to experiment with this setting, click on Tools/Sketch Tools and select Automatic Relations from the pull-down menus.

If Automatic Relations is disabled, the relationships graphically displayed by the cursor while sketching will not add relationships. This is not normally a desired function because none of the entities created while sketching will contain any intelligence.

➥ **NOTE:** *Do not forget to turn Automatic Relations back on if you turn this off for any reason.*

Adding relations to sketch geometry is easy if you remember one thing: Correct entities must be selected prior to clicking on the Add Relations icon. All this takes is a little common sense and logical thinking. For example, if placing a parallel relationship between two lines, make sure nothing else is selected except the two lines, then click on the Add Relations icon. If there is something else selected already, either click in an open area devoid of geometry or simply press the Escape key. To add geometric relationships to selected entities, perform the following steps:

1. Select the entities to be geometrically constrained.

2. Click on the Add Relations icon or select Add Relations from the Tools/ Sketch Relations menu.

3. Select the appropriate geometric relationship from the Add Relations dialog box.

4. Click on OK.

Displaying and Deleting Relations

The Display/Delete Relations function displays geometric relationships set for a sketch entity. You can view each relation and delete unwanted relationships. A geometric relation is usually associated with another sketch entity, but not always. For instance, a line can be constrained to be horizontal by itself. If there are two or more entities involved and the relation is deleted from one of these entities, the relation is removed from all entities involved.

Normally, the entity in question is selected prior to clicking on the Display/Delete Relations icon. This brings up a dialog box showing the relations for that entity. If no entity is selected first, the same dialog box appears, showing all relations to any entities in the sketch. The Display/Delete Geometric Relations dialog box is shown in the following illustration.

The Display/Delete Geometric Relations dialog box.

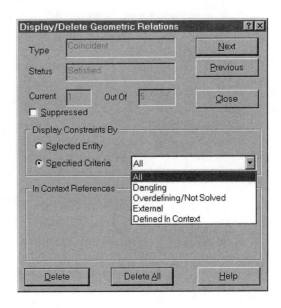

To view a feature's geometric relationships, perform the following steps:

1. Select the sketch entity in question.

2. Select the Display/Delete Relations icon, or select Display/Delete Relations from the Tools/Sketch Relations menu, or click the right mouse button with the pointer over the entity.

3. Select Next or Previous to cycle through each relationship for the selected entity. The Current and Out Of boxes will tell you which constraint you are viewing out of the total present.

4. If needed, select Delete to remove the geometric relation shown, or select Delete All to remove all relations from the entity.

5. Select Close to close the dialog box.

If you want to view the other constraints within the sketch, continue with the following steps:

1. In the Display Constraints By pull-down menu, select the Specified Criteria option.

2. From the drop-down list, select the criteria that best suits your requirements. Common choices are All, Overdefining/Not Solved, and Dangling.

3. Select Next or Previous to cycle through each relationship for the selected criteria.

4. Select Delete or Delete All as needed.

5. Select Close to close the dialog box.

Scan Equal

The Scan Equal function can be a time-saving shortcut for adding relations. It reviews a sketch for entities of equal length or radii, and allows you to set geometric relationships automatically.

Scan Equal can be used when there are a number of entities that should be grouped together via the Equal Length/Radii constraint. These entities need to be the same size for the function to recognize them as equal length or radius. This command is not used that often in practice, but has been included here for reference. It is sometimes convenient to use this command for imported geometry that needs to have constraints added. To scan a sketch for equal length or radii, perform the following steps:

1. Select the Scan Equal icon or select Scan Equal from the Tools/Sketch Relations menu. This opens the "Scan for equal radii and line lengths" dialog box, shown in the following illustration.

2. Select Set Equal to constrain the highlighted set of entities. If the dialog box is obscuring your view of the work area, just drag it out of the way.

3. Select Find Next to move to the next set of entities and repeat the process.

4. Select Close to quit this command.

The "Scan for equal radii and line lengths" dialog box.

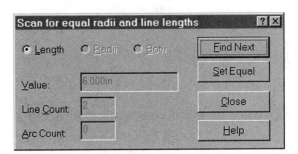

Constrain All

The Constrain All function is used to add geometric relationships to unconstrained imported DXF or DWG files. The entire sketch is reviewed and applicable geometric constraints are added to the sketch, which you are informed of onscreen, as shown in the following illustration. Normally, just basic constraints are added, such as horizontal, vertical, and perpendicular. This may change as the SolidWorks software develops. To add geometric constraints to an unconstrained sketch, perform the following steps:

1. Select Constrain All from the Tools/Relations menu.

2. The system will display a dialog box showing how many constraints were added to the sketch.

3. Select OK to continue.

SolidWorks informing you how many constraints (relations) were added.

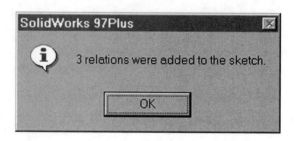

It should be noted that the sketch must not contain any constraints whatsoever. That is why this function is best used after importing AutoCAD DXF or DWG files. It is always best to add constraints and dimensions to such files. AutoCAD dimensions will import, but they will not contain parametric information. It is actually best to turn off any extraneous layers, such as dimensions or text, before importing AutoCAD files into SolidWorks. (This is covered more fully in Chapter 11.)

Derived Sketch

A derived sketch can be used to copy existing sketch geometry. This allows one sketch to drive a number of identical part features. The new sketch is dependent on the parent sketch. Any changes to the parent sketch are shown in the derived sketch. It should be noted that derived sketches do not contain any dimensions precisely for the reason that they are dependent on their parent sketch geometry. Therefore, no dimensions will automatically be created in the 2D layout, and reference dimensions will probably need to be added manually.

Sometimes the need for a specific design intent overrides the luxury of having SolidWorks automatically import dimensions into the 2D layout. This process has been placed here for reference. It should be noted that a derived sketch cannot be created until you get a little farther into creating feature geometry. You might find it convenient to come back to this section at a later time. To create a new sketch based on an existing sketch, perform the following steps:

1. Make sure you are not in an active sketch.

2. Select the parent sketch from FeatureManager using the left mouse button.

3. Hold down the Control key and select the planar face you would like to apply the sketch to.

4. Select Derived Sketch from the Insert menu.

5. Locate the new sketch as desired using sketch dimensions or constraints.

6. Build the feature, which is covered in Chapter 6.

An Interactive Sketching Exercise

This example involves the selection of a sketch plane or face, as well as sketching entities; dimensioning to impart design intent; and modification of existing sketch entities. In the following example, a sketch is created for the features named Base Profile, Bearing Hole, and Adapter Mtg Bracket, shown in the following illustration. These features have rectangles surrounding their names so that you can identify them. The chapters that follow build solid features, create an assembly, and produce a drawing using this example.

The adapter bracket.

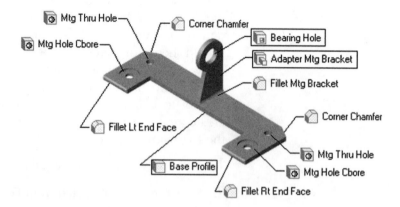

When starting a part, you should identify the features that constitute the part, such as the features named in the previous illustration. You should also consider the best method for locating and dimensioning the sketch geometry so that the dimensions will incorporate your design intent. Default planes can be used as a basis for creating sketch geometry. Identification of the adapter bracket's planes is shown in the following illustration.

Identifying the best planes for the adapter bracket's initial features.

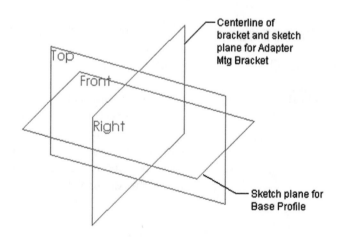

When selecting the base feature, review the part for a major shape that defines the part. For this example, the feature's base profile would be a good choice. This was created using one sketch. This keeps the sketch fairly simple and allows for easy modification.

The orientation of the base feature could be per the normal assembly position, a standard orientation based on drawing views, or according to a plane that makes viewing the part in an isometric view easier. This example uses the initial orientation of the bracket in the final assembly.

Do not worry too much about the part's final orientation in any future assemblies because individual parts can be moved, rotated, and mated as needed when the time comes. To start sketching, select the plane named Front and click on the sketch icon. The Orientation function can be used to sketch in a normal (2D) view orientation. The sketch can be created in a 2D or 3D orientation.

When creating the sketch entities, do not be concerned with their precise sizes. Dimensions that will control the size and position of the sketch will be added later. The following sequence of illustrations shows the steps used to create the sketch. Note how the cursor changes when sketching various types of information.

Sketch creation, step 1.

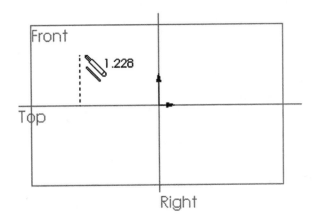

Sketch creation, step 2.

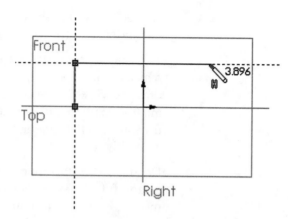

Sketch creation, step 3.

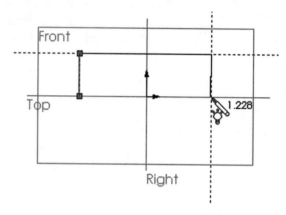

Sketch creation, step 4.

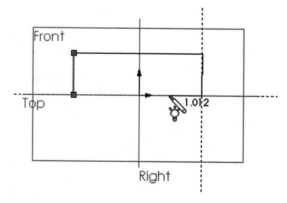

Sketch creation, step 5.

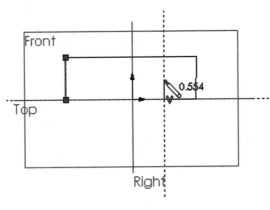

Sketch creation, step 6.

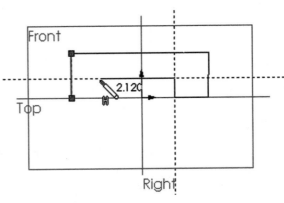

Sketch creation, step 7.

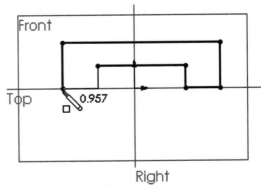

Now that all of the sketch entities have been created, as shown in the following illustration, the dimensions that control the size of the sketch can be added. Note the black sketch lines in the sketch geometry. This means the lines are constrained. This happened during sketching, and if you were paying attention to the cursor, you were already are aware of this. The black lines are constrained coincident with the origin point. Because the origin is anchored to one location, anything constrained to it will be further restricted in movement.

Completed sketch profile.

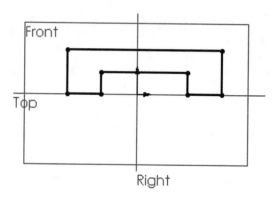

When adding dimensions, keep in mind what dimensions may need to be changed later. Placing dimensions is important because they drive the geometry of the sketch. This is not required in AutoCAD. If the SolidWorks user is concerned about the people in the manufacturing department having enough dimensions to build the part, consider this: When a sketch is fully defined, it needs no more dimensions to define the geometry within the sketch.

Also, when a detailed drawing is created, all of the dimensions placed on the part will be brought into the drawing. Rest assured that there will be enough information on the drawing to complete the project. If not, you can add reference dimensions in the part or in the drawing.

The completed sketch has all sketch entities shown in black. This is another visual clue that all sketch entities are fully constrained. Fully constraining sketch geometry is not necessary, but is a good practice. Underconstrained geometry can sometimes behave erratically. The following illustration shows a fully defined sketch.

Fully defined sketch geometry.

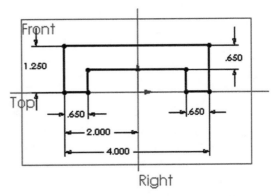

The next step would be to create the solid feature. This is explored in Chapter 6. The following illustration shows a base feature for a solid model.

Base feature for a solid model.

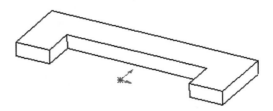

Summary

Sketching is the foundation of parametric, feature-based solid modeling. Building strong sketching skills is an important step for a new user and should not be taken lightly. The method used to create sketch entities, and to dimension and constrain geometry, will determine the design intent of the feature, as well as how easily the model can be modified.

Be aware of what the cursor and SolidWorks visual cues are telling you during the sketch process. Focus on how best to dimension and constrain sketch geometry to allow for easy editing and to capture the design intent of the feature.

6 Parts

Introduction

This chapter discusses how to create and modify solid features within SolidWorks. These features are described using graphical examples and step-by-step instructions. The 2D sketching techniques and tools learned in Chapter 5 will be applied in this chapter to create solid features that add or subtract material from a part. The order and method of creating these features determine the parametric characteristics of the part, and define the design intent imparted to the solid model.

There is a wide range of feature types explored in this chapter. Because SolidWorks is a design tool, this chapter will also explore the capabilities present in SolidWorks for making design changes to a feature's definition and dimensions.

Prerequisite

This chapter requires that you have a good working understanding of the basic sketch tools and techniques needed to create valid 2D sketch geometry. Defining geometry by adding dimensions and constraints should also be understood, along with the system feedback used in creating sketch geometry and the techniques used for understanding and correcting an overdefined sketch. How to correctly select specific entity types, such as an edge or face, is also necessary.

Content

The "Reference Geometry" section describes reference geometry (e.g., planes and axes) used within SolidWorks. Reference geometry used on a regular basis is covered early in the chapter, with some of the more obscure reference geometry commands covered later. The section "Types of Features" describes the various types of SolidWorks solid modeling features, both applied and sketched. The "Modifying a Feature" section describes how to modify an existing feature through various means.

Features can be changed, added, or removed—anywhere in the design process— after a part has been defined. The section "Advanced Part Topics" describes some of the more advanced topics related to part modeling. This section introduces these features and provides insight as to how they can be applied to a design.

The "Thin Features" and "Sheet Metal Parts" sections describe thin features and how SolidWorks can create a sheet metal part from a thin feature. SolidWorks contains functions specific to thin feature and sheet metal parts. The sheet metal functionality defines both the folded model and the flat pattern created by SolidWorks automatically from the thin feature part.

Objectives

After reading the "Reference Geometry" section, you should understand the uses of planes and axes and be able to identify the methods used to create these reference entities. With completion of the section "Types of Features," you should understand the various types of solid features and how they can be applied, and you should understand when different types of features should be created.

When you have completed the "Modifying a Feature" section, you should understand the various methods for redefining or editing existing features. You should also understand how and why features would be suppressed and how rollback can be used to organize features into functional groups. Upon completion of the section on advanced part features, you should understand what design tables are, how to select a configuration created by a design table, what equations are and how they are defined, what a configuration is and how it can be used to define optional versions of a part or assembly, what a base part is used for, and how a new part is derived from an existing part.

When you have finished the "Thin Features" and "Sheet Metal Parts" sections, you should understand what a thin feature part is and how it is created, and the difference between a thin feature and a sheet metal part. You should also know the components of a sheet metal part and how they can be used to create, modify, and document sheet metal parts.

Part Planning

Because a solid model consists of many different features that have many complex dependencies, planning is required to ensure that a flexible part is created that incorporates all of the design intent. A parametric solid model requires more planning than a simple wireframe because of all of the interdependent relationships that can be created.

The main elements of a part should be identified and prioritized. Specifically, a base feature and initial sketching plane should be determined prior to beginning a part. Functional features should be created in order of importance. Less important features should, when possible, be created near the end of the part. This helps minimize impact if these features are changed or deleted.

Similar design features should be functionally grouped. For example, if a set of drill holes are going to be placed around the perimeter of a part, and counterbores and chamfers added, it would make sense to add all of the holes first, then all of the counterbores, then the chamfers.

This is much more logical than adding a hole, then a counterbore, then a chamfer, then another hole, and so on, especially if all of the chamfers are the same size and can be added as part of the same feature definition. This makes the part more easily understood, mostly because like features are grouped together and the part itself is created on the CAD system in a manner similar to its physical creation.

The Rollback function can be used to analyze a part, whether created by you or another individual. Rolling a part back accomplishes what many of us wish we could do when creating real prototype models, which is going back in time to add a feature you wish you had added earlier, or simply to see the process of how the features were created. When analyzing a part, the Rollback bar can step through the part one feature at a time, graphically displaying the part, feature addition by feature addition.

Because FeatureManager is a chronological list of features, Rollback can step back through time to a point before certain features were created. It would be great if we were all perfect planners, knowing exactly how a part should be built. However, we are not. With Rollback, if you forget to put in a feature, you can step back in time and add it at any step in the process. The model will update accordingly, as if the feature had been added at that point in time.

When creating a solid model, you need to determine how many features should be used to define a part, and in what order. Making a part with too many simple features can produce a part in which finding specific features later on becomes quite a chore. A part with a small number of complex features produces an inflexible model with sketches that are difficult to control. A good rule of thumb is to work between these two extremes. Group geometry functionally, keeping in mind the possibility of changes and modifications that may need to be made later.

General Feature Creation Order

As discussed in Chapter 5, the best plane should be chosen with which to create the first sketch. The first sketch should be a profile that will most accurately define the overall shape of the part. After this base feature is created, you create features that more significantly define the part's shape, such as bosses or holes. Adding features less likely to be modified early in the creation process will result in less likelihood of downstream effects causing unforeseen problems to other features.

Draft and shell features should be added at a fairly early stage because of their geometric nature. It is best to add fillets toward the end of the design process if this is considered feasible in the design of the part. Fillets add complexity to a part, making for a larger draw on system resources both computationally and graphically. In general, you should leave complex features such as threads or variable radius fillets for the end of the design process. If at all possible, try to maintain the following order when adding features once the base feature has been created:

- Create the main functional part features such as bosses and cuts. Create the most important features and those least likely to change.
- Insert any draft or shell features.
- Insert fillets and complex geometry last.

If the solid model will not allow you to follow the suggested creation order, do what you have to do. From a software standpoint, SolidWorks does not care about the order. The creation order is a suggestion only, not a requirement. When creating a solid model from an AutoCAD standpoint, the order in which geometry is added to the part is not as important an issue. Because there are no parametrics or external references to existing geometry, there are no internal conflicts that may arise within the part.

For example, if a rectangular base plate is created in AutoCAD, and a circular boss is then placed on top of that plate, it makes absolutely no difference if the base plate is removed or if the circular boss had been created before the base plate. In SolidWorks, the base plate could not be deleted because the boss is dependent on it. The order of creation of features is important for this and other reasons, which are explored in this chapter.

Types of Features

The first feature in a part is called its *base feature*. This is usually an extrusion but can be any sketched feature type. All subsequent sketched features that add material to a part are called *bosses*. If material is being taken away, the sketched feature is considered a *cut*. There are other feature types that do not require sketch geometry, and these features are known as *applied features* because they are directly applied to the solid model.

AutoCAD allows the creation of various types of primitive shapes, and offers various methods of creating extrusions and revolved features. In the SolidWorks sense of the word, these cannot be called features because the AutoCAD shapes do not have their own unique attributes the way a SolidWorks part feature does. That is, an AutoCAD solid does not contain information pertaining to dimensions, end condition specifications, external associations to existing geometry, and so on.

The shape and orientation of the base feature (see illustration at left) should be chosen carefully because all other features are extensions of the base feature. The plane used to sketch the base feature's profile should correspond to the front, top, or right-hand face of the part.

Base-Extrude

A simple base feature.

This is not a requirement, only a good technique for new users who may find adjusting to the 3D qualities of solid modeling a bit confusing. If you do have a design in mind, decide what would be the best way to orient the design in space, then decide what the best plane for the base feature's profile would be and sketch on that plane.

Assume you wanted to create a simple part that has a small plate with various cuts and extrusions placed on it at various locations. In AutoCAD, the process of building a solid model would consist of creating solid shapes and then performing a number of Boolean operations. In Solid-Works, the same thing is accomplished by sketching the first profile and using that profile to create the feature. This process of creating a sketch and then defining the feature is performed repeatedly to build up the solid model. A simple rectangular profile could have been used to create the base feature shown in the previous illustration.

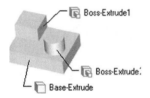

Boss features defined by extruding sketch geometry.

Instead of performing Boolean unions or subtractions, SolidWorks defines parametric bosses or cuts. These two categories of sketched features are described in the sections that follow.

Boss

A boss adds material to a part. A boss can be defined by using the Extrude, Sweep, Revolve, or Loft commands. The illustration at left shows two examples of simple boss extrusions.

Cut

A cut subtracts material from a part. A cut can be defined by using the Extrude, Sweep, Revolve, or Loft commands. The illustration at left shows two examples of simple cut extrusions.

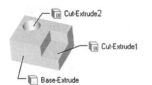

Cut features defined by extruding sketch geometry.

Bosses and cuts are almost complete opposites. Procedurally, these two commands are almost identical. Do not be misled by the terminology. Just remember that a boss adds material and a cut takes it away.

Solid Features

Once the decision has been made whether to add or to remove material, it must then be decided what classification of feature should be used to complete the task. This probably sounds more difficult than it is. In most cases the choice is obvious once you know the four main feature classifications. The following is a summary of the information to this point on feature types:

- Features can be either bosses or cuts. Bosses add material and cuts remove material.

- Features can be sketched features or applied features. Sketched features require a sketch; applied features do not.

- Features are of four main types: extrusions, and revolved, swept, or lofted features.

Perhaps 90 percent of everything done in SolidWorks is based on these four feature types.

You also need to brush up on the five main steps involved in creating features. These five steps will be repeated as each sketched feature is created and the solid model built.

1. Select a plane or planar face.

2. Enter sketch mode (by clicking on the Sketch icon).

3. Create the sketch.

4. Add dimensions and constraints.

5. Create the feature.

As discussed in the Chapter 5, AutoCAD's function analogous to the sketch plane is the User Coordinate System (UCS). The UCS plane would be specified, and the geometry would be created, whether it be wireframe geometry or solid geometry. Accuracy is very important in AutoCAD because the ability to modify a dimension to reshape the part does not exist.

If working with a solid model, geometry must be added or subtracted to achieve the desired shape of the model. If a mistake is made, it can be very difficult to correct. Even if you were the most accurate and error-free AutoCAD user, design changes would still be a fact of life.

Modifying a solid model in AutoCAD would require major work. An example is a boss that needs to be resized and relocated. An additional solid would have to be added to the file and subsequently subtracted using a Boolean operation. An additional boss would then be created, and an additional Boolean union could then be performed. In SolidWorks, a dimension or two could be changed as needed.

For the descriptions of the four feature classifications that follow, it is assumed you have already completed the first four steps. In other words, the sketch has been created and you are ready to create the feature.

Extrude

Extrude is probably the most commonly used of all features. This particular feature extrudes a profile a specified distance. Either a boss or cut can be extruded. The sketch plane should be either a plane or a planar face on which a 2D profile will be created. A closed profile, by default, will extrude as a solid feature. An open profile will always extrude as a thin feature. (Thin features are covered later in this chapter.)

Follow the general guidelines for sketching presented in Chapter 5. Summed up, these guidelines state that a sketch should be a closed non-self-intersecting profile. There will be exceptions to this rule, which are discussed later, but that is a good general rule to follow. An extruded boss is shown in the following illustration.

An extruded boss.

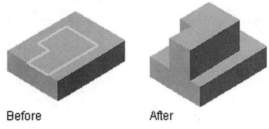

Before   After

To create an extruded boss feature from an existing sketch profile, perform the following steps:

1. Select Insert/Boss.

2. Select Extrude… to open the Extrude Feature dialog box.

3. Select End Condition Type. Blind is the default selection, which is very common. Leave this set to Blind for now.

4. Specify a depth by entering a value in the Depth field, or use the up/down increment arrows.

5. Observe the preview on the screen and click on Reverse Direction if necessary.

6. Select OK to complete this function.

To create an extruded cut feature, perform the previous steps, but use Insert/*Cut*/Extrude... instead.

End Condition Types

End conditions are nothing more than a way of determining how far a sketch will be extruded. The end condition types may vary slightly, depending on whether you are performing a cut or a boss, and depending on other variables discussed later in this chapter. The following are the SolidWorks end condition types. The illustration that follows shows end type results.

Blind	Extrudes a profile a specified distance.
Through All	Extrudes a profile through the entire part. Most commonly used for cuts.
Up to Next	Extrudes up to the next surface encountered.
Up to Vertex	Extrudes up to a selected vertex point, which you must specify.
Up to Surface	Extrudes up to a surface you specify.
Offset from Surface	Extrudes a profile to an offset distance from a surface you specify.
Mid-Plane	Extrudes a part equally in both directions.

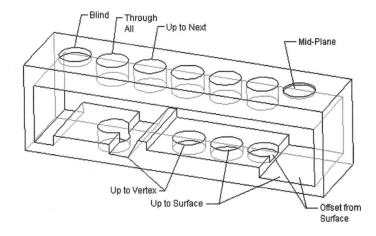

End conditions and what the results might look like.

Other Extrude Attributes

There are other options that can be found in the Extrude dialog box, such as Reverse Direction, the function of which should be self-evident if you are looking at the preview onscreen. The following is a list of these options and the functions they perform:

Depth	Enter the extrusion depth or click on the up and down arrow buttons to increment or decrement the depth value. This is not always present, depending on the end condition type.
Reverse Direction	This is a toggle switch that reverses the extrusion direction.
Flip Side To Cut	This toggle switch is only available during a cut operation. It toggles the portion of the material to be cut away.
Selected Items	This box is only active if there are items to select, such as with the end condition types Up To Vertex or Up To Surface. You should select the appropriate entity type, which will be listed in this box.
Draft While Extruding	Check to add draft to the extruded feature.
Angle	Enter the draft angle or click on the up and down arrow buttons to increment or decrement the draft angle value.
Draft Outward	This is a toggle switch that controls whether a draft will be inward or outward.

Both Directions	Check to select whether the extrusion should be extruded in one or two directions. This is different from the Mid-Plane end condition type in that Mid-Plane allows for extruding in equal amounts in opposite directions, whereas Both Directions allows for specifying separate end condition types for either direction.
Settings For	When Both Directions is selected, the Settings For pull-down menu is used to define the properties for Direction 1 and Direction 2.

AutoCAD does have an Extrude command in release 13. If you are familiar with this command in AutoCAD, the equivalent SolidWorks functionality will seem similar. The Depth option in the SolidWorks End Condition dialog box is analogous to AutoCAD's "Height of extrusion" option while performing the Extrude command. Both programs have the ability to add draft during the extrusion process. There is no need to convert geometry into regions or anything of that sort in SolidWorks. The program is a solid modeler by nature; therefore, regions and wireframe geometry are not necessary.

Revolve

The Revolve function creates a boss or cut feature from a profile revolved about a centerline. A centerline entity must be used for creating this feature. A common mistake for a new SolidWorks user is to attempt to create a revolved feature with an axis. This will not work. Also, the centerline must exist in the current sketch, and not reused from an existing sketch. A closed profile, by default, will extrude as a solid feature. An open profile will create a thin feature.

There are a few general rules regarding revolved features. First, there must be a centerline in the current sketch that will become the revolved feature. In addition, you will want to adhere to the following guidelines when creating a revolved feature. The following illustration shows a revolved feature.

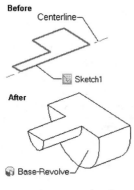

Before

Centerline

Sketch1

After

Base-Revolve

*A boss revolved
180 degrees.*

• The sketch should not touch the centerline at one isolated point. This results in invalid geometry. Think of an object having substance but no thickness. Such an object might exist in theory, but not in the real world, where mathematics define solid geometry. If the solid model requires mathematical definition with imaginary numbers, it cannot be created in SolidWorks.

• The sketch should not cross the centerline. This results in self-intersecting geometry.

Revolved features are previewed in the graphics area. If the Revolved Feature dialog box is obscuring your view, drag it out of the way. To create a revolved feature from an existing sketch profile, perform the following steps:

1. Select Insert/Boss.

2. Select Revolve… to open the Revolve Feature dialog box.

3. Enter the angle of rotation.

4. Toggle Reverse to change the rotation direction if needed.

5. Select OK to complete the operation.

To create a revolved cut feature, perform the previous steps, but use Insert/*Cut*/Revolve… instead.

End Condition Types

There are end condition types associated with revolved features, just as there are with extruded features, but not nearly as many. These end condition types are:

One Direction	Revolves a profile in one direction only. You must specify the angle.
Mid Plane	Revolves a profile in both directions at the same time. The angle you specify is the total angle revolved.
Two Directions	This allows you to specify angles for both clockwise and counterclockwise directions.

Other Revolve Attributes

The Revolved Feature dialog box contains an option to revolve as a thin feature. Thin features will be discussed separately in a later section. For now, the following are the options you need to be aware of when dealing with the Revolved Feature dialog box:

Angle	Enter the angle to revolve the sketch profile.
Reverse	Click on to reverse the revolve direction (clockwise or counterclockwise).
Revolve as	Click on to select whether to revolve a solid or thin feature. This option is only accessible for closed profiles.

As with AutoCAD, SolidWorks requires some way to define the axis of rotation when revolving geometry. AutoCAD requires two points to define the axis of rotation, whereas SolidWorks requires a centerline. You must also supply the rotation angle in each program. Keep in mind that SolidWorks does not accept negative dimensions. Instead, you must use the Reverse check box to alternate between clockwise and counterclockwise.

Sweep

The sweep feature is created using a closed profile (sweep section) and a trajectory curve (sweep path). The profile (sweep section) is used to define the shape of the swept section, and the trajectory (sweep path) defines the direction and path of the sweep. Optionally, a guide curve can be used to control the sweep profile.

As with any other feature created with SolidWorks, there are a couple of simple rules that should be followed to ensure the feature is created without error. The Sweep function is considered to be a slightly more advanced feature of SolidWorks. There are a larger number of computations that must be performed, and the graphics are more difficult to display because of the shading requirements that need to be met. The guidelines to keep in mind while performing a sweep are as follows. The illustration that follows shows a simple swept feature.

- *The sweep trajectory must start on the same plane as the sweep profile.* This condition does not always have to be established with a constraint. If the trajectory's start point just happens to be on the profile's plane, the sweep will work, as long as the other listed conditions are met. Sometimes, however, you may find it necessary to implement the Pierce constraint. The Pierce constraint will allow a curve to pierce a point on the profile's plane, thereby anchoring the profile to the trajectory.

- *A sweep trajectory must not be self-intersecting.* This simply means that the trajectory should not come into contact with itself.

- *A swept feature must not intersect itself.* This sounds similar to the previous guideline but is actually different. Imagine a helix. The helix itself does not intersect itself. However, if a large enough circle were used as a profile, the circle would intersect itself as it swept along the helix. This constitutes self-intersecting geometry, which is not permissible in Solid-Works.

The following is a step-by-step procedure for creating a swept feature. Keep in mind that two sketches must be created before a sweep can be performed.

1. Create the sketch that will define the profile. (A sweep profile must be closed. There is no option for creating a thin feature during a sweep operation.)

2. Create the sketch that will define the sweep trajectory. Usually this would be an open trajectory, but that is not necessary. For instance, a circle can be swept along another closed profile, such as a circle, to create a donut.

3. Exit from the active sketch.

4. Select Insert/Boss.

5. Select Sweep… to open the Sweep dialog box.

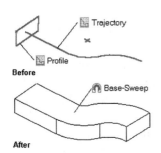

A simple swept feature.

6. Click in the Sweep Section box and select the sweep profile from the graphics area or from FeatureManager.

7. Click in the Sweep Path box and select the sweep path from the graphics area or from FeatureManager.

8. Click on OK to complete the operation.

To create a swept cut feature, perform the previous steps, but use Insert/*Cut*/Sweep... instead.

Sweep Guide Curves

Guide curves can be used to alter a sweep section. It is mandatory that the sweep section have a pierce relation added in order to attach the sweep section to the guide curve. If this were not the case, the sweep profile would not have any association with the guide curve and would not know enough to change its shape to "follow" the guide curve.

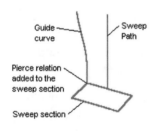

Elements of a swept feature using a guide curve.

A guide curve can be defined by a sketch or feature edge, or through the use of 2D or 3D curves defined by x-y-z coordinates. The sweep path and the guide curve do not need to be the same length. The length of the sweep is determined by the shorter of the two objects. More than one guide curve can be used to alter the shape of the sweep section. The illustration at left shows the elements of a guide curve sweep. To create a swept feature using an optional guide curve, perform the following steps:

1. Create the sketch that will define the profile. Once again, the sweep profile must be closed.

2. Create the sketch that will define the sweep trajectory. This profile should be an open trajectory if the plan is to implement a guide curve.

3. Exit from the active sketch.

4. Select Insert/Boss.

5. Select Sweep... to open the Sweep dialog box.

6. Click in the Sweep Section box and select the sweep profile from the graphics area or from FeatureManager.

7. Click in the Sweep Path box and select the sweep path from the graphics area or from FeatureManager.

8. Select the Advanced tab.

9. Select Guide Curve(s) from the graphics area or from FeatureManager.

10. Click on OK to complete the operation.

Optional Guide Curve Creation

Creating a guide curve does not need to be a feat of technical expertise. A guide curve can be a simple sketch used to further define the shape of a profile as it sweeps along a trajectory. If needed, a guide curve can also be a set of coordinates that defines a curve through 3D space. This obviously results in a much more complex solid feature. Such complex curves are beyond the scope of this book.

Other Sweep Attributes

There are other options you may have noticed in the Sweep dialog box. Most of these options are not used on a regular basis. The Sweep command itself is not as commonly used as Extrude or Revolve. However, there are some features of SolidWorks that are just very nice to have around when needed. This section covers most of the additional options that can be implemented when performing a sweep.

These obtained are contained in two tabs present in the Sweep dialog box. These are the Sweep tab and the Advanced tab. The Orientation/Twist Control selection box under the Sweep tab contains a number of options, and controls how the sweep profile moves along the path and guide curves. These options are:

Follow Path	The profile will remain tangent to the sweep path.
Keep Normal Constant	The profile will remain parallel to the original profile sketch plane during the course of the sweep.
Follow Path and 1st Guide Curve	The original angle between the profile and path remains constant, and the twist is based on a vector between the path and the first guide curve.
Follow 1st and 2nd Guide Curves	The original angle between the profile and path remains constant, and the twist is based on a vector between the first and second guide curves.

There are additional optional settings in the Advanced tab. These are:

Up/Down	Click on to move the selected guide curve up or down the guide curve list box to change its order of priority. This will result in a somewhat different shape, depending on the twist control.
Maintain Tangency	This option is only relevant if the entities in the sweep profile are tangent, meaning the individual line or arc segments in the profile. Maintaining tangency reduces segmentation lines in the resultant swept surface.
Show Intermediate Profiles	This option will calculate a number of intermediate profiles that represent cross sections of the solid geometry. It is essentially a preview of the swept feature. This gives you an idea of what the outcome of the sweep will look like without SolidWorks having to perform all of the calculations necessary to complete the entire operation.

During a sweep, geometric conditions can sometimes cause a feature to either fail or not be produced. When defining the sweep section, sweep path, and guide curves, you may create geometry that cannot be geometrically solved. The other factor is control of tangency, orientation, and twist. These options can be changed to alter the sweep geometry created along the sweep and guide curves.

If the sweep section turns or twists too sharply, the geometry may not be valid. Usually, this is caused by self-intersecting geometry being created. Take a simple scenario, where a circle 10 millimeters in diameter is swept along a path. The center of the circle is positioned on the path.

Now visualize the path having a bend in it that is less than 5 millimeters. In other words, the path contains a bend that is less than the circle's radius. During the sweep, the circle would begin to kink in on itself as it followed its tangent course along the path. Once again, you would have self-intersecting geometry, as shown in the illustration at left.

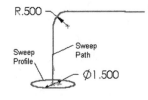

R.500

Sweep Profile

Sweep Path

⌀1.500

This geometry would result in a self-intersecting sweep.

The following are troubleshooting tips if your sweep is failing:

- Review the sweep section, sweep path, and the optional guide curves to determine if the sketch geometry can physically produce a solid feature. See if it can be corrected by modifying the sketch geometry of the sweep section, sweep path, or guide curve.

- Ensure that the sweep path start point is on the same plane as the sweep section.

- Ensure that the correct sketches are listed in the Sweep Section and Sweep Path list boxes and that they are not reversed.

- If the sweep is a boss, make sure it touches existing geometry. If it is a cut, make sure it is not cutting empty space. Otherwise, a disjointed-feature error will be encountered.

Sweeping in SolidWorks is much more powerful than in AutoCAD. Sweeping a region in AutoCAD would normally be done with the Extrude command, specifying the Path option. A spline can be used as the path to create a variety of swept shapes. The profile is automatically aligned perpendicular with the path.

In SoldWorks, this is not an issue. There are very few limitations when creating a swept trajectory in SolidWorks. The Sweep command is a separate command and not just an extension of the Extrude function. A SolidWorks profile does not need to be perpendicular to the trajectory, guide curves can be used, and the profile can be swept tangent to the trajectory or with its orientation left constant throughout the sweep.

Loft

Loft is used to create a solid boss or cut from multiple closed profiles. Multiple guide curves can be optionally selected, as with the Sweep feature. A common "connection point" for each profile should be consistent to avoid twisting the solid.

The sketching planes for each profile do not have to be parallel, and each section does not need to have the same number of edges. For example, a loft can be created between a circle and a square, a series of ellipses, or between a triangle and a point, to name a few. Optionally, a guide curve can be used to define a loft direction. The guide curves can be used to alter the loft profile or as a guide for twist. A guide curve can be defined by a sketch, part edges, or construction curves. The illustration at left shows a lofted feature.

Creating a Lofted Feature

To create a feature defined by multiple closed profiles (a lofted feature), perform the following steps:

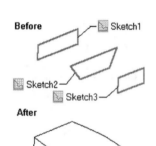

A lofted feature.

1. Create the sketch profiles. There must be at least two profiles, and they should be closed. If open profiles are used, a surface, not a solid, will be created.

2. Make sure you exit out of sketch mode after the last profile has been created.

3. Select the sketch profiles in the order you would like the loft to occur. Remember to hold the Control key down when selecting more than one. The sketches can be selected from FeatureManager or from the graphics area. If selected from FeatureManager, twisting may occur and SolidWorks will inform you of this fact with a warning. If the sketch profiles are selected from the graphics area, select each profile near a common vertex; this will help SolidWorks determine the loft and how the profiles should be connected.

4. Select Insert/Boss.

5. Select Loft... to open the Loft dialog box.

6. Select OK to complete this function.

To create a lofted cut feature, perform the previous steps, but use Insert/*Cut*/Loft... instead.

Other Loft Attributes

Lofting is not very complicated from a user's standpoint. From a software standpoint, however, it is quite an achievement. There are options that allow you to define some very interesting shapes. The following is a list of those options and what they perform:

Profiles	Field displays the name of selected loft profiles. Pick inside this field to add or remove sketch profiles.
Guide Curves	Field displays the name of the selected guide curves. This is an optional field. Guide curves do not need to be used. Pick inside this field to add or remove guide curves.
Maintain Tangency	This option is only relevant if the entities in the sweep profile are tangent, meaning the individual line or arc segments in the profile. Maintaining tangency reduces segmentation lines in the resultant swept surface.
Advanced Smoothing	Check if you want SolidWorks to perform extra calculations on any arcs in the loft profiles that will result in a smoother surface.
Close along Loft Direction	Check to connect the last profile to the first profile. This requires at least three profiles.
Move Up/Down	Click to change the order in which the profiles are lofted. This is usually determined during the selection process, but can be altered here.

Very interesting and complex shapes can be created using the loft process. However, it is not a foolproof procedure. The following are a few tips to help you when trouble-shooting a failed loft:

- Review the loft profiles and the guide curves to determine if the geometry created is physically attainable. In other words, can it exist in the real world? It is possible to create geometry that is impossible to manufacture, but it is not possible to create geometry that cannot exist in the real world. Change the geometry to see if it can be corrected by modifying the sketch geometry of the loft profiles or the guide curves.

- Ensure that the profiles were selected in the correct order.

- Select profiles from the graphics area instead of FeatureManager.

- Ensure the loft profiles were selected using the same relative location on the profile sketches. The loft preview should show you what will be the common vertex points between profiles.

There is no counterpart in AutoCAD for a SolidWorks Loft feature. There is not even a valid workaround for creating similar solid shapes. About the best that can be done is to use some of AutoCAD's surfacing commands to try to achieve a shape similar to what might be created using the SolidWorks Loft command.

The following table describes the characteristics used to determine the solid feature used for a boss or cut. Use this list if you have a particular shape or profile in mind but are not certain how to best create the feature. Sometimes there is more than one choice for a particular shape or profile. This table is meant to get you pointed in the right direction, and not as a rigid set of rules.

Options	Extrude	Revolve	Sweep	Loft
One profile	x	x		
One profile and one trajectory			x	
Multiple profiles				x
Cylindrical feature	x	x		
Project geometry along a curve			x	
Able to use optional guide curves			x	x
Drafted feature	x	x	x	x

Feature Names

Naming features makes a model easier to understand because the named features are then much easier to find in FeatureManager. Keep names short, and as meaningful as possible. Meaningful names help document the purpose and design intent of a feature. The following are the default system names for dimensions, features, and components:

- Dimension names are found in the Dimension Properties dialog box. Right click on the dimension to access its properties. The following are examples of dimension names.
  - D1@Sketch1 (if a sketch dimension)
  - D1@Feature_name (if a feature dimension)
- Part feature names are found in FeatureManager. The following are examples of feature names.
  - Base-Revolve
  - Cut-Extrude2
  - Shell1
- Assembly component names are found in the FeatureManager of Assemblies. The following is an example of a component name.
  - Part1, or more precisely, *Part_name* (where *Part_name* is the actual name of the part file)

By defining meaningful names, you can associate a feature's function, grouping, or purpose by reviewing the defined name and creation order. There is an option that prompts you for a feature name after it has been created. This option is selectable by checking the "Name feature on creation" field in the General tab in the Tools/Options menu. The following are examples of SolidWorks default names and what you might use for a new name:

- *Default name:* D2@Sketch2
  New name: Diameter@ScrewProfile
- *Default feature name:* Base-Extrude
  Renamed feature: Mounting Plate Profile

Because AutoCAD is not a feature-based program, there is no such thing as a feature, and therefore no need to name one. Likewise, there is no distinction between a feature and a sketch. An AutoCAD file is typically either a wireframe, a 2D layout, or a solid model. Feature names are irrelevant.

Parent/Child Relationships

Parent/child relationships are created when a feature uses a reference of an existing feature (e.g., sketch plane or feature edge) or when a new feature cannot exist without an existing feature. A *parent* is a feature that other features have referenced or are based on. This reference could be defined by dimensioning to the edge or face, by using the Convert Entities or Offset Entities sketch tools, or by sketching the feature on the face of another feature.

A *child* is a feature that references another feature. Child features are dependent on parent features. If a parent feature is deleted, the children are not able to exist because they are dependent on the parent. The FeatureManager design tree is used to query existing parent/child relationships.

Unnecessary parent/child relationships should be kept to a minimum. When selecting edges or faces for dimensions or geometric references, you should be aware that a relation to the selected entity has been created. If the parent is removed, the child will fail.

Always select edges or faces in a view orientation that allows a clear view of what is being selected. Selecting an edge viewed by a normal projection may select the edge or face, or another feature directly behind the desired entity. Using an isometric orientation can produce better results, simply because it is easier for you to see what is going on.

If unwanted relationships do exist, the features can be redefined to eliminate the dimension or geometric reference that created the relationship. When investigating parent/child relationships, items to look for include a sketch plane, converted or offset edges, geometric relations, or dimensions. The easiest method for investigating parent/child relationships is to right click the sketch or feature in FeatureManager and select Parent/Child. All parent/child relationships will be displayed. To display the parent/child relationships for a sketch or feature, perform the following steps:

1. Right click on the sketch or feature in FeatureManager.

2. Select Parent/Child.

3. Select OK to close the Parent/Child dialog box.

To remove an unwanted parent/child relationship, you must remove any references to the parent geometry. This can sometimes be accomplished by editing the relations of a sketch (see Chapter 5). In other cases, it is impossible to remove the parent/child relationship. Take this simple example: if a hole is created through a block, the hole is a child of the block and the block is a parent to the hole. Without the block, there will be no hole. Removing references is not an option.

Parent/child relationships are a derivative of a feature-based program. It could be argued that AutoCAD has a form of parent/child relationships. For instance, if a hole were made through a block, the hole could not exist without the block. Therefore, the block must be a parent of the hole. This is a correct assumption in the AutoCAD environment, but the implications of this relationship are more substantial in SolidWorks.

Because features are created in a specific chronological order in SolidWorks, a parent feature exists at a place in time before the child. This in itself is not remarkable. However, the time a feature was created can in essence be altered so that it exists at an earlier stage in the design process. Features can be reordered to exist at different locations in time.

Parent/child relationship plays an important role with regard to this reordering capability. A child feature cannot be reordered to exist before its parent. AutoCAD does not have anything in its software code similar to this. In AutoCAD, Boolean operations can be performed at any time without regard to the order of events. As long as the desired shape is obtained, that is all that matters.

Other Feature Functions

Holes

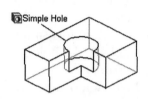

Simple hole.

Counterbored hole using Hole Wizard.

The following sections describe other SolidWorks feature functions. These include holes, fillets/rounds, chamfers, shells, ribs, draft, and mirror.

Simple holes are used to quickly insert a single hole on a model face. Hole Wizard is used to define complex hole geometry (e.g., countersunk or counterbored) using a set of easy-to-use menu selections. The hole definition can be modified or redefined after insertion. The hole location can be precisely defined by redefining the sketch after insertion. Otherwise, the hole location is defined by the selected location on the sketch face.

Using Hole Wizard

The following is a list of the types of holes that can be automatically created using Hole Wizard. The illustrations at left show a simple hole and a hole using Hole Wizard.

- Simple (this creates a simple straight-hole feature)
- Tapered
- Counterbored
- Countersunk
- Counterdrilled
- Simple drilled
- Tapered drilled
- Counterbored drilled
- Countersunk drilled
- Counterdrilled drilled

The following illustration shows a screen shot of Hole Wizard and the current options for hole types.

Hole Wizard.

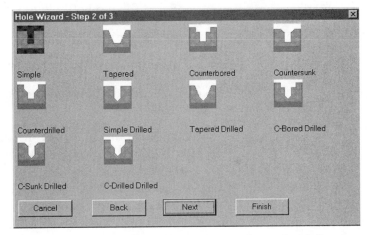

To add a circular hole to a part, perform the following steps:

1. Select on the face where the hole is to be created.

2. Select Insert/Features/Hole/Simple from the pull-down menus.

3. Specify the End Condition Type and the Diameter.

4. Select OK to complete this function.

It should be noted that after using this procedure to add a simple hole, the locating sketch must then be edited in order to accurately locate the center of the hole. In most cases, it is easier simply to create a circle and use Cut/Extrude instead. In the case of a more complex hole type, Hole Wizard will save you steps. To create a hole using Hole Wizard, perform the following steps:

1. Pick on the face where the hole is to be created.

2. Select Insert/Features/Hole Wizard from the pull-down menus.

3. Select the End Condition Type and Depth.

4. Select Next to go to the next step.

5. Select the type of hole to be created.

6. Select Next to continue.

7. Enter the dimensional parameters for the hole.

8. Select Finish to complete the procedure and insert the hole.

Again, it should be noted that after adding a hole using Hole Wizard, the locating sketch must be edited in order to dimension or constrain the center of the hole. There are two sketches created when using Hole Wizard. The first sketch is the locating sketch, which consists of nothing more than a point. This point can be dimensioned or constrained just like any other sketch geometry.

The second sketch is created by SolidWorks automatically using the parameters entered by the user. This sketch cannot be edited, but the definition of the hole can be edited if the parameters must be changed. Use the right mouse button to edit the definition, and the original Hole Wizard dialog boxes will appear.

Other Hole Attributes

The various options that might appear in the Hole Wizard dialog boxes are totally dependent on what end condition type is selected. These options are identical to the End Condition options listed in the section covering extrusions earlier in this chapter.

The parameters that must be specified in the last dialog box are dependent on the hole type selected. For example, if a countersunk hole type is selected, a countersunk depth and diameter must be entered. These values are shown in a preview that tells you which dimensions are related to which parameters. The actual terminology does not need to be known (see the following illustration).

Entering parameters for a countersunk drilled hole.

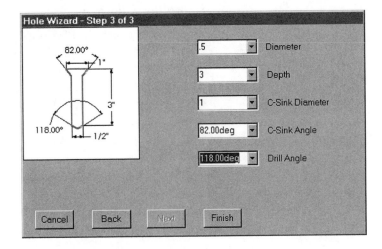

Again, AutoCAD has no such counterpart to the Solid-Works Hole Wizard. In order to reproduce the functionality Hole Wizard provides, the AutoCAD user would have to recreate the exact opposite of the hole to be created. It would probably be easiest to draw half the profile in AutoCAD, change the profile into a region, then revolve the region and perform a Boolean subtraction operation once the desired hole shape was moved to the appropriate location on the part. It is much easier to plug the information into a dialog box such as those provided in SolidWorks' Hole Wizard.

Fillet/Round

The Fillet/Round feature will create a fillet or round on specified part edges. SolidWorks does not care whether it is a fillet or a round, and there is no need to specify one or the other. If an interior edge is selected, a fillet will be applied, and if an exterior edge is selected, a round will be applied. There is absolutely no difference in the implementation of this command from a user standpoint. From this point on, the Fillet/Round command will simply be referred to as Fillet.

Using the Fillet Function

The creation order and grouping of fillets will affect how a part can be modified. This order and grouping will also determine tangency conditions for the fillet. Selecting multiple edges allows you to add fillets for all edges selected at one time. This works fine as long as all selected edges will have the same radius. Edges with fillets of differing radii must be added as independent features.

Fillets should be added to the model toward the end of the modeling process. Many fillets are inserted for cosmetic reasons and should not burden the model early in the design process. This will result in a performance gain by the user. It may also limit unnecessary parent/child relationships and keep the model less complicated, which makes for easier editing.

The creation order and grouping of fillet edges will determine the blending of fillets. Blending is the manner in which fillet intersections are formed. When inserting fillets, you should group edges that are similar in function and radius. Grouping too many fillets into the same feature can make the part difficult to modify. If every edge were made into a separate feature, there would be too many features in the part. Try to find a reasonable middle ground. Limiting the number of filleted edges per fillet feature to nine of fewer seems to work well. The illustration at left shows a fillet feature.

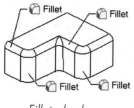

Filleted edges.

When adding a fillet, it is possible to select either an edge or a face. If a face is selected, every edge on the face will be filleted. The edges or faces to fillet can be selected either before or after the Fillet command is entered. This is the case with most commands. With regard to the Fillet command and certain other dialog boxes, the Control key does not need to be held down when selecting more than one entity. For this reason, it is easier to select entities after the Fillet dialog box is open. To insert a constant radius fillet, perform the following steps:

1. Select Fillet from the Insert/Features menu.

2. Select the edges or faces to be filleted.

3. Enter the fillet radius.

4. Leave Propagate To Tangent Faces selected if the fillet should continue along every tangent edge it encounters.

5. Select OK to accept the changes and close the dialog box.

Variable radius fillets can also be added to a part. The main difference in creating a variable radius fillet is how the radii are entered. To insert a variable radius fillet, you would perform the following steps:

1. Select Fillet from the Insert/Features menu.

2. Select the edges to be filleted.

3. Select the type of fillet (variable) and whether to continue the fillet along tangent edges by checking Propagate To Tangent Faces.

4. Select a vertex from the list box and enter the radius. This must be done for each vertex.

5. Select OK to continue.

Other Fillet Attributes

Not all of the additional options available in the Fillet dialog box are straightforward and self-explanatory. The following is a list of these additional attributes, with explanations of each.

Propagate Along Tangent Edges	Check to continue the radius (fillet) along all tangent edges until a non-tangent corner is encountered. If this option is not selected, the fillet will continue in a linear fashion at each end of the edge selected until it runs out of material to fillet. Adjacent edges will be mitered as needed to blend with the filleted edge.
Smooth Transition	Available with the variable fillet type only. The tangent lines of the fillet will be parallel with the filleted edge at each end of the fillet.
Straight Transition	Available with the variable fillet type only. The radius varies linearly.

The following are fillet attribute types:

Fixed Radius	Fillet with one radial value.
Variable Radius	Fillet with multiple radial values. Radial values can be set for each vertex of the selected edges.
Face Blend	Extends two or more faces and fillets the intersection. This fillet type can literally swallow up entire faces without resulting in geometry errors.

The following are Overflow attribute types:

Default	The system selects which method to use, depending on the geometry selected.
Keep Edge	Blends the target surface smoothly, but the fillet surface may be broken. In other words, the fillet radius will change in order to accommodate the edge encountered by the fillet.
Keep Surface	Blends the fillet surface smoothly, but the target surface may be broken. The fillet's radius will remain unchanged, and the edge where the fillet is overlapping will change to accommodate the fillet.

AutoCAD's Fillet command is similar to SolidWorks' in that edges are selected and a radius is supplied. The Chain option is similar to SolidWorks' Propagate To Tangent Faces option. When used, these options will continue the fillet along tangent edges. This is where the similarities end. SolidWorks allows you to select from a wide variety of options that control the attributes of the fillet, such as the overflow characteristics when a fillet runs off the face of a feature, thereby interfering with the fillet's face properties.

Variable radius fillets and face blends can also be created in SolidWorks. In addition, the Parasolids solid modeling kernel that SolidWorks uses is much more powerful than AutoCAD's. Try this simple experiment: Create a solid block in AutoCAD and fillet one edge at half an inch. Now create another fillet using the Chain option and place it on the edges that wrap around one end of the first fillet. Give it a radius greater than half an inch, and AutoCAD will return an error. SolidWorks will complete the Fillet without flinching, and blends the two fillets at the corner. As another example of the power of SolidWorks' Fillet command, it is possible to create a solid cube and fillet every face to create a sphere.

Chamfer

Chamfer will create a beveled edge on selected edges at a given distance and angle. Chamfers can be performed on multiple edges at one time, similar to the fillet function. The two parameters that must be entered are distance and angle. The distance is the distance from the edge being chamfered, and the angle is the angle of the beveled edge as measured from the face where the distance was applied.

Using the Chamfer Function

Chamfer features do not slow down your computer's performance hit like fillet features do. This is due mostly to the fact that fillets require rounded edges with a large computational overhead, and chamfers do not. The illustration at left shows examples of chamfer features. To create a chamfer on selected edges, perform the following steps:

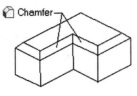

Chamfer features.

1. Select Chamfer from the Insert/Features menu.

2. Select the edges or faces to be chamfered.

3. Enter the chamfer Distance and Angle.

4. Checking Flip Direction will reverse the direction the distance is measured.

5. Select OK to continue.

Other Chamfer Attributes

Distance, Angle, and Flip dimensions are the only parameters needed for a chamfer. As with fillets, it is easiest to select entities after the dialog box is open because the Control key does not have to be held down to select multiple entities. Likewise, selecting a face will chamfer all edges on that face. Chamfers will always propagate along tangent faces. Unlike with Fillet, there is no switch to toggle propagation on or off.

AutoCAD's and SolidWorks' chamfer commands have about the same functionality; however, SolidWorks' command is easier to implement. The command provides you with a user-friendly dialog box in which to enter information.

Shell

The Shell feature creates a constant wall section on the inside or outside of a solid part. At least one face must be selected as the open face. The open face is the face removed during the Shell operation. Multiple shell thicknesses can be defined as an added option, which in SolidWorks terminology is known as a *multi-thickness shell.*

Using the Shell Function

The most important decision that needs to be made with a shell is when to insert the shell feature. It is usually desirable to create a shell early in the design process. A shell essentially hollows out a solid model; therefore, it follows that if many features have been added, the shell operation will have to work overtime to shell out many features that do not necessarily need to be shelled.

SolidWorks is very intuitive when it comes to the shell process. For instance, if a rib has been added to a part and the rib has a thickness greater than half the shell wall thickness, the rib will be included with the shell. What happens if the shell wall thickness increases beyond half the rib's thickness?

One might think the shell operation would fail, but the software is intelligent enough to know it cannot shell the rib and ignores it. Nevertheless, play it safe and shell geometry as soon as you can. This will keep the part from becoming too complex before the shell feature is implemented. The illustration at left shows a shell feature.

To create a shell, perform the following steps:

A shelled part.

1. Pick the faces to be removed during the shell process.

2. Select Shell from the Insert/Features menu.

3. Enter the wall Thickness.

4. Select OK to continue.

To create a shell with multiple wall thicknesses, perform the following steps:

1. Pick the faces to be removed during the shell process.

2. Select Shell from the Insert/Features menu.

3. Enter the wall Thickness.

4. Click in the Multi Thickness Faces box and select additional faces that will require a different wall thickness.

5. Enter the wall thickness by highlighting the desired face in the Multi Thickness Faces box and specifying the thickness. This should be done for each face listed.

6. Select OK to continue.

Other Shell Attributes

Another shell attribute is Shell Outward. This option specifies whether the wall thickness will remain on the inside of the part or be added to the outside. If wall thickness is added to the inside of the part, it is as if the part has been "hogged out" and a wall thickness left behind. If adding wall thickness to the outside of the part, it is as if the entire original model has been removed, and a wax coating of a desired thickness remains. The following guidelines might help if you are experiencing difficulties creating a shelled part:

- At least one end must be removed for a shell feature.
- Surfaces can be selected or deselected after the dialog box has been brought up.
- The face or faces for a *multiple-thickness* shell must be selected after the dialog box has been brought up.
- Click the cursor in the Multi Thickness Faces field prior to selecting faces that are not to have the default thickness.
- Prior to selecting OK, make sure there is a selected face in the Faces To Remove field.

AutoCAD does not have a shell command. It would be possible in AutoCAD to create a solid, copy it, rescale the copy, and then subtract it from the original, but this is a very crude workaround at best.

Rib

A rib is an open sketch used to create a thin-walled rib feature. The rib sketch does not need to be geometrically constrained to the walls of the part. The advantage to a rib is that a simple sketch can be used to produce this feature. SolidWorks does most of the work needed to create the rib.

Using the Rib Function

The sketch geometry for creating a rib must be on a plane that intersects the solid geometry the rib will extend to. The rib must be within the extents (boundary) of the current part geometry. A portion of the rib sketch cannot protrude outside the existing part geometry because SolidWorks requires existing boundary edges the rib can be extended to. The Rib command has limited extrusion end conditions compared with the Extrude function, but allows for a bare minimum of input from you in order to create the rib. The illustration at left shows a rib feature.

There are a few simple rules that must be followed in order to implement the rib feature. New users tend to find this function difficult. To insert a rib, perform the following steps:

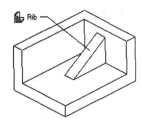

A rib feature.

1. Select the sketch plane that intersects the solid model. This plane should extend in the same direction you want the rib to extrude to. The rib geometry *will not* extrude perpendicular to the plane, as a normal extrusion would.

2. Select the Sketch icon or select Sketch from the Insert menu.

3. Create a line that will define the height of the rib with respect to the face it should be extruded to. The length of the line is not important, as long as it fits within the boundaries of existing geometry.

4. Select Rib from the Insert/Features menu.

5. Enter the Thickness for the rib and click on Next.

6. Enter the material direction by selecting Flip Side of Material and observing the preview arrow.

7. Select Finish to complete the rib.

Other Rib Attributes

Because the rib feature does not follow the general rule of extrusions being perpendicular to the sketch plane, it can confuse new users. All of the additional options encountered in the Rib dialog boxes are included in the material that follows to try to eliminate any confusion. The additional options are as follows:

Single Side	Check to create the rib on one side of the sketch plane only.
Reverse	Check to reverse the direction for a single side rib. The direction arrow indicates the direction in which the rib thickness will be applied.
Mid Plane	Check to create the rib split equally on both sides of the sketch plane. This is the most common setting.
Thickness	Enter the rib thickness by picking inside the field and entering the value, or pick the up/down arrows to increment/ decrement the thickness value.

The second dialog box contains the following options:

Flip Side of Material	Check to reverse the extrusion direction for the rib. The preview arrow indicates the direction of extrusion. Obviously, this should be toward the part.
Next Reference	To create a rib with multiple segments using draft angles, click on the Next Reference button until the arrow shows on the entity from which you want to start the draft angle. This can only be accomplished on a rib sketch that has more than one segment.
Enable Draft	Check to create draft on the rib feature.
Angle	Enter the rib draft angle by picking inside the field and entering the value, or pick the up/down arrows to increment/ decrement the draft value.
Draft Outward	Check this feature to draft outward. If drafting inward, keep in mind that drafting to the point of making material disappear will result in an error.

It is possible to create the same types of ribs in AutoCAD that SolidWorks creates using the Rib command. However, it is much easier in SolidWorks once you have been through the routine once or twice. The dialog box is helpful and steps you through the process. When using the Rib tool, all you have to do is draw a line, add a dimension, plug in a few parameters when asked, and SolidWorks does the rest, going as far as including draft if needed.

Draft   Draft is used to create a tapered surface on selected faces from a neutral draft plane or parting line. Draft is used to add an angle to a part face. Draft is typically used by designers of injection molded parts and casting to allow the tool to release from the part.

Neutral plane draft is defined by selecting a plane or face to be used as the neutral axis of the draft feature. Selecting a curve to define the axis of rotation for the draft face creates parting line draft. The Split Line function can be used to create a curve that can be used with the Parting Line function to create nonplanar parting lines. The following illustrations show a neutral plane draft and a parting line draft.

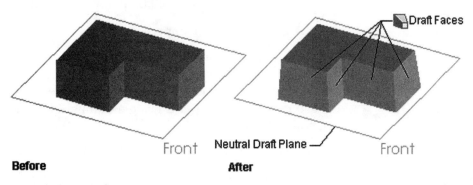

Neutral plane draft.

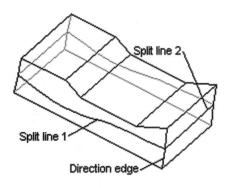

Parting line draft.

To create a drafted face using a neutral draft plane, perform the following steps:

1. Select Draft from the Insert/Features menu.

2. Select Neutral Plane as the Type of Draft.

3. Click in the Neutral Plane list box and select a neutral plane.

4. Click in the Faces to Draft list box and select the faces to be drafted.

5. Enter the Draft Angle.

6. The Reverse Direction field can be checked to reverse the draft direction. The preview arrow points in the direction the mold will be removed from the part.

7. Select OK to continue.

The Split Lines and Parting Lines commands will be discussed later in this chapter. The method for creating draft using a parting line has been included here for reference. To create a drafted face using a parting line, perform the following steps:

1. Select Draft from the Insert/Features menu.

2. Select Parting Line as the Type of Draft.

3. Click in the Parting Line list box and select the parting lines that will be used for drafting. There is no need to hold down the Control key.

4. Enter the Draft Angle.

5. Click in the Direction of Pull list box and select an edge that will indicate the direction the mold will be pulled from the part.

6. The Reverse Direction field can be checked to reverse the draft direction. The preview arrow points in the direction the mold will be removed from the part.

7. Select OK to continue.

The previous description shows how draft can be added as a separate feature. However, you have seen other ways in which draft can be applied. One method is to incorporate draft directly into sketch geometry. This can be done by using angled lines and then extruding the sketch. Draft can also be applied during the extrusion operation itself. (See the section on extruding in this chapter.)

Draft is not an option in AutoCAD, at least not as a command. There are valid workarounds for this function, and draft can be added when extruding a profile, but there really is no comparison. AutoCAD has no way of creating draft from a parting line that may be a curved parting line running around the outside of a curved part. Trying to create something such as this is a scary prospect in AutoCAD, but quite easily performed in SolidWorks.

Mirror

In Chapter 5 you learned that sketch geometry can be mirrored in SolidWorks. Feature geometry can also be mirrored. Additionally, there are options for mirroring an entire part to create a symmetrical part or to create a completely new mirror-image part. These functions are discussed in the following section.

Mirroring Features

The Mirror Feature function is used to create a copy of a feature mirrored about a plane or planar face. The new feature is a child of the parent feature. Any changes to the parent feature will be reflected in the mirrored feature upon rebuild. Mirror Feature can be used to mirror a single part feature or groups of features that have already been mirrored or patterned. When mirroring sketch geometry, a centerline suffices, but a plane or planar face must be used to create a 3D mirror of solid feature geometry. The following illustration shows a mirrored feature.

Mirrored feature.

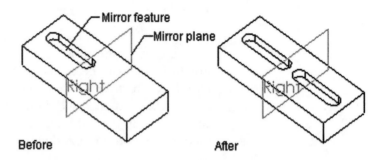

Before   After

To mirror individual part features, perform the following steps:

1. Select Mirror Feature from the Insert/Mirror/Pattern menu. The mirror plane will be shown in the Mirror Plane field.

2. Click in the Mirror Plane field and select a plane or planar face from existing feature geometry.

3. Click in the Items to Copy field and select the features to be mirrored. More than one feature can be mirrored at once. A preview will be displayed.

4. Select OK to continue.

If an AutoCAD model has not yet been turned into a complete solid, it is possible to mirror individual components in the model. If working in wireframe, this is not an issue. SolidWorks allows mirroring features at any time. Like AutoCAD, a plane is needed that can be used to mirror across. AutoCAD does not require an actual plane, just the representation of one, such as three points, which would define a plane. SolidWorks actually requires a plane entity or a planar face on a part.

Mirror All

Mirror All creates a mirrored feature that is a reversed copy of the active part and is attached to the original part about the mirror face. The new feature is a child of the parent feature. Any changes to the parent feature will express themselves in the mirrored feature upon rebuild. This function is used to define half a symmetrical part and produce the other half by mirroring the geometry. This can reduce the time required to model, change, or add features to symmetrical part models. A part face must be selected to define the mirror plane. The following illustration shows the Mirror All function in action.

A part created with Mirror All.

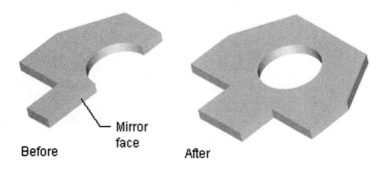

The steps needed to perform this operation are quite simple and are as follows:

1. Select the planar face on the part to be mirrored.

2. Select Insert/Pattern/Mirror/Mirror All.

This command is most similar to AutoCAD's 3D Mirror command in that it will allow you to mirror a part about a plane to create a new part. In SolidWorks, the mirrored image must be attached to the original. This is not necessary in AutoCAD, and there is no relationship to the original, as in SolidWorks. If a mirror image of a part is required to create a new part, SolidWorks' Mirror Part command, described in the material that follows, is needed.

Mirror Part

Mirror Part is used to create a new derived part that is a reversed copy of the active part. This function requires a plane or planar face in order to create the new part. A new part is created, and the Save or Save As command can then be used to redefine the name and file location. Any modifications to the original part will also update the mirrored part because the newly created mirrored part is a child of (dependent on) the original parent part. As features are added to the mirrored copy, the original part is not updated. The following illustration shows a mirrored part.

A mirrored part.

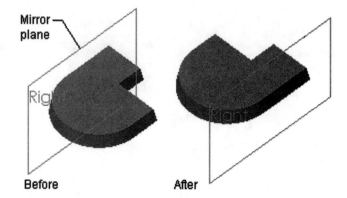

To create a mirror copy of a part, perform the following steps:

1. Select a face or plane that defines the mirror plane for the new part.

2. Select Mirror Part from the Insert menu. The new part will be created and become the active part. The existing part will not be altered in any way.

3. Select Save from the File menu to rename the derived part.

Be aware that the new part is dependent on the original. This means that moving, renaming, or deleting the original will make it more difficult or impossible to open the mirrored part. SolidWorks gives you an option to Browse for a parent file in such cases. However, if the original has been deleted, you will be out of luck, and the mirrored file might as well be deleted from the hard drive.

Pattern Features

A linear pattern creates a linear copy of a feature by adding parameters that control the number, direction, and distance between the first feature (parent) and the copies (children). Linear patterns can be made in one or two directions at a time. A circular pattern creates a copy of a feature by adding parametric parameters, which control the number, direction, and angle between the first feature (parent) and the copies (children).

All features created by the linear pattern are dependent on the parent geometry. Any changes to the parent geometry are reflected in the pattern features. Individual pattern members may also be deleted after the pattern has been inserted. To perform this function, select the pattern feature to be removed and select Delete from the Edit menu or press the Delete key and select Delete Pattern Instance.

Patterning features is more efficient than either creating a large number of features or creating one large feature through the use of a very large and often complex sketch. It is also quicker and easier to change a parameter and rebuild the model than to change a large number of individual features and parameters. The pattern feature is easier to manipulate and modify without having to redefine the original sketch. It keeps the sketch simple as additional features are sketched. Pattern features also produce fewer features than creating each identical feature separately. The following illustration shows a linear pattern.

A linear pattern.

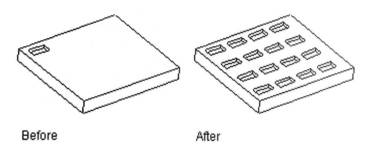

Before   After

To create a linear pattern, perform the following steps:

1. Select the features to be patterned. This is most easily accomplished by selecting the features in Feature Manager rather than in the sketch area, for the sole reason that items are named out for you, which means that selection is not impeded by view orientation or other entities on the part.

2. Select Linear Pattern from the Insert/Pattern/Mirror menu.

3. Select the edge or linear dimension that defines the vector for the First Direction. When this is done, the Edge/Dim Selected check box will contain a check mark. Reverse Direction can be checked to reverse the pattern creation direction. A preview arrow displays the pattern creation direction.

4. Enter the Spacing. This is the distance from the start of one instance to the start of the next.

5. Enter the Total Instances.

6. If a two-directional pattern (typically rectangular) is required, select Direction 2 and repeat steps 3 through 5.

7. Select OK to continue.

Circular patterns can be created in a similar fashion. However, one difference with this function has to do with the items that can be selected to determine the pattern direction. Because this is a circular pattern, a linear dimension cannot be used. Instead, an angular dimension, edge, or axis must be selected. For the sake of continuity, the Edge/Dim Selected check box retains the same name. A circular pattern is shown in the following illustration.

A circular pattern.

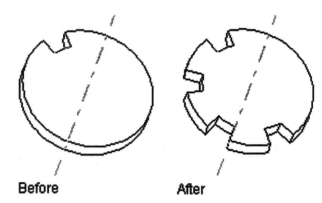

Before   **After**

To create a circular pattern, perform the following steps:

1. Select the features to be patterned. Again, use Feature Manager to select features.

2. Select Circular Pattern from the Insert/Pattern/Mirror menu.

3. Select the axis, edge, or angular dimension that defines the center of the pattern rotation. When this is done, the Edge/Dim Selected check box will contain a check mark. Reverse Direction can be checked to reverse the pattern creation direction between clockwise and counterclockwise.

4. Enter the Spacing. This is the angle between instances.

5. Enter the Total Instances.

6. Select OK to continue.

SolidWorks' Pattern Attributes

The following list includes the pattern attributes previously discussed, as well as some that have not.

First Direction	The direction to which the values shown will be applied (linear only). Select Second Direction to define a linear pattern in two directions.
Reverse Direction	Pick to reverse the direction of the pattern.
Spacing	The spacing between pattern features.
Total Instances	Total number of features in the pattern, including the parent feature.
Items to Copy	Displays the numbers of features that will be patterned. The Control key must be held down in this dialog box.
Instances Deleted	Displays the deleted instances in the feature pattern. The feature number is displayed by row and column if linear, or by number if circular.
Vary Sketch	This is a somewhat obscure option. Sketch geometry for the feature being patterned must be constrained to existing edge geometry, typically by using the Offset Entities sketch tool. As the feature is patterned, its dimensions change to maintain the relationship with existing edge geometry.

SolidWorks is very similar to AutoCAD when it comes to creating patterns. AutoCAD names this function differently, but it accomplishes the same thing. AutoCAD's Array is analogous to SolidWorks' Pattern. Features are the only entities that can be patterned. AutoCAD users might initially make the mistake of trying to pattern sketch geometry in SolidWorks. This is not possible. Make sure to turn any sketch geometry into a feature before patterning. After that, almost every other option is the same, such as number of instances to pattern, distance between instances, and so on.

AutoCAD's resultant pattern will be a set of individual entities with no connection to one another. SolidWorks will create parent/child relationships; therefore, any change to the original will result in the patterned features updating automatically. This is actually very similar to creating a block pattern in AutoCAD, modifying the block, then reinserting the block to have it update all of the occurrences of the block in the drawing.

Pattern Deletion

Portions of a defined pattern may be omitted by deleting a pattern instance. After the pattern (linear or circular) has been inserted, pattern features can be deleted or added back to the pattern. The pattern feature to be deleted must be selected within the graphics window by selecting a pattern feature face. This is because individual pattern instances are not listed in FeatureManager and simply cannot be selected any other way. The following illustration shows a pattern deletion.

What a pattern might look like after having instances deleted.

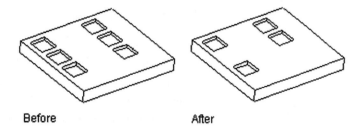

Before   After

To delete a selected pattern instance, perform the following steps:

1. Select a face on the pattern features to be removed. Click on the Delete key or select Delete from the Edit menu.

2. Select Delete Pattern Instances from the Options field. The following illustration shows the dialog box displayed when deleting a pattern instance.

3. Select OK to continue.

The Pattern Deletion dialog box.

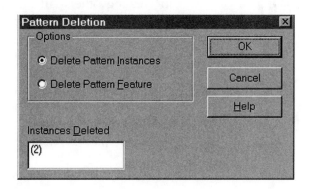

To retrieve a deleted pattern instance, perform the following steps:

1. Right click on the pattern feature in FeatureManager and select Edit Definition.

2. Select the desired instance from the Instances Deleted field.

3. Press the Delete key or select Delete from the Edit menu.

4. Select OK to continue.

In summation, the following are points to keep in mind regarding linear and circular patterning of features:

- Any changes to the original feature are reflected in the patterned features.

- To select multiple features to pattern, hold the Control key down while selecting.

- The number of features selected for the pattern appears in the Items to Copy field.

- Portions of the pattern may be deleted by selecting a face, rather than an edge of an instance.

- The Instances Deleted field displays the deleted instance by number for circular patterns, and by row and column for linear patterns.

Reference Geometry

Reference geometry is used to define special features known as reference entities, whose only function is to aid in creating other part and assembly features. These features are simple in nature and can be used to parametrically drive the location of other part and assembly features. Reference geometry can be used to define and document important part and assembly faces, along with many other very useful functions, which will be discussed in this section. All nonsolid geometry is considered reference geometry and can be found in the Insert/Reference Geometry menu. Two important uses for reference geometry are:

- When a part face is not available to act as the sketch plane, a plane can be created for the 2D sketch and the feature can be created from the new location.

- When a sketch face will be used by more than one feature, it is helpful to create a common reference plane because this minimizes parent/child relationships. All sketches will then reference the plane as opposed to the face of an existing feature. Creating a common reference plane also allows you to name the plane, which helps document the design intent of the part.

Planes

Planes are reference entities used to define construction surfaces for sketching and model creation. Planes can also be used to define important part function or mating surfaces. The default plane names can be changed under the Tools/Options menu by selecting the Planes tab. The names of the default planes can be defined so that all new parts will have the default plane names changed.

The names should be changed to Front, Top, and Right. To change the names of the planes in the current part, the slow double click method of renaming items in Feature-Manager must be used. The default planes with typical names are shown in the following illustration.

Default planes.

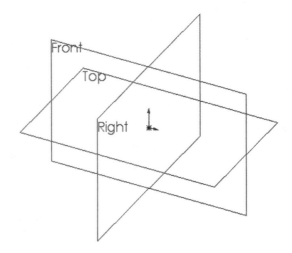

A plane should be renamed to help document the intent or use of the plane. This visually helps anyone viewing the document to understand the use of the plane. For example, if a plane were created to sketch a mount bracket feature, the name of the plane might be Mounting Bracket Plane.

The visual size of a plane can be changed by selecting the plane, then dragging the handles to resize the plane. It should be noted that the visual representation of a plane makes no difference as to where sketch geometry can be created. All planes theoretically extend infinitely in all directions. To turn on or off the ability to view planes globally, check the Planes option in the View menu. To view planes or hide planes independently, right click on the plane and select Show or Hide.

Planes can also be created through the use of existing geometry. For example, basic geometry states that any three points can be used to define a plane. This is one of seven creation methods available for defining a plane. Different geometry is required, depending on what method is used to define a plane. The following series of illustrations shows seven planes created seven different ways, each using its own geometry.

Plane offset from an existing plane:

An offset plane.

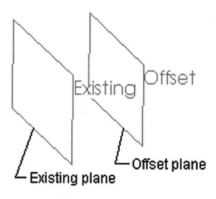

Plane inserted at an angle from an existing plane passing through an edge:

Plane created using the At Angle option.

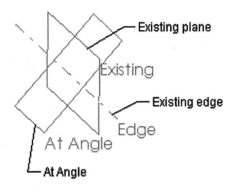

Plane using three sketched points or vertices:

Plane created using the 3 Points option.

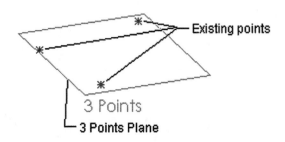

Plane parallel to an existing plane and passing through a vertex:

Plane created using the Parallel Plane @ Point option.

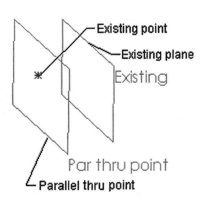

Plane passing through an edge and a sketched point or vertex:

Plane created using the Line & Point option.

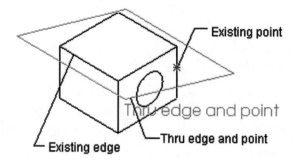

Plane perpendicular to a line (known as a curve) passing through a sketched point or vertex:

Plane created using the ⊥ Curve option.

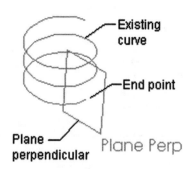

Plane tangent to a cylindrical surface where it passes through the intersection points of an edge and a plane:

Plane created using the On Surface option.

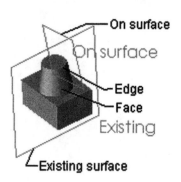

Resizing a plane has already been discussed, but for reference, the steps for resizing a plane follow. Remember that a plane's size is for visual aid only and that the plane actually extends infinitely in all directions. To resize or move a plane, you would perform the following steps:

1. Select the plane with the left mouse button.

2. Select one of the plane's resize handles with the left mouse button and drag to resize the plane. These handles appear at each corner of the plane boundary and at the center of each boundary segment. Select the plane boundary to move the plane instead of resizing.

AutoCAD does not make use of planes. The closest analogy would be modifying the UCS to create entities on a different plane. However, as an entity in the drawing database, plane entities do not exist in AutoCAD.

Axes

An axis is used for dimensional reference and circular pattern creation. All cylindrical features and cylindrical surface sections have an axis. These axes are called *temporary axes*. Axes that are created by the user are referred to as *reference axes*. To display temporary axes, check Temporary Axes in the View menu. To display reference axes, check Axes in the View menu. At left is an image of an axis created with one of the six axis creation methods available in SolidWorks.

An axis should be renamed to help document its intent or use. For example, if an axis were created to denote the *x*-axis centerline of a part, the axis might be named Centerline X. The extents (size) of an axis can be changed by selecting the axis and grabbing one of its handles and dragging the axis length.

Axis created in SolidWorks.

As previously mentioned, there are various ways of defining an axis, just as there are ways of defining a plane. The method used depends on the reference geometry available for creating the plane. The following are the various

SolidWorks methods of creating an axis, with a graphical representation of the entities used to create each axis.

Axis created using a temporary axis:

Axis created using the One Temporary Axis option.

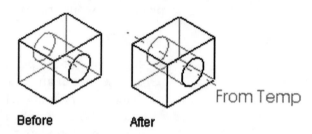

Before   **After**

Axis at the intersection of two planes:

Axis created using the Two Planes option.

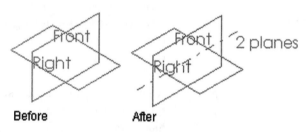

Before   **After**

Axis using two points:

Axis created using the Two Points/Vertices option.

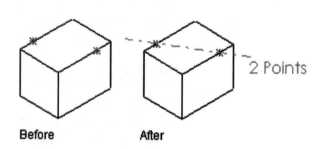

Before   **After**

Axis using one edge:

Edge converted into an axis using the One Line/ Edge option.

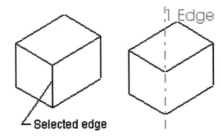

Selected edge   1 Edge

Axis using a cylindrical surface:

Creating an axis using the One Surface option requires selecting one cylindrical surface.

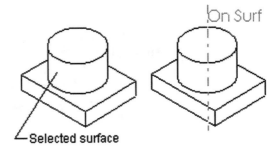

Selected surface   On Surf

The following are other facts to keep in mind when using an axis:

- Axes can be resized and renamed. Temporary axes cannot.
- Reference and temporary axes may be used for adding reference dimensions, relationships, plane creation, and assembly constraints.
- Axes are displayed with a "+" symbol when viewed normal to an existing axis (i.e., head-on).

Surfaces

Surfaces can be defined or imported to define reference surfaces for solid feature creation. For example, surfaces can be used as a depth reference for an extruded or cut feature, thickened to create solid geometry, and used to cut through existing geometry. The surface and solid features use 2D sketches to define the geometry for the feature. The surfacing functions are located in the Insert/ Reference Geometry menu.

With the exception of the Import Surface and Offset Surface functions, surfaces use the same creation procedure as their solid feature creation counterparts. Take, for example, the Extruded Surface function. If a sketch is created and this operation is begun, the same dialog box used for creating an extruded solid feature is opened. However, you still need to determine an end condition and depth, and whether or not draft should be applied. Refer to the "Types of Features" section within this chapter for a further explanation of the various dialog boxes encountered when creating extruded, revolved, swept, or lofted features.

For some time now, AutoCAD has offered the ability to create a variety of surface types. Some very complex and interesting surfaces can be created. SolidWorks also has the ability to create a variety of surfaces, but what can actually be accomplished with those surfaces is somewhat limited. This holds true for AutoCAD as well. There is a distinct difference in the nature of the geometry, and in the nature of software programs, when discussing solid modelers versus surface modelers. Normally, the two do not mix.

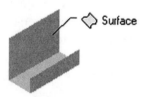

Combination surface/solid modeling packages are usually the domain of high-end software. AutoCAD has an add-on package called AutoSurf that allows for the creation of surfaces. To date, there is no add-on surface-creation package for SolidWorks. However, as previously stated, surfacing is available in SolidWorks. The series of illustrations at left and following shows what the various Solid-Works surface types typically look like.

Extruded surface.

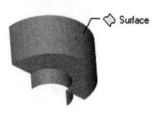

Revolved surface.

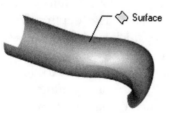

Swept surface.

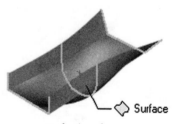

Lofted surface.

An offset surface does not have a solid counterpart; therefore, the creation of such a surface will be explained here. Offset surfaces require an existing surface or solid face to offset from. In the illustration at left, the top face of the solid part was offset a distance above the part to create the surface. To create a true offset surface, perform the following steps:

1. Select the face or surface to be offset. If adjacent faces are selected, they will remain adjacent after the offset.

2. Select Insert/Reference Geometry/Offset Surface.

3. Specify an offset Distance.

4. Use the Reverse toggle if needed to reverse the offset direction.

5. Click on OK when done.

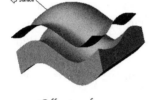

Offset surface.

Imported surfaces are usually imported as IGES files; however, ACIS (.SAT) and Virtual Reality Modeling Language (VRML=*.WRL) files can also be imported. Files imported in this fashion are left as surface files that can be used to edit existing solid geometry or to create new solid geometry. Generally speaking, single surface files are brought in using this method. Multiple surface IGES files, when imported via the IGES File Open command, are knitted together by SolidWorks to form a solid. (This is covered in more detail in Chapter 11.)

Projected Curves

The Projected Curves command projects a sketched curve onto a model face. This curve can be used to define sweep trajectories and split lines, and to project text on a nonplanar face, to name two possibilities. In the following illustration, Projected Curve has been used to project a sketch onto the nonplanar face of a container. To project a curve onto a face, perform the following steps:

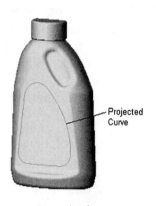

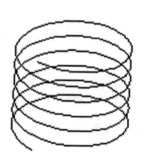

A result of using Projected Curve.

1. Create a sketch. The profile can be open or closed, as required.

2. Exit the sketch.

3. Select the sketch and the face to be projected to. Remember to hold down the Control key when selecting more than one entity.

4. Select Projected Curve from the Insert/Reference Geometry menu.

It is also possible to create a 3D spline by projecting two orthogonal 2D curves into one 3D curve. The resultant curve will have the shape of each of the separate curves when viewed perpendicular to their respective sketch planes.

Helixes

The Helix function creates a reference curve that can be used to define a sweep trajectory for thread profiles and springs. A helix can be used as a trajectory for a cut or boss sweep. A circle is used to define the diameter of the helix. The helix can then be defined by specifying the pitch and revolution, height and revolution, or height and pitch. It should also be pointed out that a spiral can be created from within the Helix dialog box.

The sweep sketch profile must start at the endpoint of the sweep trajectory (the helix) or be pierced by the helix when performing the actual sweep once the helix has been created. If a plane does not exist at the start point of the helix, one must be created before sketching the sweep profile. Use the Perpendicular Curve option to create a plane for a helical sweep, as described earlier in this chapter. A helix curve is shown in the illustration at left. To create a helix, perform the following steps:

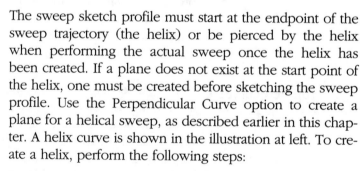

Helix curve.

1. Sketch a circle that defines the diameter of the helix. It is recommended that a diameter dimension be applied, as this dimension will control the diameter of the helix.

2. Exit the sketch.

3. Select the circle sketch.

4. Select Helix from the Insert/Reference Geometry menu.

5. Specify the parameters for defining the helix (see the following section).

6. Select OK to continue.

Helix Properties

Before creating a helix, it would benefit you to know a little bit more about the parameters involved. The following list of helix properties available in SolidWorks should help you on your way when creating a helix:

Defined By	Defines which combination of pitch, height, and revolution will be used. The three alternatives are Pitch & Revolution, Height & Revolution, and Height & Pitch.
Pitch	Pitch, with reference to threads, is the distance from thread peak to thread peak. The distance on the helix is measured along the height of the helix from revolution to revolution (coil to coil).
Height	Total height of the helix.
Revolution	Number of helix revolutions.
Taper Helix	Check to apply a taper angle to the helix.
Angle	Taper angle. Enter a new value in the field or use the up/down arrows to increment/decrement the value.
Taper Outward	Check to taper the helix outward.
Starting Angle	Angle to start the helix measured with respect to the circle used to define the helix diameter. Enter a new value in the field or use the up/down arrows to increment/decrement the value.
Reverse Direction	Check to reverse the helix creation direction.
Clockwise	Check to create the helix in a clockwise direction.
Counterclockwise	Check to create the helix in a counterclockwise direction.

There are usually some very good AutoLisp routines that can be found to create geometry such as spirals (see the following section) and helix shapes. However, there is no counterpart command to create a helix from within the

AutoCAD program itself. Also, generally speaking, most Lisp routines require command line input and do not make very good use of dialog boxes, such as the dialog box for creating a helix or spiral in SolidWorks. Once again, these curves are parametric and can be easily modified in SolidWorks.

Spirals

Spirals are created from within the Helix dialog box. This option is found in the Defined By drop-down list box. If Spiral is selected, only Pitch and Revolution need to be specified. CW or CCW can still be specified. Clicking on Reverse will create the spiral inside the circle instead of outside. Starting Angle has the same effect it does when creating a helix.

Split Lines

Split Line is used to create a nonplanar curve for the Draft feature, to create variable radius fillets on edges without vertex points, and anywhere it is necessary to break a single surface into two or more surfaces. The Parting Line option in the Draft command will use the curve created by the Split Line function to create draft. The split line can be defined on multiple part faces at once. Many designs require the parting line of the injection molded or casting tool to jog the mating surfaces between the ejector and stationary side of the tool. The illustration at left shows a split line. To create a split line, perform the following steps:

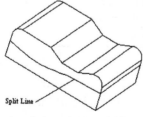

A split line that could be used for adding draft.

1. Create a sketch that will be projected onto the desired faces. The sketch should extend beyond any edges to be projected to.

2. Select Split Line from the Insert/Reference Geometry menu.

3. Select the Projection split line type (Silhouette will not be covered here).

4. Select Next to continue.

5. Click in the Sketch to Project list box and select the sketch.

6. Click in the Faces to Split list box and select the faces to be split by the sketch.

7. Click on Single Direction if projecting in only one direction.

8. Ensure the projection direction preview arrow is pointing toward the part.

9. Select Finish to complete the process.

Curves

There are two methods of creating curves through points in space in order to achieve a 2D or 3D curve: Curve Through Reference Points and Curve Through Free Points. Curve Through Reference Points is used to create a curve based on existing points in a part. Curve Through Free Points is used to create a curve from a set of data points you specify, or from a set obtained through a file. These points can be read from an external text file with a TXT or SLDCRV extension. The illustration at left shows a curve created through reference points.

Make sure you are not in an active sketch before attempting to insert a curve using either method described in the following material. Otherwise, the functions will be grayed out. To create a curve through a set of existing points, perform the following steps:

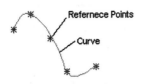

Curve created through reference points.

1. Select Curve Through Reference Points from the Insert/Reference Geometry menu.

2. Select the points that define the curve.

3. Select OK to continue.

To create a curve from an external point file, perform the following steps. An external point file list is shown in the illustration that follows. It is the dialog box you will see when initiating this command. Make sure to check out the

preview displayed on your screen as points are entered in
the dialog box.

1. Select Curve Through Free Points from the Insert/Ref-
   erence Geometry menu.

2. To begin entering points, double click anywhere in a
   blank line (below the XYZ headings) and begin entering the *x-y-z* coordinates for the curve.

3. If importing coordinates from a text file, click on the
   Browse button. The coordinates will be imported
   once the file is selected.

4. Highlight a row and click on Insert if another row of
   x-y-z coordinates needs to be inserted into the existing set. The new row will appear above the highlighted row.

5. If coordinates need to be deleted, highlight the row
   and press the Delete key.

6. Select OK to continue.

*Curve created "on the fly"
by entering external
reference points.*

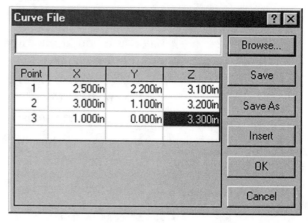

This is an area in which AutoCAD outperforms Solid-
Works. Creating a 3D spline entity in AutoCAD is as easy
as entering the Spline command and punching in coordinates onscreen. Grips can be used to modify the spline.
SolidWorks does offer a way of creating 3D splines, and it
is similar to AutoCAD's method, but the process requires

a few more steps. There is no way to "drag" the spline geometry in SolidWorks, although the definition of the spline can be modified and coordinates changed on the fly.

Modifying a Part

This section describes the functionality available within SolidWorks to change the definition or references for an existing feature. One of SolidWorks' strengths is the ability it gives you to change or modify a feature once it has been created. The ability to easily redefine a part or assembly can mean the difference between being productive and having to redo existing work.

This section is where the main differences between AutoCAD and SolidWorks really start to become apparent. Because of SolidWorks' parametric nature, any dimension (for that matter, every aspect of a part definition) can be accessed at any time and modified to reshape a part. The ease and flexibility that this provides is essential to a designer. AutoCAD does not offer an equivalent.

Edit Definition and Other Edit Functions

The properties and attributes used to define a feature (i.e., end condition, depth, values, creation direction, and so on) can be changed after the original feature has been created. The same dialog box that came up during the creation of the feature is used for Edit Definition. To change a feature's definition, perform the following steps:

1. Right click the feature in the FeatureManager design tree.

2. Select Edit Definition.

3. Redefine the feature's original properties as desired.

4. Click on OK when finished.

Edit Sketch

A sketch can be redefined after creation. The reason for redefining a sketch instead of modifying dimensions would be to add or subtract sketch entities or to make a number of "what if" changes without rebuilding the rest of the part. To change a sketch used to define a feature, perform the following steps:

1. Expand the feature tree if necessary in order to see the sketch below the feature in question. Do this by clicking the "+" sign in front of the feature name in the FeatureManager design tree.

2. Right click the sketch in the FeatureManager design tree.

3. Select Edit Sketch.

4. Redefine the sketch as needed.

5. Rebuild the part when done to see the changes. This can be done by clicking the Rebuild icon or just exiting the sketch.

Edit Sketch Plane

The sketch plane used to create a 2D sketch can be changed after the feature has been defined. This allows the sketch feature to be changed to another face or plane, thereby changing its orientation. To change the sketch plane for a sketch, perform the following steps:

1. Expand the feature tree if necessary in order to see the sketch below the feature in question. Do this by clicking the "+" sign in front of the feature name in the FeatureManager design tree.

2. Right click on the sketch in the FeatureManager design tree.

3. Select Edit Sketch Plane.

4. Select the new sketch plane.

5. Select Apply to continue.

List External References

When a feature is created referencing another assembly component, this is referred to as an *in-context feature*. SolidWorks identifies these references within the Feature-Manager design tree and allows you to recall the referenced components to change the in-context features. To list external references, perform the following steps:

1. Right click the sketch, feature, or part in the Feature-Manager design tree.

2. Select List External Refs. A dialog box will appear listing all applicable external references.

3. Select OK to close the dialog box.

Undo

Undo reverses the effects of recent actions. This function is available in all modes (i.e., sketch, part, assembly, and drawing). It may be accessed by pressing the Control + Z keys or by clicking on the Undo icon. Undo also allows for returning sketch geometry to its original state after dragging the sketch. This allows you to investigate many "what if" scenarios without committing to any of these modifications.

AutoCAD's Undo command is quite a bit more powerful than SolidWorks'. The knowledge that the Undo function is there sometimes gives the user more confidence than they might otherwise have. If you are an AutoCAD user accustomed to using the Undo command frequently, you might want to try to break out of that habit.

SolidWorks has an Undo function, but not everything can be undone. It should be pointed out, however, that because of the powerful editing characteristics of Solid-Works, an Undo command is not as important as it is in AutoCAD, where editing is severely limited with regard to solids. Also bear in mind that SolidWorks does not have a Redo command. If a feature is created that is not quite what you expected, it is much easier to edit the feature than it is to delete it and recreate it in SolidWorks. If the feature is deleted, you must then recreate it if you decide that deleting was not the smartest decision. The Undo list box is shown in the following illustration.

➥ **NOTE:** *Once a rebuild is performed, the Undo list box is wiped clean.*

The Undo drop-down list box.

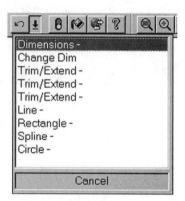

When multiple commands are selected from the pull-down list, all functions from the selected command and above are undone. Single or multiple commands can be undone depending on the icon selected. Care should be taken when selecting Undo, as the command cannot be reversed (Redo). To undo recent changes, perform the following:

1. Select the Undo icon or select Undo from the Edit menu.

To undo recent changes by selecting from an item in a list, perform the following steps:

1. Open the Undo list box (see the previous illustration).

2. Select an item on the list, which will undo the selected action and all actions above the selected item.

Rebuild

Rebuild is the function used to update dimensional changes and to rebuild a part any time modifications have been made. You can select when to rebuild a part. A number of changes can be made without rebuilding the part. When all changes are complete, the part can be rebuilt to change the geometry based on new dimensions.

The Rebuild function is available within the Modify dialog box. For instance, when a sketch dimension is double clicked to modify the dimension, the Modify dialog box appears. The dimension value can be changed, and by selecting the Rebuild button, the changes are displayed in the part and the Modify box is left open.

The Modify dialog box is also used in sketch mode. Double click on a sketch dimension to change the value. Changes to sketch dimensions within sketch mode are automatically rebuilt unless Automatic Solve is unchecked in the Tools/Sketch Tools menu. The difference between rebuilding each change is that a number of "what ifs" can be reviewed without rebuilding the rest of the part geometry. To rebuild any model parameter changes, simply click on the Rebuild icon or select Rebuild from the Edit menu.

Rollback

Rollback is used to roll a model back to an earlier creation state, prior to the position of the rollback bar. The rollback bar is a FeatureManager design tree indicator of the current display state of the part or assembly. Parts and assemblies are shown in a sequential or history-based order in the FeatureManager design tree.

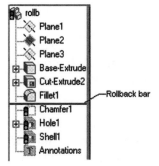

The rollback bar.

The rollback bar allows you to go back to an earlier creation state in the FeatureManager's chronological history of events, or to step through the feature list to analyze a part to see how it was built. Any new features or assembly components will be inserted above the position of the rollback bar in the FeatureManager design tree. The illustration at left shows the rollback function.

Keeping features logically grouped can make interpreting and modifying a part or assembly easier. When modifying or adding features to a previously defined functional area, use Rollback to position the rollback bar in the desired area. New features for the functional group are added in the same location in the FeatureManager design tree.

The rollback function can also be used to edit an area of a part. Instead of modifying a feature and rebuilding the entire model, only the changed portion is rebuilt. This can speed up the modification of parts and assemblies because only a small number of features are rebuilt. This technique can be used very effectively on large parts and assemblies. This allows for many "what if" scenarios to be tried without rebuilding many unrelated features.

The rollback bar can be positioned at a desired location backward or forward. The bar can be repositioned at any time to easily view the model in many different states. By setting the rollback bar to the beginning and stepping through each feature, you can review how the part or assembly was created. There are two methods of rolling back a model. The first method is as follows:

1. Select the feature to define how far the model will be reverted.

2. Select the Rollback icon or select Rollback from the Edit menu.

When the mouse cursor is placed over the rollback bar, it changes into a small hand. To roll back a model using the second (and preferred) method, perform the following:

1. Select the rollback bar with left mouse button and drag it to the desired location in FeatureManager.

To cancel rollback mode, perform the following:

1. Select the rollback bar with the left mouse button and drag the rollback bar to the bottom of FeatureManager, after the word *Annotations*.

Rollback is similar to a smart AutoCAD Undo command. It is as if a part can be undone without actually really undoing anything. Nothing is deleted or undone, but nearly the same thing is accomplished, as if you were going back in time to before the rolled-back features were created.

Suppressing Features

Suppressing features temporarily blanks the display of selected features and removes them from memory. However, the features have not been deleted and can be redisplayed (unsuppressed). Suppressing features can be used to simplify a model for easier creation, to temporarily avoid unwanted parent/child relationships, or to minimize part complexity for part editing and complex assembly management.

When a feature is suppressed, the feature's children are automatically suppressed. The children can automatically be unsuppressed when the parent is unsuppressed by using the Unsuppress With Dependents command. Otherwise, the children remain suppressed. Turn on the Dependency Editing toolbar in order to have access to the icons used in the following example. Click on View/Toolbars to toggle toolbars on. To suppress features, perform the following steps:

1. Select features from FeatureManager. Hold the Control key down to select multiple features.

2. Select the Suppress icon or select Suppress from the Edit menu.

It is also possible to suppress a feature by accessing its properties, but it is much easier to use the icon on the Dependency Editing toolbar. To unsuppress features, perform the following steps:

1. Select features from Feature Manager to be unsuppressed. Hold the Control key down to select multiple features.

2. Select the Unsuppress icon or select Unsuppress from the Edit menu.

To unsuppress features with dependent children, perform the following steps:

1. Select features from FeatureManager to be unsuppressed. Hold the Control key down to select multiple features.

2. Select the Unsuppress With Dependents icon or select Unsuppress With Dependents from the Edit menu.

There are a number of guidelines that go along with suppressing and unsuppressing features. These are:

- The first feature of the part cannot be suppressed.
- Children are suppressed when the parent feature is suppressed.
- A suppressed feature will be shown in gray in FeatureManager.
- The Control key can be used to select multiple features for suppression.
- The Shift key can be used to select a range of features in the FeatureManager design tree. Select the first feature, hold down the Shift key, and select the last feature in the range. This also works for selecting parts in Assembly FeatureManager.
- Features can also be suppressed or unsuppressed from the Property dialog box. Right click the feature and select Properties.
- Children are unsuppressed when the parent is unsuppressed only when the Unsuppress With Dependents function is used. Otherwise, the children have to be unsuppressed independently.
- Parents are unsuppressed when a child is unsuppressed.

Advanced Part Features

Many of the topics covered in this section are not commonly used in all disciplines. Your particular company may find certain of these features very valuable. You might want to skim over this section to see if any of the topics pertain to your applications.

Annotations

Model annotations are used to define engineering characteristics and parameters directly on a part. The important features and characteristics can be defined and used later in the design process (e.g., drafting or manufacturing).

Model annotations can be used to add specific design intent during the modeling phase of the design. Often, this information is added near the end of the design phase.

This allows the person who created the design to define important characteristics at the time the part and assembly are created. This information can also be used downstream to add important comments and design intent annotations without the need for detailed drawings.

For a complete explanation of how to create an annotation, see the "Drawing Symbols" section in Chapter 8. The methods used to define the annotation are the same whether they are created within a drawing view, part, or assembly. The following illustration shows an example of model annotations.

Model annotations.

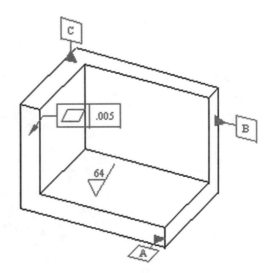

The following are types of model annotations:

- Cosmetic Threads
- Notes
- Datum Target Symbols
- Geometric Tolerance
- Surface Finish Symbols
- Feature Dimensions
- Reference Dimensions
- Weld Symbols
- Datum Feature Symbols

To display model annotations, perform the following steps:

1. Right click Annotations in FeatureManager.

2. Check Display Annotations.

To display only certain model annotations, perform the following steps.

1. Right click Annotations in FeatureManager.

2. Select Details to open the Annotation Properties dialog box (see the following illustration).

3. Uncheck Display All Types.

4. Check the desired annotations to be displayed.

5. Select OK to continue.

The Annotation Properties dialog box.

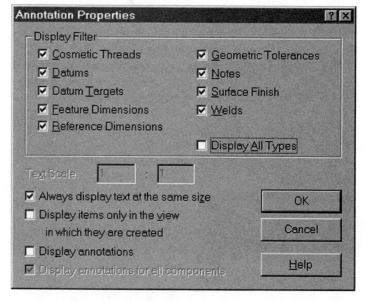

To insert a model annotation, perform the following steps:

1. Select the desired face or edge. This is where the leader arrow will be attached.

2. Select the desired annotation from the choices in the Insert/Annotations menu.

3. Enter the annotation object information, if applicable.

To edit a model annotation, perform the following steps:

1. Double click on the annotation.

2. Edit the object.

3. Select OK to continue.

Design Tables

The Design Table function is used to insert an embedded Microsoft Excel spreadsheet to drive dimension parameters for feature suppression. Microsoft Excel is required to use this function, and no other spreadsheet type is currently supported, although any OLE-compliant software can have files embedded into a SolidWorks document.

Only one design table can be inserted into a part. The menu structure when inserting or editing design tables is the Microsoft Excel menu. When design table insertion or editing is complete, the menu structure reverts back to the SolidWorks menus. The following illustration shows a design table.

Design table.

	D3@Sketch2	Hole1
Part 1	1.75	1	——Row
Part 2	2.5	0
Part 3	3.5	0

```
        Column          Value or visiblity
                    Parameter or Feature name
   Design table configuration name
```

Function of Design Tables

Design tables can be used to change feature sizes or to suppress unwanted features. Design tables create part configurations and are used to create multiple models from one part file. A configuration can be used to define a subset, feature, or assembly component to create simplified parts and assemblies, exploded assemblies, or optional versions of a design. To recall a design table configuration, select the Configurations tab at the bottom of the FeatureManager design tree and select the desired configuration name.

After insertion, the design table is embedded into the SolidWorks document and no longer references the original spreadsheet. Therefore, any changes to the original worksheet will not affect the part unless it is reinserted into the part. Design tables are embedded objects, not linked. A linked document differs from an embedded document by the fact that a linked document still references the values in the original document. Insert Object can be used to insert a linked OLE object into SolidWorks.

The value defined by the cross-reference between row 1 (dimension or feature names) and column 1 determines design table configurations. The value in cell row 1, column A, is left blank. Any cell without a corresponding row and column value is ignored. Design table values and configurations should be documented so that anyone can view the design table and determine the intent for the configurations and any dimensional references. The best way to do this is to change sketch and dimension names prior to creating the design table, and create notes on the second sheet of the spreadsheet that explain what is being accomplished in the table.

The first row of the spreadsheet defines the names of the variations (e.g., Part 1, Part 2, and Part 3). The second and subsequent rows control dimension values or feature display (D3@Sketch2 and Hole1). The cross-reference cell value can determine the size or visibility of a feature. Features can be suppressed by leaving the field blank. Entering a number 1 or "yes" (or anything except 0) in the field shows features. Entering the number 0 will suppress a feature.

If you want only one configuration, a design table can still be used to drive dimension parameters. The configuration named Default is included with every part and can be redefined using design tables; however, it is best to create a new configuration in the spreadsheet by using a name other than Default. This is just a failsafe, so that the default configuration can be fallen back on if needed.

The design table should be properly annotated so that the design intent and dimension references can be clearly understood by others who might read it. However, this is not mandatory. There are two methods for annotating design tables: using text strings or using embedded cell comments. Embedded cell comments can be added by selecting Comments from the Insert menu in Microsoft Excel 97 or higher. All embedded cell comments can be displayed by selecting Comments under the View menu. Embedded cell comments are displayed when passing the cursor over a cell with a red triangle in the upper right-hand corner (Microsoft Excel 97).

Dimension names inserted into a spreadsheet must be in the form of full dimension names. The dimension name for a sample base feature, for instance, would be D1@Base-Feature1, and not just D1. Dimension names are case sensitive; therefore, the name must be entered exactly as shown. Dimension names can be found by selecting the dimension and pressing the right mouse button and selecting Properties.

The dimension name appears in the Full Name field. Dimension names can be copied and pasted into the design table using the right mouse button. By defining meaningful dimension, feature, and component names, you can associate the feature's function, grouping, or purpose by reviewing the defined name and creation order. The following are some examples:

- *Dimension name:* D2@Sketch2
  Renamed dimension: Diameter@ScrewProfile

- *Feature name:* Base-Extrude
  Renamed feature: Mounting Plate Profile

To insert a design table, perform the following steps:

1. Create a Microsoft Excel spreadsheet that has configuration names starting in row 2, column 1, and extending down column 1. Do not leave empty cells in column 1.

2. The dimension names or feature names start in row 1, column 2, and continue across row 1. It is best to copy and paste these dimension names into the spreadsheet to help eliminate typographical errors. Do not leave empty cells in row 1.

3. Enter dimension values for the respective revisions.

4. Save the design table when done. It can be helpful to save the design table with the same name as the part it will be embedded in. It might also be helpful to put the spreadsheet in the same directory.

5. Back in SolidWorks, select Design Table from the Insert menu.

6. Select the Excel Spreadsheet to be inserted. Solid-Works will inform you either of errors or that the table insertion was successful. If successful, SolidWorks will display the configurations created.

7. Edit the spreadsheet, if necessary. Click outside the spreadsheet in the sketch area when finished.

To activate a design table configuration, you would perform the following steps. The ConfigurationManager icon is shown in the following illustration.

1. Select the ConfigurationManager icon from the bottom of FeatureManager.

2. Double click on the desired configuration or right click the configuration name and select Show.

*The design table
configuration.*

ConfigurationManager
icon

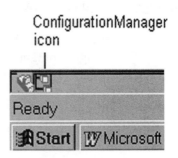

AutoCAD does not have the ability to import a design table in the same fashion as SolidWorks. It is possible to make database connections that achieve similar results, but it is not something to be attempted by the inexperienced.

Edit Design Table

Existing design tables can be added to, changed, or deleted. Design tables are embedded Microsoft Excel spreadsheets that contain information used to drive dimensional parameters for SolidWorks parts, as previously described. If configurations are added to a design table, the configurations are automatically added to the part by SolidWorks. Dimension and feature names can be added or deleted, and dimension values in the spreadsheet can be modified. To edit a design table, perform the following steps:

1. Select Design Table from the Edit menu.

2. Add, delete, or change values in the Microsoft Excel design table as needed.

3. To finish, click anywhere outside the design table.

To delete a design table, perform the following steps:

1. Select Delete Design Table from the Edit menu.

2. Select Yes or Yes to All to continue. Select No to skip the selected item. Select Cancel to abort.

Equations   Equations are used to define mathematical relationships between model dimensions. For example, an equation can be defined to set a part feature equal to half the total length, height, or width of the part. Another example might be adding an equation to adjust the distance between items in a pattern should the number of instances increase or decrease. The possibilities are quite numerous. The following illustration shows an example of an equation.

"Length_base@sketch1"=("Width_base@sketch1"/2)+.125

|

Dimension names
enclosed in quotes

An equation.

Dimension and feature names should be redefined to help convey and document the design intent of the part. Without these names, it can be difficult to understand the intent of the design. Meaningful names can help a user understand the function or purpose of an equation when editing the equations. Without logically named features and dimensions, the user has to investigate design intent. By defining meaningful names, the user can associate dimension names found in the equations with what is being defined by an equation.

If any dimensions or feature names are going to be changed, this should be done before adding equations. In older versions of SolidWorks, equations would become invalid if names were changed after equations using those names were added. As of this writing (SolidWorks date-code 97/341), equations will automatically update if the associated feature name is modified. If you possess a recent copy of SolidWorks, ignore this warning.

Like design tables, equations are case sensitive. Dimension names in an equation need to match the dimension names on the part precisely. One mistyped character will cause the equation to fail.

One other steadfast rule when creating an equation involves the location of the dimension names with respect to the equal sign. Any dimension name on the left of the equation is a driven dimension. Any dimension on the right is a driving dimension. Once a dimension is made driven by adding it to an equation, it cannot be altered by double clicking the dimension in the sketch area.

Because of AutoCAD's lack of parametric technology, creating equations is simply out of the question. Intelligent relationships between geometry in AutoCAD cannot be obtained without the use of an add-on software package. To add an equation in SolidWorks, perform the following steps:

1. Select Equations from the Tools menu.

2. Select Add from the Equation Editor list box.

3. Double click the feature or sketch in FeatureManager whose dimension you would like to access.

4. Select the dimension. It will be placed in the New Equation dialog box.

5. Complete the equation by entering values, mathematical operators, or dimensions.

6. Select OK to continue.

7. Click on the Rebuild icon or select Rebuild from the Edit menu.

To edit an existing equation, perform the following steps:

1. Select Equations from the Tools menu.

2. Select Edit All to edit the equations listed.

3. Edit the desired equation using standard word processing techniques (i.e., backspace, Delete key, and so on).

4. Select OK to exit out of all dialog boxes.

To delete an existing equation, perform the following steps:

1. Select Equations from the Tools menu.

2. Select the equation to be deleted.

3. Click on the Delete button.

4. Select OK to continue.

In summation, remember these guidelines when working with equations:

- Dimensions driven by equation values are not editable by double clicking on the dimension.

- To determine the name of a dimension, right click on the dimension and select Properties. The name of the dimension can be found in the Full Name field. This typically is not needed when adding equations, because selecting a dimension enters its name in the Add Equation dialog box automatically.

- Equations can be deleted by selecting the equation and pressing the Delete key.

- Dimensions on the left side of the equation are driven. Driving dimensions are on the right-hand side.

Configurations

Configurations are used to simplify complex parts and assemblies into different named states or optional features or parts. A configuration allows you to temporarily suppress features or components that may not be required, or to show parts with various arrangements of features. Parts and assemblies will rebuild more quickly when configurations are used to suppress features that might require a large amount of computation.

Configurations are often used to suppress features or parts not currently necessary to the design process. A simplified part configuration can be used in assembly configurations to address large assembly management. Configurations might also be used to simplify a part for use with finite element analysis. This section covers part configurations only.

When a part or assembly is saved, the current configuration name becomes the default configuration. When the document is opened, this configuration is selected by default. Working-state configurations can be defined to minimize the number of components active when working on a single part. For example, you can use configurations to define a Structure Only assembly. This allows you to recall an assembly and review or modify the structure without rebuilding the complete assembly. The following illustration shows where configurations are found.

Where to find configurations.

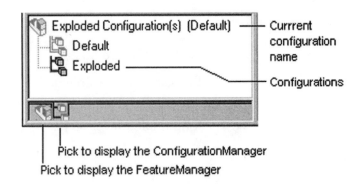

To toggle between FeatureManager and Configuration-Manager modes, select the desired icon at the bottom of FeatureManager, as described in the section "Design Tables" and shown in the illustration above. The active configuration is shown to the right of the main (top) part/ assembly ConfigurationManager icon. The configuration name is shown in parentheses to the right of the part or assembly name.

Simplified configurations can be defined to help minimize the number of active components necessary when editing an individual part, or for many other reasons, such as those previously listed. To create a new configuration, perform the following steps:

1. Add a new configuration by right clicking on the part name in ConfigurationManager and selecting Add Configuration.

2. Go back to FeatureManager and suppress or unsuppress features or components as desired. (See "Suppressing Features," earlier in this chapter.)

To open a part or assembly using a defined configuration, perform the following steps:

1. Select the Open icon or select Open from the File menu.

2. Check the Configure option at the bottom of the menu.

3. Select the file to be opened and click on Open.

4. Select the configuration state to be used.

5. Select OK to continue.

To activate a configuration within a part or assembly, perform the following steps:

1. Select the ConfigurationManager icon at the bottom of FeatureManager.

2. Right click on the desired configuration and select Show Configuration.

To delete a part or assembly configuration, perform the following steps. Be aware that the current configuration cannot be deleted.

1. Select the ConfigurationManager icon at the bottom of FeatureManager.

2. Select the desired configuration and press the Delete key.

To edit an existing part or assembly configuration, perform the following steps:

1. Select the ConfigurationManager icon at the bottom of FeatureManager.

2. Activate the desired configuration as previously described. Only the current configuration can be edited.

3. Suppress or unsuppress features or parts as needed.

In summation, the following list represents the important topics discussed in the "Configuration" section:

• The active configuration cannot be deleted. Make another configuration active and then delete the desired configuration.

• The Comment field is a good place to briefly describe the reason and function of the configuration. This field is found in the Add Configuration dialog box when adding a configuration.

• To make a configuration active, you can double click on the configuration name with the left mouse button.

• The active configuration name is displayed in parentheses following the part or assembly name in the FeatureManager design tree.

• Configurations can also be used in drawing views. A single drawing can display multiple configurations in the various views. (This is discussed in Chapter 8.)

Base Parts

The Base Part function uses an existing part file as the base feature for a new part. The original part becomes a single feature in the new part. Any changes to the parent part will be reflected in the base part. A casting is a good example of a model for which a base part such as this would be used. The parent part is the raw casting. The new part would have the machined surfaces and tapped and drilled holes.

Using the Base Part Function

Changes can be made to the parent part by right clicking on the Base Part feature in the FeatureManager design tree. Press the right mouse button and select Edit In Context. This will open the parent part in a new window for editing. Any changes to the parent part will be reflected in the base part (child) when the base part is reopened. The following illustration shows a base part.

New part
with added
features

Original
base part

*Making use
of a base part.*

An AutoCAD user might draw a comparison between a SolidWorks base part and an external reference (Xref). An Xref can be modified and then updated in the drawing file that incorporates the Xref so that the drawing will accept the new changes made to the Xref.

Differences Between Base Part, Cavity, and Derived Component Part

The Base Part function is used when a single part can be used to create a new part, as with a casting and the machined finished part. There are no assembly references for the original base part.

Cavity is used to create a cut in an assembly component while applying a shrinkage value. This requires assembly references to the cavity block (target) and the design component. This function is typically used before the Derive Component Part function to add a part shrinkage value.

Derive Component Part is used when a part needs to be created from an assembly component part. An example would be a mold base. The cavity block is created as an assembly cut using a design part. This function requires the parts to be in the assembly for the cavity to be defined.

To use a previously defined part as the base feature, perform the following steps:

1. Start a new part by clicking on the New icon or selecting New from the File menu. There cannot be any solid features in the default part. Only nonsolid features (i.e., planes and axes) can already be in the part.

2. Select Base Part from the Insert menu.

3. Select the part file name to be used as the base part.

4. Select Open to continue.

Once the base part is brought into the new part file, it is listed in FeatureManager as the base feature. Because this base feature is totally dependent on the base part, it has no dimensions. Therefore, it cannot be modified parametrically from within the new file, only from the original file used to create the base part. However, new features can be added in the same fashion as any other part. Any modifications made to the new part are not reflected back to the parent base part.

Thin Features

Thin features are used to define constant wall thickness parts. This type of feature can be extruded or revolved. Thin features are defined by default for open profiles. To create a thin feature for a closed profile, select the feature type as you normally would to create a feature (i.e., Extrude), then select Thin Feature from the box labeled Extrude As at the bottom of the Feature Definition dialog box.

Thin feature parts can also be used to create sheet metal parts. Adding the Bends feature to a thin-feature part will create a sheet metal part, which is covered in greater detail at the end of this section.

Thin-feature parts can be created in AutoCAD, but it is not an automated process as it is in SolidWorks. There is not really a counterpart for a thin-feature part in AutoCAD.

A simple thin-feature part.

In the examples that follow, it is assumed that you have already created a sketch. To create a thin-walled extruded feature, perform the following steps. The illustration at left shows an example of a thin feature.

1. Select Insert/Boss/Extrude and specify parameters as described in the "Extrude" section of this chapter.

2. In the Extrude As drop-down box, select Thin Feature. This is automatic if extruding an open profile.

3. Select the Thin Feature tab to define material thickness properties.

4. Select the thickness type from the Type field: One-Direction, Mid Plane, or Two Direction (see the section "Wall Thickness Properties").

5. Enter the Wall Thickness.

6. The Reverse option can be used to change the direction of the wall thickness. This option is only applicable for the One Direction type.

7. Select OK to continue.

To create a thin, revolved feature, perform the following steps:

1. Select Insert/Boss/Revolve and specify parameters as described in the "Revolve" section of this chapter.

2. In the Revolve As drop-down box, select Thin Feature. This is automatic if revolving an open profile.

3. Select the Thin Feature tab to define material thickness properties.

4. Select the thickness type from the Type field: One-Direction, Mid Plane, or Two Direction (see the section "Wall Thickness Properties").

5. Enter the Wall Thickness.

6. The Reverse option can be used to change the direction of the wall thickness. This option is only applicable for the One Direction type.

7. Select OK to continue.

Thin-feature Properties

There are a number of options that will be encountered while creating a thin feature. Some of the options that follow have already been discussed, but are added here for convenience. These options are found under the Thin Feature tab.

One Direction	Add wall thickness a specified distance in one direction only.
Mid Plane	Add wall thickness an equal depth in both directions.
Two Direction	Add wall thickness different lengths in either directions.
Reverse	Check to reverse the direction in which the wall thickness is added. Option available only for the One Direction type.
Wall Thickness	Enter the wall thickness or pick the up/down arrow buttons to increment/decrement the wall thickness value. Option available only for One Direction and Mid Plane types.
Direction 1 Thickness	Enter the wall thickness for Direction 1. Option available only for Two Direction types.
Direction 2 Thickness	Enter the wall thickness for Direction 2. Option available only for Two Direction types.
Auto Fillet	Check to add a fillet to each sharp corner automatically. When the box is checked, a fillet radius value can be entered in the Radius field. The Fillet Radius field is only visible when the Auto Fillet box is checked. This option is only available for open profiles.
Cap Ends	Checking this option will place a cap on either end of the thin feature, creating a hollow part. When checked, the Cap Thickness box appears and a value must be added. This option is only available when creating a thin feature as a base feature.

Sheet Metal Parts

Thin features are commonly used to create sheet metal parts. The Bends function is used to add sheet metal features and attributes, but more importantly, to define the thin-feature part as a sheet metal part as far as SolidWorks is concerned. Certain types of sheet metal features (e.g., a cut across a bend) need to be added to a model in the unfolded mode. Otherwise, the cut would not be true to shape or size when unfolded. The process used to unfold a sheet metal part is explored in this section.

The Bends function defines the thin feature as a sheet metal part and allows for inserting sheet metal parameters such as bend radius, bend allowance, bend order, and bend angle. The bend radii can be added to the thin-feature sketch or with the Bends function. The Bends function allows each individual bend to be edited when bends are added using the correct procedure. There is also the capability to add automatic bend relief.

Configurations can be used to define folded and unfolded parts. This is useful when creating detail drawings for sheet metal parts. This allows for a drawing to show the folded and unfolded views of the sheet metal part on the same sheet. The following illustrations show a sheet metal part and the sheet metal features in FeatureManager.

A sheet metal part.

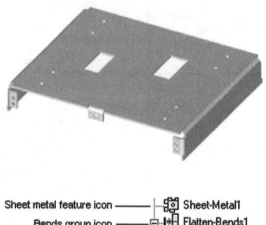

Sheet metal features in FeatureManager.

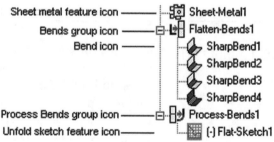

The advantages to creating a part using sheet metal features are that a flat pattern is produced automatically from the sheet metal part (flat patterns can be used to produce the part) and that there are features (e.g., a corner relief along a bend) that cannot be properly defined using features created in the bent state. Dimensions can be accurately obtained in the flattened state that automatically take into account any stretching that takes place when adding bends.

When creating a thin feature from an open profile, the radii can be added using Auto Fillet or by adding the fillets in the sketch, but the latter is not recommended when creating a sheet metal part. If it is known that the part will become a sheet metal part, the Bends feature will take care of any bends needed and will offer more flexibility. To create a sheet metal part, perform the following steps:

1. Create a thin feature using an open profile.

2. Select a face that will be held flat while inserting the bends.

3. Select Bends from the Insert/Features menu. This opens the Flatten Bends dialog box.

4. Specify the Default Bend Radius.

5. Specify the Bend Allowance.

6. Check Use Auto Relief if desired and specify the Offset Ratio.

7. Click on OK to accept the data.

There are many third-party programs for AutoCAD that will allow you to create sheet metal parts. Some of these programs are very good, but AutoCAD itself does not contain sheet metal functionality.

Modifying Bends

There are certain features that need to be defined in the flat pattern state. The sheet metal part is manufactured from a flat piece of metal. The flat part is bent to form the completed part. SolidWorks allows you to add features in the formed or flat states. To modify a bend, perform the following steps:

1. Right click the desired Sharp Bend below the Flatten Bends feature.

2. Select Edit Definition.

3. Make modifications as needed to the Radius or Bend Allowance. Bend Order can be modified, but does not serve any higher purpose other than for documentation.

4. Select OK to continue.

To add a cut or tab to the flat pattern, perform the following steps:

1. Roll back prior to the Process Bends feature.

2. Add cut features or tabs to the flat state as desired. Actually, any feature can be added at this point, but remember that this is supposed to be a sheet metal part.

3. Move the rollback bar to the bottom of the Feature-Manager feature list to reprocess the bend attributes and view the part in its folded state.

New thin features such as tabs can be added to an existing sheet metal part and have the bends added automatically. This is accomplished through the use of the rollback bar once again. To add new features to the sheet metal part and have the bends incorporated automatically, perform the following steps:

1. Roll back prior to the Sheet Metal feature.

2. Add thin features to the part as desired. When extruding a new feature, a Link To Thickness option will be present. Checking this option will link the thickness

of the new feature to the thickness of the sheet metal part. If the sheet metal part thickness is changed, all linked features will change.

3. Use Rebuild to reprocess bend attributes. Additional bends will be added to any new sharp corners.

Configurations can be used to create a configuration for the formed and flat pattern. The drawing can display both configurations. To prepare the flat pattern for use in a drawing, perform the following steps:

1. Select the ConfigurationManager icon.

2. Add a new configuration by right clicking on the part name in ConfigurationManager. A suggestion for the configuration name might be *Flat*.

3. In FeatureManager, suppress the Process Bends feature.

4. Select OK to continue.

Other Sheet Metal Attributes

The following list is a summary of the options encountered while adding bends and defining a sheet metal part:

Default Bend Radius	Specifies the default bend radius.
Thickness	Specifies the default part thickness. This is specified while creating the thin feature and is grayed out if editing the definition of the sheet metal feature.
Use Bend Table	Select this option to use a bend table from the *sldworks\LANG\English* directory (English is defined by the installed language type). The default file is named *SAMPLE.btl*. This ASCII text file contains various bend allowances based on the material thickness, bend radius, and bend angle. This file name can be copied to define various material types or manufacturing processes.
Use K-Factor	Select this option to define the bend allowance based on a ratio between material density and material thickness. Pick inside the field to change the K-factor value.

Use Bend Allowance	Select this option to define the bend allowance based on adding a set value to each bend. Pick inside the field to change the bend allowance value.
Use Auto Relief	Check to add bend relief to areas where material deformation may occur (see the following entry, Offset Ratio).
Offset Ratio	This value determines how much bend relief will be applied. The default setting is .5. What this means is that the relief cut will be half (.5) of the material thickness.
Order	Specify the order for bending the part. "0" means use the system default, which is the feature creation order. This will not affect the shape of the part.

There are two additional toolbar icons (Flattened and No Bends) that can be added to the Features toolbar using the Toolbars tab in the Tools/Customize menu. Select the Features toolbar and drag the icons to the desired position within the Features toolbar. Do not attempt this if you do not feel comfortable doing so. Customizing is usually best left to users more familiar with the program.

Summary

SolidWorks has a number of features that make producing and redefining solid parts simple. SolidWorks offers you an easy-to-use interface for creating solid modeling features. The selection of the feature type, location, and creation order of features helps define the design intent of the part and determines the ease with which the design can be modified.

Reference geometry is used to create simple geometric references that can be used to provide a sketch plane or axis, or to define parametric reference locations for features. With seven different methods of creating reference planes and six ways in which to create an axis, you should be able to create nearly any reference geometry imaginable with which to begin a sketch and create a feature.

Design tables and equations can be used to add intelligence to part features. Multiple versions can be produced and maintained from one part through the use of design tables and configurations. Equations can be used to define relationships between dimensions. Configurations are a powerful, flexible tool that can be used to define simplified versions of a part or assembly, define optional or alternate versions of a design, and define exploded versions of an assembly.

Modifying features can be accomplished quickly and easily. Right clicking on a sketch or feature allows for editing sketch geometry, sketch planes, and definitions, and for checking parent/child relationships. Double clicking on a sketch or feature accesses its dimensions. Very rarely does anything ever need to get deleted with the powerful editing tools available. "Starting over" is a phrase that can be eliminated from your vocabulary with regard to creating parts in SolidWorks.

SolidWorks allows for the creation of solid geometry, but also has built-in functions for creating thin-feature parts and surfaces. Once a thin-feature part is created, it can be turned into a sheet metal part if desired. The various features of a sheet metal part (i.e., Bends, Flat Pattern, and so on) are identified by function within the FeatureManager design tree and can be used to make changes to the sheet metal part.

There are many similarities between AutoCAD and Solid-Works, but as you can see, there are many differences in the way the user interfaces with the software and its ease of use. The largest differences exist in SolidWorks' editing capabilities. When any aspect of the part can be edited at any time—whether it be a sketch, feature definition, dimension, or any other SolidWorks component—the term *design software* begins to have new meaning.

Assemblies

Introduction

This chapter discusses how to create assemblies and use these assemblies to create and control parts within Solid-Works. An assembly is a collection of parts and subassemblies that defines the relationships between assembly components. Subassemblies can be inserted into an assembly. Any assembly inserted into another assembly is considered a subassembly.

An assembly can be used to define or check part dimensions, features, movement between components, assembly interference, and clearances. Components are positioned within an assembly by inserting mate features. A mate feature describes a geometric constraint placed between the selected assembly components. SolidWorks defines an assembly as a separate document type. The pull-down menu headings will not change when working in an assembly document, but the content of those pull-down menus will change. The logical placement of menu options and the adherence to the look and feel of part menus makes learning and using SolidWorks much easier.

Prerequisite

You should at this time have completed chapters 3 through 6 at a minimum. Of course, it would be better to have read the entire book up to this point prior to tackling assemblies. The concepts that should be firmly understood are how to select objects and correctly interpret system feedback by the use of the cursor, color schemes, and interacting with SolidWorks' FeatureManager. The implementation of constraints should be well understood, because this functionality will be directly applied to assemblies, but in a 3D perspective. Also, how to create the basic feature types discussed in the previous chapter should be understood.

Content

The "Assembly Modeling Methodology" section describes several approaches that can be taken when creating an assembly. This section also discusses what an in-context assembly feature is and how it can be applied. The section on creating an assembly describes how to create an assembly and the procedures used for this process. This section discusses the two methods used to add an assembly component (Insert Component and New Part) and the methods used to precisely assemble (mate) these components.

The "Modifying Assemblies" section describes the methods that can be used to fix, move, and rotate assembly components. SolidWorks allows for underconstrained assembly components to move or rotate independently. This can be used to simulate assembly motion when the appropriate assembly mates are added. The ability to define and change assembly component properties is discussed, along with how to edit a part in-context with the assembly (or open the part individually by selecting an assembly component). The "Advanced Assembly Features" section describes some of the advanced topics concerning assemblies. The "Example Assembly" section shows how a simple assembly can be created.

Objectives   When you have completed the "Assembly Modeling Methodology" section, you should understand the difference between top-down and bottom-up assembly modeling, be able to identify an assembly layout and the benefits that can be derived from using this type of layout, and understand what an in-context assembly feature is and how it is created. With completion of the section on creating an assembly, you should be able to insert parts into an assembly, create a new assembly component within an assembly, and mate an assembly component.

Upon completion of the "Modifying Assemblies" section, you should be able to move or rotate assembly components, view or change existing assembly component properties (i.e., file name, configuration, and so on), and edit an assembly component within the context of the assembly or open a new document window for the selected assembly component.

With completion of the "Advanced Assembly Features" section, you should be able to define a component pattern to create an array (linear or circular) of an assembly component using an existing part pattern or by defining a new pattern, understand how an assembly feature can be defined to create a cut-through assembly component as an assembly feature or for visualization purposes, check an assembly for interference between assembly components, understand the uses for the Insert Cavity and Derived Component part functions, explode an existing assembly to create a view of the assembly in the exploded state, and understand the uses for the Join function. When you have finished the "Example Assembly" section, you should be able to insert an assembly component, mate two assembly components, edit an existing assembly component within the context of the assembly, and explode the assembly.

Assembly File Management

Assemblies consist of other SolidWorks parts and assemblies known as subassemblies. When creating new parts within the context of an existing assembly, external references to these documents are created by SolidWorks. Sometimes managing the large number of parts and subassemblies can be a daunting task. The Copy Files option in the Find References dialog box can be used to create a copy of the assembly and all related components that will copy references to files created within the assembly.

All files in the assembly can then be moved to another location, such as over a network, and the externally referenced files will no longer be referenced by the assembly. Instead, the copied parts will be referenced, thereby eliminating what can sometimes be a huge amount of network traffic. This not only speeds up the overall network but makes working on the SolidWorks assembly that much more productive.

Component properties can be used to redefine file locations or replace assembly components. Parts currently within an assembly can be redefined by "pointing" SolidWorks to a new location for a replacement component. If the new component is similar in size and shape to the original part, the existing mate relationships will be maintained.

FeatureManager component (part) names can be different from the component file name when "Update component names when documents are replaced" is unchecked under the External References tab in the Tools/Options menu. However, if that particular part is replaced, the new part name will not update in FeatureManager. If this is unknown to another user, he or she might look for the wrong component.

The actual name of the part can be determined easily enough, simply by right clicking on the part, if there is any question as to the part's real name. SolidWorks gives you the opportunity to open individual parts from within the assembly, and lists the actual part name in the right mouse button menu. Likewise, the path to the original part file can be discovered by right clicking on the part in FeatureManager and selecting Component Properties.

This entire dilemma of needing to keep track of files used within an assembly and which files are externally referenced, as well as questions such as "What assemblies will be affected if I move this file?," are problems not normally encountered in most AutoCAD drawings. To be fair to AutoCAD, it is possible to create an assembly of externally referenced parts. If the externally referenced parts are changed, they can be updated from within the AutoCAD assembly drawing.

However, unlike SolidWorks, if part geometry is referenced, AutoCAD does not care what happens to the external reference. The new part maintains no connection to the referenced geometry, other than the path to that geometry. Changing a part's dimensions will not automatically affect every assembly the part is in. Also, Xrefs cannot be edited within the AutoCAD file unless the association to the original externally referenced drawing is broken. If these differences between AutoCAD and SolidWorks had to be summed up, it could be stated that AutoCAD files are not bidirectionally associative. Solid-Works files, on the other hand, are all associative to one another. This includes Part, Drawing, and Assembly files.

Assembly Modeling Methodology

An assembly can be used as a virtual prototype for a product. The assembly can be designed to mimic the location of components to determine fit and function, allow for the analysis of assembly motion for assembly components, and be used as a visualization tool for the assembled and exploded states of the assembly.

There are basically two methods that can be used to create an assembly. The top-down assembly method starts with the assembly, with components then built within it. The bottom-up method builds the components first and then assembles the components into the assembly. Skeletons and assembly layouts use simple geometry (planes, axes, and assembly sketches) that can be used to drive the size, location, and orientation of assembly components.

An effective approach to assemblies is a combination of the two approaches. The reference geometry or skeleton can be defined within the assembly. This allows the designer to identify the important features and functions within the assembly. By focusing on the design intent early in the process, you can produce robust, functional assemblies. You use top-down assembly design when in-context assembly references will be used to interrelate assembly components, or when using assembly skeletons or layouts. You use bottom-up assembly design when the parts used to create the assembly already exist, or when using customer- or supplier-defined geometry.

Skeletons and Layouts

Reference feature skeletons and assembly layouts are techniques used to define common references for part features and assembly components that use simple reference geometry and assembly layout sketches. A skeleton uses simple geometry (i.e., planes, axes, and assembly sketches) to drive the location or placement of features and assembly components. An assembly layout uses an assembly sketch to drive part geometry.

The goal of a skeleton or an assembly layout is to make simple, intelligent information available with little overhead, using an underlying sketch to control the movement of parts. The following illustration shows a robot assembly for which planes and (more importantly) an assembly sketch were used to drive the positioning of the components within the assembly. The underlying sketch has dimensions attached to it, just like any sketch would. These dimensions can be altered, and because the components in the assembly have relationships to the sketch, the components will move to accommodate these relationships.

A robot arm assembly.

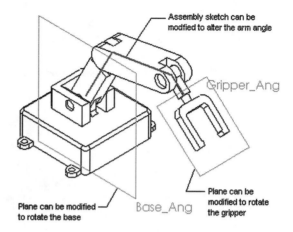

Assembly sketch can be modfied to alter the arm angle

Gripper_Ang

Plane can be modified to rotate the base

Base_Ang

Plane can be modified to rotate the gripper

This use of skeletons and assembly layouts to define the important mating features for an assembly design can be very useful. This helps the engineer or designer better plan how a design will function, and to describe movement to control the design intent and convey ideas to others. The simple sketches can also be renamed to help describe the purpose for the skeleton sketch and as a visual aid for documenting the purpose and function of a skeletal feature.

Reference Feature Skeletons

A reference feature skeleton is a framework consisting of simple features, planes, and axes used to define mating surfaces, axes of rotation, and common reference features. Combinations of features can be used, depending on the project at hand. Planes and axes are simple features that can be defined with few parent/child relationships. The ability to use simple features or reference geometry means the design intent of the assembly can be clearly defined without additional complex design work.

A reference feature skeleton can be constructed within a part or assembly. A part feature skeleton can be used to define planes or axes that will be used by more than one feature. For major functional surfaces within a part, a well-named plane can be used by many features while

creating only one parent relation to the plane. This is
sometimes a better practice than using a part face for the
same function because a part face would be dependent
on the part, whereas a plane might not. The following
illustration shows a feature skeleton.

Feature skeleton.

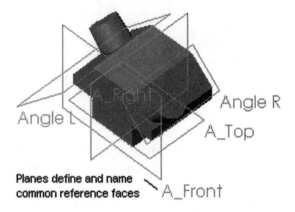

Reference feature skeletons can also be used to simplify
complex models or assemblies. When the major functional
surfaces are defined, unnecessary features or components
can be suppressed to help minimize the information
required for rebuilding the part or assembly. Configurations can also be defined to aid in suppressing the features
or components.

Assembly Layouts

An assembly layout is an assembly sketch used to drive
the location of in-context assembly features. An assembly
sketch can drive components created in assembly mode.
An in-context assembly feature is a part feature created
within an assembly. Part features that reference other
parts or assembly geometry are related to the features
they reference.

Sketches can be defined in an assembly that can be used
to define geometry in component parts. Changes made to
the assembly sketch are reflected automatically in the
parts that used this sketch geometry. Assembly layouts
use the assembly sketches to control motion or location
of assembly components. An example would be a linkage

that follows a profile created within an assembly sketch. All components related via geometric relations (i.e., parallel, collinear, fix, and so on) or dimensions move when the assembly sketch profile changes.

Using layout sketches reduces the amount of parent/child relationships. The components are related by one sketch in the assembly. Minimizing unnecessary parent/child relationships makes for parts that are easier to manipulate and redefine.

The sketch can be fully or partially constrained, depending on how you want to modify the assembly once completed. You can control the level to which the sketch is geometrically or dimensionally constrained. Adding dimensions to the sketch allows you to precisely modify the geometry, whereas unconstrained or underconstrained geometry allows for a more free-form modification of the sketch geometry. Dragging the object handles of a sketch entity can be used to modify the sketch, and therefore the assembly. The following illustration shows an assembly layout sketch.

Assembly layout sketch.

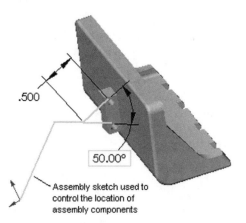

.500

50.00°

Assembly sketch used to control the location of assembly components

All and all, assembly skeletons and assembly layouts are really the same thing. Feature skeletons are the same thing as a building block for the assembly, as if it were a core component that other parts in the assembly are placed upon. All of these methods are ways of aiding in the assembly creation process and allowing for greater flexibility to the assembly when finished. When assembly components are based on a common object, whether that object is a layout or a skeleton, you have greater control over the assembly because many components in the assembly are based on that common object.

These building tools are options, not requirements. They can be useful when creating an assembly that will be used to show movement. Many assemblies will never need the aid of these tools and can be built piece by piece using mating constraints and still show everything you are trying to show, such as movement or design configurations. It is suggested that you continue with the rest of this chapter to get the full picture of assemblies before attempting to implement an assembly layout sketch for your particular assembly.

You will not find many similarities between AutoCAD and SolidWorks when it comes to creating assemblies. One of the largest portions of this chapter, and of creating assemblies, is the application of mating relationships. These are intelligent relationships between geometry, much like was done with constraints on 2D geometry within sketch mode. Because AutoCAD does not make use of constraints, or in this case mating relationships, this may be a new way of thinking.

Creating an Assembly

When creating an assembly, a plan should be developed to determine the method (i.e., top-down or bottom-up) used to create the assembly and the order of creation. The answer to the question of whether or not the assembly is going to be of the top-down or bottom-up variety is based on one condition. Are the parts built yet? If the answer is yes, or if the answer is that the parts will be built before the assembly is put together, you will be creating a bottom-up assembly. The bottom-up assembly is the easiest to create and requires two main steps. These steps are:

- Bringing the components into the assembly
- Adding mates between components to move them into place

It is almost like putting together the pieces of a puzzle. The only tricky part for new users is figuring out what mates to use (covered later in the chapter). If the SolidWorks assembly is created or ordered in the same manner as the final assembly order, and you are already aware of how the assembly components should be placed together, putting the assembly together should be fairly straightforward. When you plan an assembly, you should determine the following:

- What parts will go into the assembly?
- What is the assembly order for the product? The assembly should be defined from the first base component to the final assembly component, usually in the order it will be built in the real world.
- What is the function of each assembly component? Will an assembly skeleton or layout be needed to control these functions and define movement?
- What are the known additional features the assembly will need either during or after it is built? When starting a part or assembly, the most important features or components should come early in the design. The additional details can be defined later in the design process.
- Are there existing components or assemblies that can be used to aid in the design definition?
- Will parts brought into the assembly be used in other assemblies? If so, will the original parts be modified later? It may be best to copy components to your project directory if the original may be used in other assemblies or modified by other users.

Another type of assembly is the top-down assembly. This assembly is created when the design of certain components is not going to be known until portions of the assembly are built. The reason may be because measurements will not be known, or because certain factors in the shape of the part are difficult to determine and require existing geometry from components already placed in the assembly.

It should be noted that entire assemblies are usually not built this way. It is possible to build an entire assembly around a skeleton or assembly layout, as discussed previously, but this is not a typical real-world scenario. What is more common is when a few parts need to be built from within the context of the assembly, usually because they must reference existing geometry. (Creating in-context parts is discussed later in this chapter.)

Assembly Creation Procedure

Before actually running through the SolidWorks steps for inserting components into an assembly, you should review the factors to be considered before starting an assembly. The following is a step approach to creating an assembly.

1. Review the design concepts and determine the functional aspects of the assembly. A clear definition of the purpose and function of each component should be determined to the fullest extent possible prior to starting a part and performing any design work.

2. Determine the assembly method (top-down or bottom-up).

3. If parts will be designed within the context of the assembly, create an assembly layout.

4. Determine what should be the first assembly component. This component is usually the main component in the assembly and the one that will remain stationary.

5. Insert components into the assembly.

6. Mate the components in the assembly.

7. Check for movement. This allows you to determine if the correct mates have been added.

8. Continue adding components, mating as necessary, and checking movement to determine interaction between components.

9. If at any time during the assembly process errors are encountered, such as overdefined components,

search for the cause of the problem before continuing. Problems that are ignored will always get bigger!

Insert Component

Assemblies consist of parts and subassemblies. The assembly contains information on order and how the components are assembled. Parts or subassemblies can be inserted into an assembly by selecting the document window or by dragging the part or assembly icon from the Windows 95 or Windows NT Explorer into the assembly document window. The new component can be positioned precisely after insertion.

Assembly components can be left fully or partially unconstrained. These constraints can be added, edited, or removed at any time. Underconstrained assembly geometry can be used to simulate assembly motion. The following illustration shows the insertion of a component.

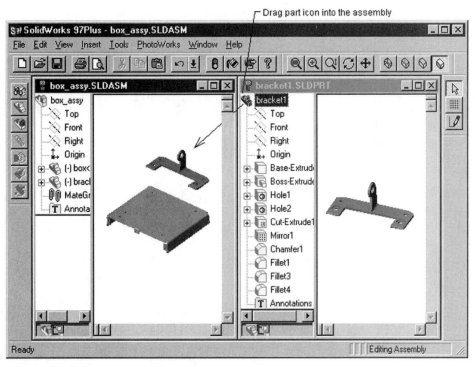

One method of component insertion.

There are three ways of bringing a component into an assembly, which are presented as steps in the material that follows. It is assumed you have already started a new assembly and no components have yet been inserted. As a reminder, be aware that the very first component brought into the assembly is usually the main component for the assembly.

By default, the first component will be fixed in space. In other words, its location will be locked and the component will not move with relation to other components. This can be altered at a later time. To unfix or "float" a component, right click on the component in FeatureManager and select Float. This is a toggle; therefore, right clicking on the same component a second time will allow you to Fix the component. The three methods of bringing a component into an assembly follow.

- *Method 1 — Inserting a component when the component file is closed. To do this, perform the following steps:*

    1. Select Insert/Component/From File from the pulldown menu.

    2. Select the type of file to be opened. Parts (*.sldprt) are selected by default. Assemblies (*.sldasm) can be chosen as well.

    3. Select the file to be opened.

    4. Select Open to complete this function.

    5. The cursor changes to a target symbol. Select the location for the part/subassembly in the graphics window by picking in a blank area of the screen.

- *Method 2 — Inserting a component when the component file is opened. To do this, perform the following steps:*

    1. Select the component name from the FeatureManager design tree of the part and drag the icon into the graphics window.

2. Release the mouse button.

- *Method 3 — Inserting a component from the Windows File Explorer. To do this, perform the following steps:*

  1. Select the component file name from Windows Explorer and drag the icon into the graphics window.

  2. Release the mouse button.

Once the part has been brought into the assembly, it can be repositioned or mated. Just remember that the first component in an assembly is fixed by default. Other components will move in relation to the first component. One part can be brought into an assembly as many times as needed. Dragging a component from FeatureManager into the assembly is an easy method to use when there are multiple instances of a part in the assembly.

However, if other occurrances of a part must be brought into the assembly and Windows Explorer is not available, it is possible to drag a component from FeatureManager to the graphics window while holding the Control key down. If you use the Insert/Component/From File method, the cursor changes when the component has been selected and needs to be placed within the assembly.

New Part

When top-down design needs to be implemented, Insert/Component/New is the option to use. This function will create a new part in the active assembly. Insert/Component/New allows you to reference assembly components for geometrical references and constraints. The term *in-context editing* refers to constructing part geometry based on assembly geometry, literally building on the component *in the context of* the assembly. The assembly components turn gray when editing new parts. The part can then be defined using existing assembly geometry references.

The advantages to creating and editing parts while in assembly mode is that the interdependent features between parts can be defined in such a way that when one of these feature changes in size or location, the other related features automatically update. Any references to external component geometry will create an in-context feature in the FeatureManager design tree. The in-context feature is a child of the parent feature. If the parent feature changes, the in-context feature will change. If the parent feature is removed, the in-context feature will fail to rebuild. When this happens, the part must be edited to remove any references made to parent geometry.

An advantage that SolidWorks enjoys during problem solving (i.e., references cannot be found, or become invalid due to the shape or size of related geometry) is that a display message will warn you of the failed reference and allow you to correct the problem. SolidWorks will also explain what happened to cause the failure. The feature within the FeatureManager design tree will have an exclamation point (!) in front of the feature or sketch name, with arrows pointing to the problem if the problem area resides in a feature that may be many levels deep within the assembly (e.g., a sketch for a feature in a part within a subassembly). To view the cause of the problem, select the feature in the FeatureManager design tree, press the right mouse button, and select What's Wrong. An explanation of the problem will be displayed.

An InPlace mate is added when inserting a component using the Insert/Component/New function. In-context parts can be moved and can be exploded for assembly-exploded views. Do not associate SolidWorks' Explode function with AutoCAD's Explode because they have nothing in common. An in-context part is created by the New (Part) function. This mating constraint can be removed and more appropriate mating constraints can be placed on the component. It may be desirable to delete the default mating constraint InPlace inserted automatically by the system with a mate or mates that better define the function of the assembly component. The following illustration shows a new part.

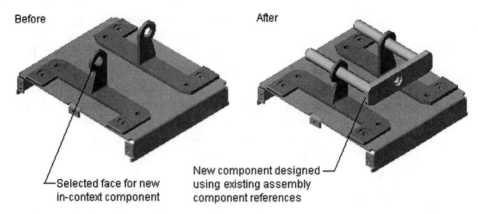

Before

After

Selected face for new
in-context component

New component designed
using existing assembly
component references

New part designed around existing geometry.

When a new part is created in an assembly, SolidWorks first asks you to give the part a name. This is because it is impossible to edit a part unless a part exists. Therefore, it must be named and saved. To create a new part in an active assembly, perform the following steps:

1. Select New from the Insert/Component menu.

2. Enter the name and file location in the Save As dialog box.

3. Select OK to continue.

4. Select a plane or planar face on which to begin sketching and to locate the new part in the assembly. SolidWorks will place you in Sketch mode.

5. Create, dimension, and constrain the sketch.

6. Create the first base feature for the new part.

7. Create more sketch and feature geometry as needed to complete the part.

8. When finished creating the part, right click anywhere in the document window and select Edit Assembly to return to the assembly.

As soon as the new part is inserted into the assembly, the assembly components will appear gray to let you know that they are no longer editing the assembly. Even though the assembly is still visible, it is the new part that is being edited. As new features are added to the part, they will appear orange. This is SolidWorks' color scheme while editing a part in the context of an assembly. As soon as the right mouse button is clicked in the graphics window and Edit Assembly is selected, the components will regain their natural colors.

Part Color

When working with assemblies, it is a good idea to change the colors of different parts. Otherwise, differentiating between the components may become a difficult task, not to mention a strain on the eyes. To modify a part's color, perform the following steps:

1. Right click on the part in FeatureManager.

2. Select Edit Part. The part will temporarily turn orange.

3. Select Tools/Options.

4. Select the Color tab.

5. Select Shading and click on the Edit button.

6. Select a color, then click on OK to exit out of all dialog boxes.

7. Right click in the graphics window and select Edit Assembly. The parts will return to their original colors.

This method will change the color of the part in the part file itself. If you want to change the color of the part in the current assembly only, perform the following steps:

1. Right click on the part in FeatureManager.

2. Select Component Properties.

3. Click on the Color button.

4. Click on the Change Color button and specify the desired color.

5. Click on OK to exit out of all dialog boxes.

This method will only affect the part in the current assembly and will *not* revert back to the original component.

Assembly Mates

Assembly constraints are used to define the alignment characteristics of assembly components. Assembly constraints allow you to define the assembly method for each component. The constraint chosen should simulate the actual assembly methodology. Using assembly mates that mimic the actual function of the component within the assembly allows you to mate assembly components in such a way that they can be manipulated for viewing their ranges of motion. Using planes instead of part faces has these advantages:

- Easier to pick a plane from FeatureManager.
- Part features can be suppressed, or simplified configurations can be used for large assembly management without omitting features used to mate the assembly.
- Planes are more robust features and less subject to change than part faces. Planes are not as dependent on existing geometry.

Using a Distance mate allows you to move the component by changing a parametric value. This can be used to simulate component movement. This technique should not be used to explode a component. The Explode function should be used to define exploded assemblies.

There are a number of mating types, and they all have their purpose. Before adding mates, ask yourself how you would like the part to move with respect to the part it is being mated to. If it were a pin, should it slide in and out of the hole? If it were a propeller, should it be allowed to spin on the shaft? If it is a hinge, should you allow for flexibility along a common axis? Perhaps the part should be firmly mated to another component without any freedom of movement. This greatly reduces the options and makes the task an easy one. The following illustration shows what will become a fully mated bracket on top of a box.

Fully mating a bracket to a box.

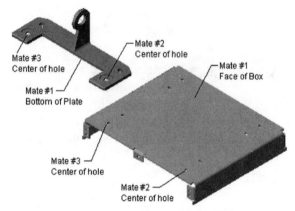

There are six ways a part can move. Different combinations of mates restrict certain movements, resulting in a limited degree of freedom of movement. These six degrees of freedom of movement are:

1. Translation along the x axis

2. Translation along the y axis

3. Translation along the z axis

4. Rotation about the x axis

5. Rotation about the y axis

6. Rotation about the z axis

What mates should be added to an assembly is dependent on how a given part should move in the assembly. The FeatureManager design tree object MateGroup is used to organize the component mates for an assembly. This is SolidWorks' way of keeping all of the mates organized. A component mate describes the type of mate and the features mated. The following illustration shows mate attributes.

*Mate attributes
of a mate feature.*

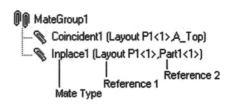

Reference 1 and reference 2 in the previous illustration refer to the selected faces or entities the mate was placed between. To add mating relationships, perform the following steps:

1. Hold the Control key down and select the planes or faces to apply the mate between. Select these items from the graphics window, not FeatureManager.

2. Select the Mate icon or select Mate from the Insert menu.

3. Add the desired mating constraint. Only one mate can be added at one time.

4. Select Apply to continue.

Mates are usually added between faces on components within an assembly. Mates can also be added to edges, origin points, and plane entities. New users should attempt to add mates between faces if possible. Faces are more limiting and more easily understood for those having problems grasping the meaning of the mating relationships. Read on to get a better understanding of the various mates and what they do.

Mating Constraint Types

In Chapter 5, you learned that it was possible to place relations between entities. These relations can be between arcs, lines, points, or any other entity type. The relations could be parallel, perpendicular, coincident, and so on. Now it is time to take that knowledge and apply it to the 3D world.

What you learned in sketching will be applied almost exactly the same way to parts within an assembly. In a sketch, the entities to be constrained are selected, the Add Relations icon selected, and the relation added. In an assembly, the faces (or other entities) are selected, the mate icon selected, and the appropriate mate applied. The process is the same, but the mechanics are different. The following are the various types of SolidWorks constraints available in the Mate dialog box:

Coincident	Constrains components so that they lie on the same plane.
Perpendicular	Constrains selected objects so that they lie perpendicular to one another.
Tangent	Constrains components so that they remain tangent to one another.
Concentric	Constrains cylindrical surfaces so that they share the same origin.
Parallel	Constrains components parallel at an unspecified distance from one another.
Distance	Constrains components so that they are a specified distance from one another.
Angle	Constrains components so that they are a specified angle from one another.

Included in the Mate dialog box are the options Aligned, Anti-aligned, and Closest. These are not mates, but alignment conditions for mates. Their meanings are as follows:

Aligned	Places a component's material on the same side of the planes selected for mating.
Anti-aligned	Places a component's material on the opposite side of the planes selected for mating.
Closest	SolidWorks decides on Aligned or Anti-aligned, whichever is closest.

The following illustration shows a simple example of the Aligned and Anti-aligned options. It is not extremely important that you understand these conditions one hundred percent. If the option for alignment is left to Closest, SolidWorks has a 50/50 shot of getting it right. You can normally ignore this setting and just apply or preview the mate. If the mate is incorrect, simply select the opposite setting.

*Aligned versus
Anti-aligned.*

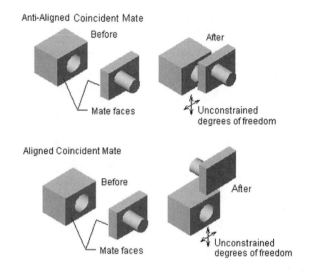

Deleting Mates

Deleting mates in SolidWorks is as easy as deleting anything else. Select the Mate from FeatureManager and press the Delete key. To delete a mate, perform the following steps:

1. Select the constraint in FeatureManager.

2. Select Delete from the Edit menu or press the Delete key.

3. Select Yes to continue and confirm the deletion.

The table that follows charts types of mating relationships for various types of geometry. Most mating relationships are fairly obvious. For instance, it would be impossible to add a concentric mate between two planes. For the sake of thoroughness, this table has been included.

	Point/Vertex	**Line/Axis**	**Plane**	**Cylinder**
Point/Vertex	Coincident Distance	Coincident Distance	Coincident Distance	Coincident Concentric
Line/Axis	Coincident Distance	Coincident Distance Parallel Perpendicular Angle	Coincident Distance Parallel Perpendicular	Coincident Tangent Concentric
Plane	Coincident Distance	Coincident Distance Parallel Perpendicular	Coincident Distance Parallel Perpendicular Angle	Tangent
Cylinder	Coincident Concentric	Coincident Tangent Concentric	Tangent	Tangent Concentric

Fixed components cannot have additional mating constraints placed on the component. If a part is fully defined in an assembly, it will appear without a prefix in FeatureManager. If it has any degree of freedom of movement, a small minus symbol will prefix its name. If the component is fixed in space, the component's name will be prefixed with an "f." The following illustration shows component constraint prefixes.

Component constraint prefixes.

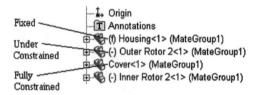

Components that have been mated should not be fixed, and vice versa. However, it is allowable, and sometimes necessary, to temporarily Fix components. If this is done, do not forget to go back later and Float the component in question. The following section provides a more detailed explanation of fixing and floating.

Modifying Assemblies

After components have been added to an assembly, SolidWorks allows the components to be edited and repositioned, and new configurations to be defined. Depending on the defined mating constraints, assemblies can simulate assembly motion.

Fix Component

Assembly components can be fixed within an assembly. A fixed component cannot be moved. The first component in an assembly is fixed by default. The fix attribute can be removed by using the Float function. Right click the component in FeatureManager and select Float. The component can now be moved. To fix the location of a component, perform the following steps:

1. Right click on the component in FeatureManager.

2. Select Fix.

To remove a component's fixed location attribute, perform the following steps:

1. Right click on the component in FeatureManager.

2. Select Float.

As mentioned previously, a fixed component will display an "f" in front of the component name in FeatureManager. Mate relationships should not be added to fixed components, and mated components should not be fixed. Usually, a plus sign (+) prefix is added before the part name in FeatureManager if it is overdefined. However, there is one exception to this, and that is if a part is fixed and constrained at the same time. The "f" prefix will be displayed instead of a plus sign, thereby hiding the fact that the part is overdefined. Be aware of this so that it does not catch you off guard.

Move Component

Assembly components can be moved, depending on their active assembly constraints or mating conditions. The assembly component will move depending on its remaining degrees of freedom. For example, if a component is constrained along the *x-y* axes, the component will move only in the *z* direction.

As you know, the first assembly component is fixed by default. This component can be moved only after Float has been applied. The assembly components added afterward are allowed to move or rotate along any unconstrained axis. Move Component can be used to show assembly motion. The assembly components are allowed to move along the unconstrained degrees of freedom previously mentioned.

As a reminder, these degrees of freedom of movement are translation along the *x-y-z* axes and rotation about the same. This totals six degrees of freedom of movement. This allows for some simple assembly motion studies but does not provide the capabilities of a complete kinematics software program. To move a component, perform the following steps:

1. Select the component in FeatureManager.

2. Click on the Move Component icon, or select Tools/ Component/Move.

3. Hold down the left mouse button and drag the component to its new location.

Move Component is similar to AutoCAD's Move command only in its ability to move an object from one point to another. In SolidWorks, unlike AutoCAD, there is no need to enter displacement values or pick base points.

Rotate Component

Assembly components can be rotated, depending on their active assembly constraints. The Rotate Component Around Centerpoint (shortened after this point to Rotate Component) function works only with unmated assembly components. Rotate Component cannot be used to show assembly motion because only completely unconstrained parts can be rotated.

Another option, Rotate Component About Axis, allows for rotating components about a selected axis or edge. Unlike its Rotate Component counterpart, this function can show assembly movement very well, as long as the mating relationships have been correctly applied. Take a look at the following illustration to see an example of what might be accomplished with the Rotate Component About Axis function.

Using Rotate Component About Axis.

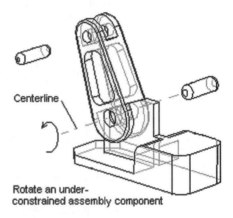

Centerline

Rotate an under-
constrained assembly component

To rotate a component that has not been mated, perform the following steps:

1. With the left mouse button, select the component in FeatureManager.

2. Click on the Rotate Component Around Centerpoint icon.

3. Hold down the left mouse button and drag to rotate the component to its new location.

To rotate a component around an axis, perform the following steps:

1. With the left mouse button, select the component in FeatureManager.

2. Hold down the Control key and select an edge or axis of rotation.

3. Click on the Rotate Component Around Axis icon.

4. Hold down the left mouse button and drag to rotate the component to its new location.

When components or assemblies are manipulated onscreen in any way, the system will temporarily turn the display mode to wireframe if Hidden Lines Removed or Hidden in Gray have been selected. This is done because attempting to recalculate hidden lines during the rotation process would result in too many computations to make redisplaying in those modes feasible. Therefore, the recalculation of hidden lines is not completed until you let go of the mouse button. The wireframe and shaded modes will offer the best performance when moving or rotating components.

Edit Part

Editing a part within an active assembly allows you to reference assembly component geometry while creating new features. This allows for other parts to be created in-context to the assembly. Creating geometry using a reference to another assembly member creates an external reference to that assembly component.

The advantage to this methodology is that design features can be logically interrelated. For example, a bearing hole can be created with .001 clearance to the mating shaft. The clearance is maintained between these components anytime the shaft dimension changes. The disadvantage is that if the parent part or feature is removed, the referenced feature will fail to find the parent part or feature and fail to rebuild.

Any time a feature or part is created with external references, an arrow is added as a suffix to the part or feature with the external reference. As previously discussed, creating parts or features in the context of an assembly automatically creates an external reference. Take a look at the following illustration to view the external reference symbol at the end of a part in FeatureManager.

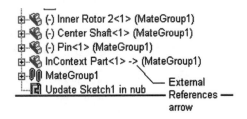

The External References arrow.

An assembly component can be opened in a new document window. This allows the document to be edited without the visual clutter of the other assembly components and ensures that no unintentional assembly references are made within the document. This is a shortcut method that allows you to open an assembly with two mouse picks: right click on the component and select Open *Filename.sldprt*. This shortcut can actually be shortened to just one mouse click if the right mouse button is held down after right clicking on the part name. Hold down the mouse button and highlight the desired menu choice. When the mouse button is released, the desired choice is selected.

The alternative to opening the part in its own window is to edit the part within the context of the assembly. Each method is presented in the material that follows. To edit a selected part file in the active assembly, perform the following steps:

1. Right click on the part name in FeatureManager.

2. Select Edit Part. The part will display as orange, and the rest of the assembly will display as gray.

3. Modify the part as desired.

4. To return to the assembly, right click in the graphics window or on the assembly name in FeatureManager and select Edit Assembly *AssemblyName.sldasm*.

To open a selected assembly component in a new document window, perform the following steps:

1. Right click on the part name in FeatureManager.

2. Select Open *PartName.sldprt*. The part file will be opened independent of the assembly.

3. To return to the assembly, click in the graphics window to make it active or select the assembly name from the Window pull-down menu.

Assembly Information

Find References in the File menu displays the file location of assembly components. This is an ideal way of seeing just what files are in the assembly and where those files are located. Optionally, you can copy these files to a new location. External file references can be lost when a file is moved or deleted. When the SolidWorks software cannot find an external file it will prompt you to locate the file. More specifically, it will ask you if you want to Browse for the file.

The advantage to using SolidWorks to copy a document is that any existing external references are kept intact. Otherwise, if the file was copied using Windows Explorer, the external file references may be missing. The following will create an external file reference:

- Components (parts and subassemblies) within an assembly (these are referenced by the assembly).
- Parts and assemblies used in drawings (these are referenced by the drawing).
- In-context assembly features. The referenced feature becomes an external reference for the part.
- The Base Part function. The base part becomes the external reference for the new part.
- The Mirror Part function. The original part becomes the external reference for the mirrored part.

To display the file location of components used in an active assembly, perform the following steps:

1. Select Find References from the File menu.

2. Select Close to exit the dialog box.

To copy the components used in an active assembly to a new location, perform the following steps:

1. Select Find References from the File menu.

2. Select Copy Files to copy the assembly and related component files to a new drive or directory.

3. Select the location of the new documents. These files will have the same file name.

4. Check Preserve Directory Structure to maintain the entire directory structure for every part listed in the dialog box. This is optional. If this is not selected, all assembly files will be placed in the location you choose.

5. Select Close to exit the dialog box.

The Copy Files function can be used to make changes to a released document in a temporary working directory. It can also be used to create a new assembly similar to an existing assembly or to explore experimental changes without affecting the original assembly. The system will prompt you prior to overwriting any files, although when copying an entire assembly it is best to create a directory specifically for that purpose.

Component Properties

Component Properties can be used to control and define specific characteristics of the parts in an assembly. These properties are used to suppress or hide a component, change the component's source file or location, exchange the component with a different part or assembly, or specify a named configuration for use in the assembly.

It is possible to control what configuration is being used in specific assemblies. For instance, a part may have many configurations, but one configuration in particular is needed for the assembly. It is possible to control, from the assembly, exactly what configuration of the part is being used within the assembly. This feature is extremely important in reducing the number of files needed to create multiple assemblies that require different revisions of the same part. The part does not have to be copied every time it needs to be placed in a different assembly.

External file references can be lost when a file is moved or deleted. When the system cannot find an external file, it will prompt you to Browse for the file. This command can also be used to replace an external file reference with a new file name. Problems may arise with geometry references if an externally referenced part is replaced. These lost external references can then be redefined or removed. Through the use of Component Properties, the following characteristics of an assembly component can be controlled:

- Component location
- Component name (if "Update component names when documents are replaced" is left unchecked in the External References tab of the Tools/Options dialog box)
- Visibility
- Suppression
- Ability to use or override default configurations for parts contained within subassemblies
- Display of defined configurations for individual parts or subassemblies
- Component color

To change a component's properties, perform the following steps:

1. Right click on the component and select Component Properties....

2. Set or change the desired properties.

3. Select OK to continue.

Not all of the properties in the Component Properties dialog box are adjustable. Some are hard coded by the software. These are pointed out in the list that follows, which contains the SolidWorks component property types and descriptions of each.

Component Name	The component name. This name is derived from the component name and cannot be changed unless "Update component names when documents are replaced" is left unchecked in the External References tab of the Tools/Options dialog box. When that option is unchecked, the component name will be independent of the actual part file name of the component.
Instance ID	Indicates the number of the component in the assembly when more than one instance of the component is present. This is not the total number of instances. It is SolidWorks' way of identifying the same components as being individual instances within the assembly. If an instance is deleted, SolidWorks will not reorder the ID to begin at number 1 for the remaining instances. This item is maintained entirely by the system.
Model Document Path	Displays the path to the component.
Browse...	Select this button to open FileManager to locate a replacement component or specify a new path to the component if it has been moved. This is only available for assembly parts, not subassemblies or subassembly components.
Use properties specified in Configuration "*<configuration name>*" of "*<subassembly name>*"	This option is only available for subassembly components. Selecting this option uses the visibility settings specified in the subassembly.
Override properties specified in configuration "*<configuration name>*" of "*<subassembly name>*"	This option is only available for subassembly components. Selecting this option uses the visibility settings of the assembly.
Suppress	Check to suppress the component. When suppressed, the component's icon will appear gray in the FeatureManager design tree and the component's tree will not be accessible. Suppressing removes the component from memory.
Show Model	Check to display the component and the component's design tree. When the component is not shown, the component's icon will appear as an outline in FeatureManager. Both Show Model and "Show Feature Detail in FeatureManager design tree" are selected together.
Show Feature Detail in FeatureManager design tree	This option is only available for subassemblies. If Show Model is unchecked, unchecking this option will show only subassembly components under the subassembly in FeatureManager. In other words, plane, origin point, and mate group information will remain hidden.

Color	Click on this button to change the component's color. This information will not revert back to the original. It will only affect the current assembly. Also, this is a great way to show interior workings of an assembly by making outer components transparent. Use the Advanced button after clicking on Color to change advanced color characteristics.
Use component's "in-use" or last saved configuration	Select this option to use the active or last saved configuration in the selected part.
Use named configuration	Select this option to use a named configuration. Select a configuration name from the drop-down list. The list will be directly connected to the configurations created for the part.

Advanced Assembly Features

This section discusses many of the advanced features available within a SolidWorks assembly document. Certain operations must be completed within an assembly because those operations require more than one part to be open at one time. Remember, unlike AutoCAD, a SolidWorks part can only contain one contiguous solid model. Operations that require multiple components, such as the Join operation or the Core or the Cavity routine, must have two or more components to be completed.

Another requirement that often comes into play in operations such as these is that a new part will be created. Therefore, it is necessary to begin a new part and save it first, much like the sequence needed when inserting a new component into an assembly.

Assembly Pattern

This function creates a pattern of a selected component using a pattern defined in another part or by defining a new pattern within the assembly. Assembly patterns can be defined with either a linear or circular pattern. Assembly patterns can be used to create a copy of an assembly component without having to insert the same component repeatedly. This pattern has parametric values that can be edited and rebuilt to display changes.

As previously mentioned, the assembly pattern can be based on an existing component feature pattern, or the pattern can be created locally within the assembly. If the pattern is based on a component feature pattern, assembly components will be child features of the component feature pattern. If the feature pattern changes, the assembly components update accordingly. The following illustration shows an assembly pattern. To create an assembly pattern based on an existing part pattern, perform the following steps:

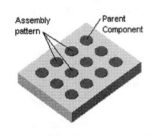

Assembly pattern. Parent Component

Assembly pattern.

1. Insert the component containing the pattern into the assembly.

2. Insert and mate the component to be patterned into the assembly.

3. Select Component Pattern from the Insert menu.

4. Select the "Use an existing feature pattern (Derived)" field.

5. Select Next to continue.

6. Pick inside the Seed Component field and select the component to be patterned from FeatureManager.

7. Pick inside the Pattern Feature field and select the pattern feature from FeatureManager.

8. Select Finish to continue.

To create an assembly pattern based on an existing part pattern, perform the following steps:

1. Insert and mate the component to be patterned into the assembly.

2. Select Component Pattern from the Insert menu.

3. Select the "Define your own pattern (Local)" field.

4. Select either the Linear or Circular option.

5. Select Next to continue.

6. Pick inside the Seed Component field and select the component to be patterned from FeatureManager.

7. Pick inside the Along Edge/Dim field and specify an edge, axis (if a circular pattern), or dimension that will define the direction of the pattern.

8. Specify First Direction or Second Direction if a linear pattern.

9. Specify the Spacing distance (angular if a circular pattern, linear distance if a linear pattern).

10. Specify the number of Instances.

11. Specify Reverse Direction if needed.

12. Select Finish to continue.

It is possible to delete instances after creating a pattern. If this is done, the deleted items will appear in the Items to Skip field when editing the definition of the Component Pattern. To delete an instance, select a surface on the desired instance and press the Delete key. SolidWorks will ask if you want to delete the entire pattern or just an instance. Make sure you specify just an instance. If at a later time you would like to undelete the instance, edit the definition of the pattern and delete the instance name from the Items to Skip field.

Assembly Features

An assembly feature is used to add features to an assembly that will not revert back to the original components. This function can also be used to show cross sections of the assembly for display purposes. Assembly features can only be made as cuts, and cannot add material to the assembly. Assembly features can be used to add important design features that would normally be machined into the assembled model. They can also be used to create some very nice demonstrations.

The Feature Scope function is used to define which assembly components an assembly feature will affect. Feature Scope can be changed after an assembly feature has been defined. Therefore, just like anything else in SolidWorks, you are never locked into a decision. Multiple assembly features in the same part can have different feature scopes. The following illustration shows an assembly feature in which a 90-degree section of an assembly has been removed.

Two components were not included in the feature scope.

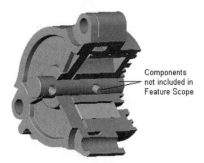

Components not included in Feature Scope

The desired feature scope should be defined prior to creating an assembly feature. Otherwise, the assembly feature will affect all parts in the assembly and Feature Scope would more than likely need to be edited. This is not a problem, but it is easier to set the feature scope beforehand. To specify the feature scope of an assembly feature, click on Feature Scope in the Edit menu. Any changes to the feature scope will affect only new assembly features. To define the scope of an assembly feature, perform the following steps:

1. Select Feature Scope from the Edit menu.

2. Select items to add to Feature Scope by selecting components in FeatureManager.

3. To delete items from Feature Scope, highlight the item in the Feature Scope list box and press the Delete key.

4. Select OK to continue.

When the assembly feature is added, only those items listed in Feature Scope will be affected. Assembly features can be only cuts or holes, as previously stated. To modify the scope of an existing assembly feature, perform the following steps:

1. Right click on the assembly feature in FeatureManager.

2. Select Feature Scope.

3. Select components in FeatureManager to be added, or highlight the component in the Feature Scope list box to be deleted and press the Delete key.

4. Select OK to continue.

At this point, you could probably piece together the steps used to create an assembly feature. To make things as easy as possible, the following steps guide you through the entire process of creating an assembly feature. It is assumed you know how to define the feature scope. To create an assembly feature using a cut, perform the following steps:

1. Define the feature scope for the assembly feature (Edit/Feature Scope).

2. Select a plane or planar face.

3. Select the Sketch icon or select Sketch from the Insert menu.

4. Sketch a profile to use as the cutting profile.

5. Dimension and geometrically constrain the profile as necessary.

6. Select Insert/Assembly Feature/Cut, and specify Extrude or Revolve.

7. Select the End Condition and Depth. Select any other option as required.

8. Select OK to complete this function.

To create an assembly feature using a hole, perform the following steps:

1. Define the feature scope for the assembly feature (Edit/Feature Scope).

2. Select on the face where the hole will be created.

3. Select Simple from the Insert/Assembly Feature/Hole menu.

4. Specify the End Condition and the Diameter.

5. Select OK to complete this function.

In summary, the following guidelines should be used when creating an assembly feature:

- The scope of an assembly feature should be defined prior to creating the assembly feature.
- The scope of the assembly can be redefined to include or exclude assembly components.
- Components should be selected after the Feature Scope dialog box has been brought up.
- An assembly feature will affect only components listed under Feature Scope.
- Assembly features will not revert back to the original components.

Interference Detection

Interference checking is used to determine if two or more components interfere with one another. This is a useful feature because assemblies can be checked for problems prior to physical prototypes. Assembly interference can be identified and corrected early in the design process. Interference detection can only be performed in an assembly.

The system will display the interference using a highlighted box showing a rectangular boundary box of the interference. This box is a representation of the interference and illustrates the smallest possible bounding area the interference could exist in. This helps illustrate the height, width, and length of the area of concern. Objects to be included in the interference check must be selected. These selected assembly components will highlight in the usual green color. There may be more than one area of interference. The following illustration shows interference detection.

Interference detection.

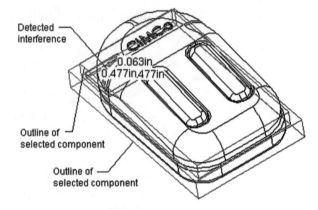

To check for component interference in an assembly, perform the following steps:

1. Select Interference Detection from the Tools menu.

2. Click in the Selected Components list box and select the components to be checked from FeatureManager.

3. Click on the Recheck button.

4. Pick the interferences listed in the Interference list to display each interference. New components can be selected by holding down the Control key and selecting or deselecting components. Select Recheck to start an interference check with the selected components.

5. Select OK to exit, or select Recheck to recheck interference with newly selected assemblies.

Each listed interference can be viewed graphically by selecting it from the Interference list. The system will graphically display where and how much interference occurred. The fields Component1 and Component2 will display the component names for the selected interference. Components can be selected before or after starting this function, as is the case with all SolidWorks dialog boxes.

AutoCAD allows for checking interference and actually creating a solid from the result. The solid can then be used in a Boolean operation to modify components in the assembly. SolidWorks does not permit this. It is up to you to find the interference and then modify the assembly as needed.

As you learned earlier, it is possible to simulate motion in an assembly. It would be ideal if the interference detection could be run at the same time motion was being applied to the assembly components. However, each position must be defined manually and checked individually within SolidWorks. Concurrent function is the domain of very high-end modelers and analysis software and is outside the limitations of SolidWorks without special add-on packages.

Insert Cavity

Assembly components can be used to create cuts in other assembly components, very similar to an AutoCAD Boolean subtraction. A common use of this function is to create a cut in a mold base or insert that defines the mold cavity. This method allows you to enter part shrinkage that takes into account the cooling of the material, which is something AutoCAD does not offer.

The mold cavity is derived from the design part geometry, and any changes to the design part will be updated in the mold cavity parts. Therefore, a standard cavity block or insert could be defined and reused. Care should be taken to create a copy of the standard part because the cavity function will change the part. Save As or Save As Copy can be used to rename the standard part.

Derive Component Part can be used to break a mold base into multiple mold parts. The cavity function is performed first to cut the design component from the mold base. The following are differences between Base Part, Cavity, and Derived Component Part. The illustration that follows shows a cavity.

- Base Part is used when a single part can be used to create a new part. An example would be a casting and the machined finished part. There are no assembly references for the original base part.

- Derived Component Part is used when a part needs to be created from an assembly component part. An example would be a mold base. The cavity block is created from the Cavity routine using a design part. This function requires the parts to be in the assembly for the cavity to be defined.

- Cavity is used to create a cut in an assembly component while applying a shrinkage value. This also requires assembly references to the cavity block (target) and the design component. This function is used typically before the Derived Component Part function. Whereas Cavity would be used to create the cut itself, Derived Component Part would be used to create both halves of the mold.

Results of the Cavity routine.

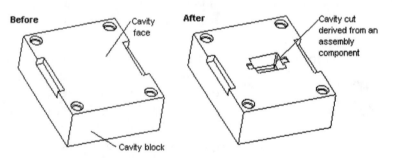

The following are the required documents when you create a cavity cut:

- Create the cavity block or mold base. This will be the target for the cavity cut.

- Create the design component used to define the cavity cut in the cavity block or mold base.

- Create an assembly that contains the cavity block and the design component. The assembly should be mated to ensure proper placement of the design components.

To create a cavity cut, perform the following steps:

1. Create the mold base.

2. Create the molded part.

3. Create a new assembly.

4. Insert both parts into the assembly.

5. Mate the mold base to the component. Distance and coincident mates are commonly used for this. Ideally, the design component should be centered within the mold base.

6. Select the Save icon or select Save from the File menu to save the assembly.

7. Right click on the mold base component in FeatureManager and select Edit Part.

8. Select Cavity from the Insert/Features menu.

9. Select the Design Component.

10. Specify a Scaling Factor, if required.

11. If a scaling factor is used, specify the Scaling Type.

12. Select OK to continue.

You might know some of the Cavity routine properties. The following expand on these properties:

Design Component	Displays the name of the design components used to define the cavity. More than one design component can be selected. Click in the list box before selecting components.
Scaling Type	Select About Centroid or About Origin. This is analogous to AutoCAD's Base Point when scaling geometry.
Scaling Factor in %	Enter the scaling (shrinkage or expansion) factor for the material being used (+/–10%).

Some important guidelines for performing the Cavity routine (sometimes called the Core and Cavity) follow. This summary is provided to help new users through this somewhat advanced topic.

- Create a backup copy of any standard parts (i.e., mold cavities) so that if they are accidentally overwritten, the original part can be retrieved.

- It may be convenient to create a directory with standard mold base sizes for common use.

- Multiple components may be placed in the mold cavity.

- The mold base normally would totally enclose the component parts, but this is not mandatory.

- The part should have a datum plane that can be used as the parting line. This will allow for easy alignment and cutting the mold components. This is a suggestion; it is not mandatory.

- Create derived component parts to split the mold into multiple parts, or use Base Part to create the halves of the mold.

Derived Component Part

A derived component part is used to break assembly components into multiple parts. All new parts are derived from the original assembly component. Any changes to the original assembly component will be reflected in the derived component parts. The example described in this section is a mold base created via a derived component part method. The following illustration shows a derived component part.

Possible results of using a derived component part.

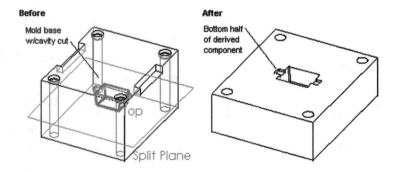

Before

Mold base
w/cavity cut

Top

Split Plane

After

Bottom half
of derived
component

To create a component derived from an existing assembly component, perform the following steps:

1. Using the left mouse button, select the desired assembly part in FeatureManager.

2. Select Derive Component Part from the File menu.

3. A new window will open with the derived part file.

4. Change or add features to the new part. In the previous illustration, a cut was performed to chop the derived part in half.

5. Save the part under a new name.

Remember, any feature that references another feature in another part or assembly is called an in-context feature. In-context features are shown in the FeatureManager design tree using the in-context arrow. This also holds true when creating parts based on other parts, such as using the Base Part or Derived Component Part functions.

Explode

Explode expands the active assembly, revealing how the assembly would be put together. This image can be used on drawings to describe assembly sequences or images for user manuals. Each assembly step can be defined within the exploded view. Only one exploded view can be defined within a configuration.

Exploded views are controlled using ConfigurationManager. This is a FeatureManager area used for setting, defining, and editing configurations. Each configuration can have its own exploded view. To set the exploded view to the default assembly state, select the configuration named Default when creating the exploded view.

Explode steps can be defined to view the exploded assembly by exploding each step of the assembly process one by one. The step editing tools (shown in the illustration of Asembly Exploder further in this chapter) allow you to define and modify multiple assembly steps with the current exploded view. Assembly steps can be added, edited, or deleted. The following illustrations show an exploded assembly and the objects within Configuration-Manager.

An exploded assembly.

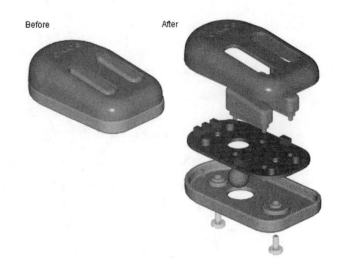

ConfigurationManager objects.

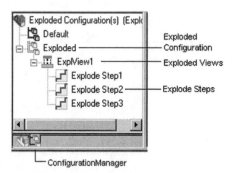

To add an exploded view to an active assembly, perform the following steps:

1. Open ConfigurationManager by selecting the configuration icon at the bottom of FeatureManager.

2. Right click on the configuration to create the exploded view and select New Exploded View.

3. Select Auto Explode to allow SolidWorks to explode the assembly automatically.

4. The exploded view may be edited as desired (see the next procedure).

5. Select OK to continue, or select Cancel to quit.

To edit an exploded view or create one manually, you would perform the following steps. The illustration that follows shows the Explode dialog box.

1. Open ConfigurationManager by selecting the ConfigurationManager icon at the bottom of FeatureManager.

2. Right click on the configuration for which to create the exploded view and select New Exploded View; or if an existing exploded view, select Edit Definition.

3. Edit, delete, or add the explode steps as desired.

4. Select OK to continue.

The Explode dialog box prior to adding an explode step.

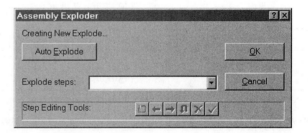

Adding the exploded view is easy, but sometimes Solid-Works does not place the components in the desired locations and the exploded view should be edited. If the Auto Explode button is not convenient, you can add steps on your own. As soon as you click on the icon for adding a step, the rest of the dialog box (shown in the following illustration) opens up to show additional attributes you can use to add your own steps in the explode process. The following are the attributes in the SolidWorks Explode dialog box:

Auto Explode	Pick to explode the current configuration.
Explode Steps	Displays the current explode step. Pick from the pull-down list or select the step editing tool arrows to show an explode step.

Explode dialog box after adding an explode step.

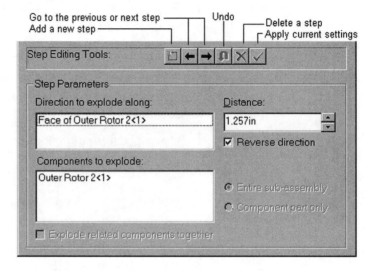

The following are the step editing tools:

New	Select to define a new explode step. Select Apply to add the explode step.
Previous	Select to list the previous explode step.
Next	Select to list the next explode step.
Undo	Select to reverse a change.
Delete	Select to delete the current explode step.
Apply	Select to show the current distance setting onscreen.
Direction to explode along	Pick an edge that defines the explode direction. To select a new edge, pick inside the field and select the desired edge. A cylindrical surface whose axial direction will define the explode direction may also be used.
Distance	Enter the distance to explode the selected component.
Reverse direction	Select to reverse the explode direction.
Components to explode	Displays the components to be exploded. Components can be added by selecting within this field and then selecting the components to be added. Components can be removed by selecting the component and pressing the Delete key.
Entire subassembly	Check to explode the entire selected subassembly. This option is only available when a subassembly has been selected.

Component part only	Check to explode only the selected component of an assembly. This option is only available when a subassembly has been selected.
Explode related components together	Check to explode related (parent/child) components together. This option is only available when selecting components with external references.

Once the exploded view has been obtained, expanding and collapsing it is only a right mouse click away. To collapse an exploded view, perform the following steps:

1. Right click on the exploded view name in ConfigurationManager.

2. Select Collapse.

To activate an exploded view, perform the following steps:

1. Right click on the configuration name in ConfigurationManager.

2. Select Explode.

In Chapter 8, you will learn how an exploded assembly can be shown in a drawing layout. Multiple exploded views can be defined, but only one can be defined per configuration. New explode steps are placed at the end of the explode step list. The name defaults to "Explode Step x," where x is the explode step number.

To edit an exploded view, the parent configuration must be active. If the exploded step is selected in FeatureManager, a dashed green line will be shown. Dragging the end of this green line is a very easy way of changing the explode distance of the exploded component. The component will be dynamically dragged onscreen as the line is dragged.

AutoCAD does not have explode capabilities. AutoCAD assembly files are a drawing file with a collection of entities within it. In this respect, the individual entities are not really separate. It is not possible to create various configurations because the separate components are actually all part of the same file. About the closest workaround for creating configurations would be to make duplicates of all entities in the file and place them on a different layer, where the entities can be moved to create the appearance of an exploded state. This is at best a cumbersome workaround. Without configuration capabilities, exploded states cannot exist.

Join

Join creates a new part out of multiple assembly components, joining them into one component. This could be used to simulate a welded assembly, or to create a part for use with analysis software. The Join command does not affect the original parts. The join operation would fail if the parts that defined the join were not available, whether because they were moved or deleted. This is because the parts are needed to define the joined component. An external reference is established to the defining components. The following illustration shows three joined parts.

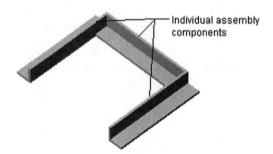

Implementing the Join command.

Similar to the Cavity routine, Join requires that you create a new part in the assembly. This new part file will become the joined part. To join two or more parts from an assembly into one part, perform the following steps:

1. Create an assembly and insert the parts to be joined.

2. Constrain the parts as necessary.

3. Click on Insert/Component/New.

4. Select a face on which to sketch. This is not overly important, as a sketch will not actually be required. However, the plane should still be selected.

5. Click on Insert/Features/Join. The Join dialog box will appear.

6. Using the left mouse button, select the parts to be joined in FeatureManager.

7. Select OK to continue.

8. To return to editing the assembly, right click on the assembly name in FeatureManager and select Edit Assembly.

AutoCAD's Union command is similar to Join. Union adds solid parts together, creating a new solid. Unlike Solid-Works, creating the new solid does not result in a new part file. SolidWorks creates a completely new part file that externally references the originals. Making changes to the originals results in the joined component being updated. This type of associativity is not present in AutoCAD. AutoCAD's unioned part could be Write Blocked out to a separate file, but there is no associativity to the originals.

Another command that follows closely behind the Join command is the ability to add weld beads to an assembly. This is discussed in the next section.

Weld Beads

Weld beads can be defined in an assembly to represent the weld beads used to weld parts together. These can be used to create detail drawings and show an added aspect of reality. The advantage of placing weld beads on an assembly is that the annotation function can be used in the drawing to document the weld beads. The engineering characteristics of the feature (weld beads) are defined at the time the beads are created. This can be easier than trying to document these characteristics when the drawings are produced. The following illustration shows a weld bead.

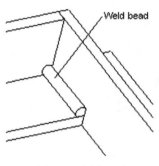

Adding weld beads.

When a weld bead is created, SolidWorks creates a new part file that contains the weld bead. The bead becomes another part file in the assembly. Before creating weld beads, it is not necessary to join the components. It is common to do so, but this is not a requirement. To add a weld feature between two part faces, perform the following steps. The illustration that follows shows the Weld Bead wizard.

1. Select Weld Bead from the Insert/Assembly Feature menu.

2. Select the weld type and click on Next to continue.

3. Select the weld shape, specify the measurements for the bead, and click on Next to continue.

4. Select the weld faces. These will be different, depending on the weld type being created.

5. Click on Next to continue.

6. Enter the name for the weld bead part file or accept the default name SolidWorks assigns.

7. Select Finish to continue.

Page 1 of the Weld Bead wizard.

Example Assembly

The robot assembly shown in the following illustration uses an assembly layout sketch. The layout sketch is used to control the angle of components in the assembly. Plane Base_Ang can be changed to rotate the robot arm. The plane Gripper_Ang can be used to rotate the gripper arm around the attachment point. Some of the components in this assembly were created using the top-down design process discussed early in this chapter. Other components were already built and simply inserted into the assembly. It is not intended that you attempt to create this assembly, as many steps have been left out regarding the actual design process.

The assembly layout is used to define the linkage between the robot components. The sketch is aligned to the center of the base and each sketch entity has a defined length. The angle of each sketch leg can be defined with an angular dimension or dragged within the sketch to the desired position. The following series of illustrations depicts a typical assembly procedure. The completed assembly is shown in the final illustration.

Step 1:
Define the function
of the assembly.

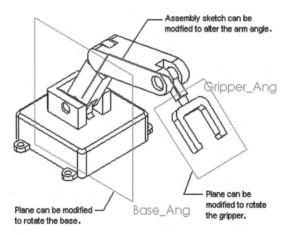

Assembly sketch can be modfied to alter the arm angle.

Gripper_Ang

Plane can be modified to rotate the gripper.

Plane can be modified to rotate the base.

Base_Ang

Step 2: Create the
assembly skeleton and
assembly control layout.

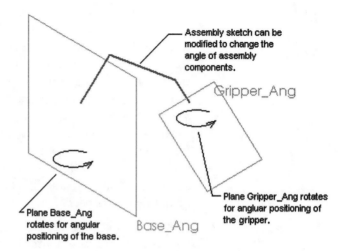

Assembly sketch can be
modified to change the
angle of assembly
components.

Gripper_Ang

Plane Gripper_Ang rotates
for angluar positioning of
the gripper.

Plane Base_Ang
rotates for angular
positioning of the base.

Base_Ang

Step 3: Incorporate
the base unit into the
assembly, and mate the
assembly and base unit
origins.

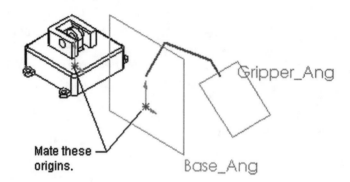

Gripper_Ang

Mate these
origins.

Base_Ang

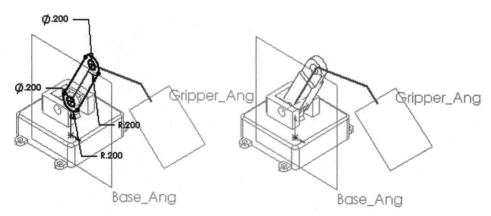

Ø.200

Ø.200

Gripper_Ang

R.200

R.200

Base_Ang

Gripper_Ang

Base_Ang

Step 4: Incorporate Arm 1 into the assembly and mate it to the base.

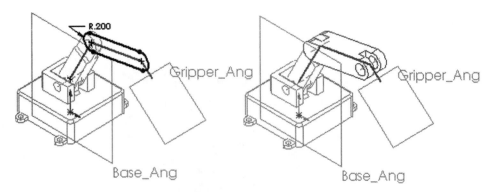

Step 5: Create Arm 2 in-context within the assembly.

Step 6: Insert the gripper brace and mate it to Arm 2.

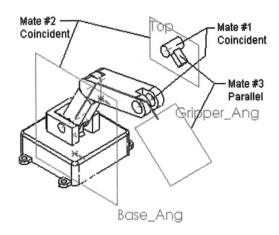

Step 7: Insert the gripper finger into the assembly and mate it to the gripper base and the plane Gripper_Ang.

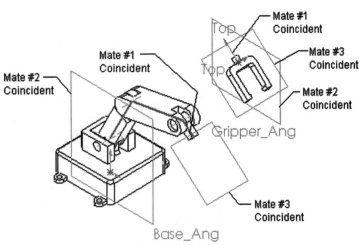

Completed assembly.

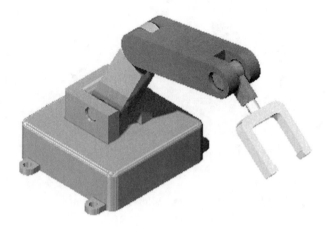

Summary

The purpose of an assembly is to create a document that can be used to define, drive, and document the design of a product. The assembly can provide information that can help define the form, fit, and function of the design. Assembly mates should be defined in a manner that allows for the simulation of the actual assembly method. If a door hinges on a pivot and can be opened, the assembly should be constructed to mimic this functionality. The assembly can be reviewed in a number of different positions to determine the clearance and fit to other assembly components.

There are two main assembly types. These are bottom-up assemblies, where parts are brought into the assembly, and top-down assemblies, where parts are created from within the assembly. In the latter, parts created will contain external references to geometry in the assembly.

Mating relationships play a big role in assemblies. Without mates, parts would be free to move without rhyme or reason. Add appropriate mates that result in a model in which components move as they would in the real world. Use the Assembly toolbar icons to move or rotate assembly components individually. Interference detection can be used to check for component interference, and Explode can be used as a visual aid and to show assembly instructions within a drawing layout.

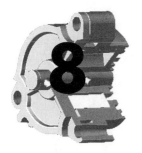

8 Drawings

Introduction

This chapter discusses how to create 2D drawings based on existing parts and assemblies. The automated process used to create drawings with SolidWorks is very user friendly and eliminates many of the tedious aspects normally associated with drafting. The ability to alter aspects of certain views, such as section lines and detail circles, can make what used to be hours of painstaking drafting nothing more than a tweak of a line or circle.

Dimensions created in a part do not have to be recreated. All of a part's dimensions can be easily inserted into a drawing with a few mouse clicks. The amount of detail and type of dimensioning or geometric tolerances can vary greatly between companies; therefore, you should establish a standard before embarking on a full-scale project. Many standards can be set in SolidWorks, such as ANSI, ISO, and JIS, to name a few.

Drawings are a unique type of document within Solid-Works, just as parts and assemblies are unique. The pull-down menu headings remain constant, as they did with assembly documents, which helps reduce confusion for the new user. What commands are contained within the pull-down menus depend on what SolidWorks document type is active at the time (i.e., part, drawing, or assembly). You will find that some of the pull-down menu commands remain the same and that the other menus display drawing commands.

Prerequisite   Because this chapter deals primarily with engineering drawings and drafting terminology, you should have at least a basic understanding of drafting. Also, many of the topics and the step-by-step procedures covered will assume that you have completed the previous chapters.

Content   The "Creating a Drawing" section describes drawing formats and sheets. These are the basic components used when creating a drawing. Drawing views, dimensions, and symbols are added after a drawing format has been established. This chapter will attempt to follow as closely as possible the actual sequence of events found when creating a drawing.

The section on creating views describes the various drawing views. Following that, the "Adding Dimensions" section describes how to display existing part or assembly annotations or create new dimensions to document a design. The section on drawing symbols describes these symbols (i.e., notes, balloons, and so on) and how they are used to add information to a drawing that dimensions do not provide.

Objectives   When you have finished the "Creating a Drawing" section, you should understand what a drawing format is and how it can be used, be able to define and import a drawing format, and understand drawing sheets and how they can be used to create multisheet drawings all within the same drawing file. Upon completion of the section on creating views, you should understand the various types of drawing views, be able to select a part or assembly for view creation, and understand how to define and manipulate drawing views.

With completion of the "Adding Dimensions" section, you should know the difference between an existing model annotation and a created dimension, be able to insert existing model annotations from a part or assembly, and be able to modify an existing dimension. When finished with the section on drawing symbols and annotations, you should understand how to add a wide range of model annotations and drawing symbols and be able to modify existing symbols, text, geometric tolerances, and any of the other annotation symbols. When you have completed the "Bill of Materials" section, you should be able to import a bill of material, including balloons.

About SolidWorks Drawings

Drawings are created as separate documents that become associated with existing parts and assemblies. This helps separate the functions of design and drafting into separate documents. The part is used in the design phase, and the drawing documents the finished product for manufacturing. This helps simplify the user interface and allows you to focus on the current task, rather than have the commands needed for parts, assemblies, and drawings all gathered in one document type and one interface.

Drawings are created using existing parts or assemblies. These part documents are created prior to creating the drawing, although the reverse can also be true. Not all that long ago, drafters and designers created 2D layouts that represented a model before the model was ever built. Now, through the use of solid modeling programs such as SolidWorks, a part can be created, checked, and visualized before the layout is ever started.

Most of the dimensions needed for a part are actually added while designing the part. It would be foolish to have to recreate all dimensions for a drawing; therefore, SolidWorks allows the importation of all part dimensions directly into a drawing layout. The dimensions and annotations (i.e., surface finish, geometric tolerance, and so on) can all be extracted from the part or assembly to help produce the detail drawing. The following are a few uses of drawings:

- Detail drawings for parts. Detailed drawings are used to display the dimensions used to create and document a design. The drawing should have sufficient views to display the desired dimensions.

- Design layouts can be created from assemblies. These layout drawings, which display important design-related features or functions, can be produced from a part or assembly.

- Quick reference drawings can be produced to measure a feature or dimension value. The purpose of this type of drawing is similar to the design layout but is simpler in nature. Quick prints can be used to impart information to others without creating a complete layout.

- Exploded assembly drawings can be produced from an assembly. An assembly can be exploded to indicate the assembly direction and order for those manufacturing the assembled product.

- Assembly drawings can be used to produce a bill of materials.

SolidWorks documents are fully associative. This means that any changes made to the part or assembly used to create a drawing will be automatically updated in the drawing. The display within the views is automatically cleaned up for hidden line removal or hidden lines in gray (or dashed) display modes.

The part or assembly is designed in the currently selected unit of measure (i.e., inches, mm, cm, and so on) at a scale of 1:1. This is similar to AutoCAD, wherein parts are normally drawn at full scale. Parts are not normally scaled until they are printed. This is typical of SolidWorks. AutoCAD's use of Paper Space allowed for different scaling of viewports. Again, this is similar to SolidWorks, where the drawings are created using views that can be displayed at a different view scale (i.e., 1:2, 2:1, and so on) than the part or assembly. Drawing formats and sheets are created using a selected paper size. The drawing views are scaled to fit within the selected paper size.

You do not have to be concerned with the paper space versus model space AutoCAD uses to simulate the various document types within SolidWorks. An approach wherein a part is created full size and drawing views are scaled to display the part or assembly is more flexible and easier for most users to work with. A drawing is shown in the following illustration.

A SolidWorks drawing.

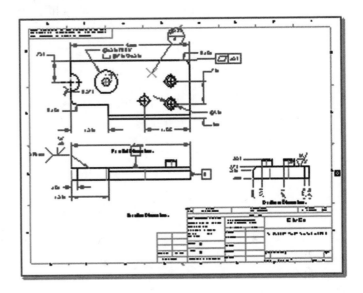

Creating a Drawing

Drawings are created as a means of documenting a part or assembly. A drawing can contain more that one part or assembly. As a matter of fact, a drawing can contain absolutely any combination of parts or assemblies of any configuration from any file. A drawing is a document that references the part or assembly used to define the drawing views. Because of this, if the original part used to create the drawing is somehow misplaced or deleted, the drawing will fail to open.

Drawings, or 2D layouts as they may be referred to in this chapter, can be used as a design tool by creating drawing views and dimensions that show the critical design dimensions of a part or assembly. As the design progresses, this drawing can be used as a reference to check these features and can even be used to make modifications to the part. Because drawings are bidirectionally associative with the part or assembly contained within it, any change made to a dimension will affect the part or assembly. Some companies do not want people viewing the drawings to have this capability. For those companies, this function can be disabled during the installation of the SolidWorks program.

Starting a new drawing is the same as starting a new part or assembly, but with one extra dialog box (shown in the following illustration). To start a new drawing, perform the following steps.

1. Click on File/New, or select the New icon.

2. Specify Drawing from the New dialog box.

3. In the Template to Use dialog box, specify Standard, Custom, or No Template for the template to use.

4. If No Template is selected, specify a Paper Size to use.

5. Click on OK.

Selecting a template to use.

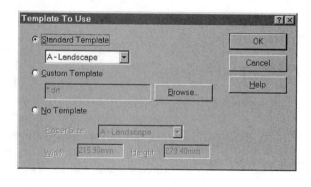

Creating a Standard 3 View Layout

Once a drawing is started, the next item on the agenda is usually bringing the part or assembly into the drawing. There are three methods for bringing a part or assembly into a drawing in order to achieve the standard top, front, and right-side engineering layout. The following are the steps required to create a standard engineering drawing using any of the three methods available:

1. Open Windows Explorer.

2. Drag the part or assembly file into the drawing window.

or

1. Open the part or assembly.

2. From the top of FeatureManager, drag the part or assembly name to the drawing window.

or

1. Click on Insert/Drawing View/Standard 3 View, or click on the Standard 3 View icon.

2. Click in the window of the part or assembly to be inserted into the drawing.

Any one of these methods will produce top, front, and right-side views of the part or assembly used. AutoCAD makes use of layers to separate 2D geometry from 3D geometry. Also, Paper Space can be used to create specific views within AutoCAD. None of the AutoCAD process is automated as it is in SolidWorks. If working with solids in AutoCAD (or even wireframe), it is a chore to create section views, manipulate scales for specific views, organize layers so that the proper entities are visible, and so on. It is certainly possible, and there are methods for all of these routines, but SolidWorks automates all of these processes.

One advantage AutoCAD has over SolidWorks is its ability to include attributes within blocks or template files. Inserting a drawing template or title block can be arranged so that it automatically asks you for all of the appropriate title block information during the import process. Templates can be set up in SolidWorks quite easily, but the template information usually needs to be edited for each drawing. The material that follows contains further explanation of the drawing formats (templates) and template options available.

Drawing Formats (Templates)

Templates are used to define drawing formats. These templates can be customized to suit your company's requirements. Drawing formats will be one of the first things that need defining when creating a drawing. Existing drawing formats, logos, and so on can be imported via DXF- or DWG-formatted files.

There are existing formats included with SolidWorks that can be customized to your requirements, or existing title blocks can be inserted via DXF or DWG file formats. These files are located in the \sldworks\data directory. A company logo can be inserted as a DXF, DWG, or OLE object.

The Edit Template function can be used to customize desired formats. Save the formats and then back up the format directory. It is a very good idea to back up formats into another directory and make these files read-only so that they cannot be changed or deleted. SolidWorks will replace standard format names when the software is updated. Having a backup copy ensures that your custom formats are not overwritten. The following is information that could be included in a drawing format. The illustration that follows shows a drawing format.

- Company name
- Revision
- Approved by/Date
- Scale
- Part Number
- Drawn by/Date
- Checked by/Date
- Sheet Number

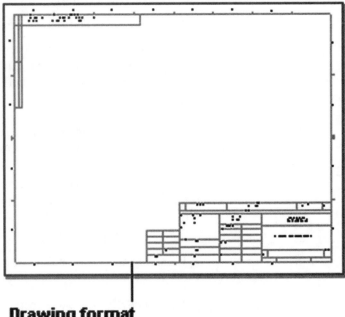

Typical drawing format.

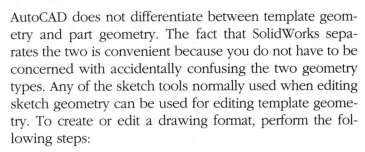

Drawing format

AutoCAD does not differentiate between template geometry and part geometry. The fact that SolidWorks separates the two is convenient because you do not have to be concerned with accidentally confusing the two geometry types. Any of the sketch tools normally used when editing sketch geometry can be used for editing template geometry. To create or edit a drawing format, perform the following steps:

1. To redefine a standard template, select the template name from the Standard Template field. To redefine an existing custom template, select Custom Template and enter the custom template name. To start a new, blank template, select No Template and specify a paper size.

2. Right click anywhere in a blank area on the sheet and select Edit Template.

3. Make any desired changes or additions to the format.

4. Select Save Template from the File menu.

5. Select the new format name by selecting Custom Template, or select Standard Template to overwrite an existing standard template.

6. Select OK to continue.

Once again, it is recommended that you make a copy of the new templates using Windows Explorer. These should be kept in a directory outside the SolidWorks directory. To import an existing drawing format from a DXF or DWG file, perform the following steps. The illustration that follows shows the import of a DXF or DWG file as a template.

1. Open the DXF or DWG drawing by selecting the Open icon, or by selecting Open from the File menu.

2. Select DXF or DWG from the Files of Type field.

3. Select the file to be opened.

4. Select OK to continue.

5. The Open DXF/DWG File dialog box will appear. Select the "Import to template" check box.

6. Click on OK.

7. Make any desired changes or additions to the format.

8. Select Save Template from the File menu.

9. Select the new format name by selecting Custom Template, or select Standard Template to overwrite an existing standard template.

10. Select OK to continue.

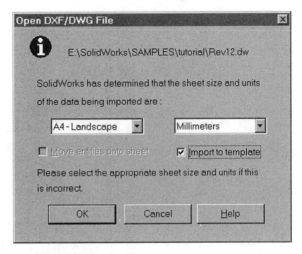

Importing a DXF or DWG file as a template.

It is typically easier to start with an existing template when making your own templates because this gives you something to work from. Back up all templates into a different directory before creating new templates so that there will be copies of the originals, and back up all new templates into a separate directory to keep them in a safe place. New releases to SolidWorks will overwrite any template changes made to the original files in the Solid-Works\Data directory. All drawing templates will have a .drt file extension.

Drawing Sheets

Drawing sheets are used to create a drawing using multiple drawing formats instead of one larger, single-format drawing. Using multiple sheets can allow for more space on individual sheets. This also allows for more information in one drawing file but less crowding on individual sheets. The tabs at the bottom of the drawing allow for easy navigation between different drawing sheets. Sheets can be added or removed depending on your needs. The following illustration shows an example of drawing sheet tabs.

Drawing sheet tabs for moving between sheets.

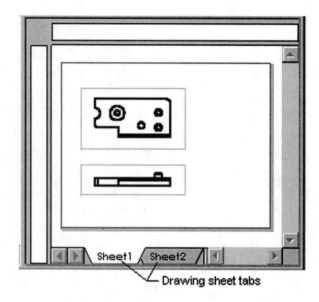

Drawing sheet tabs

Adding Drawing Sheets and Changing Properties

To add a new drawing sheet, perform the following steps:

1. Select Sheet from the Insert menu, or right click on a drawing sheet tab and select Add.

2. Select the format template, drawing scale, paper size, title, and type of projection (first or third).

3. Select OK to continue.

To delete a drawing sheet, perform the following:

1. Right click on the drawing sheet tab to be deleted and select Delete.

To change drawing sheet properties, perform the following steps:

1. Select Sheet Setup from the View menu, or right click on the desired tab and select Properties.

2. Edit the desired sheet properties.

3. Select OK to continue.

Drawing Sheet Properties

When editing the properties of a drawing sheet, the current template or sheet size can be changed, along with the drawing sheet scale and many other options. The following is a list of the various options available to you.

Name	Name of the drawing sheet. This is the name that appears on the sheet's tab.
Paper Size	Size and orientation of the sheet. Width and Height are only selectable for a custom paper size.
Width	Width of the sheet. Pick inside the field to change.
Height	Height of the sheet. Pick inside the field to change.
Scale	Scale of the entire drawing sheet. Pick inside each field to change. Be aware that individual drawing views can have their scale changed independently of the sheet.
Template	Select the template name to use for the sheet.
Type of Projection	Check first angle to view objects from the front and projected back. Check third angle to view objects from behind and projected forward. This method is primarily used in the USA, Canada, and parts of the UK.
Next Section Label	The next default section letter. Pick to change the default for the next section.
Next Detail Label	The next detail letter. Pick to change the default for the next detail.
Next Datum Label	The next datum letter. Pick to change the default for the next datum.

Activating Drawing Sheets

Because it is possible to have multiple drawing sheets, it would benefit you to know how to alternate between these drawing sheets. This is a very simple procedure. To make the next drawing sheet active, perform the following:

1. Select the sheet name from the sheet tab at the bottom of the drawing, or select Next Sheet from the View menu.

To make the previous drawing sheet active, perform the following:

1. Select the sheet name from the sheet tab at the bottom of the drawing, or select Previous Sheet from the View menu.

AutoCAD does not use sheets in the same sense that SolidWorks does. The closest way to simulate drawing sheets in AutoCAD would be to have independent layers in AutoCAD's Paper Space. Layers would have to be turned on and off to view the specific "sheets." It is much easier to click on a tab to view a sheet, as in SolidWorks.

Creating Views

Drawing views are created to display different orientations or snapshots of a part or assembly. The drawing view's alignment, orientation, and hidden line display are controlled and updated automatically when any changes are made to the part or assembly. Drawing views can be used to create views of parts or assemblies. These views display a part or assembly using orthographic views and can be projected using first- or third-angle projection. More than one part or assembly can be displayed within a single drawing.

Drawing views are used to display different view orientations of the same part or assembly. The scale of the view is independent of the actual part or assembly. The scale of the drawing views can be different from the part or assembly, and different views within the drawing can have different view scales. The illustration at left shows the standard three views.

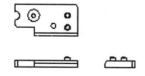

Standard 3 views

The three standard views.

AutoCAD does have the ability to create any of the views SolidWorks can. However, the process is much more cumbersome. Model geometry must either be duplicated in order to create the other "view" in model space, or viewports must be created and set up within Paper Space and then the geometry and layers manipulated to create the desired view. SolidWorks creates snapshots of the model, which update as the model changes. Crosshatch is created automatically, not manually. Projected and auxiliary views are automatically projected.

Alignments between views are automatic and adjustable. The list is quite extensive. Without getting into every last difference between AutoCAD and SolidWorks, suffice it to say that many of the procedures used to create drawing views will probably be a lot easier and much more user friendly than those the AutoCAD user is accustomed to.

Because the methods for inserting the three standard views of top, front, and right side into a drawing layout have already been discussed, the rest of this section is devoted to the remainder of the view types accessible to the SolidWorks user. It will be assumed at this point that you have already created a new drawing and have the standard three-view layout inserted into the drawing.

Activating Views

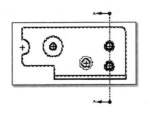

An activated view has a red border.

For specific geometry to be associated with a particular view, that view must be activated. Activating a view is simple enough. What is most important is that you remember to do it! To activate a view, either double click on the view border, or right click on the view border and select Activate View. If the view is not activated before adding a detail circle or section line, the view options of Detail View or Section View will not be available. The illustration at left shows an activated view.

Activating a view before adding geometry serves another function. If the view is moved to a different location, any geometry added to the view while it was active will move with the view.

Projected Views

Orthographic view

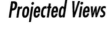

A projected view.

To create an orthographically projected view from an existing view, perform the following steps. The illustration at left shows a projected view.

1. Select the view to project from.

2. Click on the Projection icon or select Projection from the Insert, Drawing View menu.

3. Select the side and location for the new view. For instance, clicking on above the selected view will project a new view above it.

Relative to Model View

One of the view types you can specify is the relative-to-model view. This takes a little bit of input on your part, but can be used when a precise orientation needs to be created normal to a particular face. To create a view oriented relative to model faces, perform the following steps:

1. Select the Relative to Model icon, or select Relative to Model from the Insert/Drawing View menu.

2. Use the Window menu to activate the part window.

3. Click on a face of the part.

4. Select the orientation for the selected face in the dialog box that appears (see the following illustration).

Drawing View Orientation dialog box.

1. Click on a second face.

2. Select the orientation for the second face.

3. Make the drawing the active window.

4. Select the location for the new view on the drawing. (The illustration that follows shows a view oriented relative to model faces.)

View relative to model.

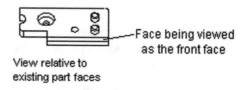

Named Views

A named view allows you to bring any previously saved view into the drawing. This can be a system view already defined by SolidWorks, a view named by you, or the current model view. First, take a look at how to save a specific view within a part. Open a sample part to use in this example and follow along with these steps:

1. Rotate the model until the desired view is obtained.

2. Click on View/Orientation to open up the Orientation dialog box.

3. Click on the Add button.

4. Name the view.

5. Click on OK to complete the procedure.

Notice that the new view with the name you gave it is listed in the View Orientation list box. Double click on the view name to go to that view, just like you would to go to any other view listed in the Orientation dialog box.

Now that you know how to create any named view, take it one step further and import that named view into the drawing. To create a view from a named part or assembly orientation, perform the following steps. The illustration at left shows a named view.

1. Select the Named View icon, or select Named View from the Insert/Drawing View menu.

2. Use the Window menu to activate the part or graphics window.

3. Select in the part or graphics window.

4. Select a view from the Orientation menu list. A single click on it is all that is needed.

5. Use the Window menu to activate the drawing window.

6. Select the location for the new view on the drawing.

Named view (Iso)

Sample of a named view; in this case, an Isometric view.

Auxiliary Views

An auxiliary view is used to show a planar face straight on that otherwise would not appear normal to the screen. Sometimes there are details that are difficult to distinguish on the surface of a part unless that surface is being displayed in a plane view. Many times the only way to see the surface straight on is to use the relative-to-model view or auxiliary view.

In SolidWorks, selecting a model edge allows a view to be projected perpendicular from that model edge so that the face of that model edge can be viewed parallel to the screen. To create an auxiliary view from a selected model edge, perform the following steps. The illustration at left shows an auxiliary view.

1. Select the edge to project the auxiliary view from. The view will be defined perpendicular to the selected edge.

2. Click on the Auxiliary icon, or select Auxiliary from the Insert/Drawing View menu.

Auxiliary views must be from an angled edge. Otherwise, if the edge is horizontal or vertical, SolidWorks thinks you are trying to create a projected view. Projected views are created slightly differently than auxiliary views. Read on for the procedure used to create a projected view.

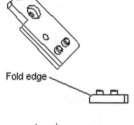

Fold edge

Auxiliary view.

Detail Views

Detail views are used to show an area of a view at a larger scale. The detail view allows for detailing a feature at a larger scale than the rest of the drawing. A detail view will update automatically with any changes to the original view or geometry, just as any other view in SolidWorks would. A detail or section view is related to the view (as a child) used to define the section or detail view. If the parent view is removed, the views created from this view will also be removed. The following illustration shows a detail view.

Detail view.

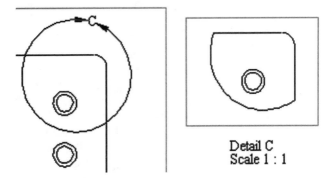

Detail C
Scale 1 : 1

To create a blown-up detail of an existing view, perform the following steps:

1. Activate the view to create a detail view.

2. Create a circle that defines the boundary of the detail view.

3. Select the circle.

4. Select Detail from the Insert/Drawing View menu or select the Detail View icon.

5. The detail view will be created. Select the detail view border with the left mouse button and drag it to the desired location.

To change the detail view label, perform the following steps:

1. With the left mouse button, double click on the Detail label.

2. Enter the new detail letter. The detail view name will update automatically.

When creating a detail view, remember that detail view notes are associated with the detail letter after insertion. Therefore, both values can be modified and the other value will update automatically. To change the name of a detail view, double click with the left mouse button and type in the new name. These properties can also be changed by right clicking on the detail view and selecting

Edit Properties, or by selecting Properties from the Edit menu. To reposition the detail view letter, select the detail letter and drag the mouse to the new location. It is also possible to drag the position and size of the detail circle itself. The detail view will automatically update, but may need repositioning.

Detail and section views have something in common as far as the mechanics involved with creating the views. Geometry must be added to the view in each case. This is not too surprising, considering that detail circles are needed for detail views and section lines are needed for section views. What is significant is how SolidWorks keeps track of the geometry that needs to be created.

Section Views

A section view is used to show a cutaway view showing the interior detail of a part in an assembly. This view does not affect the part or assembly components sectioned for the drawing view. The drawing section is used only for visualization purposes within the drawing.

A section view differs from a part section view and an assembly cut. A part section view is used only within a part to view a cutaway. A part section cannot be displayed within another document. An assembly feature cut is used to create a cutaway for visualization purposes. An assembly feature can be displayed within a drawing, but the section lines are not created and managed automatically like a drawing section view would be. Actual assembly section views can be created within a drawing for this purpose.

Creating a Section View

Activating a view and sketching a line that defines the section line creates a section view. This line can be one segment or can be a number of contiguous (joined) segments. These line segments are then turned into a section line, and the view can be defined from the section line. A detail or section is related to the view used to define the section or detail view. If the parent view is deleted, the

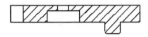

SECTION B-B
Scale 1 : 1

Basic Section view.

views created from this view will also be removed. The illustration at left shows a section view.

As with detail views, section views require geometry to be added to the view. Before this is done, the view must be activated so that SolidWorks can associate the geometry with the correct view. Section views require centerlines, which can then be turned into section lines or used to create section views directly. To create a section view, perform the following steps:

1. Activate the view.

2. Sketch a centerline across the geometry to be sectioned. The centerline should extend all the way across the geometry for a complete section view.

3. Select the centerline.

4. Select the Section View icon, or select Section from the Insert/Drawing View menu.

5. The section view will be created. With the left mouse button, select the section view border and drag it to the desired location.

Crosshatching

Crosshatching properties for section views can be changed. Crosshatching is created automatically when a section view is created. Unlike AutoCAD, crosshatching cannot be created as a separate entity. The crosshatching pattern can be changed when the default crosshatching characteristics are not sufficient for a section view due to the size or pattern type. The illustration at left shows section view crosshatching. To modify an existing section's crosshatching, perform the following steps:

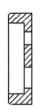

SECTION A-A
Section view crosshatching.

1. Right click on the crosshatching to be modified and select Crosshatch Properties.

2. Edit the values as desired (see the following illustration of this dialog box).

3. Select OK to continue. Select Apply to make the change but keep the Crosshatch Properties dialog box active for further changes.

Crosshatch Properties dialog box.

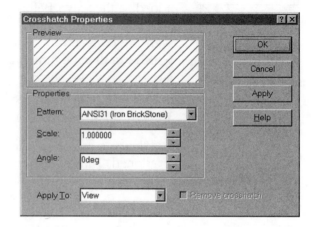

The following are adjustable pattern properties and other options within the Crosshatch Properties dialog box.

Preview	Shows a preview of the crosshatching with the specified changes.
Pattern	Pick different crosshatch patterns from this list.
Scale	Crosshatch scale. Enter a higher value to make the crosshatching smaller. Enter a new value in this field or select the up/down arrows to increment/decrement the scale value.
Angle	Crosshatch angle. Enter a new value in this field or select the up/down arrows to increment/decrement the angular value.
Apply To:	*Select the scope of change from the following:*
View	All faces or components in the active section view.
Component	Selected faces of an assembly.
Region	Selected surfaces.
Remove crosshatch	Check to remove crosshatching from this section view.

The default crosshatch type is ANSI31 (Iron Brick Stone). The default crosshatch pattern can be defined for the current drawing or for all new drawings by setting the values in the Crosshatch tab in the Tools/Options menu.

Aligned Section Views

Aligned section views are very similar to section views but with one difference. The section line itself must contain two segments that should not be orthogonal. During the creation of the aligned section view, SolidWorks "unfolds" the section line so that the view is perpendicular to each section line segment. The illustration that follows shows an aligned section view.

Aligned section view.

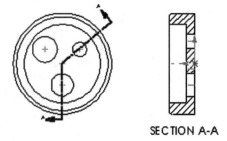

SECTION A-A

Take a look at the illustration that follows to get a better idea of the various section lines that can be created in SolidWorks.

Section lines that can be created in SolidWorks.

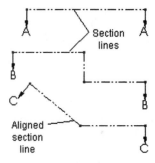

Creating an Aligned Section View

Aligned section views are used most often for cylindrical parts, but an aligned view can be used anywhere a two-segment angled section line needs to be created. To make an aligned section view, perform the following steps:

1. Activate the view.

2. Sketch a centerline across the geometry to be sectioned. The centerline should extend all the way across the geometry for a complete section view. If the part is cylindrical, the point where the section lines meet should usually be at the center of the part. However, this is not a requirement.

3. Select the centerline.

4. Select the Aligned Section View icon or select Aligned Section from the Insert/Drawing View menu.

5. The section view will be created. Select the section view border with the left mouse button and drag it to the desired location.

To modify the direction of the section line arrows, double click on the section line. To change the properties of a section line, perform the following steps:

1. Right click on the section line and select Properties.

2. Change the desired values (see the list that follows).

3. Select OK to continue.

Section Line Properties

A common mistake made by new users when attempting to edit a section view is to edit the properties of the section view, when in reality it is the section line itself that must be addressed. Right clicking on the section line and selecting Properties will bring up a dialog box with the following options. The illustration that follows shows the Section Line Properties dialog box.

Label	Section line text label.
Change direction of cut	Check to change the direction of the section cut. This can also be accomplished by double clicking on the section line.
Scale with model changes	Check to make the section scale change with the drawing sheet.
Partial section	A section view shows only the geometry cut by the section. If the section line does not pass completely through the geometry, check this option.

Display only surface cut	Only the portion of the model cut by the section line will be shown. Geometry behind the cut will not be shown.
Font	Uncheck the Use Document's Font field to make the Font button selectable. Select the Font button to change the section line text font. This works well for setting the size of the section line labels.

The Section Line Properties dialog box.

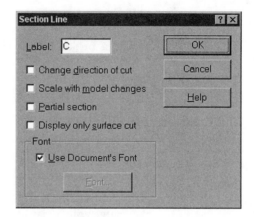

Sometimes it may be desirable to create a simple section line without creating a section view. To do this, follow the same procedure for adding a section view up to the point where the view is actually inserted. Instead of adding a section or aligned section view, click on Insert/Make Section Line. This will change the centerline into a section line without creating a new view.

One other comment on section views should be made. If the scale of a section view is modified, the text associated with the view will alter to display the new scale. The reverse is also true. By modifying the text associated with a section view, the scale of the view is changed as well.

Broken Views

Broken views are used to display one or two ends of a view with the middle portion removed. This type of view can be used to show details on long parts that would normally not fit on the paper. A typical application would be a tube or pipe with detail on both ends and the center removed to fit the part on a smaller drawing. This also

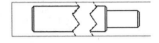

Broken view

Broken view.

allows the part to be shown at a greater scale than would be possible if the entire geometry was required on the drawing. A broken view is shown in the illustration at left.

Broken views can be created in AutoCAD, but once again this is a manual procedure that must be done by cutting and trimming entities, adding break lines, and modifying dimension values to read correctly. SolidWorks automates this process in a way you should be coming to expect. To create a broken view, perform the following steps:

1. Select the view.

2. Select Horizontal Break or Vertical Break from the Insert menu.

3. Position each of the breaks by selecting a break line with the left mouse button and dragging the break line to the desired location.

4. Right click on the view and select Break View. The view will be broken at the break line positions.

To remove a broken view, perform the following:

1. Right click on the view and select Unbreak View.

To change break line types or move the break lines, perform the following steps:

1. Select the break line with the left mouse button and drag it to a new position.

2. Right click on one of the break lines and select Straight Cut, Curve Cut, or Zig Zag Cut to change the break line type.

Only one broken view can be created per view. However, more than one broken view can exist on a drawing. Dimensions will read accurately when applied to the broken view.

Empty View

Empty views are just what they sound like: views without geometry. SolidWorks includes this function so that you can create a view, make it active, and add geometry that will move with the view border. In this respect, you can "create" their own views from scratch. With all of the functionality SolidWorks provides, this function does not seem very useful.

Modifying and Aligning Views

Preexisting views can have their attributes (i.e., scale and alignment) changed. The alignment of views is defined by the creation method of the view. Alignment properties can be removed or added to existing views. Views that have other drawing views projected or created from them can also have their alignments broken. Moving a view requires that you select the view's border and drag the view by its border. Sometimes increasing or decreasing the size of the view's border is needed to make moving the view easier. To move a view or resize a view's borders, perform the following steps. The illustration at left shows view handles used for resizing the view.

1. Select the view by selecting on the view boundary with left mouse button.

2. Select one of the view's resize handles with the left mouse button. These handles appear at each corner of the view boundary and at the center of each boundary segment.

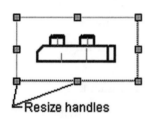

Resize view handles.

3. Drag the handle to the desired size or position. The view border cannot be resized to the point where the geometry will not fit in it.

To change a view's properties, perform the following steps:

1. Right click on the view and select Properties.

2. Change the drawing scale if desired.

3. Select OK to continue.

In the last example, you may also have noticed the ability to change a drawing view's configuration. This is possible only if other configurations already exist in the part or assembly. Any configuration present in the part or assembly can be viewed within a particular view. To access a particular configuration, perform the following steps:

1. Right click on the view and select Properties.

2. In the Configuration Information section, select Use Named Configuration.

3. Specify the configuration name from the drop-down list.

4. Select OK.

It is sometimes necessary to break the alignment of a view so that it can be moved to a different location. To break an existing view alignment, perform the following steps. The illustration at left shows a broken view alignment.

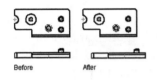

Broken view alignment.

1. Right click on the view whose alignment you want to break and select Break Alignment.

To align a view horizontally, perform the following steps. The illustration at left shows a view aligned horizontally.

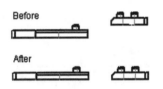

Horizontal view alignment.

1. Select the view to be aligned horizontally.

2. Press the right mouse button and select Align Horizontal.

3. Select the target view to set the alignment.

To align a view vertically, perform the following steps. The illustration that follows shows a view aligned vertically.

1. Select the view to be aligned vertically.

2. Press the right mouse button and select Align Vertical.

3. Select the target view to set the alignment.

Vertical view alignment.

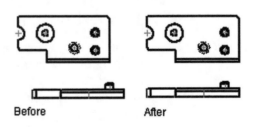

To reset the view alignment to its original default alignment state, perform the following. The illustration that follows shows a reset view alignment.

1. Right click on the view whose alignment should be returned to its default state and select Default Alignment.

Reset view alignment.

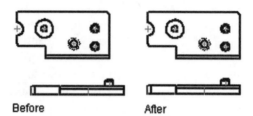

Before   After

To temporarily hide a view, perform the following:

1. Right click on the view to be hidden and select Hide View.

When a view is hidden, its border is still selectable. By selecting the view's border, it is possible to restore a hidden view. To restore a hidden view, perform the following:

1. Right click on the border of the hidden view and select Unhide View.

There are a few things before closing this section on drawing views that should be mentioned. Drawing views can be copied and pasted to other drawing sheets. View borders are shown with a green border when they are selected, and a selected view can be moved, deleted, or activated. Their borders are shown with a light gray edge when they are not selected or activated. These borders will not print, but the borders can be turned off, if you prefer, in the Drawing tab of the Options dialog box. Remember to activate a view before adding geometry. Otherwise, geometry will not be associated with the view and will not move with the view. When activated, a drawing view is outlined in red.

Adding Dimensions

Dimensions are added to a drawing to communicate the design intent of the part and to identify the critical functions and inspection dimensions. The dimensions discussed within this section are discussed within the context of drawing creation. (Chapter 5 discusses creating 2D sketch dimensions to create part features.)

AutoCAD's dimensioning commands seem fairly straightforward and easy to implement. However, if you have had to change the characteristics of just a few dimensions, you know the difficulties that can arise in changing a dimension's properties. There are many system variables that must be modified manually or through the use of a dialog box. In addition, a dimension style must then be saved and a dimension updated in order to be able to use the specified style. SolidWorks does away with all that by incorporating a global setting for all dimensions and the ability to modify any dimension's properties to achieve the desired result.

The dimensions used to create the 2D sketches can be used to annotate the drawing. These dimensions are referred to as model dimensions. The Dimension, Horizontal Dimension, and Vertical Dimension commands can be used in sketch mode to create model dimensions. These modifiable dimensions are used to drive the part feature size.

The Dimension, Horizontal, Vertical, Baseline, and Ordinate Dimension commands can be used to create dimensions within the drawing. These dimensions are referred to as reference dimensions. These dimensions cannot be used to drive the model geometry. They show the size of the feature and will change value only if the geometry changes. Model dimensions are shown in black. Reference dimensions are shown in gray, with parentheses being an optional trait.

Model Dimensions Versus Reference Dimensions

The following are points to keep in mind when comparing model dimensions and reference dimensions:

- Model dimensions reuse sketch dimensions from a part, eliminating the time required to redefine layout dimensions.

- Model dimensions can be changed within the drawing and the corresponding drawing views and part will update automatically.

- Dimension parameters and annotations can be defined within a model during feature creation. These parameters could be tolerance values, appended or prefixed text, geometric tolerances, and so on. The advantage to defining these parameters during feature creation is that a designer can capture design intent when the feature is defined and not have to go back later and try to remember the intent for the feature. For companies that employ engineers, designers, and draftspersons, the person who creates the model can also define the engineering attributes for the design.

- Reference dimensions can be added when and where it makes sense in creating a drawing.

- Reference dimensions cannot be altered and cannot change model geometry.

AutoCAD does not differentiate between model dimensions and reference dimensions. It has no need to, because there are no parametric relationships to be concerned with. Dimensions cannot alter model geometry; therefore, all of AutoCAD's dimensions might be thought of as reference dimensions.

Model Dimensions and Annotations

Model dimensions are the sketch dimensions used to define part geometry. Annotations are additional attributes that can be defined within a part or assembly and displayed in a drawing. Model dimensions shown on a drawing can be modified, and the model geometry will update after the Rebuild command has been issued. Model dimensions are shown in black, and reference dimensions are shown in gray. The following are types of model annotations:

- Cosmetic Threads
- Datum Targets
- Geometric Tolerance
- Notes
- Surface Finish

- Reference Dimensions
- Feature Dimensions
- Welds
- Datums

Model dimensions and annotations can be added to an entire view, feature, or assembly component. For this to occur, the proper object must be selected from the drawing's FeatureManager. The following list includes a brief description of each optional object that can have annotations added within a particular view. The illustration that follows shows model annotations.

View	Select the view or views to display annotations. The selected types of annotations are displayed within the selected views.
Feature	Select the feature or features to display annotations. The selected types of annotations are displayed for the selected features.
Component	Select the assembly component or components to display annotations. The selected types of annotations are displayed for the selected assembly components.

To display model annotations by view, perform the following steps:

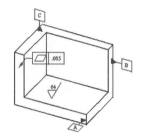

Model annotations.

1. Select the views to display model dimensions. To select multiple views, hold down the Control key and select the desired views.

2. Select Model Annotations from the Insert menu.

3. Select the types or annotations to be inserted. All Types can be selected to display all model annotations within the selected view. The default selection is Dimensions.

4. Select OK to continue.

To display model annotations using only selected features, perform the following steps:

1. Select the specific features to display model annotations. Multiple features can be selected by holding down the Control key and selecting the desired features.

2. Select Model Annotations from the Insert menu.

3. Select the types or annotations to be inserted. All Types can be selected to display all model annotations within the selected view. The default selection is Dimensions. The Import From field displays Selected Feature.

4. Select OK to continue.

To display model dimensions using only selected assembly components, perform the following steps:

1. Select the specific assembly components to display model annotations. Multiple components can be selected by holding down the Control key and selecting the desired features.

2. Select Model Annotations from the Insert menu.

3. Select the types or annotations to be inserted. All Types can be selected to display all model annotations within the selected view. The default selection is Dimensions. The Import From field displays Selected Component.

4. Select OK to continue.

Creating Reference Dimensions

Reference dimensions are added to a drawing as individual dimensions, as opposed to importing them, as in the previous procedure. This type of dimension is not parametric and cannot be used to drive model geometry. The default dimension type is point-to-point, point-to-line, and line-to-line, as shown in the following series of illustrations. When selecting a single line to dimension, the dimension lines are inserted parallel to the selected line. Generally speaking, adding reference dimensions is done the same way as when dimensions are added to sketch geometry. The mechanics are the same.

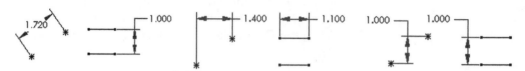

Reference dimensions.   *Horizontal reference dimensions.*   *Vertical reference dimensions.*

The Dimension command will place the dimension value in a direct line between the two points. A dimension can be placed between two vertices, a single sketch entity, or two sketch entities.

If you require a refresher course on how to insert dimensions, see Chapter 5, regarding inserting dimensions. Once again, adding dimensions in a sketch is exactly the same as adding reference dimensions. However, there are a few extra dimension types that can be added to a drawing as reference dimensions. These are covered next.

Baseline Dimensions

A baseline dimension is a reference dimension that uses a common endpoint and displays dimensions in the same manner as a horizontal or vertical dimension. A baseline dimension will follow any changes to geometry used to create the dimension. To create a baseline dimension referencing one start point, perform the following steps. The illustration at left shows baseline dimensions.

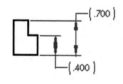

Baseline dimensions.

1. Select Baseline Dimension from the Tools/Dimensions menu, or press the right mouse button and select the dimension type.

2. Select the edge to be used as the baseline origin.

3. Select each additional edge or vertex to be dimensioned.

4. Click on the first dimension's text location to place all dimensions.

Ordinate Dimensions

An ordinate dimension is a reference dimension that uses a common endpoint and displays dimensions with a single extension line. An ordinate dimension will follow any changes to geometry used to create the dimension. The type of ordinate dimension (point-to-point, horizontal, or vertical) would be selected based on the same reasoning as the other dimension types. To create parallel point-to-point ordinate dimensions referencing one start point, perform the following steps. The illustration at left shows ordinate dimensions.

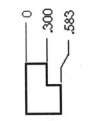

Ordinate dimensions.

1. Select Ordinate Dimension from the Tools/Dimensions menu, or press the right mouse button and select the dimension type.

2. Select the edge to be used as the ordinate origin.

3. Select the text location.

4. Select additional edges or vertices to be dimensioned.

5. Select the text location. Repeat steps 4 and 5 until all ordinate dimensions have been placed.

To create horizontal ordinate dimensions referencing one start point, perform the following steps. The illustration at left shows horizontal ordinate dimensions.

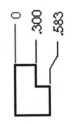

Horizontal ordinate dimensions.

1. Select Horizontal Ordinate Dimension from the Tools/Dimensions menu, or press the right mouse button and select the dimension type.

2. Select the edge to be used as the ordinate origin.

3. Select the text location.

4. Select additional edges or vertices to be dimensioned.

5. Select the text location. Repeat steps 4 and 5 until all ordinate dimensions have been placed.

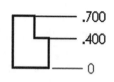

*Vertical ordinate
dimensions.*

To create vertical ordinate dimensions referencing one start point, perform the following steps. The illustration at left shows vertical ordinate dimensions.

1. Select Vertical Ordinate Dimension from the Tools/ Dimensions menu, or press the right mouse button and select the dimension type.

2. Select the edge to be used as the ordinate origin.

3. Select the text location.

4. Select additional edges or vertices to be dimensioned.

5. Select the text location. Repeat steps 4 and 5 until all ordinate dimensions have been placed.

To add new ordinate values to an existing set of ordinate dimensions, perform the following steps:

1. Select an ordinate dimension with the left mouse button.

2. Press the right mouse button and select Add to Ordinate.

3. Select a new item to be measured, and click on it again to place the dimension.

4. Select additional edges or vertices to be dimensioned.

5. Select the text location. Repeat steps 4 and 5 until all ordinate dimensions have been placed.

To align ordinate dimensions in a drawing, perform the following steps:

1. Select an ordinate dimension with the left mouse button.

2. Press the right mouse button and select Align Ordinate.

To jog an ordinate dimension, perform the following steps:

1. Select the ordinate dimension.

2. Press the right mouse button and select Jog.

3. Drag the text to jog the dimension.

Linked Dimensions

Linked dimensions are usually added in a part to control design intent, but they can also be added in a drawing. A linked dimension allows a single dimension name to drive many dimensions. The equation function could be used for the same purpose, but the link function can be used to do the same thing more quickly when a number of dimensions are required to be the same value. If an equation is used, all of the dimensions need to be added to separate equations.

Equations are useful when mathematical operators are required. Linked values can be used for equalities. When dimensions are linked, they all have the same name. If one of the dimension values is changed, all of the linked dimensions will change. Reference dimensions cannot be linked because they are driven. Linked dimensions require that they drive the geometry of the part. To create a linked dimension, perform the following steps:

1. Right click on the dimension and select Link Value.

2. Specify a name for the Link Value.

3. Select OK to continue.

4. Right click on the next dimension to be linked and select Link Value.

5. Type in or select the link name from the drop-down list.

This ability to link dimension names is strictly a Solid-Works feature. AutoCAD has nothing that can be compared with linked dimensions. AutoCAD dimensions do not have names with which to link. Because of this lack of underlying intelligence within the dimension entities, the ability to create equations or linked values does not exist.

Modifying Dimensions

Existing dimensions can have any attribute changed through their dimension properties. Model dimensions are created within the part and are used to drive the size of part features. Reference dimensions are created in the drawing and do not drive the size of part features, but will automatically update when part geometry is modified.

The option to disable or enable changing model dimensions in a drawing to update model geometry is selectable during installation and can be optionally disabled. When this option is disabled, model dimensions cannot be changed within the drawing. This is usually a decision made by management and is not something you can change.

Moving dimensions between views can be accomplished while holding down the Shift key. Hold the Control key down while dragging dimensions to be copied to other views. Only orthographically correct views are allowable. In other words, if SolidWorks cannot make the dimension look reasonably correct in a view, such as a horizontal dimension on edge, it will not place it there. The following are methods used to modify a dimension.

Double click on	Double clicking on a model dimension with the left mouse button will bring up the Modify dialog box. This dialog box allows you to change the dimension value and rebuild the feature. Double clicking on a feature will display its dimensions.
Properties	Right click on the dimension to be modified and select Properties. Dimension attributes (i.e., font, decimal precision, tolerance, and so on) can be changed. Multiple dimensions can be selected for this function by holding down the Control key, selecting the dimensions, and then right clicking on the dimensions.
Dimension handles	Selecting a dimension will display selection points (handles) that can be used to change the location of the dimension, dimension text, extension line length, or slant.

A dimension's handles can be picked and dragged to the desired location. Handles are similar to AutoCAD's grips in the way they are selected and dragged to a new position. The following illustration shows dimension handles.

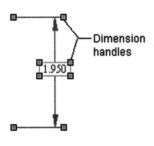

Dimension handles.

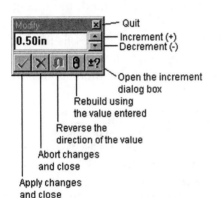

The Modify dialog box and its icons.

A model dimension can be changed within any type of SolidWorks document (i.e., part, assembly, or drawing). The Modify dialog box appears when you double click with the left mouse button on a model dimension. The advantage to using the Modify dialog box is that different dimensional values can be tried before rebuilding the entire model. To change a model dimension value, perform the following steps. The following illustration shows the Modify dialog box.

1. Using the left mouse button, double click on the dimension.

2. Enter the new value in the value field.

3. Select from the optional functions available within the Modify menu.

Dimension attributes can be changed or redefined after a dimension has been created. The attributes for both model and created dimensions can be changed via the Properties function. Setting dimension properties within the Options dialog box only changes the format of new dimensions. To make changes to the default values for dimensions, select the Detailing tab from the Tools/ Options menu. This topic is covered in the "Preferences Settings" section in Chapter 3. To change an individual dimension's properties, perform the following steps:

1. With the left mouse button, select the dimensions to be changed. Hold down the Control key to select multiple dimensions. Multiple dimensions can also be selected by picking a corner of a rectangle and dragging it to define the opposite corner. All dimensions that fall within the rectangle will be selected.

2. Press the right mouse button and select Properties.

3. Change the desired parameters.

4. Select OK to continue.

Dimension Properties

When the previous procedure is implemented, the dialog box that opens contains specific properties for various dimension types. Some of the property values in the list that follows may not be present in all Dimension Properties dialog boxes. The following are the more common properties:

Value	The dimension's value. Select to change the value of a model dimension. Select Rebuild to update the model once the dialog box is closed. This option is selectable only for model dimensions.
Name	To change the name of a dimension, pick inside the field and enter the new name. The new name must be unique to the part.
Full Name	Full name assigned by the system. This name can be referenced in design tables, equations, or notes. The full name's syntax could be *<DimensionName>@<SketchName>*, *<DimensionName>@<FeatureName>*, or *<DimensionName>@<FeatureName>@<PartName>*, depending on where the dimension name originates (such as in an assembly).
Arrows	Select an arrow type from the pull-down menu. The arrow will automatically be placed outside the extension line when Smart has been selected.
Display Precision	Uncheck "Use document's precision" and press the Precision button to set the primary, dual, and angular dimension decimal precision.
Font	Uncheck "Use document's font" and press the Font button to select a different dimension text font.
Driven	Checked when other dimensions or parameters drive a dimension.
Read Only	Check to disallow any modification of model dimensions in the drawing.
Display with Parentheses	Check to display parentheses on drawing-created dimensions.

Modify Text	Select to prefix and append text strings and symbols to the dimension. The dimension remains fully associative with the part/assembly geometry.
Tolerance	Select to define a tolerance type and values for the selected dimension.
Display as Dual Dimension	Check to display a dimension formatted with a dual unit of measure.

To edit the decimal precision, perform the following steps:

1. Right click on the dimension and select Properties.

2. Uncheck "Use document's precision" to set the primary and alternate (dual) dimension decimal precision.

3. Select the Precision button.

4. Select the decimal precision for primary, secondary, and angular dimensions.

5. Select OK to return to the Dimension Properties menu.

6. Select OK to continue.

SolidWorks uses Windows fonts, which offers many fonts, sizes, and styles to SolidWorks documents. To edit a dimension's font type, perform the following steps:

1. Right click on the dimension and select Properties.

2. Uncheck "Use document's font" to set the dimension's font properties.

3. Click on the Font button.

4. Select the desired font characteristics.

5. Select OK to return to the Dimension Properties menu.

6. Select OK to continue.

The visibility of the extension and dimension lines is definable within SolidWorks. To edit witness line visibility, perform the following steps:

1. Right click on the dimension and select Properties.

2. Click on the Display button.

3. Select the items to be displayed or suppressed. The dimension graphic will display the changes as they are made.

4. Select OK to return to the Dimension Properties menu.

5. Select OK to continue.

Text can be added before, after, above, or below a dimension. This function can be used to add symbols to the dimension. The dimension value is displayed in the form <DIM>. Any symbol is also displayed with a less than and greater than symbol (<symbol name>). Anything displayed with the less than and greater than symbols is being controlled by SolidWorks. If the "<>" symbols are removed, the text will not read correctly. To add or change prefixed or appended text to a dimension, perform the following steps:

1. Right click on the dimension and select Properties.

2. Click on the Modify Text button.

3. Select the items to be added or modified. The Preview field will display the changes as they are made.

4. Select OK to return to the Dimension Properties menu.

5. Select OK to continue.

It is possible to modify a dimension's properties in AutoCAD, but it is just not as user friendly as it is in Solid-Works, where there are no messy variable names to deal with, such as DIMALT, DIMASO, or DIMLFAC. Solid-Works takes care of all of these settings, and lets you make modifications by right clicking on a dimension and changing its properties.

Dimension Text Properties

This section expands on the previous procedure for modifying text and adding symbols. For reference, the illustration that follows shows the Modify Text of Dimensions dialog box.

Dimension Text: (Field 1)	Text entered in this field will be inserted above the dimension.
Dimension Text: (Field 2)	Text entered in this field will be inserted on the dimension line.
Dimension Text: (Field 2)	Text entered in this field will be inserted below the dimension.
Preview	Select to insert a symbol at the cursor location.
Add Symbol	Check/uncheck this field to display/suppress the first witness line.
Add Value	Select to add the dimension value back into field 2. The dimension value cannot be changed in this dialog box. The dimension value can only be displayed in field 2. The dimension value will appear as <DIM>. This option is only available if for some reason the value has been removed from field 2.

*The Modify Text
of Dimensions dialog box.*

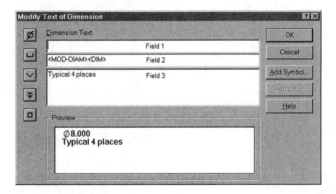

Tolerances can be defined on dimensions. When a model dimension is modified, the tolerance is also displayed on the dimension when selected within the part. To change a dimension's tolerance properties, perform the following steps:

1. Right click on the dimension and select Properties.

2. Click on the Tolerance button.

3. Select the desired tolerance characteristics. The preview field in the lower right-hand corner of the dialog box will display the changes as they are made.

4. Select OK to return to the Dimension Properties
menu.

5. Select OK to continue.

Tolerance Properties

The Dimension Tolerance dialog box, shown in the following illustration, has a number of options that should be
elaborated upon. Use the illustration that follows this list
to reference the various tolerance options described in it.

*Dimension Tolerance
dialog box.*

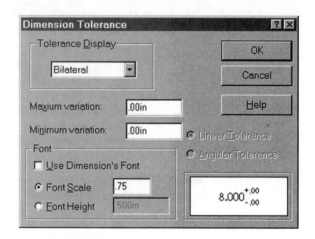

Tolerance Display	Select a tolerance type from the pull-down menu. Select None to display no tolerance. The preview field in the lower right-hand corner displays the selected tolerance type and limit values.
Maximum Variation	Display the upper tolerance limit. Pick inside the field to change the value. Symmetrical tolerance types are defined by the value in this field.
Minimum Variation	Display the lower tolerance limit. Pick inside the field to change the value.
Use Dimension's Font	Uncheck to set font scale and height. The Font Scale and Font Height fields are not selectable with this field checked.
Font Scale	Check to select a tolerance font scale value. Pick inside the field to change the value.
Font Height	Check to select a font height for the tolerance font. Pick inside the field to change the value.
Linear Tolerance	Field checked for linear dimensions.
Angular Tolerance	Field checked for angular dimensions.

Tolerance types.

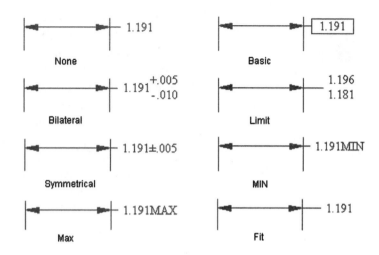

Drawing symbols are 2D entities added to a drawing to document the design intent. These symbols communicate the additional information (i.e., note, surface finish, weld symbol, and so on) that dimensions cannot convey. Model annotations can be defined within the part or assembly and displayed on the detail drawing. The following are annotation features that can be defined on a part or assembly. The illustration that follows shows model annotations.

Drawing Symbols

- Cosmetic Threads
- Datum Targets
- Geometric Tolerances
- Surface Finish Symbols

- Datums
- Dimensions
- Notes
- Weld Symbols

Samples of model annotations.

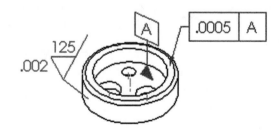

Drawing symbols in AutoCAD are created through a much different process than in SolidWorks. There are third-party programs that will allow an AutoCAD user to insert symbols, but if that type of software is not available, other means must be devised. For instance, it is possible to create symbol libraries within AutoCAD and then insert those symbols as needed into a drawing. This is usually accompanied by specifying x and y scaling, rotation angle, and so on. This is really just a workaround because AutoCAD does not have symbol creation methods of its own. There is the ability to create a few symbols, such as the degree symbol, by using the %% codes, but this is inconvenient.

Notes

Notes are used to insert text, labels, and balloons on a SolidWorks drawing. The note can also be made a hyperlink to a WWW (World Wide Web) page or to another location on the local computer or over the network. This HTML document can be located on the Internet or an intranet.

In SolidWorks, notes can be produced in a model or drawing. You can also use an external program (e.g., Microsoft Word) to cut and paste them via the clipboard as a text string into the drawing. This allows for functions such as spell checking to be performed prior to a text note being inserted into a drawing. The following illustration shows examples of a note, balloon, and hypertext link.

It is important to remember to select a location for the note prior to executing the command. The command will not be accessible otherwise. To insert a text note into a drawing, perform the following steps:

1. With the left mouse button, select the origin for the note.

2. Select the Note icon, or select Note from the Insert menu.

WWW Web link — Hyper-link
Example Note — Plain note

Balloon

Samples of a note, balloon, and hypertext link.

3. Enter the text in the Note Text field. Define any additional options.

4. Select OK to continue.

AutoCAD's text commands have come a long way from the simple TEXT command. SolidWorks lacks the capabilities of AutoCAD release 13, such as its formatting of text and specification of line justifications, page anchor points, and overflow type. Changing text styles and colors within the same paragraph is outside the ability of SolidWorks at this time. On the other hand, it is possible to create active hypertext links to notes within a SolidWorks document.

Note Properties

The following list describes the various properties found within the Note Properties dialog box.

Note Text	Displays the text as it is entered.
Angle	Enter the text angle or pick the up/down arrows to increment/decrement the angle value.
Add Symbol	At any point in the note, the Add Symbol button can be selected to insert standard drafting symbols.
Display with Leader	Check to add a leader to the note.
Arrow Style	Select an arrow style from the pull-down menu when Display with Leader has been checked.
Display with Bent Leader	Leave this field unchecked to use a straight leader for the note. Check this field to place a tail before the note text.
WWW link	Pick to enter a WWW URL (i.e., *http://www.solidworks.com*) link to jump to when selected.
Balloon Style	Select the balloon style from the pull-down list.
Size	Select the balloon size from the pull-down list.
Use document's font	Uncheck "Use document's font" to set dimension font properties. Select the Font button to define a new font style.

Editing a Note

To change the contents of an existing note, perform the following steps:

1. With the left mouse button, double click on the note.

2. Modify the parameters of the note as previously described.

3. Select OK to continue.

Symbol Properties

Symbol Properties are very self-explanatory, but have been included in the list that follows for reference. Describing all of the various symbols is outside the scope of this book. The following illustration shows the Symbols dialog box.

The Symbols dialog box.

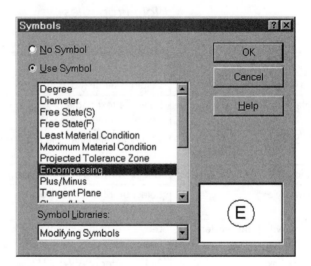

No Symbol	Check to disallow the display of symbols.
Use Symbol	Check to allow for the display of symbols.
Symbol Field	Select the desired symbol from the pull-down list. The list displays symbols from the selected symbol library. The field in the lower right-hand corner will display a preview of the selected symbol.
Symbol Libraries	Select a symbol library from the pull-down menu.

To insert a note with the leader option, perform the following steps:

1. Select the leader attachment point (where the arrow will point to).

2. Select the Note icon, or select Note from the Insert menu.

3. Enter the note text. Check the Display with Leader option.

4. Select OK to continue.

5. Drag the text location.

To insert a note with the balloon option, perform the following steps:

1. Select the balloon leader attachment point.

2. Select the Note icon, or select Note from the Insert menu.

3. Enter the note text. Specify the Balloon Type and Size.

4. Select OK to continue.

5. Drag the balloon location.

To relocate the attachment point of a leader or note, perform the following steps:

1. Using the left mouse button, select the note.

2. Select the attachment end of the leader. The leader can be attached to an edge or face. The cursor will display valid conditions as the cursor passes over these features.

3. Drag the end of the leader to its new attachment point.

4. Drag the note to the desired location.

Notes can be cut into the clipboard and pasted into the current drawing or other drawing and applications. Simply paste any notes copied to the clipboard into the text box when inserting a note. Drawing notes can also be associated with a view. Activate the view or select a model edge or face and insert the note. When the view or model reference moves, the note will move.

Balloons   This command inserts a balloon in a drawing. Balloons can be used to label features and relate them to items on a bill of material. Various types of balloons can be defined. The item in the balloon can be an item number, quantity, or custom value. The following illustration shows balloon styles.

Balloon styles.

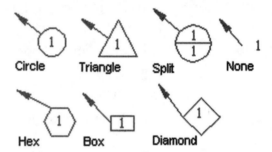

To insert a note with the balloon option, perform the following steps:

1. Select the balloon attachment point.

2. Select the Note icon, or select Note from the Insert/Annotations menu.

3. Enter the note text. Specify a balloon Style and Size.

4. Select OK to continue.

5. Drag the balloon with the left mouse button to the desired location.

To insert a balloon using the balloon icon, perform the following steps:

1. Select the Balloon icon, or select Balloon from the Insert/Annotations menu.

2. Select the balloon attachment point.

3. Drag the balloon with the left mouse button to the desired location.

To edit a balloon, perform the following steps:

1. Double click the left mouse button to automatically open the Note dialog box.

2. Add, edit, or delete the balloon's definition.

3. Select OK to continue.

A couple of points to remember when creating balloons are:

- Balloons can be edited using the same methods as notes.
- Default balloon characteristics can be defined under the Detailing tab in the Tools/Options dialog box.

Center Marks

Center marks show the centerpoint of an arc or circle. The illustration at left shows a center mark. To insert a center mark, perform the following steps:

Center mark.

1. Select the Center Mark icon, or select Center Mark from the Insert/Annotations menu.

2. Select any arcs or circles with which to add center marks.

To change the attributes of a center mark, perform the following steps. The illustration that follows shows the Center Mark dialog box.

1. Double click on the center mark with the left mouse button.

2. Edit the display attributes.

3. To change the default properties, uncheck the "Use document's defaults" field.

4. Select OK to continue.

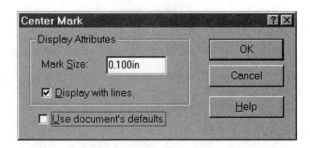

The Center Mark dialog box.

Geometric Tolerances

ANSI geometric tolerance symbols and datum symbols can be added to a drawing or part to define the position, shape, or form of a feature. These symbols can be added to a drawing or model directly using the annotation function. These symbols can also be displayed within a drawing. The illustration at left shows geometric tolerance symbols. To insert a geometric tolerance symbol in a drawing, perform the following steps:

Geometric tolerance symbols.

1. With the left mouse button, select the location for the geometric tolerance symbol .

2. Select the Geometric Tolerance icon, or select Geometric Tolerance from the Insert/Annotations menu.

3. Click on the GCS button and select the type of tolerance. The preview field in the lower left-hand corner will display the symbol as it is created.

4. Select OK to return to the Geometric Tolerance menu.

5. Enter the value for Tolerance 1, and set whether or not the diameter symbol is to be included.

6. Enter whether any material conditions apply (i.e., MMC, LMC, or RFS).

7. Repeat for the additional tolerances.

8. Set whether the tolerance is to apply to a projected tolerance zone.

9. Enter a Datum identifier, if applicable.

10. Select OK to continue.

11. Drag the tolerance note to the desired location if Display with Leader was checked in the Options menu.

Geometric Tolerance Properties

The following list describes the various properties within the Geometric Tolerance dialog box. Use the following illustration for reference.

The Geometric Tolerance dialog box.

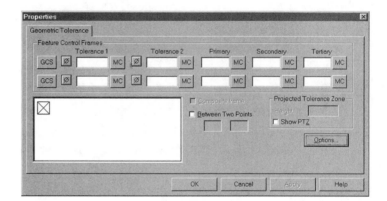

GCS	Pick the GCS button to change or define the GDandT symbol field. This can be defined for the first and second lines of the geometric tolerance symbol.
Tolerance 1	Pick inside the field to enter the first tolerance value. Select the diameter symbol if applicable. Select the MC button to define the material condition if applicable. This field can be defined for the first and second lines of the symbol.
Tolerance 2	Pick inside the field to enter the second tolerance value. Select the diameter symbol if applicable. Select the MC button to define the material condition if applicable. This field can be defined for the first and second lines of the symbol.
Primary	Pick inside the field to enter the primary datum letter. Select the MC button to define the material condition if applicable. This field can be defined for the first and second lines of the symbol.
Secondary	Pick inside the field to enter the secondary datum letter. Select the MC button to define the material condition if applicable. This field can be defined for the first and second lines of the symbol.

Tertiary	Pick inside the field to enter the tertiary datum letter. Select the MC button to define the material condition if applicable. This field can be defined for the first and second lines of the symbol.
Composite frame	Control both the form and orientation of a profile feature. The top specifies the locating tolerance zone and the bottom the form and orientation.
Between Two Points	Check to add a symbol used to define two locations to constrain the tolerance. Enter the two point names in the field below the check box.
Show PTZ	Check to specify a tolerance zone located at true position extending away from the primary datum. A projected tolerance zone is used to control perpendicularity of threaded or press-fit hole features with the mating part.
Height	Projected tolerance zone height. Pick inside this field to enter a new value. This field is selectable only with Show PTZ checked.
Options...	Pick to select leader and font characteristics for the symbol.

To set optional properties for a geometric tolerance symbol, perform the following steps:

1. Insert the geometric tolerance symbol as previously described.

2. Select the Options button.

3. Select the desired optional symbol characteristics.

4. Select OK to return to the geometric tolerance menu.

5. Select OK to continue.

6. Drag the tolerance note to the desired location if Display with Leader was checked.

Optional Geometric Tolerance Properties

The Options button found within the Geometric Tolerance dialog box opens another dialog box. The characteristics described in the list that follows can be found in this dialog box, shown in the following illustration.

Options for geometric tolerancing.

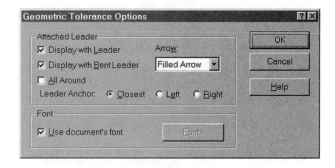

Display with Leader	Check to display the symbol with a leader attached to the selected origin.
Display with Bent Leader	Check to add a leader tail before the symbol.
All Around	Check to add a circle around the intersection of the leader and the leader tail.
Leader Anchor	Select the leader tail placement direction.
Arrow	Select an arrow style from the pull-down menu when Display with Leader has been checked.
Use document's font	Uncheck "Use document's font" to set the dimension font properties. Select the Font button to define a new font style.

To edit a geometric tolerance symbol, perform the following steps:

1. Right click on the geometric tolerance symbol and select Properties, or double click with the left mouse button to automatically open the Geometric Tolerance dialog box.

2. Add, edit, or delete the symbol's definition.

3. Select OK to continue.

To relocate a geometric tolerance or datum feature symbol, perform the following steps:

1. With the left mouse button, select the origin or text of the symbol.

2. Hold the button down and drag the datum point to its new location.

3. Release the mouse button.

The geometric tolerance symbols are inserted, by default, using the document's font. For a more complete description of the principles of geometric tolerancing and dimensioning, refer to *ANSI Y14.5M, Dimensioning, and Tolerancing.*

Annotations can be turned off globally within any Solid-Works document. If drawing annotations are not visible, right click on the Annotations feature in FeatureManager and select Display Annotations.

Datum   ANSI geometric tolerance datum, datum point symbols, and datum points can be created within SolidWorks. A datum symbol describes the alpha reference (i.e., A, B, C, and so on) for a datum plane. A datum point is used to aid in the measurement of geometric tolerances. A datum point is used to define specific locations for the definition of a reference datum plane. An example would be to define three points that define a reference plane.

Inserting a Datum Feature Symbol

A datum point symbol is used to define properties for datum points. These symbols can be added to a drawing or a model directly using the annotation function. These symbols can also be displayed within a drawing. The illustration at left shows a datum. The following illustration shows a datum point and datum point symbol. To insert a datum feature symbol, perform the following steps:

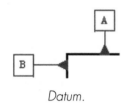

Datum.

1. Select the Datum Feature icon, or select Datum Feature Symbol from the Insert/Annotations menu.

2. Select the origin of the datum feature symbol.

3. Drag the datum feature to the desired location.

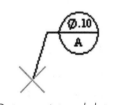

Datum point and datum point symbol.

To edit a datum feature symbol, perform the following steps:

1. Double click on the Datum Feature icon, or right click on the Datum Feature icon and select Properties.

2. Enter the desired datum feature symbol characteristics. The preview field in the upper left-hand corner will display the specified datum feature symbol.

3. Select OK to continue.

To insert a datum target point, perform the following steps:

1. Activate the view by double clicking on it with the left mouse button.

2. Select the Datum Target Point icon, or select Datum Target Point from the Insert/Annotations menu.

3. Select the datum target point origin.

To insert a datum target symbol, perform the following steps:

1. Select the datum target point.

2. Select the Datum Target icon or select Datum Target Symbol from the Insert/Annotations menu.

3. Enter the desired datum target characteristics. The preview field in the upper left-hand corner will display the specified datum target symbol.

4. Select OK to continue.

Datum Target Symbol Properties

Refer to the following illustration for the options present in the Datum Target Symbol dialog box. The list that follows describes the properties contained in this dialog box.

*The Datum Target Symbol
dialog box.*

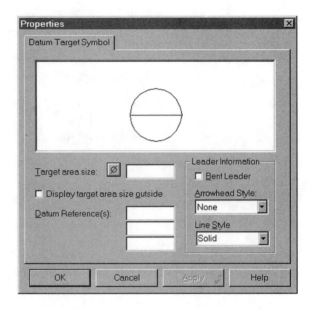

Target area size	Enter the target size for measuring the target area. The Diameter symbol can be selected to indicate a diameter target area.
Display target area size outside	Check to display the target area outside the symbol. Typically this is done when the target area note is too long or large and would be more easily read outside the symbol.
Datum Reference(s)	Enter the datum reference letters.
Bent Leader	Leave this field unchecked to use a straight leader for the note. Check this field to place a tail before the note text.
Arrowhead Style	Displays the arrowhead style. Select a new arrowhead style from the pull-down menu.
Line Style	Displays the leader line font style. Select a new line style from the pull-down menu.

To edit a datum target symbol, perform the following steps:

1. Double click on the datum target symbol, or right click on the datum target symbol and select Properties.

2. Enter the desired datum target characteristics. The preview field in the upper left-hand corner will display the specified datum target symbol.

3. Select OK to continue.

To relocate a datum target symbol or datum target point, perform the following steps:

1. With the left mouse button, select the origin or text of the symbol.

2. Hold the left mouse button down and drag the datum point to its new location.

3. Release the mouse button.

Weld Symbols

Weld symbols are used to denote the manufacturing method and processes used to fasten parts using welding processes. These symbols can be added to a drawing or model directly using the annotation function. These symbols can also be displayed within a drawing. The illustration at left shows weld symbols.

Inserting a Weld Symbol

To insert a weld symbol in a drawing, perform the following steps:

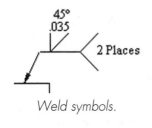

Weld symbols.

1. Select the weld symbol attachment point.

2. Select the Weld Symbol icon, or select Weld Symbol from the Insert/Annotations menu.

3. Enter the desired weld characteristics.

4. Select OK to continue.

5. With the left mouse button, drag the weld symbol to the desired location.

Welding Symbol Properties

There are numerous welding symbols. Describing all of them is outside the scope of this book. However, the list that follows describes the most commonly used properties. Refer to the following illustration of the ANSI Weld Symbol dialog box.

The ANSI Weld Symbol dialog box.

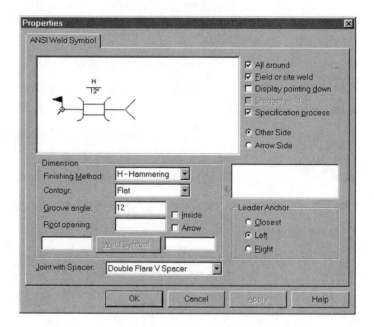

Dimension (top)	Specifies the weld characteristics for the top (near side) of the weld.
Groove angle	Angular opening for groove weld. Pick inside the field to change the groove weld opening angle.
Root opening	Distance between weld members. Pick inside the field to change the root opening distance.
Weld size	The text field preceding the weld symbol is used to indicate weld size. Pick inside the files to enter a new weld size.
Weld Symbol	Click on the Weld Symbol button to select a symbol type. Select a weld symbol from the Symbol field. Select OK to continue.
Pitch or length of weld	The text field following the weld symbol is used to indicate the pitch or length of the weld. Pick inside the files to enter a new pitch or weld length.
Dimension (bottom)	Specifies the weld characteristics for the bottom (opposite side) of the weld.
Groove angle	Angular opening for groove weld. Pick inside the field to change the groove weld opening angle.

Root opening	Distance between weld members. Pick inside the field to change the root opening distance.
Weld size	The text field preceding the weld symbol is used to indicate weld size. Pick inside the files to enter a new weld size.
Weld Symbol	Click on the Weld Symbol button to select a symbol type. Select a weld symbol from the Symbol field. Select OK to continue.
Pitch or length of weld	The text field following the weld symbol is used to indicate the pitch or length of the weld. Pick inside the files to enter a new pitch or weld length.
All around	Check to indicate a weld completely around the specified joint.
Field or site weld	Check to display the field weld symbol. Field welds designate a weld done at the work site.
Specification process	Check to enter a text string in the tail section of the weld symbol. This area is used to specify a weld process or number of welds. Enter the text string in the field following the check field.

Surface Finish Symbols

Surface finish symbols are used to describe the manufacturing methods, surface roughness, and machining direction for a part surface. These symbols can be added to a drawing or model directly using the annotation function. These symbols can also be displayed within a drawing. The illustration at left shows surface finish symbols.

Surface finish symbols.

Inserting a Finish Symbol

To insert a surface finish symbol, perform the following steps:

1. Select the surface finish symbol attachment point. This should be an edge or surface.

2. Select the Surface Finish Symbol icon, or select Surface Finish Symbol from the Insert/Annotations menu.

3. Enter the desired surface finish characteristics. The surface finish symbol is displayed as changes are made.

4. Select OK to continue.

5. With the left mouse button, drag the surface finish symbol to the desired location.

Surface Finish Properties

The properties that can be added using the Surface Finish Symbol dialog box are described in the list that follows. The following illustration shows the Surface Finish Symbol dialog box.

The Surface Finish Symbol dialog box.

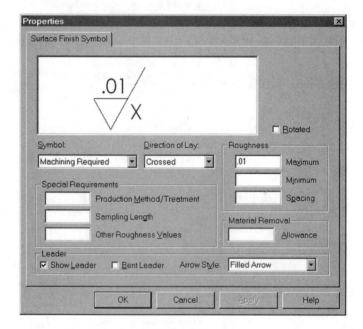

Symbol	Display the current surface finish symbol type. Select a new symbol from the pull-down list. Basic, Machining Required, or Machining Prohibited can be selected.
Direction of Lay	Displays the surface finish direction or pattern.
Roughness	Defines height deviation and spacing between the peaks and valleys of the surface.
Minimum	The maximum arithmetic-average height deviation of the surface from the mean line in the profile. Pick inside the field to change this value.
Maximum	The minimum arithmetic-average height deviation of the surface from the mean line in the profile. Pick inside the field to change this value.
Spacing	The maximum allowable distance between repetitive features of the surface pattern. Pick inside the field to change this value.

Special Requirements	Defines any necessary requirements.
Production Method/ Treatment	Specify the production method or process. Pick inside the field to change this value.
Sampling Length	Specify the length of surface to be measured. Pick inside the field to change this value.
Other Roughness Values	Specify the width cutoff value. Pick inside the field to change this value.
Material Removal	Specifies the amount of material to be removed by machining. Pick inside the field to change this value.
Leaders:	
Show Leader	Check to show a leader pointing to the surface.
Bent Leader	Check to specify bent leader type.
Arrow Style	Displays the currently selected arrowhead type. Select a arrowhead type from the pull-down list.

Cosmetic Threads

Cosmetic threads are used to display the major diameter of a thread. They appear as dashed lines indicating cosmetic arcs. These symbols can be added to a drawing or model directly using the annotation function. These symbols can also be displayed within a drawing. The following illustration shows cosmetic threads.

Cosmetic threads.

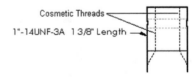

Cosmetic threads must first be placed in the part before they can be inserted into a drawing. To insert a cosmetic thread in a drawing, perform the following steps:

1. On the part, select a circular edge on which to start the cosmetic threads.

2. Select Insert/Annotations/Cosmetic Threads.

3. Specify the thread parameters.

4. In the drawing, select the views intended to display cosmetic threads.

5. Select Cosmetic Threads from the Insert/Annotations menu.

6. Select OK to continue.

Hole Callouts

Hole callouts are used to annotate circular features. These features can be cylinders, or simple, countersunk, counterbored, or tapped holes. These symbols can be added to a drawing or model directly using the annotation function. These symbols can also be displayed within a drawing.

The hole callout feature uses the information defined by the Simple Hole or Hole Wizard commands to help automate detail drawing creation. The illustration at left shows a hole callout. Hole callout information can also be automatically obtained from an extrusion, whether a cut or boss. To add a hole callout, perform the following steps:

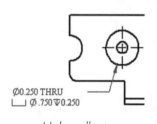

Hole callout.

1. With the left mouse button, select the circular feature to be dimensioned.

2. Select the Hole Callout icon, or select Hole Callout from the Insert/Annotations menu.

3. The Modify Text dialog box will appear with the recommended hole callout displayed in the preview box.

4. Select OK to continue.

Bill of Materials

A bill of materials (BOM) is created on drawings to describe component names, part number, and the number of instances for each component in the assembly. This BOM is created from assembly component properties. AutoCAD does not currently have functionality similar to SolidWorks' BOM, but there are third-party programs that may provide this feature.

The item number is derived from the creation order of the assembly. This order is displayed within the FeatureManager design tree from top to bottom. The BOM will display only unique assembly components. Multiple assembly components are noted within the Quantity field. Any changes to the assembly are updated within the BOM. A BOM can be added only to an assembly. The following illustration shows a bill of materials.

ITEM NO.	QTY.	PART NO.	DESCRIPTION
1	1	Exploded Base	
2	2	Exploded Pin	
3	1	Exploded Cover	

Bill of materials.

Inserting a Bill of Materials

To insert a BOM, perform the following steps:

1. With the left mouse button, select a drawing view. The view should contain the parts in the assembly to be included in the BOM.

2. Select Bill of Materials from the Insert menu.

3. Select the desired options, which are described in the section that follows.

4. Select OK to continue.

5. Enter any other desired information in the spreadsheet.

6. Select outside the spreadsheet to close Excel and return to SolidWorks.

7. Resize the BOM as needed.

8. Select outside the BOM a second time to deselect the spreadsheet.

Bill of Material Properties

The Bill Of Materials dialog box contains options described in the list that follows. Use the following illustration as reference for the options described in the list.

The Bill Of Materials dialog box.

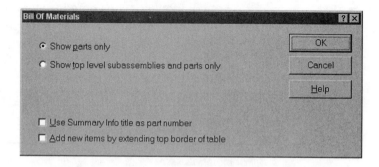

Show parts only	Check to show only parts in the BOM. Subassembly components will be listed separately.
Show top level subassemblies and parts only	Check to show subassemblies and parts in the BOM. Subassemblies will not have their parts listed separately.
Use Summary Info title as part number	Check to use a component's Summary Info title field for the part number.
Add new items by extending top border of table	Check to add new items to the top of the table.

To update a BOM, perform the following steps:

1. Select the drawing view used to create the BOM.

2. Select Bill Of Materials from the Insert menu. The existing BOM will update to show any additions or deletions.

3. Enter any other desired information in the spreadsheet.

4. Select outside the spreadsheet to close Excel and return to SolidWorks.

5. Resize the BOM as needed.

6. Select outside the BOM a second time to deselect the spreadsheet.

To move or resize a BOM, perform the following steps:

1. With the left mouse button, select the BOM. Do not double click on the spreadsheet, as this will open Excel and put you in edit mode for the spreadsheet.

2. Drag the spreadsheet window to the desired size from the small black handles on the spreadsheet's edges.

3. Select outside the spreadsheet to close the BOM.

A few other notes regarding spreadsheets (BOMs) merit mention. Specifically, Microsoft Excel is required to use this function. Also, the default template for BOM creation is Bomtemp.xls and is located in the SolidWorks/LANG/ <language> directory (where <language> is English by default).

Summary

Drawing formats can be imported from your existing CAD systems using a DWG or DXF file format. SolidWorks allows for multisheet drawings within the same drawing file. Drawing views are created to display different orientations of parts and assemblies. These drawing views are associative to the part or assembly used to create them. Any changes to the part or assembly are automatically updated in the drawing. Changes made to the drawing's model dimensions will update the part or assembly. This is a function that can be disabled during installation.

Drawing views also benefit from the ability to automatically display them with hidden lines removed or hidden lines in gray or dashed. SolidWorks allows you to define the views without spending time cleaning up views for hidden line removal or updating geometry changes. Dimensions can be added to 2D sketch geometry for a solid model and then reused on drawings, or recreated inside the drawing as reference dimensions. The advantage to using model dimensions is that these dimensions do not have to be recreated in a drawing.

Annotations can be defined within parts and assemblies to assign engineering attributes. The advantage to defining these attributes during the design phase is that the designer or engineer that created the design can assign an attribute (i.e., surface finish, geometric tolerance, and so on) when design criteria are first established. This can be easier than performing this task later or having someone else less familiar with the design add these attributes.

SolidWorks' ability to create all of the standard views from a solid part file and have that geometry update when design changes are made results in significant time savings. The ability to drag detail circles and section lines to obtain best overall views can result in countless hours saved on the drafting floor.

Rendering

Introduction

This chapter discusses the lighting and shading capabilities of SolidWorks. Models can be created and edited while a wide array of light sources and color options are active. Other uses of implementing these features include such venues as marketing and design reviews, customer presentations, advertising and promotion, and production of manuals and documentation.

Prerequisite

Chapters 6 and 7 should be understood. It is not necessarily essential to comprehend how every feature is created, nor is it mandatory that every aspect of assemblies and mating relationships be completely understood. What is important, however, is the theory behind feature-based modeling and knowing that a part consists of individual features and that an assembly consists of individual parts. This will be important when discussing the properties of these individual features and parts.

Content

Within this chapter you will find procedures on lighting, making use of colors, modifying color and lighting properties of individual features, and saving images. The section on lighting describes the types of light sources available and how light can be added, changed, or deleted. Light sources alter the way a model appears within SolidWorks. Lighting can add a quality to a part that makes it look as though it were made of certain materials, such as, for example, glossy plastic or transparent resin.

The section "Feature Colors" explains how to modify a part in numerous ways with regard to color options. Specifically, you will see how to make certain colors apply to certain feature types. In addition, a section on feature properties explains how individual features can be altered to display specific properties and how this can apply to individual faces.

PhotoWorks is an optional module that produces photo-realistic images of parts and assemblies. A comparative description, including reasons a SolidWorks user might want to purchase PhotoWorks, is provided at the end of the chapter.

Objectives

With completion of the "Lighting" section, you should be able to define, change, or delete a light source, and should understand how these light sources are saved with a document. The section "Advanced Shading Characteristics" steps you through the process of modifying light properties. These properties can be light emission qualities, transparency, or a number of others.

When you have worked through the "Feature Colors" section, you should be able to define or change a feature's shaded color properties and understand how these color settings are stored within documents. You should have a perspective on global settings versus independent feature color settings. You should also understand how assembly parts can have their colors changed and how to control whether these changes are propagated to the original part.

Lighting Sources

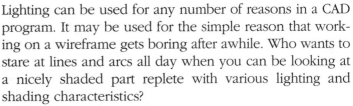

Lighting can be used for any number of reasons in a CAD program. It may be used for the simple reason that working on a wireframe gets boring after awhile. Who wants to stare at lines and arcs all day when you can be looking at a nicely shaded part replete with various lighting and shading characteristics?

Lighting may also be used for other, more business-oriented reasons. Because AutoCAD is more suited to the architectural market, lighting may be used to enhance an image of a building, perform sun and shadow studies, and display light source options for interior decorating possibilities. The list is endless. AutoCAD requires an add-on package to complete these tasks. It should be noted that with the release of version 14, a rendering package is now included with AutoCAD.

SolidWorks makes use of lighting for various purposes. Because SolidWorks is suited to the mechanical design market, its lighting capabilities are somewhat different from those required for an architectural program. For example, sun and shade studies are admittedly not very important for a mechanical part that may very well wind up buried inside an assembly.

Where lighting is sometimes more important is during the design process. When viewing a part in a more realistic manner, editing the part not only becomes a more enjoyable task, it becomes much more efficient. Finding possible flaws in the design is easier than if the same part or assembly were being displayed in a simple wireframe. AutoCAD's shading capabilities are not comparable to SolidWorks' out-of-the-box functionality. Even with release 14, it is still not possible to dynamically rotate a shaded part in AutoCAD.

Now that AutoCAD release 14 has included the AutoShade add-on with the AutoCAD main program, it arguably has a better rendering package than SolidWorks. However, as nice as AutoCAD's 2D renderings may be, they are still static images that cannot be rotated, panned, or zoomed during the design process. AutoCAD's AutoShade feature allows for walkthrough animations, but that is a different topic that goes beyond the scope of this book. If photorealistic renderings are needed, PhotoWorks is the solution for SolidWorks users.

One more piece of important information should be noted. Any and all of the lighting and color changes discussed in this chapter are saved with the part file. If a part's color or lighting is changed in any way, and the part is saved, expect to see the changes the next time the part is opened.

Light Sources

Light Sources is actually a name of a dialog box available in SolidWorks. Adding a light source is a function found in both parts and assemblies. The Light Sources dialog box is shown in the following illustration.

The Light Sources dialog box.

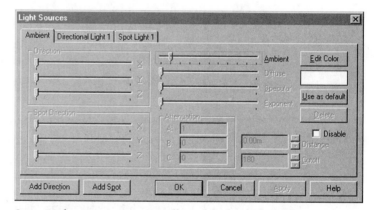

Spot Light 1 is not normally added by default, and must be added by the user if desired. Steps outlining how to employ this option are provided in material to follow. Three light source styles (ambient, directional, and spot) can be combined to produce a realistic lighting effect. These styles are defined as follows:

Ambient Light	A light source applied evenly from all sides of the object (see the previous illustration). Most of the settings in the Ambient tab section are grayed out because they do not apply to ambient lighting.
Directional Light	A light source applied from a distance (see the following illustration). The sun would be a perfect example of a directional light source. Light is radiated from a specific direction, but shines uniformly on the part from its specified location.

Directional Light tab in the Light Sources dialog box.

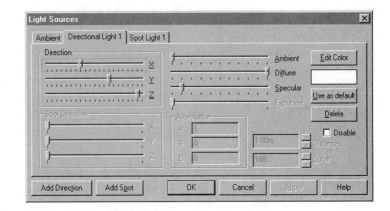

Spotlight	A tightly focused directional light source (see the following illustration). Like directional light sources, spotlights have a source position, but also have a direction the spotlight is pointing in. This creates a definite spot on the part that gradually diminishes as the light cone expands. An example of this type of light source would be a flashlight or an automobile's headlights.

Spot Light tab in the Light Sources dialog box.

Modifying Light Source Properties

This section discusses the three types of light sources previously mentioned, and describes the functions the various settings in each of the light source tabs perform. If you are working along with this book in SolidWorks, open a part to use as a subject for the lighting experiments contained in this section.

An excellent part for this topic is Camera.sldprt. This part, shown in the following illustration, can be found in the Samples\examples directory under your main Solid-Works directory. This assumes that the sample files were loaded when SolidWorks was installed.

The first and most straightforward of the three lighting tabs is Ambient. This lighting source tab will be discussed first, followed by the Directional and Spotlight lighting sources.

Camera part with default lighting characteristics.

Ambient Lighting Options

Ambient lighting options include Ambient, Edit Color, "Use as default," and Disable. Descriptions of these options and their functionality are provided in the following list.

Ambient	With this option, you set the amount of ambient light that comes from all directions by positioning a slider. Move the slider to the left to decrease, or right to increase, the value. This option is found under, and has the same functionality in, all three light source tabs.
Edit Color	This option sets the color of the light source. White is generally best for ambient light sources. This setting does not change the color of the part, only the light source that shines on the part. Depending on the display settings determined in the Windows Display dialog box and your graphics card memory, the number of colors available to you may be different. For graphic arts and CAD programs, nothing short of 4 Mb of memory and 16 million colors is recommended. Edit Color is found under, and performs the same function in, all three light source tabs.

Use as default	This option sets whatever changes are made to the Ambient or Directional tabs as the default settings for future parts. This option, however, is not available under the Spot Light tab. Be careful using this option, as it may be difficult to get back to the "factory set" settings if you decide changes are not acceptable. "Use as default" is found under, and performs the same function in, all three light source tabs.
Disable	This option disables the current tab's light source. This option is not recommended for the default ambient light source. Disable is found under, and performs the same function in, all three light source tabs.

Directional Lighting Options

The Directional tab includes the same options as the Ambient tab, along with additional options. These options—Position, Diffuse, Specular, and Delete—are described in the following list.

Position	This option is used to define the direction of the light source using x, y, and z coordinates. It is sometimes difficult to tell exactly what is happening behind the scenes when adjusting the slider bars. However, these adjustments will give you a real-time update of how changes affect a part. Drag the Light Sources dialog box out of the way so that you can see changes occur as you use the slider controls.
Diffuse	This option sets the amount of diffuse light applied from one direction. Diffuse light scatters equally when it bounces off a surface, making the surrounding area appear equally as bright. With this option, you move the slider to the left to decrease, or right to increase, the amount of diffuse light.
Specular	This option sets the amount of specularity applied to a particular light source. Specular light tends to bounce off an object in a particular direction, giving the object a shiny quality. A glossy surface will have a high specularity value (see the following illustration). With this option, you move the slider to the left to decrease, or right to increase, the value.
Delete	The Delete button deletes the current tab light source. This button is available for all light sources except the default Ambient light source.

Spot Light Lighting Options

The Spot Light tab includes the same options available under the Ambient and Directional tabs, along with the following options. The illustrations that follow show camera part with a specularity setting of about 60 percent and a spot light source added to the camera part.

*Camera part shown
with a specularity set
at about 60 percent.*

*Spot light source added
to the camera part.*

Spot Position	This is the location the spot light originates.
Spot Direction	Used to define the direction of the spot light beam using *x, y,* and *z* coordinates. This is the direction the spot light beam arrives from.
Exponent	Sets the degree of beam focus. Move the slider to the right to increase the beam's focus. Think of this as the fuzzy quality around the light where it strikes the object. The Cutoff option, described in material that follows, controls the beam's cone angle.
Attenuation	This is the property that decreases the intensity of the light as the light's distance from the light source increases. Note that the light source itself is not increasing in distance. Rather, it is the distance the light is from the source. It might help to think of the light waves diminishing in intensity the farther they get from the light bulb. Attenuation is the speed of this diminishing intensity. The distance of the light source itself is determined according to the formula found in the next entry, Distance. Attenuation is determined according to the following formula: (where d = Distance) $1/(a+b*d+c*d^2)$.
Distance	Sets the distance from the light source to the object. The up arrow increases the distance and the down arrow decreases the distance. Values can be between -1,000 and +1,000.
Cutoff	Used to set the spread of the light cone for a spot light source. The defualt value for the setting is 180, the range of which is 0 to 90 or 180. Settings between 90 and 180 are not allowed. Experiment with this to find an acceptable value for your specific part.

Take a look at the following illustration to see what settings were used for the Spot Light settings. The Spot Position and Direction settings were left at their default values.

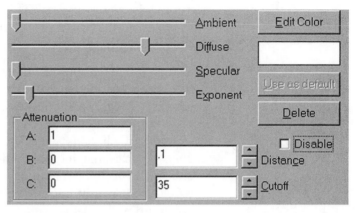

Settings used for the Spot Light source in the previous illustration.

Adding a Light Source

All that is required to access functionality for adding a light source is to click on the Add Direction button or Add Spot button at the bottom of the Light Source dialog box. To add a light source, perform the following steps:

1. Select Lighting... from the View menu.

2. Select Add Direction to add a directional light source, or select Add Spot to add a spot light source.

3. Edit the lighting properties. Use the definitions previously listed for reference if needed.

4. Continue adding light sources as needed, or select OK to close the dialog box and accept changes.

Colors

Now that you can change the light sources for a part or assembly, it is time to move on to bigger and better things. At this stage of the book, you should have a sense of what modifying the color of a part entails. This has been mentioned in a few places, but for the sake of convenience, the steps for changing a part's color follow. To change the color of a part, perform the following steps:

1. Click on Tools/Options....

2. Select the Color tab.

3. In the System area, select Shading.

4. Click on the Edit button and select a color that compliments the part.

Okay, so maybe you do not care about choosing a color that compliments the part. If you prefer purple bearings, who is to judge? In seriousness, though, the color of parts plays an important role when creating an assembly. For example, if all parts were left as their default shade of gray, you can imagine how difficult it would be to differentiate the components in an assembly? In some cases it would be a nearly impossible task. Consider the idea of color coding by using particular colors for particular part types.

AutoCAD generally associates colors with layers. Solid-Works does not have the need for layers, but colors still need to be managed. This can be done on a global level, per part, or for individual features or faces. AutoCAD is not feature based; therefore, when two or more solids are combined, the lesser components take on the traits of the master solid. For this reason, contiguous solid models in AutoCAD can be one color only when shaded.

Advanced Shading Characteristics

Individual parts can have any one of six settings adjusted that control the lighting characteristics of the part. These settings are found in the Color tab of the Options dialog box. To open the Material Properties dialog box, shown in the illustration that follows, perform the following steps:

1. Click on Tools/Options….

2. Select the Color tab.

3. In the System area, select Shading.

4. Click on the Advanced button to open the Material Properties dialog box.

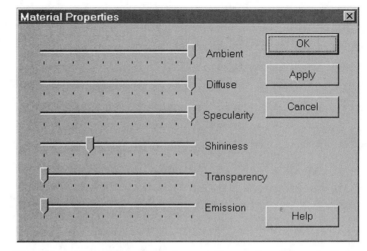

The Material Properties dialog box.

There are slider bar adjustments for each of the six lighting characteristics available. These characteristics are:

Ambient	Light reflected and scattered by other objects
Diffuse	Light reflected from the surface of a part and scattered equally in all directions
Specularity	An object's ability to reflect light
Shininess	Determines the reflective nature of a part
Transparency	Determines the amount of light that can pass through an object
Emission	Determines how much light is projected from the surface of a part

Camera part with transparency set at about 75 percent.

Through the use of these settings, it is possible to create some very interesting-looking parts and assemblies. The transparency setting alone is excellent when working with an assembly whose inner workings need to be shown. The use of these settings, combined with Solid-Works' ability to show movement through the use of mating tools, makes for some very impressive visuals.

The Material Property adjustments will update a part onscreen automatically. If the dialog boxes are in the way, drag them to the side or pan the part to the opposite side so that the adjustments can be observed on the part. The illlustration at left shows the camera part with a transparency set at about 75 percent.

Feature Colors

In addition to being able to make modifications to an entire part, SolidWorks allows you to specify colors for individual features. One way this is accomplished is through the use of the bottom half of the Colors tab, shown in the following illustration.

Colors can be associated with individual features.

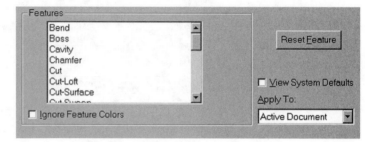

More than twenty features are listed in the Features section. Using the Apply To option, any changes made can apply to the current drawing, future drawings, or both. As always, be careful when changing default settings. To specify that you would like certain features to have specific colors, complete the following steps:

1. Click on Tools/Options....

2. Select the Color tab.

3. In the Features list box, select the feature whose color you would like to change.

4. Click on the Edit button to modify the color of the selected feature.

5. Continue this process until the desired feature colors are modified.

6. Use the Apply To function to specify whether or not the new settings should be applied to the current drawing (Active Drawing), future drawings (System Defaults), or both (All Possible).

7. Click on OK when finished.

There are two other options that should be noted: Ignore Feature Colors and Reset Feature. Ignore Feature Colors will ignore any feature color settings that have been made because this box has been checked and is active. This is a desirable feature when you want to temporarily disable feature colors. Reset Feature is a button that resets any selected feature to the same color the part is currently set at. The current part color is set by the Shading option in the System list box previously discussed.

Feature Properties

There is another way to change the color of part features that allows for a much greater degree of flexibility. Part features can have any color of the rainbow, independent of part color or feature color. These features can also have independent lighting characteristics, as described earlier in this chapter. Once again, the key to accessing this functionality is the right mouse button. The following steps outline this process:

1. In FeatureManager, right click on the feature whose color you would like to change.

2. Select Properties....

3. Click on the Color... button. This opens the Entity Property dialog box.

4. Click on Change Color to use a color other than the feature's current color settings.

5. Click on Advanced to modify the Material Properties (lighting characteristics) of the feature.

6. Click on OK to exit out of each dialog box and accept changes.

This can be a very convenient alternative to having every feature of a certain type be the same color. By accessing a feature's properties, color and lighting can be controlled on a much more selective scale. It is also possible to change the properties of a single face, instead of an entire feature. The process is very similar to the previous one. The following steps outline this process. The illustration at left shows the camera part with some of its face properties changed.

Camera part after changing some face properties.

1. In the Sketch area, right click on the face whose color you would like to change.

2. Select Face Properties....

3. Click on the Color... button. This opens the Entity Property dialog box.

4. Click on Change Color to use a color other than the face's current color settings.

5. Click on Advanced to modify the Material Properties (lighting characteristics) of the face.

6. Click on OK to exit out of each dialog box and accept changes.

Assembly Parts

All of the functionality described in this chapter can be applied to SolidWorks parts and assembly features. There are no differences between the two. There is only one other aspect regarding changing the color of a part inside an assembly that should be addressed. Depending on how the part's color is changed will make a difference as to whether or not those changes propagate back to the original part, and possibly any other assemblies the part may be in. The following are the possible scenarios for changes made to a part's color:

Scenario 1: Color changes made to the part are intended to affect the original part and any associated assemblies. To change the color of the part, perform the following steps:

1. In FeatureManager, right click on the part.

2. Select Edit Part. The part is now being edited, not the assembly.

3. Click on Tools/Options....

4. Select the Color tab.

5. Select Shading and make changes, as described earlier in this chapter.

Scenario 2: Color changes will affect only the part in the current assembly. To change a part's color in the current assembly only, perform the following steps:

1. In FeatureManager, right click on the part.

2. Select Component Properties....

3. Click on the Color button.

4. Make desired color changes, as described earlier in this chapter.

If you use this second method, you do not have to worry about other people getting upset with you for changing part colors in their assembly. This is because any changes made to the color of the part with the Component Properties Color button will not revert back to the original part.

Saving Images

Once all lighting and color enhancements have been implemented, it might be nice to save an image or two. SolidWorks currently has no built-in way of accomplishing this, but probably will in future releases. PhotoWorks, however, discussed in the next section, will save to a number of file types of any resolution.

How do you save an image in SolidWorks? The first option requires you to go out and buy a screen capture utility. That is how many of the images in this book were created. There are at least a half dozen such products on the market. Do a little research before spending much.

The second option is built into your computer. Windows 95 and NT both allow copying of the entire screen to the clipboard by pressing the Print Screen key on your keyboard. This takes the entire screen; therefore, the image needs to be cropped. It can then get pasted into any program.

PhotoWorks

SolidWorks' PhotoWorks is analogous to AutoCAD's AutoShade. PhotoWorks allows for the creation of photo-realistic style renderings, complete with procedural or texture bitmapped material properties. It also gives you the ability to modify and create custom material libraries, which is a function very similar to AutoShade. Procedural material properties go one step further than standard bit-mapped images. By using mathematical algorithms, specific material properties can be obtained. This process works especially well for materials such as metals, glass, and even water or diamond.

AutoCAD's AutoShade gives you tools for creating elaborate scenes, complete with trees and shrubs, as well as a variety of other options. PhotoWorks, on the other hand, is more suited to the mechanical market instead of the architectural market. Settings can be created and backgrounds displayed to give the impression, for example, that items are sitting on a tabletop surrounded by walls, or in an open environment with wispy clouds in the background. Photographs can be used to complete the effect. Shadows can be turned on to heighten the realistic effect.

Full ray tracing and anti-aliasing are available in Photo-Works for those individuals who are very discriminating and want the highest quality renderings. File output can be in the common TIFF or TARGA formats, as well as BMP and Postscript. If rendering to a file, the resolution is limited only by your machine's hardware and the length of time you are willing to wait for the process to take place. Very high resolutions can be keyed in, and large, E-size drawings can then be plotted with excellent results.

SolidWorks has excellent shading and lighting functionality, but if your business requires a higher degree of quality, PhotoWorks is the way to go. Applications include professional-looking catalogs, sales brochures, presentations, advertising, and any other number of possibilities. Talk to your vender or reseller to obtain more information on PhotoWorks.

Summary

Adding light sources or modifying colors and lighting characteristics are all options that will increase the Solid-Works user's efficiency by making a model easier to understand. By diversifying the colors of various part features or assembly components, not only is the model more aesthetically appealing, it simplifies the editing process because of the greater degree of contrast these changes invoke. Adding transparency to an assembly or placing a spotlight on a part are just a few ways that can help get a point across or convey information about a solid model.

Any modifications made to lighting sources, colors, advanced color options, or part properties are saved with the part. Expect to see the changes the next time the part or assembly is opened. Use the Print Screen key on the keyboard to save an image of the screen to the clipboard, where it can then get pasted into another program, such as the Windows Paint program or a text document. Photo-Works is an add-on package that creates photorealistic images that can be used in a variety of ways, such as for business promotions and advertising.

10 Printing

Introduction

This chapter discusses how to print a SolidWorks document using any printer available within the Windows operating system. Output can also be directed to a file if you wish to save a copy of the output, or send the file to another user, customer, and so on. Parts, assemblies, and drawings can be printed using this utility.

Prerequisite

You should have at least a basic understanding of the Windows 95 or Windows NT 4.0 operating system. Almost all of the printing parameters and the actual job of printing are handled by the operating system, not Solid-Works. For this reason, it helps if you are somewhat familiar with Windows so that any problems that arise can be addressed and the causes of such problems can be more easily tracked down.

Content

The sections of this chapter follow the logical order in which printer settings should be defined. The "Printing Basics" section gives you background information needed before using the print function. The section on defining a printer or plotter describes how a new printer or plotter can be added to Windows. The "Page Setup" section describes how to define paper size, margins, and header or footer values for a SolidWorks document. Line weights are addressed in the "Print Settings" section. The section on printing a document describes how to preview and print any type of SolidWorks document.

Objectives

When finished with the "Printing Basics" section, you should be aware of the fundamentals of printing and how printing is handled by the hardware and software. Upon completing the section on defining a printer or plotter, you should be able to identify what printers are installed and the steps required to define a new printer. You should be able to change page setup values (i.e., paper size, margins, header, and footer) at the end of the "Page Setup" section, and at the conclusion of the section on printing, you should be able to preview and print any type of SolidWorks document.

Printing Basics

Printing in SolidWorks is compatible with all printers and plotters defined under the Windows 95 or Windows NT operating system. The drivers for printers or plotters are obtained from the manufacturer, or from the Windows operating system setup disks or CD-ROM. The same procedure is used whether the output device is a printer or plotter.

The actual task of sending print information to the printer or plotter is the domain of the operating system. SolidWorks does not have any part in this. If the print preview can be displayed, SolidWorks has upheld its end of the bargain.

Loading or installing print drivers should be done before any printing is even attempted. Once again, this is done through the operating system, not SolidWorks. AutoCAD users will probably be well aware of the difficulties in setting up and configuring a printer. Whether or not to use an AutoCAD driver or a Windows driver was a common dilemma when initially setting up an AutoCAD printer or plotter.

These decisions do not concern the SolidWorks user. The SolidWorks program was written specifically for the Windows operating system and takes full advantage of this fact. If a printer or plotter is set up correctly through Windows, SolidWorks can print to it.

The Argument for Hard Copy

Obtaining hard-copy output is still an important, often necessary, task when working with engineering drawings. Few companies are operating in a completely electronic environment. Some companies are still using drawing boards. If you or your company are trying to convert to an electronic environment, SolidWorks has methods available for distributing documents electronically.

If it is necessary to be able to print from workstations other than where SolidWorks is installed, SolidWorks has a document viewer that allows any user with a PC to access SolidWorks documents (i.e., parts, drawings, and assemblies) for viewing and printing. It is not necessary to have SolidWorks installed. For that matter, the user or company does not even have to own a copy of Solid-Works. This is a free document viewer available from SolidWorks that can be obtained from the SolidWorks web site at *http://www.solidworks.com.*

Even when a document can be distributed electronically, there are still advantages to producing a hard copy of a drawing. It is easier to read the entire drawing with a large, formatted plot than on a computer monitor. Often it can be difficult to see the entire drawing on a monitor. The plot can produce a much larger image of the same drawing, and mistakes or design changes can be more easily recognized. The SolidWorks document viewer does not have red lining or mark-up capabilities. Therefore, a printed drawing can be a way of checking or marking changes on a drawing.

Quick Printing

Quick prints can be made of parts or assemblies without a drawing being made. There are many cases for which a print of a screen shot of a part or assembly can be made to effectively communicate or document a design element. This can be performed with or without a document's related dimensions. This can be done if scale is not a factor, because there is no way to set the scale of a part or assembly when printing the image onscreen. This is obviously not the case with regard to drawings.

Performing a quick print of the screen in AutoCAD is difficult if you are trying to print a shaded part. AutoCAD automatically regenerates the model during the print process, thereby placing the model back to its wireframe state. This is not an issue in SolidWorks.

If it is a shaded image you desire, you would print the screen from a part or assembly. Shaded views cannot be placed in a drawing using the usual methods described in Chapter 8, but objects can be embedded into a drawing. This might be a company logo, a shaded picture of a part, an AVI movie file, or any other object. The list goes on and on.

This would be accomplished using the Windows clipboard. Inserting objects can be done in SolidWorks using the Insert/Object...command. This is a capability that uses standard Windows functionality and is beyond the scope of this chapter. Any Windows program worth its weight should be able to perform such tasks.

The quality of the prints obtained from printing a screen shot of your SolidWorks model are only limited by your artistic eye for color and the quality of the printer's output. See Chapter 9 for options on changing the color or lighting characteristics of a part or assembly. If the print is being sent to a bubble-jet printer, the results are certainly not going to be as dramatic as what might be seen sending the print to a thermal wax printer.

Printing SolidWorks Documents

The three types of SolidWorks documents (parts, drawings, and assemblies) have different characteristics when printing or plotting. The following list describes these characteristics for the three types of documents. The routines for printing these document types are discussed later in the chapter.

Parts	Parts are printed using the current zoom scale and view orientation. The document will be printed as it is currently shown onscreen. The active display mode (i.e., wireframe, hidden in gray, hidden removed, or shaded) will be used to create the output file.
Assemblies	Assemblies are printed using the current zoom scale and view orientation. The document will be printed as it is currently shown onscreen. The active display mode (i.e., wireframe, hidden in gray, hidden removed, or shaded) will be used to create the output file. Assembly printing options and functionality are exactly the same as for parts.
Drawings	Drawings will print a full-size copy of the active sheet regardless of the current zoom scale. Scale for drawings is determined by the Page Setup dialog box and through the drawing itself. Multiple-sheet drawings (i.e., Sheet1, Sheet2, and so on) can be printed individually or singly using the print range function in the File/ Print menu, as described later in the chapter.

Defining a Printer or Plotter

SolidWorks uses the Windows print system for producing printed output. Whether a printer is going to be used for AutoCAD, SolidWorks, or any other program makes no difference. Defining a printer is done the same way, which is explained in material to follow. There are advantages to using the standard Windows print system, two of which are:

- More printer and plotter drivers are available. Device manufacturers no longer have to produce application-specific drivers. The manufacturer produces a driver for Windows 95 or Windows NT and all applications that run in Windows can then make use of these drivers. Many printer drivers are included with the Windows operating system and more can be obtained by contacting your vender or from the Internet.

- Any printer, local or remote, can be accessed using standard Windows functionality. You do not have to relearn a new interface to print a document. The same printer setup dialog box used to produce a printed document from a Microsoft Office application can be used to print a drawing from Solid-Works.

Adding a printer in the Printers folder.

Printing devices are defined by selecting Printers from the Windows Start button and clicking on Settings to open the printer setting's folder. The location, driver, port, and printer name must be supplied to set up a printer. Using the left mouse button, double click on the Add Printer icon to start the new printer wizard (see the illustration at left).

A series of dialog boxes will ask you questions concerning the location, type, name, and driver to define the printer. Whenever a new printer is added, make sure you respond with a "yes" when asked if you want to print a test page during the new printer installation process. This will let you know that everything is functioning correctly.

Printer Configuration

A printer can be attached directly to your computer (local) or attached to another computer on a network (a remote computer). When accessing a remote printer, your computer must be connected to the same network and the printer must be accessible by remote users. For a further explanation, use the Windows help index to search for "printer sharing." This can be found by performing the following steps:

1. Double click on My Computer.

2. Click on the Help pull-down menu.

3. Select Help Topics.

4. Select the Index tab.

5. Type in the words *printer sharing.*

6. Select the option you would like to see help for, and click on the Display button.

If you have more than one printer, the printer you use most often can be defined as your system default printer. This means that all printed documents will be sent to this printer unless you select another output device. This is defined using the Printers window previously described. Right click on the printer to be set as the default printer and select Set As Default. Only one printer can be selected as the default printer.

Printer/Plotter Attributes and Customization

The system attributes for a printer can be defined or redefined by modifying the settings for the printer in question. Right click on the printer's icon and select Properties. The printer attributes (i.e., ports, paper size, dithering, and so on) can be set or modified.

Different printers allow for a varying degree of customization. There are literally hundreds of different printers on the market. These range from standard letter-size dot matrix printers to 60-inch wide inkjet plotters and everything in between. Describing all of the settings for various printers and plotters is outside the scope of this book. Refer to the manufacturer's documentation for specific information regarding the settings for your individual printer or plotter.

Page Setup

The Page Setup function allows you to define paper margin values, paper orientation, print scale, and line weights for the active document. The page setup functions should be used to change specific attributes for the current document. These changes only affect the current document and are saved within the document file.

To set default parameters that will affect all documents, the system attributes for a printer can be defined or redefined by the method described earlier in this chapter using the Windows folder. The Page Setup routine in SolidWorks is specific to SolidWorks and is not a part of the Windows operating system. The Page Setup dialog box is shown in the following illustration.

*The Page Setup
dialog box.*

Almost all programs have some sort of page setup utility. AutoCAD's print setup dialog box was a fairly complex array of options somewhat intimidating for new users. SolidWorks' interface is much more basic. There is also a preview function similar to AutoCAD's Full Preview option. The various settings in the Page Setup dialog box are described in material to follow.

Page Setup Options

There are two tabs in the Page Setup dialog box: one labeled Printer, shown in the previous illustration, and another labeled Header/Footer. The Printer tab will be discussed first, starting with setting margins. The Header/Footer tab follows this section.

Paper Margins

A margin is the distance from the outside edge of the paper to the available print area. The minimum margin differs for each printer. Think of margins as the white border around the printed image. If the print area exceeds the margin boundaries, portions of the image may get clipped.

Even though a printer's margins can be set manually, this is not recommended for most day-to-day printing chores. One example of why you might want to increase the print margins is in the case of publishing. Take, for example, a person that has to run off some prints that are going to be placed in a binder. The default margins are set too small and when the holes are punched in the printed pages, portions of the data has holes punched through it. In this case, it would benefit you to increase the left margin to an inch or so. However, this is usually not the case; therefore, leave Use Printer's Margins checked.

Page Orientation

The Page Orientation function determines the direction in which output is sent to a printer. The Print Preview function can be used to determine if the page orientation is correct with regard to the data being printed. Generally speaking, Portrait is used for most text documents and Landscape for CAD drawings. If the preview function shows the document in an undesirable manner, you can change the page orientation prior to sending the file to the printer. The Portrait option orients the long side of the paper vertically. The Landscape option orients the long side of the paper horizontally.

Scale

The Scale function is used to reduce or enlarge a printed image to fit into a desired paper size or format. The Scale To Fit check box is checked by default. This will automatically scale the output to fit the selected paper size. The scale is defined by a percentage value. Uncheck the Scale To Fit check box to activate the Scale option so that the image can be reduced or enlarged as needed.

It should be noted that the Scale option should not be used to scale drawing views for the sake of fitting the views on a particular sheet size. Drawing views are scaled to fit on a drawing when the views are initially created, as described in Chapter 8. Sheet size is also determined when the drawing is initially created. For this reason, it is best to print or plot drawings at 100 percent. This is extremely critical if individuals will be taking measurements from the print.

If you are printing a drawing file, and the scale of the geometry has already been scaled to fit a specific sheet size (i.e., half scale, quarter scale, 1:10, and so on), uncheck Scale To Fit and print with Scale set to 100 percent. If you are printing a part or assembly, or if the drawing scale does not matter, leave Scale To Fit checked and let SolidWorks scale the image to fit the paper.

Line Weights

A line can be defined as having a thin, normal, or thick line thickness. This is determined in the Options dialog box and can be changed. The material that follows explains how this is accomplished, followed by material on modifying line weight settings in the Page Setup dialog box. Perform the following steps to see how line thickness settings are attached to the various line types in SolidWorks. The illustration that follows shows the Line Fonts tab.

1. Select Tools/Options....

2. Select the Line Fonts tab.

3. Click on a line type in the Type of Edge list box to see a preview of that line type.

4. Adjust Line Style and Line Weight as needed.

The Line Fonts tab.

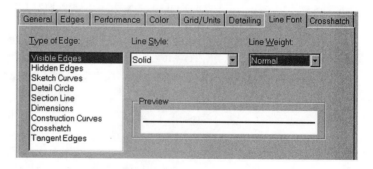

SolidWorks breaks up lines into nine categories. These are:

- Visible Edges
- Hidden Edges
- Sketch Curves
- Detail Circle
- Section Line
- Dimensions
- Construction Curves
- Crosshatch
- Tangent Edges

Each of these line types can have its line style and weight adjusted. The default settings for these line classifications are acceptable for most users. It is recommended that the default settings not be changed. Take note, however, that in the Line Weight drop-down list box there are three options: Thin, Normal, and Thick. These settings are directly related to the Thin, Normal, and Thick settings in the Page Setup dialog box.

For example, consider visible edges. Visible edges are defined as having a line weight setting of Normal. What this means to you is that all visible edges, when printed, will use the value specified in the Line Weights section of the Page Setup dialog box for normal lines. What that actual value is depends on your printer. Different printers require different settings for line weights. A laserjet may require a slightly thicker setting because the lines sometimes have a tendency to print so fine that they are almost invisible.

What all this really boils down to is: Do not mess with the line fonts in the Options dialog box. Specify a reasonable line width in the Page Setup dialog box and leave it alone.

How can you determine what is a reasonable line width? Try the following series of steps for the printer in question. You will need to know how to create a part and a drawing because the steps for creating these have been omitted from the following steps. The illustration that follows shows a drawing file for testing line weights.

1. Create a simple part. An extruded rectangle will serve the purpose.

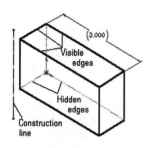

Drawing file for testing line weights.

2. Create a new drawing. A standard A-size sheet will be fine. Do not bother with a template because you will not need one.

3. Select Tools/Options… and select the Line Font tab. Set Construction Curves to Thick. This needs to be done because there are no lines that use the Thick setting by default.

4. Bring in an Isometric view of the part and display the view with Hidden Lines in Gray (or dashed).

5. Draw a centerline (otherwise known as a construction line) and add a dimension if you want.

6. Print the drawing.

Now you have a simple drawing containing all three types of line thickness. Experiment with the thin, normal, and thick line weight values in the Page Setup dialog box until good settings are found for your specific printer.

For example, for a Canon bubble jet printer, the line weight settings .010, .015, and .025 inches would probably work well for thin, normal, and thick line weights, respectively. These settings might not be ideal for your printer or plotter, but they might serve as a place to start. Do not forget to set Construction Curves back to thin! If you are wondering why the word *curves* is used, it is because this term that refers to arcs, lines, or splines.

Print Setup

This button performs one function, and that is to take you to the Print setup dialog box, shown in the following illustration, for your printers. The information in your Print dialog box may be different, but the layout will be the same.

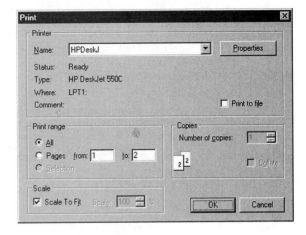

The Print dialog box.

The various options found in the Print Setup dialog box are in the Windows realm. Therefore, they will not be discussed in detail here.

Headers and Footers

Header properties define text added to the top of the printed document, and footer properties define text added to the bottom. The Header/Footer tab is used to add titles, sheet numbers, date, time, and file name to a printed document, to name a few options. Standard header and footer values are available for selection, or custom header and footer values can be defined. The properties defined for a header or footer affect only the active document. The following illustration shows header and footer print locations with regard to a standard drawing document.

Header and footer print location.

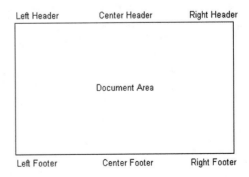

Header/Footer Options

The Header/Footer attributes option is accessed within the Header/Footer tab of the Page Setup dialog box, as shown in the following illustration.

Specifying header and footer properties.

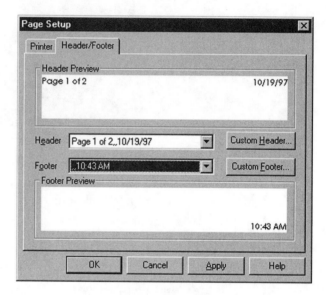

Header and footer areas have three sections each: left, center, and right. Standard header and footer values are available from the drop-down list boxes within the Header/Footer tab. A custom header or footer can also be defined to include the following system attributes. The illustration that follows shows customization of a header or footer.

Page number	Prints the current sheet number being printed.
Number of pages	Prints the total number of sheets in the document.
Date	Prints the current date. Convenient for knowing when the document was printed.
Time	Prints the time the document was printed.
File name	Prints the file name of the active document.

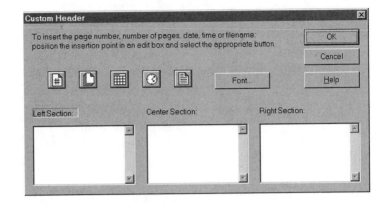

Customizing a header or footer.

The dialog box for customizing a header or a footer looks exactly the same. The only difference is where Solid-Works places the text, which will either be on the top or bottom of the document being printed. SolidWorks uses its own codes for keeping track of header and footer information. Do not be concerned with this, as it is simply the program's way of doing things.

The system attributes (or codes) SolidWorks uses are pre-fixed with an "&," followed by the system value enclosed in brackets. Feel free to type spaces or text before, after, or in between the codes to customize the header or footer information even more. For example, you can create a string to display the current page and the total pages with the word *page* before the page number and the word *of* between these values. To see how this is done, perform the following steps:

1. Click on either the Custom Header or Custom Footer button.

2. Click in the section box where the information should be placed, which would be either Left Section, Center Section, or Right Section.

3. Type in the word *Page*.

4. Click on the page number icon (see the following illustration).

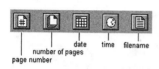

number of pages | date | time | filename
page number

Icons available for customizing a header or footer.

5. Type in the word *of.*

6. Click on the Number of Pages icon (see the illustration at left).

7. Click on the Font button to set the font and font size. A small font size, such as 8 point, is common for header or footer data.

8. Click on OK to accept the changes and exit out of the dialog boxes. When you get back to the Page Setup dialog box, you will notice a preview of the header or footer information.

In the header or footer customization dialog box, the code string will appear as follows:

Page &[pagenum] of &[pages]

In the preview window of the Page Setup dialog box, the same information will appear as follows:

Page 1 of 1

A Quick AutoCAD Comparison

As mentioned earlier in this chapter, the Page Setup dialog box is specific to SolidWorks. AutoCAD has the ability to manage line weights and pen settings on a much larger scale. Line weights can be associated with pens or with colors. AutoCAD also gives you the ability to draw polylines with varying degrees of thickness, even within the same line segment if you require it. SolidWorks does not have this fine degree of control when it comes to line weights and line types. As of this writing, there are only three line weight settings.

In the area of creating headers or footers, SolidWorks is superior to AutoCAD. In AutoCAD, there are workaround methods of placing information on a drawing that looks like a header or footer, but the process is not automated, as in SolidWorks.

Printing a Document

The Print Preview function allows you to get a sample of output prior to sending the print to the printer or plotter. This allows for corrections to the header, footer, and margin values before spending the time required to produce hard-copy output. Not only does the Print Preview option save time, it can also save money. Paper and ink can be quite expensive. Printer quality has gotten better as the printer prices have fallen, and that trend will more than likely continue. However, bubble jet ink cartridges are expensive if you have to constantly replace them.

Print Preview

The Print Preview option is found under the File pulldown menu, right where you would expect it. Print Preview is closest in functionality to AutoCAD's Preview feature with the Full option selected. Like AutoCAD's Full Preview, Print Preview provides the ability to zoom in and make some last-minute checks before sending a document to the printer. Changes can be made to Page Setup values if the previewed image is not correct. The following illustration shows the Print Preview toolbar.

The Print Preview toolbar.

Almost everything in the Print Preview window is self-explanatory. Included are the Next and Previous buttons, which take you to the next or previous sheet to be printed. This is convenient because drawings can have multiple sheets. Also included is a button named Two Page for viewing two pages at once.

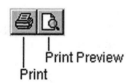

The Print icon located on the Standard toolbar.

Two Page will place two sheets onto the computer screen at the same time; therefore, do not expect to see a great deal of detail. The data will probably be too small to see. Use Zoom In and Zoom Out if you need to check details at the last minute. Note that the Two Page option is not available if the current preview is zoomed in. The illustration at left shows the Print icon on the Standard toolbar.

Printing a Document

To print a document, select the Print icon or select Print from the File menu. If using the Print Preview function, click on the Print button. An advantage to using the Print command in the File menu as opposed to the Print icon is that the Print dialog box will appear when the document is printed. This allows you to select multiple copies, change the printer, and so on.

The Print icon will print a single document using the currently defined print properties and using the default printer if more than one printer has been defined. If you want to print using another printer (other than the default), use the File/Print command and select the desired printer.

Summary

SolidWorks allows you to access any output device, local or network, available within the Windows operating system. Printers are defined outside SolidWorks, which means that you no longer need to maintain the drivers and configure printers or plotters within the CAD system. The print services (i.e., devices, location, name, spooling, and so on) are handled and maintained at the operating system level.

Printing properties defined outside SolidWorks are those for printer drivers, printer locations, and the default system printer. Printing properties defined within Solid-Works are those for headers and footers, page margins, line weights, print scale, and paper orientation (landscape versus portrait). The SolidWorks Print command uses the standard Windows Print dialog box, which is the same for any Windows application. Use Print Preview to preview what will be sent to the printer or plotter, thereby saving time and money otherwise wasted on inaccurate prints.

Import/Export

Introduction

This chapter discusses how to import and transfer Solid-Works parts, assemblies, and drawings to other CAD systems. The Import/Export function is used to communicate with external sources, import data, and reuse existing data. SolidWorks includes all file import/export formats within the base product and does not require you to purchase add-on modules.

Content

The "DXF and DWG" section describes the import/export capabilities with respect to AutoCAD DXF and DWG formatted files. The section on IGES describes the import/export capabilities with respect to IGES formatted files. The "Stereolithography" section describes the import/export capabilities with respect to stereolithography (STL) formatted files used primarily for rapid prototyping. The section on miscellaneous formats describes the other import/export capabilities within SolidWorks. These formats include STEP, ACIS, Parasolid, and VRML.

Objectives

With completion of the "DXF and DWG" section, you should be able to import and export files using these formats, and understand what type of SolidWorks documents are created when using these file types. After you have finished the section on IGES, you should be able to import and export files using this format, and you should understand what type of SolidWorks document is created when importing this file type.

Upon completing the "Stereolithography" section, you should be able to export files using this format. When you have completed the section on miscellaneous formats, you should be able to import and export files using these formats.

Basics

Files are imported and exported using the Open and Save As commands. This makes saving or opening files of other files types nearly as easy as saving a native Solid-Works file because the commands are exactly the same. The Open and Save As dialog boxes are shown in the following two illustrations. These commands allow you to specify a file type, either for importing (Open) or exporting (Save As). This simplistic and logical approach sometimes catches the new user off guard because he or she is looking for an Import or Export command when there is none to be found. This is because these commands are built into the Open and Save As dialog boxes.

Data imported from an external source can be manipulated within a SolidWorks document (i.e., part, drawing, or assembly) and stored as either a SolidWorks document or in the original file format. One advantage to keeping the file in a SolidWorks format is the ability to add parametric features to the document.

The Open dialog box.

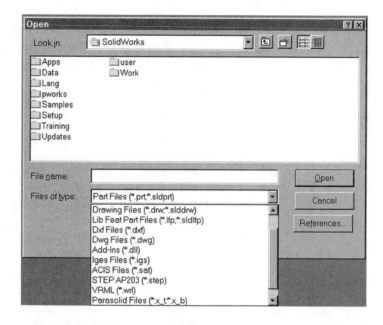

The Save As dialog box.

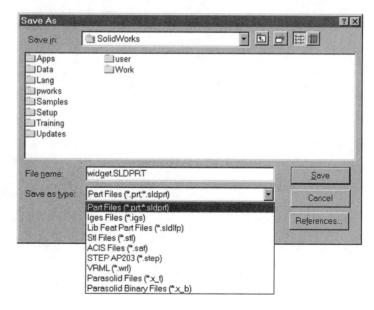

Some formats can only be imported as SolidWorks parts, and some as drawings. The reverse is true as well. This is obvious for certain types of formats. For example, it would not be possible to export a solid model as 2D wireframe geometry. Likewise, it would not be possible to take a 2D AutoCAD layout and import it as a SolidWorks 3D part file. The material that follows explores exactly what is possible within SolidWorks and discusses the best methods of translating various file types. First, however, take a look at the types of formats available for importing and exporting for SolidWorks part files.

SolidWorks Import/Export Formats for Parts

The following list contains the various file import and export options for SolidWorks parts. Some export options may be better than others for the particular program you are translating to. It is often a good idea to use a practice file to run some tests and determine the best translator to use. That way, it is also possible to inform clients or customers of the best file type to use when exchanging data, to ensure that important data is not lost or corrupted.

IGES	Initial Graphics Exchange Format file type used to transfer information between dissimilar systems. This file type has an *IGS* extension and is one of the more widely accepted file translation formats.
STL	Stereolithography file type used for rapid prototyping. This file type has an *STL* extension and is available for export only.
VRML	Virtual Reality Markup Language file type. This file type has a *WRL* extension. These file types are usually exported for use on the Internet, but can be imported as a surface.
STEP AP203	ISO STEP (International Standards Organization Standard or Exchange of Product Model Data) formatted file type. This file type has an *STEP* extension.
ACIS	ACIS formatted file type. This file type has an *SAT* extension and is AutoCAD's native solid format.
Parasolid	Unigraphics formatted file type. This file type has an *X_T* extension.
Parasolid Binary	Unigraphics binary formatted file type. This file type has an *X_B* extension.

SolidWorks Import/ Export Formats for Assemblies

Import and export options for assemblies are not quite as numerous as for parts. The nature of assemblies makes translating more difficult. The following are the import and export options for assemblies.

IGES	Initial Graphics Exchange Format file format.
VRML	Virtual Reality Markup Language file type. This file type has a *WRL* extension.
STEP AP203	ISO STEP (International Standards Organization Standard or Exchange of Product Model Data) formatted file type. This file type has a *STEP* extension.
ACIS	ACIS formatted file type. This file type has an *SAT* extension.
Parasolid	Unigraphics formatted file type. This file type has an *X_T* extension.
Parasolid Binary	Unigraphics binary formatted file type. This file type has an *X_B* extension.

SolidWorks Import/Export Formats for Drawings

When exporting or importing 2D geometry, the formats are logically going to be different from 3D geometry due to the nature of the data. Therefore, the formats for drawings will be different than for parts and assemblies. Also, as you can see, there are not a huge number of options when it comes to translating 2D geometry. Thankfully though, the DXF and DWG translators are very good and widely accepted. The following are the import and export formats for DXF and DWG are:

DXF	AutoCAD Data eXchange Format file type. This file type has a *DXF* extension.
DWG	AutoCAD drawing file type. This file type has a *DWG* extension.

Changing and Setting Document Export Preferences

Default settings for import and export characteristics can be defined by selecting the Export Settings tab from the Tools/Options menu. Settings for IGES, Parasolid, DXF/DWG, STL, and ACIS can be defined within the Export Settings dialog box. These settings are discussed throughout the chapter, as they are applicable to the individual chapter sections.

DXF and DWG

Using the Open and Save As commands, a DXF or DWG formatted file can be used to import or export drawing documents. Import or export of DXF or DWG files works for drawing documents only. It would be pointless to bring an entire 2D DXF or DWG file into a part document because the information would be useless.

When a DXF or DWG file is opened, it automatically imports as a SolidWorks drawing. There are cases in which portions of the material could be used to create a solid model. In this case, it is possible to bring portions of a 2D drawing into a part file for use as sketch geometry. AutoCAD versions 12, 13, and 14 DWG or DXF files are supported. The specific version can be defined by selecting the Import/Export tab from the Tools/Options menu and selecting the desired version (see the following illustration). Centermarks, detail circles, section lines, and note symbols are supported for DXF export.

Setting DXF and DWG export options.

Depending on what version of AutoCAD you are exporting to, it may also be desirable to limit the font export to AutoCAD standard fonts only. Not all AutoCAD users have the same Windows True Type fonts, especially if they are using the DOS version of AutoCAD. Make sure you check the appropriate option for font export, shown in the previous illustration.

DWG or DXF legacy data can also be imported into a SolidWorks sketch using the Sketch From Drawing command. Once geometry is in the sketch, geometric constraints and dimensions can be placed on the geometry. This allows you to add parametric capabilities to static 2D geometry. Multiple sketches can be used from one 2D drawing to define a 3D solid model. You can also break 2D drawings into individual sketches to define multiple features. First, however, step through how to import a

DWG or DXF file, and take a look at how to get data from that drawing into a SolidWorks sketch.

Importing a DXF or DWG Formatted File

To import a DXF or DWG formatted file, perform the following steps:

1. Select the Open icon, or select Open from the File menu.

2. Change Files of Type to specify DXF Files (*.dxf) or DWG Files (*.dwg).

3. With the left mouse button, select the file to be opened.

4. Select Open.

SolidWorks will automatically translate the file. If there is geometry you would like to use within a SolidWorks sketch, perform the following steps:

1. Begin a new part file, or open the part file to import the data into.

2. Select a plane or planar face to sketch on.

3. Enter sketch mode.

4. From the Insert menu, select Sketch From Drawing. Notice that the cursor changes.

5. Switch to the drawing that has the data to be imported into the sketch.

6. Place a window around the geometry to be imported. Do this by picking with the left mouse button and dragging the opposite corner. The geometry will automatically be imported into the sketch in the part.

Once the geometry is imported into the sketch, there are two things you will probably want to accomplish right away. The first thing you will notice is that the geometry is in the wrong location and needs to be moved. This is because the AutoCAD UCS x-y coordinate of 0,0 directly correlates to the SolidWorks origin point. (Every AutoCAD user knows that the UCS is almost always at the bottom left-hand corner of the work area.)

First, use the Constrain All function found in the Relations menu under Tools. This will add as many of the basic constraints to the sketch as SolidWorks can add. Usually, these consist of the simple constraints, such as horizontal, perpendicular, vertical, and parallel. You will have to add others, along with dimensions. Next, use the Modify tool found in Sketch Tools under the Tools menu. Modify will allow you to translate the entire sketch closer to the origin point. You can then more fully define the geometry as necessary and create the feature.

Exporting a DXF or DWG Formatted File

Only SolidWorks drawing files can be saved as DXF or DWG files for reasons already discussed. The following are the steps required for exporting these file types:

1. Select Tools/Options/Import/Export.

2. Select the version of DXF or DWG file to be exported (R12, R13, or R14).

3. Click on OK to accept the changes.

4. Select Save As from the File menu.

5. Specify the file name to save as.

6. Change "Save as type" to DXF Files (*.dxf) or DWG Files (*.dwg).

7. Select Save to accept the data.

IGES

IGES data files are used to transfer information from one type of CAD system to another. This is a neutral file format that can be interpreted by other systems. IGES file import or export works with part and assembly documents only. When native file formats are not available as an export type on both systems, an IGES format is typically used to exchange geometric model data.

When importing a closed, contiguous IGES surface file, SolidWorks will sew the surfaces into a solid if possible. If the IGES file contains open or noncontiguous surface data, SolidWorks will import the surfaces without sewing a solid and generate an error log file. This error message means only that the imported data cannot be "knitted" into a solid. This warning message can be ignored if the surfaces are not meant to be a solid feature (i.e., a single surface).

Supported Entity Types

If the IGES import was successfully knitted, SolidWorks will treat the new solid model like a base part. Features can be added or material removed from the original model. When importing IGES files, use trimmed surfaces (IGES entity type 144) whenever possible. Trimmed surfaces are the surface types understood by SolidWorks. All entities supported for IGES translation have numbers associated with them. This is nothing more than a method of identifying the various entities used by the IGES file format. The numbers are nothing the average user needs to memorize, but they are included here for reference purposes. This is not a complete listing. The following entity types are supported for import and export.

IGES Entity Type	Entity Name
144	Trimmed (parametric) surface
142	Curve on a parametric surface
128	Rational B-spline surface
126	Rational B-spline curve
122	Tabulated cylinder
120	Surface of revolution
112*	Parametric spline curve
110	Line
102	Composite curve
100	Circular arc
* Export only.	

Trimmed Surfaces

IGES files can be exported as various "flavors." This means that some programs use a slightly different IGES file type, or that they can read specific entities supported by the IGES translator better than others. For this reason, there are seven export options for the IGES export function. Once again, this setting can be found in the Import/Export section of the Options tab (see the following illustration).

IGES export options.

The following is a listing of the various IGES flavors and the surface types supported by each.

Export Format Types	Exported IGES Entity Types
Standard	144, 142, 128, 126, 122, 120, 110, 102, 100
ANSYS	144, 142, 128, 126, 110, 102, 100
COSMOS	144, 142, 128, 126, 110, 102, 100
MasterCAM	144, 142, 128, 126, 110, 102, 100
SurfCAM	144, 142, 128, 126, 110, 102, 100
SmartCAM	144, 142, 128, 126, 110, 102, 100
TEKSOFT	144, 142, 128, 126, 110, 102, 100

3D Curves—Wireframe Representation

Never export 3D curves if translating files for use in another solid modeling package. Most solid modelers do not understand simple wireframe geometry. This export option is for software that understands wireframe geometry only, or for use in surface modeling software. The following are the export IGES entity types for wireframe geometry.

Type of 3D Curve	Exported IGES Entity Types
B-splines (entity 126)	126, 110, 102*, 100
Parametric splines (entity 112)	112, 110, 102*, 100
* Exported only if you select the Duplicate Entities option in IGES Preferences.	

Report Files

SolidWorks creates a report file, *<filename>.rpt*, that lists the entities that were imported and that can be used to investigate import errors. When errors do occur during the import process, an error log file, *<filename>.err*, is created describing what occurred. You should review this file to ensure that the import function performed properly and all entities were processed, or were sent to a knowledgeable technical support representative to help diagnose translational errors. The report file is an ASCII text document that can be opened with any text editor or word processor (e.g., Notepad or Microsoft Word).

➡ **NOTE:** *When reporting problems to a vendor, customer, or SolidWorks, include a copy of this report file for reference. This can help pinpoint problems.*

Individual surfaces can be imported using Insert/Reference Geometry/Imported Surface. This import technique is different from using the File/Open dialog box in one major way. When using File/Open, SolidWorks attempts to knit the surfaces to form a solid. When using the Import Surface function, no knitting of the surfaces is attempted.

IGES surfaces that do not form a closed solid can be imported, and used in subsequent feature creation, such as by thickening the surface or using the surface to cut geometry already in the model. Individual surfaces can be exported as IGES file types using File/Save As. To save only certain surfaces, hold down the Control key a select the surfaces to be exported. Then select File/Save As and specify the IGES file type.

When Trimmed Surfaces is selected in the Import/Export tab (see the illustration at the beginning of this section), check the Pop-up Dialog Before File Saving option to display a menu with all of the IGES "flavors" prior to exporting the IGES file. This is a nice option when you frequently want to export IGES files to a variety of programs but do not want to have to enter the Options dialog box prior to every export to verify settings.

When problems occur while exporting IGES files, change the Settings For option under the Import/Export tab for the IGES settings menu to another that may better match the requirements on the target system. For example, if you are exporting to a software program not listed in the IGES Settings For list box, it is sometimes a hit or miss operation to find a setting that works the best. Try changing to an alternate setting if the first try does not work. Also, the Trim Curve Accuracy option sometimes plays a part when knitting surfaces. Setting the Trim Curve Accuracy to High creates a larger IGES file, but it might be just enough to make a successful IGES translation to an otherwise uncooperative software program.

Importing an IGES Formatted File

You have been through the ins and outs of IGES translation. Now run through the steps for importing an IGES file.

1. Select the Open icon, or select Open from the File menu.

2. Change "Files of type" to IGES Files (*.igs).

3. Select the IGES file to be opened.

4. Click on the Open button. SolidWorks will import the file.

If a large file is being imported, possibly in the multiple megabyte range, the import process may take a few minutes. This depends on your hardware as well. If Solid-Works cannot successfully import the file on its first pass, it will loosen the tolerance and try again. This continues for a few passes until SolidWorks either completes the translation or until the tolerance cannot be loosened any more and SolidWorks abandons the translation with a message to you to this effect.

Exporting an IGES Formatted File

Exporting is a very simple process. To export an IGES formatted file, perform the following steps:

1. Select Save As from the File menu.

2. Change the file name and location, if desired, using the Save As dialog box.

3. Change "Save as type" to IGES Files (*.igs).

4. Select Save to continue. SolidWorks will write the IGES file to the destination selected.

Stereolithography

Stereolithography (STL) formatted files are typically used by rapid prototyping processes. This process produces a triangulated meshed part that other systems can use for viewing, prototype creation, or machining. Accuracy for STL files is set by selecting an appropriate display quality from the STL dialog box. This dialog box is accessed from the Tools/Options menu in the Import/Export section by selecting the STL Options button. The STL output file can also be previewed by checking the Preview option in the STL export settings dialog box. The following illustration shows the various settings present in this dialog box.

The STL dialog box.

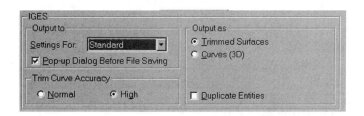

STL File Content

STL files consist of polygons. These polygons can be large or very small. Their size depends on the tolerance required. This is the reason for the preview circles in the STL dialog box, and for the ability to set the deviation. Using a quality (polygon size) that is too large will result in a smaller STL file, but a prototype that would probably not serve the purpose it was needed for. Prototyping machines will actually build a part using the settings built into in the polygon file for creating the prototype.

A good prototype file will have smaller polygons and therefore a smoother surface. The output file can be defined as an ASCII or binary file. The advantage to an ASCII file is that the file can be read with a text editor.

However, this is almost never needed. The advantages of a binary file far outweigh an ASCII text file; therefore, unless specifically requested, you should create a binary file. They are smaller and are read by the prototyping machines faster. The following illustration shows an STL polygon file.

STL polygon file.

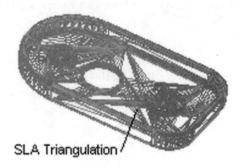

SLA Triangulation

There are a number of STL viewers on the market that allow you to measure features, calculate mass properties, spin a model, and cut cross sections in an STL part. It is not possible to import an STL file into SolidWorks, but the steps for exporting such a file follow.

Exporting a Stereolithography File

To export a stereolithography file, perform the following steps:

1. Select Tools/Options.

2. Click on the Import/Export tab.

3. Click on the STL Options button.

4. Select Show STL Info Before File Saving if you would like to see a preview of the STL file before saving it.

5. Specify the Binary file type.

6. Specify the Deviation and Angle Tolerance as required. Higher is better, but results in a much larger file and longer processing times. Experiment with these settings to find an appropriate middle ground.

7. Click on OK twice to exit out of both dialog boxes.

8. Select Save As from the File menu.

9. Change the file name and location, if desired, using the Save As dialog box.

10. Change "Files of type" to STL File (*.stl).

11. Select Save to continue.

12. If Show STL Info Before File Saving has been checked in the Import/Export tab, select Yes to continue or No to abort.

Miscellaneous Formats

A number of other formats can be imported and exported within SolidWorks. These formats, and why you would want to use each format, are discussed in the material that follows.

ACIS

An ACIS formatted file can be imported or exported using the Open and Save As commands. This file format can be interpreted by other systems that use the ACIS solid modeling kernel. ACIS file import or export works only for SolidWorks part files. ACIS surfaces can also be imported into a SolidWorks part file by implementing the Import Surface command found in the Insert/Reference Geometry menu.

Importing an ACIS-formatted File

To import an ACIS-formatted file, perform the following steps:

1. Select the Open icon, or select Open from the File menu.

2. Select the target directory.

3. Change "Files of type" to ACIS Files (*.sat).

4. Select the ACIS file to be opened.

5. Select Open to complete this function.

Exporting an ACIS-formatted File

To export an ACIS-formatted file, perform the following steps:

1. Select Save As from the File menu.

2. Change the file name and location, if desired, using the Save As dialog box.

3. Change "Save as type" to ACIS Files (*.sat).

4. Select Save to continue.

Parasolids and STEP Files

It would be redundant to walk through the steps for the Parasolids and STEP translation process, whether it be for importing or exporting. The procedure is exactly the same for IGES, ACIS, Parasolids, or STEP files. The only exception is when importing: the correct "Files of type" file extension needs to be selected. When exporting, make sure to select the appropriate "Save as type" file extension.

Parasolids is the solid modeling kernel used by Solid-Works and Unigraphics, to name a couple. There are a number of other proprietary modeling kernels in use. Always make it a point to know what modeling kernel is being used by the program you are translating to. If that information cannot be obtained, at least know what formats are acceptable to the target program.

STEP appears as though it may begin gathering steam in the near future. STEP is currently used by CATIA, a high-end design software in use by many large companies, and other software as well. It remains to be seen whether or not STEP overtakes IGES as the most popular translating standard.

VRML

The VRML function allows you to save an active part or assembly as a VRML (Virtual Reality Markup Language) formatted file. This file can be viewed with an Internet browser with a VRML plug-in. The VRML viewer is a plug-in option for web browsers. The VRML formatted file of a part or assembly can be viewed and navigated (panned and zoomed) with an Internet browser or a VRML viewer. Instructions on where to find a VRML viewer are available on the SolidWorks web site. To export a VRML formatted file, perform the following steps:

1. Select Save As from the File menu.

2. Change the file name and location, if desired, using the Save As dialog box.

3. Change "Save as type" to VRML (*.wrl).

4. Select Save to continue.

It is also possible to import VRML files using the Import Surface function in the Tools/Reference Geometry menu.

Summary

When working with vendors or customers to transfer files, it is a good practice to determine the type of system they have, available translators, and preference of file format types. When working with a system unfamiliar to you, it may be useful to provide a number of formats. The vendor or customer can then try another format if a problem does occur with the first attempt.

The difficulty with importing and exporting data typically arises due to one of the translators not understanding the format used by the other translator. Both translators must work together for successful results. If one end does not produce or read the data correctly, an error can occur. The log file generated by SolidWorks can be used to determine the cause of the problem. There are inherent difficulties involved with translating. If it is at all possible, translate using the same proprietary kernel format (i.e., Parasolids for moving between Unigraphics and Solid-Works) rather than involving a secondary format.

Customizing
SolidWorks

Introduction

There are aspects of the SolidWorks user interface that can be tailored to your preferences. This chapter discusses customizing SolidWorks. The options for doing so are different from AutoCAD's customization options. This chapter also discusses automating repetitive tasks using a programming language (e.g., Visual Basic or C++) or a SolidWorks macro. This chapter is meant to give you an overview of the programming capabilities present in SolidWorks and how Visual Basic language can be used to expand on the SolidWorks software.

Prerequisite

It is essential that you have a very good understanding of the SolidWorks program before attempting any customization. Making changes to the SolidWorks interface can result in a very different look and feel for the program and make the learning process much more difficult than it might otherwise be. Learning SolidWorks is not nearly as difficult as learning nearly any other CAD program, but the learning should be done before manipulating the interface.

Content

There are three main ways in which the SolidWorks software can be customized that will be discussed in this chapter. The first section describes how to use some of the options to change the way SolidWorks operates. The next section will go into greater detail with regard to using the Customization dialog box to alter the SolidWorks interface to a greater extent. Finally, this chapter provides an introduction to programming languages for automating repetitive tasks. This is intended to offer only an idea of what capabilities are available and where to look for further reference material on programming languages and how they can be used within SolidWorks.

Objectives

After reading through this chapter, you will be able to set up the SolidWorks environment based on your preferences. You will also be able to customize toolbars, menu commands, and keyboard shortcuts. Additionally, you will be made aware of the options available for creating user-defined programs and macros and know where to find additional reference material on the subject of programming.

User Preferences

SolidWorks, like many software programs, contains ways to customize its interface. These customization methods are not quite as extravagant as AutoCAD's—wherein you have the ability to modify pull-down menus and define custom Lisp routines within those menus—but there are ways to change many aspects of the program that are actually quite similar to AutoCAD's customization capabilities. The Customize dialog box allows you to make more drastic changes than should sometimes be performed; therefore, you need to be careful with this function.

Before diving into that aspect of the program, you will explore a more tame approach to customizing in SolidWorks. Many of the user preferences can be found under Tools/Options. Some were discussed in Chapter 3. All of the various options will not be covered at this time, as these have already been defined in Chapter 3. Only the options that will in some way alter the appearance of SolidWorks are mentioned in this chapter.

What is now the Options dialog box started out being called User Preferences when SolidWorks was first released. The following sections describe some of the option tabs that can be used to alter the way SolidWorks behaves.

General Tab

The General tab under Tools/Options has many settings that can be toggled on and off. Others, such as the View Rotation section, require more user input. View Rotation defines how sensitive the mouse will be when rotating a model onscreen. When clicking the Rotate icon, a smaller movement of the mouse will result in a greater amount of rotation if the slider bar is moved to the right. The angle amount listed in the same section defines how far the model will be rotated when using the keyboard shortcut keys. In this case, the keyboard shortcut keys refer to the arrow keys. In the following illustration, the model will rotate 15 degrees any time the arrow keys are pressed.

The General tab in the Options dialog box.

In the General section of the same tab, checking "Maximize document on open" will result in documents always filling up the entire work area when opened. This is usually desirable.

The Sketch section of the General tab has some settings relative to how SolidWorks looks to the user. For instance, "Display arc centerpoints" will project all arc centerpoints to the current sketch plane when in sketch mode. This is convenient when trying to sketch to centerpoints. However, when you are working on a part that has many arcs, the arc centerpoints have a tendency to clutter up the display. "Display entity points" will show entity endpoints as small dots. These dots will also display a specific color if they are fully defined. The color scheme follows the standard color scheme used by SolidWorks. Black represents fully defined, blue represents underdefined, and red represents overdefined.

Color Tab

This is one of those places that will get you in trouble if you are not careful. SolidWorks has default colors it uses to display certain entities or conditions. One example is overdefined sketch geometry being displayed in red. This is not something a user will normally want to change, but the capability exists nonetheless. The following illustration shows the Color tab from the Options dialog box.

The Color tab in the Options dialog box.

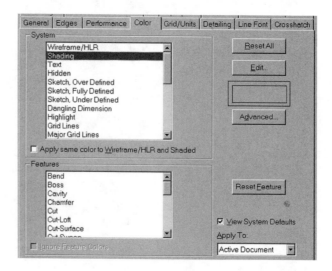

If you click on the View System Defaults button, the System list expands to show all of the options in SolidWorks that can have their color settings altered. Simply highlight the option to be changed and click the Edit button to specify a new color. It is almost too easy to make modifications to the system defaults; however, SolidWorks gives you a way out if things get too messed up. All you have to do is click on the Reset All button to reset everything in the Color tab back to default color schemes.

Customize Command

Similar to AutoCAD, SolidWorks gives you the ability to modify toolbars and pull-down menus. Where the difference lies is in the extent to which these changes can be made. For example, AutoCAD allows the creation of new toolbars complete with the ability to make your own icons. SolidWorks allows for adding and deleting icons, but only to the extent of what icons are available to begin with. In SolidWorks, you cannot create your own icons or make new toolbars.

Pull-down menu customization is similar to AutoCAD to the extent that items can be removed from the menus. However, what can be added to SolidWorks pull-down menus is limited by what originally came with the software. The Customize dialog box contains three tabs that allow you to make modifications. The options within these tabs are discussed in the material that follows.

Toolbars

Toolbars contain icons (functional buttons) that serve as shortcuts to pull-down menu functions. Each toolbar's content is grouped per various commonly used menu functions. SolidWorks contains a total of 12 toolbars, whereas AutoCAD contains over 50. SolidWorks toolbars were listed in Chapter 1, but the names of all the toolbars can be found in the Toolbars dialog box (see the following illustration). Click on View/Toolbars to view the Toolbars dialog box. Notice the check boxes with which to turn the individual toolbars on and off.

The Toolbars dialog box also contains the options Large Buttons and Show Tooltips. Tooltips are the yellow hint boxes that appear when the cursor is held stationary over an icon for longer than a second. These are helpful, and it is difficult to imagine why anyone would want to turn them off. The Large Buttons option displays the icons in a larger size for those who may have a difficult time making out the small icons. These also help if you have a very large monitor running at high resolution. Sometimes at high resolutions, icons can get very small, making work very difficult.

Toolbars can also be customized to your specific requirements so that only commonly used icons are displayed. You do this by adding or removing function buttons using the Customize dialog box. However, a toolbar must be active to be customized. The following illustration shows the toggling of toolbars on and off.

Toggling toolbars
on and off.

Toolbar Activation

Toolbars automatically appear based on the current type of open document (i.e., sketch, part, or assembly). When a document type different from the current document is opened, the appropriate toolbar is automatically activated. The only toolbars that really should be active all the time are the Standard, View, and Sketch toolbars, simply because they are used constantly no matter what drawing type is open. The Drawing, Assembly, and Sketch toolbars automatically activate according to document type. Another example would be the Macro toolbar, which turns on automatically if you are playing or recording a macro. To manually activate a toolbar, perform the following steps:

1. Select Toolbars from the View menu.

2. Check the desired toolbars to toggle them on or off.

3. Select OK to close the dialog box.

Toolbar Customization

As stated previously, toolbar icons can be added or removed from toolbars. To customize a toolbar, perform the following steps. The illustration that follows shows the Toolbar customization tab. Currently, the Web toolbar and the Selection Filter toolbar cannot be modified.

1. Activate any toolbars to be customized.

2. Select Customize from the Tools menu.

3. Select the Toolbars tab.

4. Drag the button to be removed from the desired toolbar. Drop it anywhere outside the toolbar to delete it. To add a button, drag an icon from the dialog box to the toolbar. The button should appear on that toolbar.

5. Resize the toolbar if needed by dragging the edge of the toolbar similar to resizing a program window in Windows. Sometimes this must be done before the new icons will show up on the toolbar to which they were dragged.

6. Select OK when finished.

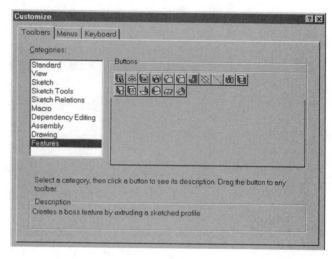

Toolbar customization tab.

Menus

You may wish to simplify a menu or remove an unwanted command. You can rename or remove commands from pull-down menus by performing the steps that follow. Only commands listed within the Customize dialog box (see the following illustration) may be added or removed. In SolidWorks, user-definable commands and functions cannot be added to a menu, as they can be in AutoCAD. It is possible in SolidWorks to add commands and alter menus using Visual Basic programming language, but this is outside the abilities of most users, and outside the scope of this book.

Menu customization tab.

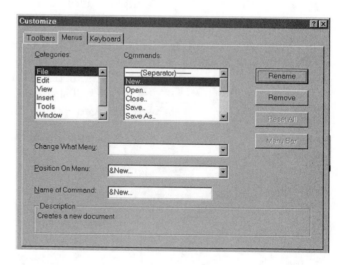

It is highly recommended that new users do not attempt to customize pull-down menus. This section has been added for reference and for the benefit of those with a good understanding of the SolidWorks program. To customize a pull-down menu, perform the following steps:

1. Select Customize from the Tools menu.

2. Select the Menus tab.

3. Select from the Categories list the menu to be modified.

4. Select from the Commands list the menu command to be modified.

5. Rename or Remove menu items as desired. Only predefined menu selections can be added. User-definable menu items are not allowed.

6. Use Position On Menu to relocate menu items.

7. Use the Name of Command field to alter the names of menu items.

8. Select OK to complete this function.

Keyboard Shortcuts

Keyboard shortcuts assign commonly used SolidWorks functions (e.g., Orientation or Measure) to keyboard keys. This can make it easier and quicker to access these functions. Only functions listed within the Tools/Customize/ Keyboard menu can be assigned a keyboard shortcut. Additional keyboard shortcuts can be defined by selecting the Keyboard tab in the Tool/Customize menu. Some keyboard shortcuts have already been established within SolidWorks, such as the following:

Rotate the model	Arrow keys
Rotate the model 90 degrees	Shift + Arrow keys
Rotate clockwise/counterclockwise	Alt + left/right
Pan	Ctrl + Arrow keys
Zoom in	Z
Zoom out	z
Rebuild the model	Ctrl + B
Redraw the model	Ctrl + R

The F2 through F9 function keys are good candidates for a keyboard shortcut. Unlike AutoCAD, these keys are typically not assigned to any functions in SolidWorks. You may want to create some simple labels to place above your defined function keys for easy reference. The keyboard shortcut customizations tab is shown in the illustration that follows.

➤ *NOTE: Do not redefine the F1 function key, as this key is the default system help key.*

Keyboard shortcut customization tab.

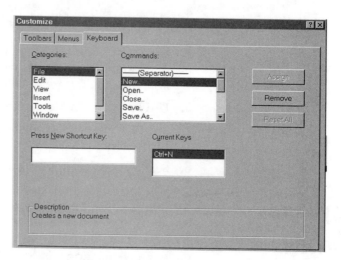

AutoCAD uses the ACAD.PGP text file for controlling what shortcuts (aliases) are assigned to specific commands. There is no need to modify a text file within SolidWorks. You simply select the command from the Customize dialog box in the Keyboard tab and press the desired key. Once again, it is not possible to define new commands or macros. You are limited to commands previously defined by SolidWorks. To customize a keyboard shortcut, perform the following steps:

1. Select Customize from the Tools menu.

2. Select the Keyboard tab.

3. Select the desired menu command to which to Assign a new shortcut key.

4. Press Assign to set the new shortcut.

5. Select OK to complete this function.

You can also select Remove in this tab to remove a shortcut key, or you can Reset All shortcut keys to their original default state. If a shortcut is already listed in the Current Key list box, it is recommended that a new shortcut not be assigned.

Programming Languages

SolidWorks offers two methods to further customize and automate design tasks. These are a macro programming language and an application programming interface (API) included with SolidWorks. The macro programming language allows you to automate repetitive tasks. The API allows Visual Basic and C++ programs to access Solid-Works functions.

Macros

The macro programming language can be used to automate repetitive tasks or create features that are geometrically similar but that have different dimension values. If a macro is created, and in the process a dimension is added, when the macro is played back SolidWorks will pause for the user to input a dimension value of their choice. Macros can be defined without any programming knowledge. A macro will record the steps taken and allow you to input values during playback. Files created with a macro have an .swb file extension. The macro programming language is described in the SolidWorks help file \sldworks\lang\english\Swxbasic.hlp.

NOTE: *The English directory may differ depending on the installed language or languages.*

The following procedures describe how to record, edit, and run a macro. To record a macro, perform the following steps:

1. Select Record from the Tools/Macro menu.

2. Perform the steps that define the macro.

3. Select Stop from the Tools/Macro menu.

4. Enter the macro file name (<filename>.swb).

5. Select OK to complete this function.

To edit a macro, perform the following steps:

1. Select Edit from the Tools/Macro menu.

2. Select the macro file name to be edited.

3. Select Open to complete this function.

4. Edit the macro as needed to add or delete macro functions.

5. Select Close from the File menu when complete. There is no Save function. The file will be saved automatically when closed.

When editing a macro, the Macro editor window will be active. The macro code itself will be displayed in the window. This can be modified as needed. The Macro editor with a sample macro is shown in the following illustration.

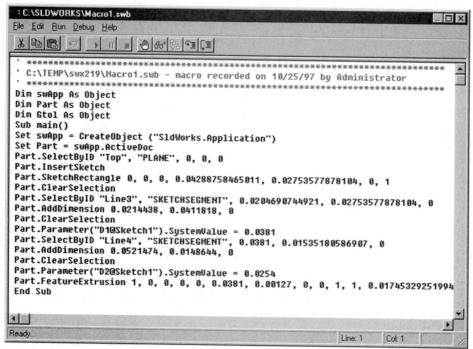

```
' C:\SLDWORKS\Macro1.swb
File  Edit  Run  Debug  Help

'  **************************************************************************
'  C:\TEMP\swx219\Macro1.swb - macro recorded on 10/25/97 by Administrator
'  **************************************************************************
Dim swApp As Object
Dim Part As Object
Dim Gtol As Object
Sub main()
Set swApp = CreateObject ("SldWorks.Application")
Set Part = swApp.ActiveDoc
Part.SelectByID "Top", "PLANE", 0, 0, 0
Part.InsertSketch
Part.SketchRectangle 0, 0, 0, 0.04288758465011, 0.02753577878104, 0, 1
Part.ClearSelection
Part.SelectByID "Line3", "SKETCHSEGMENT", 0.0204690744921, 0.02753577878104, 0
Part.AddDimension 0.0214438, 0.0411818, 0
Part.ClearSelection
Part.Parameter("D1@Sketch1").SystemValue = 0.0381
Part.SelectByID "Line4", "SKETCHSEGMENT", 0.0381, 0.01535180586907, 0
Part.AddDimension 0.0521474, 0.0148644, 0
Part.ClearSelection
Part.Parameter("D2@Sketch1").SystemValue = 0.0254
Part.FeatureExtrusion 1, 0, 0, 0, 0, 0.0381, 0.00127, 0, 0, 1, 1, 0.01745329251994
End Sub
```

The Macro editor.

To run a macro, perform the following steps:

1. Select Run from the Tools/Macro menu.

2. Select the macro file name to be run.

3. Select Open to complete this function.

When running a macro, it may be necessary to input dimension values. SolidWorks automatically pauses anytime user input is required.

The API

A Visual Basic or C++ program can access a wider range of functions and features using the SolidWorks API. Creating an API program requires programming skills. See the API documentation and training guide on how to automatically add functions and menus to SolidWorks. Examples of programs that access the API, which can be accessed through a Visual Basic or C++ program, are given in the training guide. Additional help can be found in the Windows help file *Samples\Appcomm\API_help.hlp*.

⊶ **NOTE:** *The API documentation and training guide can be accessed through the SolidWorks technical support Web site at http://www.solidworks.com/html/ Contacts/apisup.htm.*

To run a Visual Basic program, see the procedure for running a macro presented previously. Visual Basic programs can also be made to run as a standalone (.exe) program. To run a C++ program, select an Add-in (*.dll) file type accessed with the File/Open command. This will add the program to the current session.

It is also possible to click on Tools/Add-Ins and select the check box for the add-in program you would like to activate or deactivate. These are third-party programs that must be purchased separately. Not all programs conform to this function and may not appear in the Add-In dialog box. This is similar to AutoCAD's Applications list box that automatically loads lisp routines when the AutoCAD program is started. The Add-In dialog box is shown in the following illustration.

The Add-In dialog box.

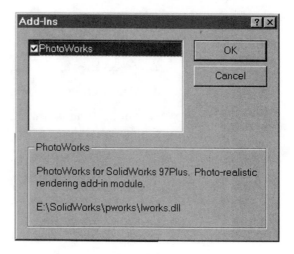

Summary

Adding keyboard shortcuts for frequently used functions that do not have a toolbar icon can reduce the number of menu picks required to access a SolidWorks function and therefore increase your productivity. Macros can be used to create simple automated tasks in SolidWorks. This function requires little or no programming experience. Visual Basic or C++ programs can be written to access the SolidWorks API to provide access to a wide range of SolidWorks functions and to automate functions specific to your company's needs. Creating programs of this type requires programming experience.

There are similarities between AutoCAD and SolidWorks with regard to the ability to customize the interface. Unlike AutoCAD, SolidWorks does not allow you to add new commands that do not currently exist within the program. However, with a little Visual Basic programming experience, a SolidWorks user can create customized routines that can accomplish nearly any task. Also, because Visual Basic is a widely accepted language, many resources are available for the motivated and the curious SolidWorks user.

Appendix

AutoCAD/SolidWorks Functionality Cross-reference

This appendix is divided into two sections: Command Cross-reference and Sketch Entities Cross-reference. It should be noted that many of the cross-referenced commands can only be associated with the listed AutoCAD commands by using a stretch of the imagination. This appendix is not intended as a function-for-function cross-reference, but as a resource for the AutoCAD user moving into the SolidWorks environment. Remember that Solid-Works and AutoCAD are fundamentally different packages, even if many of the commands seem similar. SolidWorks requires a different mindset than the traditional 2D or wireframe way of thinking.

Command Cross-reference

The following table lists AutoCAD and equivalent Solid-Works functionality, with pertinent notes about individual entries and an indication of the modes in which each function operates. All SolidWorks commands are shown in boldface. SolidWorks pull-down menus are also listed where applicable, in the form <menu name>/<function name>. Any function that has a SolidWorks toolbar icon is denoted with a "*" (i.e., File/Open*).

Not all AutoCAD commands have a direct counterpart in SolidWorks. Many of the commands listed in the follow-

Appendix

ing table will show only the closest similar command in
SolidWorks, or no command at all, in which case a reference note is typically included.

AutoCAD/SolidWorks Command Cross References

AutoCAD	SolidWorks	Notes	Mode
About	Help/About SolidWorks 97Plus	-	A D P
ACISIN	File/Open*	Files of type: ACIS files (*.sat).	P
ACISOUT	File/Save As	Files of type: ACIS files (*.sat).	P
ALIGN	Tools/Relations/Add	-	A
	Insert/Mate	-	S
AMECONVERT	None.	SolidWorks will not read AME files.	-
APERTURE	Dynamic object selection.	No need for an aperture.	All
APPLOAD	File/Open*	Files of type: Add-ins (*.dll).	All
	Tools/Add-ins		All
ARC	Tools/Sketch Entities/Centerpoint Arc*	-	D S
	Tools/Sketch Entities/Tangent Arc*	-	D S
	Tools/Sketch Entities/3 Point Arc*	-	D S
AREA	Tools/Measure	-	A D P
ARRAY	Linear Pattern, Circular Pattern	-	A P
ARX	None.	-	-
ASEADMIN	Insert/Object	OLE-compliant database application.	A D P
ASEEXPORT	Insert/Object	OLE-compliant database application.	A D P
ASELINKS	Insert/Object	OLE-compliant database application.	A D P
ASEROWS	Insert/Design Table	-	P
ASESELECT	Insert/Design Table	-	P
ASESQLED	Insert/Object	OLE-compliant database application.	A D P
ATTDEF	File/Properties	Entity attributes unavailable.	A D P
ATTDISP	None.	SolidWorks does not use attributes.	-
ATTEDIT	None.	-	-
ATTEXT	None.	-	-
ATTREDEF	None.	-	-
AUDIT	Tools/Check	Checks for invalid geometry.	P
BASE	Insert/Mates/Distance	-	A

AutoCAD	SolidWorks	Notes	Mode
BHATCH	Insert/Drawing View/Section Insert/Drawing View/Aligned Section	Use Properties to change crosshatching attributes.	D
BLIPMODE	None.	Blips do not exist in SolidWorks.	-
BLOCK	Insert/Component/From File	Parts in an assembly are similar to blocks.	A
BMPOUT	Print Screen key.	Part of Windows OS; copies screen to the clipboard.	All
BOUNDARY	A series of line segments is created when sketching entities using endpoints.	When the option Automatic Relations is selected, a relation constraint keeps endpoints attached to one another.	D S
BOX	Insert/Boss/Extrude	Create the sketch of the wedge.	P
BREAK	None.	Trim/Extend can be used as a workaround.	D S
CAL	Enter the expression when inputting the value. Tools/Measure	Input expressions using mathematical operators (+, -, /, *, parentheses) Measure distances, radii, perimeter, area, and so on.	All All
CHAMFER	Insert/Features/Chamfer*	-	P
CHANGE (POINT)	Display/Delete Relations Drag endpoints.	Select the objects to be changed first. Unconstrained entities can be dragged.	D S D S
CHPROP	Tools/Options/Colors Properties	Select the objects to be changed first. Right click on the object to be changed.	D P S D P S
CIRCLE	Tools/Sketch Entities/Circle	-	D S
COLOR	Tools/Options/Colors	-	D P S
COMPILE	None.	-	-
CONE	Insert/Boss/Revolve or Loft File/Open	Create the sketch first. Use a library part. Files of type: Lib Feature Part files (*.lfp *.sldlfp).	P P
CONFIG	None.	Uses standard Windows devices.	-
COPY	Edit/Copy*	-	All
COPYCLIP	Edit/Copy*	-	All
COPYHIST	None.	-	-
COPYLINK	Edit/Copy*	-	All
CUTCLIP	Edit/Cut*	-	All

AutoCAD	SolidWorks	Notes	Mode
CYLINDER	Insert/Boss/Revolve	Create the sketch first.	P
	Insert/Boss/Extrude	Create the sketch first.	P
	File/Open	Use a library part. Files of type: Lib Feature Part files (*.lfp *.sldlfp).	P
DBLIST	None.	Individual objects could be selected to view the Properties information.	-
DDATTDEF	None.	SolidWorks does not use attributes.	-
DDATTE	None.	-	-
DDATTEXT	None.	-	-
DDCHPROP	Tools/Options/Colors	Select the objects to be changed first.	D P S
	Properties	Right click on the object to be changed.	D P S
DDCOLOR	Tools/Options/Colors	Define default colors for objects.	A P
DDEDIT	Double click on the text to change.	-	All
DDEMODES	Tools/Options/Colors	Select the objects to be changed first.	D P S
DDGRIPS	Geometry can be dragged.	Dragged only; no editing while dragging.	D S
DDIM	Tools/Options/Detailing	Set or change default dimension values.	D S
	Select dimensions, press the right mouse button, and select Properties.	Change selected existing values.	All
DDINSERT	Insert/Library Feature	-	-
DDLMODES	None.	-	-
DDLTYPE	Tools/Options/Line Font	Global setting only.	D P S
DDMODIFY	Right select entity and select Properties.	-	All
DDOSNAP	Dynamic snapping.	Replaces the need to manually change snap modes.	All
DDPTYPE	None.	-	-
DDRENAME	Slow double click the object in FeatureManager.	Same as Windows OS.	All
DDRMODES	Tools/Options/Grid Units*	Tabbed dialog box name.	All
DDSELECT	Uses standard Windows conventions for multiple selections (Ctrl and Shift).	-	All
DDSTYLE	None.	-	-
DDUCS	None.	Uses the selected plane or face, or the default origin.	-

AutoCAD	SolidWorks	Notes	Mode
DDUCSP	None.	Uses the selected plane or face, or the default origin.	-
DDUNITS	Tools/Options/Grid Units*	Tabbed dialog box name.	All
DDVIEW	View/Orientation	-	All
DDVPOINT	View/Orientation	-	All
DELAY	Programming can be done via a SolidWorks macro, Visual Basic, or C++.	-	-
DIM	Tools/Dimensions/Parallel* Tools/Dimensions/Horizontal Tools/Dimensions/Vertical Tools/Dimensions/Baseline Tools/Dimensions/Ordinate Tools/Dimensions/Horizontal Ordinate Tools/Dimensions/Vertical Ordinate	Intelligent dimension tool icon will insert any dimension type listed at left. SolidWorks dimension tool knows what dimension to apply, depending on the entities selected.	D S D S D S D D D D
DIMALIGNED	Tools/Dimensions/Parallel*	Intelligent dimension tool.	D S
DIMANGULAR	Tools/Dimensions/Parallel*	Intelligent dimension tool recognizes an angular dimension versus a linear dimension.	D S
DIMBASELINE	Tools/Dimensions/Baseline	Intelligent dimension tool.	D
DIMCENTER	Insert/Annotation/Center Mark	-	D
DIMCONTINUE	None.	-	-
DIMDIAMETER	Tools/Dimensions/Parallel*	Intelligent dimension tool recognizes a circular feature and places a diameter dimension. A circle will produce a diameter dimension and an arc a radius dimension by default. To change, use the Properties function.	D S
DIMEDIT	Select the dimension. Reposition handles will appear, and the text or extension can be dragged to the new location. Select the dimension, press the right mouse button, and select Properties.	- Pick Display to change extension or dimension line properties.	D S D S
DIMLINEAR	Tools/Dimensions/Parallel*	Intelligent dimension tool.	D S
DIMORDINATE	Tools/Dimensions/Ordinate Tools/Dimensions/Horizontal Ordinate Tools/Dimensions/Vertical Ordinate	- - Intelligent dimension tool.	D S D S D S
DIMOVERRIDE	Right click dim and select Properties.	-	D S
DIMRADIUS	Tools/Dimensions/Parallel*	Arcs are dimensioned as radial by default.	D S

AutoCAD	SolidWorks	Notes	Mode
DIMSTYLE	Right click the dim and select Properties.	-	D S
	Tools/Options/Detailing	Global setting.	D S
DIMTEDIT	Select the dimension text and drag it.	-	D S
DIST	Tools/Measure	-	All
DIVIDE	Trim/Extend *	Temporary dimensions and entities may be required.	D S
DONUT	Insert/Boss/Revolve	Use a circle to revolve.	P
DRAGMODE	Uses dynamic drag by default.	-	-
DSVIEWER	None.	-	-
DTEXT	Insert/Annotations/Note	The text is entered in the dialog box.	D
DVIEW	View/Modify/Perspective	Camera and target angles can be simulated by rotating and panning the part.	A P
DXBIN	None.	-	-
DXFIN	File/Open*	Files of type: DXF files (*.dxf).	D
DXFOUT	File/Save As	Files of type: DXF files (*.dxf).	D
EDGE	Select the edge, press the right mouse button, and select Properties.	-	D
EDGESURF	None.	-	-
ELEV	Insert/Reference Geometry/Plane	Use an offset plane to set the elevation of a part. Use Extrude to set thickness.	P
ELLIPSE	Tools/Sketch Entity/Ellipse	-	D S
	Tools/Sketch Entity/Centerpoint Ellipse	Creates an elliptical arc.	D S
END	File/Exit	-	A D P
	File/Close	-	-
ERASE	Edit/Delete	-	All
	Del key.	-	-
EXPLODE	None.	It is possible to explode a solid by exporting it as a wireframe IGES, but it cannot be read back into SolidWorks.	-
EXPORT	File/Save As	Select file type.	A D P
EXTEND	Trim/Extend*	Intelligent tool used for trimming and extending entities.	D S
EXTRUDE	Insert/Boss/Extrude	Add material to the part.	P
	Insert/Cut/Extrude	Subtract material from the part.	P
FILES	File/Find References	Use to copy files with external references (drawings and assemblies).	A D P
	File/Save As	Change name and/or location.	A D P
	Windows Explorer.	Use to rename or delete files.	A D P

AutoCAD	*SolidWorks*	*Notes*	*Mode*
FILL	None.	-	-
FILLET	Insert/Features/Fillet Round	-	P
	Tools/Sketch Tools/Fillet	-	S
FILTER	Select an object filter from the pull-down menu.	Filter toolbar can be activated under the View/Toolbars menu.	All
GIFIN	Insert/Object	-	A D P
GRAPHSCR	None.	-	-
GRID	Tools/Options/Grid Units*	Tabbed dialog box name.	All
GROUP	None.	-	-
HATCH	None.	Crosshatching automatically created for section views.	D
HATCHEDIT	Right select crosshatch, and select Crosshatch Properties.	-	D
HELP	Help/SolidWorks Help Topics	General help.	All
	Help	Help button with a dialog box active.	All
HIDE	View/Display/Hidden Lines Removed	Display with hidden line removed. Model can be dynamically rotated.	A P
ID	Tools/Measure	Select both the origin and vertex.	All
IMPORT	File/Open	Select file type.	A D P
INSERT	Insert/library Feature	Library features are very similar to blocks.	P
INSERTOBJ	Insert/Object	-	A D P
INTERFERE	Tools/Interference Detection	Select the parts to check between.	A
INTERSECT	None.	SolidWorks does not use Boolean operations.	-
ISOPLANE	None.	No need to sketch isometric views.	-
LAYER	None.	Configurations can be used for some of this functionality.	A D P
LEADER	Insert/Annotation/Note	Hold down the Ctrl key and select the locations prior to inserting the note for multiple leaders.	D
LENGTHEN	Trim/Extend*	Entities can also be dragged.	D S
LIGHT	View/Lighting	Add directional or spot lights.	A P
LIMITS	Edit/Properties	Edit the drawing sheet size with the sheet selected.	D
LINE	Tools/Sketch Entity/Line	-	D S
LINETYPE	Tools/Options/Line Font	Global setting.	All
LIST	File/Properties	-	A D P

AutoCAD	SolidWorks	Notes	Mode
LOAD	None.	-	-
LOGFILEOFF	A log file is created by default.	-	All
LOGFILEON	A log file is created by default.	-	All
LTSCALE	Automatic	Scaling is based on view scale.	D
MAKEPREVIEW	File/Print Preview	-	All
MASSPROP	Tools/Mass Properties	-	A P
MATLIB	PhotoWorks/Edit Material	Optional PhotoWorks module.	A P
MEASURE	Tools/Measure	-	All
MENU	None.	Pull-down menus cannot be modified.	-
MENULOAD	None.	-	-
MENUUNLOAD	None.	-	-
MINSERT	Insert/Assembly Pattern	-	A
MIRROR	Tools/Sketch Tools/Mirror	-	S
MIRROR3D	Insert/Pattern Mirror/Mirror Feature	Mirror single features.	P
	Insert/Pattern Mirror/Mirror All	Mirror complete part.	P
MLEDIT	None.	-	-
MLINE	None.	-	-
MLSTYLE	None.	-	-
MOVE	Select objects and drag to the new location.	Fully constrained features will not move.	D P S
	Tools/Component/Move Component*	-	A
MSLIDE	None.	-	-
MSPACE	None.	No need for separate paper and model space in a SolidWorks document.	-
MTEXT	Insert/Annotations/Note	Format per note only.	All
MTPROP	Right click text and select Properties.	-	D
MULTIPLE	Tools/Options/General	Uncheck Single Command per Pick.	All
MVIEW	Insert/Drawing Views	Any number of views in a drawing.	D
MVSETUP	Edit/Properties.	Change the sheet's properties.	D
NEW	File/New *	-	A D P
OFFSET	Tools/Sketch Tools/Offset Entities	-	S
OLELINKS	Insert/Object	-	A D P
OOPS	Edit/Undo*	-	All
OPEN	File/Open*	Select type of file to open.	A D P
ORTHO	Tools/Options/Grid Units tab	Set snap angle to 90 degrees.	D S

AutoCAD	SolidWorks	Notes	Mode
OSNAP	Tools/Sketch Tools/Automatic Relations	Intelligent cursor snaps to geometric points and adds relations automatically.	D S
PAN	View/Modify/Pan*	More similar to RTPAN in Release 13_c4.	All
PASTECLIP	Edit/Paste*	-	All
PASTESPEC	Insert/Object	-	A D P
PCXIN	None.	OLE can be used to attach PCX files (or any other raster format) to a SolidWorks document.	-
PEDIT	Select the spline and drag the spline handles (points).	Polyline entities with AutoCAD characteristics do not exist in SolidWorks.	D S
PFACE	None.	-	-
PLAN	View/Orientation/Normal To	Select a plane or planar face first.	A P S
PLINE	Draw lines endpoint to endpoint.	Line will not have pline characteristics.	D S
PLOT	File/Page Setup File/Print Preview File/Print*	- - -	All All All
POINT	Tools/Sketch Entity/Point*	-	D S
POLYGON	None.	-	-
PREFERENCES	Tools/Options	Dialog box split into various tabbed sections.	All
PSDRAG	None.	Objects display after drag.	All
PSFILL	None.	-	-
PSIN	Insert/Object	-	A D P
PSOUT	None.	-	A D P
PSPACE	SolidWorks drawing.	Create a drawing with views.	D
PURGE	None.	Delete unwanted entities.	All
QSAVE	File/Save*	-	A D P
QTEXT	None.	-	-
QUIT	File/Exit File/Close	- -	A D P A D P
RAY	None.	-	-
RCONFIG	None. PhotoWorks/Options/Image Output tab.	Windows is used to define output. Specify file type to save as.	All A P

AutoCAD	SolidWorks	Notes	Mode
RECOVER	None.	A backup file can be created by selecting the backup option in the General tab in the Tools/Options menu.	All
RECTANG	Tools/Sketch Entity/Rectangle*	-	D S
REDEFINE	Tools/Customize/Menus Tools/Customize/Keyboard	The Reset All button can be used to return to the default condition. Ibid.	All -
REDO	None.	-	-
REDRAW	View/Redraw*	Refreshes graphics.	All
REDRAWALL	View/Redraw*	Refreshes graphics.	All
REGEN	Edit/Rebuild*	Rebuilds geometry.	All
REGENALL	Edit/Rebuild*	Rebuilds geometry.	All
REGENAUTO	None.	SolidWorks will not prompt before rebuilding.	All
REGION	None.	Regions are not necessary.	P A
REINIT	None.	-	-
RENAME	Perform a slow double click on the item in FeatureManager. Edit the objects Properties.	Works like renaming files in Windows OS. -	All All
RENDER	PhotoWorks/Render	Optional PhotoWorks module.	A P
RENDERUN-LOAD	Tools/Add-Ins	Uncheck PhotoWorks to remove from memory.	A P
REPLAY	PhotoWorks/View Image File	Optional PhotoWorks module.	A P
RESUME	Tools/Macro/Pause Macro	-	A D P
REVOLVE	Insert/Boss/Revolve Insert/Cut/Revolve	Adds material to the part. Subtracts material from the part.	P -
REVSURF	Insert/Reference Geometry/Revolved Surface	-	P
RMAT	PhotoWorks/Select Material PhotoWorks/Edit Material PhotoWorks/Copy Material PhotoWorks/Paste Material	Optional PhotoWorks module. Ibid. Ibid. Ibid.	A P A P A P A P
ROTATE	Tools/Sketch Tools/Modify Dimension objects to rotate.	Rotates an entire sketch. Modify the dimension to rotate entity.	S P S
ROTATE3D	Insert/Reference Geometry/Plane/At Angle Tools/Component/Rotate	Features can be placed on rotating planes. Rotates parts in 3D space.	P A
RPREF	PhotoWorks/Options	Optional PhotoWorks module.	A P
RSCRIPT	A macro or Visual Basic program can be used to produce a self-running script.	-	All

AutoCAD	SolidWorks	Notes	Mode
RTPAN	View/Modify/Pan*	Real-time panning.	All
RTZOOM	View/Modify/Zoom*	Real-time zooming.	All
RULESURF	Insert/Reference Geometry/Extruded Surface	-	P
SAVE	File/Save*	-	A D P
SAVEAS	File/Save As	Select file type.	A D P
SAVEASR12	File/Save As	Select Release 12 from Tools/ Options/Import Export tab.	D
SAVEIMG	PhotoWorks/Options/Image Output	Set output to Render to File.	A P
SCALE	Tools/Sketch Tools/Modify	Affects a single sketch.	S
	Insert/Features/Scale	Affects the entire part.	P
SCENE	View/Lighting	Controls the lighting and adds new lights.	A P
	View/Orientation	Controls the view orientation.	All
SCRIPT	Programming can be done via a SolidWorks macro, Visual Basic, or C++.	-	-
SECTION	Insert/Drawing View/Section	-	D
	View/Display/Section View	For display purposes only.	P
	Insert/Assembly Feature/Cut	Ibid.	A
SELECT	Select multiple objects by holding the Ctrl key down. Drag a window around objects to be selected	.Objects can be deselected using the same method.	All All
SETVAR	Use Tools/Options to change settings.	SolidWorks has no variables, per se.	All
SHADE	View/Display/Shaded	Image can be dynamically rotated.	A P
SHAPE	None.	-	-
SHELL	None.	Not required for a Windows application.	-
SHOWMAT	PhotoWorks/Select Material	Optional PhotoWorks module.	A P
SKETCH	None.	Not to be confused with SolidWorks Sketch mode.	-
SLICE	Insert/Drawing View/Section	-	D
	View/Display/Section View	For display purposes only.	P
	Insert/Assembly Feature/Cut	Ibid.	A
SNAP	Tools/Options/Grid Units tab*	-	D S
SOLDRAW	Insert/Drawing View	Select the type of view to be created.	D
	View/Orientation	Select or define a new orientation.	A P
SOLID	None.	-	-

AutoCAD	SolidWorks	Notes	Mode
SOLPROF	Insert/Drawing View	Select the type of view to be created.	D
	View/Orientation	Select or define a new orientation.	A P
SOLVIEW	Insert/Drawing View	Select the type of view to be created.	D
	View/Orientation	Select or define a new orientation.	A P
SPELL	None.	Spell checker currently not available.	-
SPHERE	Insert/Boss/Revolve	Create the sketch of the wedge.	P
SPLINE	Insert/Sketch Entity/Spline*	-	D S
SPLINEDIT	Select the spline and drag the spline handles (points).	-	D S
STATS	PhotoWorks/Options	Optional PhotoWorks module.	A P
STATUS	File/Properties	View file information.	All
STLOUT	File/Save As	Files of type: Stl files (*.stl).	P
STRETCH	Select the objects endpoint and drag to the new location.	Stretching is normally done through the use of parametric dimensions.	D S
STYLE	Tools/Options/Detailing	Set the default text and dimension fonts.	D S
	Select the object and select Edit/Properties, or press the right mouse button and select Properties.	Change existing text and dimension fonts.	D S
SUBTRACT	Insert/Cut	Create a sketch and select the cut type.	P
	Insert/Assembly Features/Cut	Create a sketch to cut through the assembly.	A
SYSWINDOWS	Window/Cascade	Basic Windows OS functionality.	All
	Window/Tile Horizontal	Ibid.	All
	Window/Tile Vertical	Ibid.	All
TABLET	None.	SolidWorks uses the mouse and keyboard for all functions.	All
TABSURF	Insert/Reference Geometry/Extruded Surface	-	P
TBCONFIG	Tools/Customize/Toolbars	-	All
TEXT	Insert/Annotations/Note	-	A D P
	Insert/Sketch Entity/Text	For creating text features.	S
TEXTSCR	None.	-	-
3D	None.	3D solids created through Insert/Boss.	P
3DARRAY	Create two linear or circular patterns.	-	-

AutoCAD	SolidWorks	Notes	Mode
3DFACE	Insert/Sketch*	One plane (surface) at a time.	S
3DMESH	None.	-	-
3DPOLY	Insert/Reference Geometry/Curve though Reference Points	-	S
	Insert/Reference Geometry/Curve though Free Points	-	S
3DSIN	None.	Use a supported file format.	A P
3DSOUT	None.	Use a supported file format.	A P
TIFFIN	Insert/Object	OLE-compliant database application.	A D P
TIME	File/Properties	-	All
TOLERANCE	Insert/Annotation/Geometric Tolerance	-	A D P
TOOLBAR	View/Toolbars	Toggles toolbars on/off.	All
TORUS	Insert/Boss/Revolve	Create the sketch of the wedge.	P
TRACE	None.	-	-
TREESTAT	None.	Handled automatically.	-
TRIM	Trim/Extend*	Intelligent tool used for trimming and extending an object.	D S
U	Edit/Undo icon	Rebuild wipes undo list clean.	All
UCS	Insert/Sketch	Select plane or planar face first.	A P S
UCSICON	View/Origins	-	All
UNDEFINE	Tools/Customize/Menus	The Reset All button can be used to return to the default condition.	All
	Tools/Customize/Keyboard	Ibid.	-
UNDO	Edit/Undo icon list box	Rebuild wipes undo list clean.	All
UNION	None.	All parts must be contiguous.	P
	Insert/Features/Join	Assembly components can be joined.	A
UNITS	Tools/Options/Grid Units tab*	-	All
VIEW	View/Orientation	Double click on to select view.	All
VIEWRES	Tools/Options/Performance	Slider bar adjustments.	All
VLCONV	View/Lighting	-	A P
	PhotoWorks/Select Material	Optional module.	P
	PhotoWorks/Edit Scene	Ibid.	A P
VPLAYER	Configurations can be defined to selectively display objects.	-	A D P
VPOINT	View/Orientation	Select Isometric, Trimetric, or Dimetric.	A P S
	View/Modify/Rotate	Dynamically rotate the model.	A P S

AutoCAD	SolidWorks	Notes	Mode
VPORTS	Window/New Window Use the split window handles.	- The horizontal and vertical split window handles are located next to the scroll bars.	All All
VSLIDE	None.	-	-
WBLOCK	File/Save As	Save as type Library Feature (*.lfp).	P
WEDGE	Insert/Boss/Extrude File/Open	Create the sketch of the wedge. Use a library part. Files of type: Lib Feature Part files (*.lfp *.sldlfp).	P -
WMFIN	Insert/Object	-	A D P
WMFOPTS	None.	-	-
WMFOUT	None.	A screen capture program can be used to capture the screen.	All
XBIND	None.	OLE can be used to attach files to a SolidWorks document.	A D P
XLINE	Right select an entity and select Properties.	Entities can be changes to construction lines, but they will not be infinitely long.	D S
XPLODE	Save as an IGES wireframe.	File cannot be imported back into SolidWorks.	A P
XREF	Insert/Base Part	Part will be updated if the original base part is modified.	P
XREFCLIP	None.	-	-
ZOOM	View/Modify/Zoom to fit* View/Modify/Zoom to area* View/Modify/Zoom up down*	Similar to Zoom/All. Similar to Zoom/Window. Similar to RTZOOM.	All - -

Key to abbreviations: Mode or SolidWorks document type: A = Assembly, D = Drawing, P = Part, S = Sketch.

Sketch Entities Cross-reference

The following table contains sketch entities cross-referenced between the AutoCAD and SolidWorks environments. In many cases, commands in SolidWorks function much differently than their AutoCAD counterparts, such as is the case with the arc commands. However, through the application of constraints and dimensions, the same objective can be reached. The AutoCAD entity is listed first, followed by the equivalent SolidWorks entity, followed by SolidWorks functionality notes.

AutoCAD/SolidWorks Sketch Entity Cross-references

AutoCAD	SolidWorks	Notes for SolidWorks
Line	Line	Pick start point and drag endpoint.
Construction Line	All sketch entities	Must modify properties. Entities such as lines will not extend infinitely.
Polyline	Line	Lines drawn end-to-end stay attached to one another but otherwise do not exhibit same characteristics as AutoCAD polylines.
3D Polyline	Curve Through Free Points	Key in X-Y-Z coordinates.
Multi-Line	Line	Must draw the lines separately. Relation (parallel) placed automatically by system.
Spline	Spline	2D only.
Curve Through Free Points	Curve Through Free Points	2D or 3D.
Arc Three Points	3 Pt Arc	Pick and drag endpoints; pick and drag radius.
Arc Start Center End	Centerpoint Arc	Pick center and drag radius; pick and drag arc segment length.
Arc Start Center Angle	3 Pt Arc	Ibid.
Arc Start Center Length	3 Pt Arc	Ibid.
Arc Start End Angle	3 Pt Arc	Ibid.
Arc Start End Direction	3 Pt Arc	Ibid.
Arc Center Start End	Centerpoint Arc	Ibid.
Arc Center Start Angle	Centerpoint Arc	Ibid.
Arc Center Start Length	Centerpoint Arc	Ibid.
Arc Continue	Tangent Arc	Pick endpoint of a line or arc and drag the arc's length.
Circle Center Radius	Circle	Pick center and drag radius.
Circle Center Diameter	Circle	Drive with a dimension.
Circle 2 Points	Circle	Drive with constraints.

AutoCAD	SolidWorks	Notes for SolidWorks
Circle 3 Points	Circle	Drive with constraints.
Circle Tan Tan Radius	Circle	Add tangent relations.
Donut	None	Create as a revolved feature.
Ellipse Center	Ellipse	Pick center and drag first axis radius; pick and drag second axis radius.
Ellipse Axis End	Ellipse	Ibid.
Ellipse Arc	Centerpoint Ellipse	Same as Ellipse, then pick arc start point and drag arc endpoint.
Polygon	Line	Drive with constraints and dimensions.
Rectangle	Rectangle	Pick and drag opposite corners.
Point	Point	Pick to place point.

Illustrated Glossary

Align—To line up objects such as views or vertex points.

SECTION B-B

Aligned section view—A section that rotates a portion of the section line normal to the section view, usually for a cylindrical part.

Arc—A sketch entity defined by a portion of the circumference of a circle.

Arrow—A triangular-shaped symbol at the ends of dimension lines.

Assembly—A collection of parts or subassemblies.

Assembly configuration—A configuration created to suppress a group of parts or subassemblies to simplify the assembly or create alternative assemblies.

Auxiliary view—A projected view defined from an angled surface.

Axis1

Axis—Axis of rotation, or the center of a cylinder.

1

Balloon—A circle that encloses a label used to identify objects, often in a bill of material.

Base feature—The first main feature defined in a part.

Base part—Use of an existing part as the basis of a new part.

Baseline dimension—A set of dimensions that uses a common reference origin and first extension line.

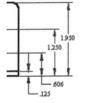

1.950
1.250
.606
.125

Boss—A feature that adds volume to a model.

Boss

Broken view—A partial view showing both ends of a part, with the center removed.

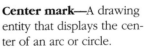

Cavity—A hollow area created by subtracting a part from a solid area. The cavity can be used to create a mold for the part that created the cavity.

Center mark—A drawing entity that displays the center of an arc or circle.

Centerline—A sketch entity used to define symmetry, rotate a sketch, or show reference.

Chamfer—A feature that cuts along an edge defined by a distance and angle.

Circle—A circular or round sketch entity.

Circular pattern—To copy features around a central point of rotation and specify the included angle and number of copies.

Component—Part in an assembly.

Configuration—A subset of features in a part or assembly that can be used to define an alternative or simplified part or assembly.

Constraint—Geometric relation used to control the behavior of sketch entities.

Construction geometry—Sketch entities converted to reference entities to help define geometric relationships.

Convert edge—To use an existing model edge as sketch geometry.

Cosmetic thread—A cosmetic feature used to define and detail threads.

Cursor—The graphical display of the operating system pointing device (mouse). Cursor graphics change depending on the action being taken.

Cut—To remove volume from a model.

Datum—A reference plane used to define a geometric tolerance.

Derived part—A new part created from and referenced to another part. The new part is derived from the existing part.

Design table—A Microsoft Excel spreadsheet used to drive model and dimension parameters.

Detail view—A blow-up view of a specific area on an existing view to show greater detail.

Dialog box—A graphical user interface (GUI) menu.

Dimension—A feature that displays the size or length of a feature.

Document—A file that contains information for an application. SolidWorks document types include parts, drawings, and assemblies.

Draft—To tilt or angle a surface, usually for tool ejection for plastic molded parts and castings.

Drawing—Detail drawing of a part or assembly.

Drawing formats—The title block format that contains standard drawing information (i.e., drawn by, title, part number, and so on).

Drawing sheet—A drawing that contains a drawing format, views of the part or assembly, dimensions, and notes. A drawing can contain multiple drawing sheets. Only one sheet is visible at a time.

DWG—AutoCAD drawing file. Used to import information into a SolidWorks drawing or transfer data between programs.

DXF—AutoCAD data exchange file. Used to import information into a SolidWorks drawing or transfer data between programs.

Edge—Single outside boundary of a feature.

Ellipse—An oblong arc/circle defined by a major and a minor axis.

Entity—An object within a SolidWorks document (i.e., line, arc, note, feature, and so on).

Embedded OLE object—A Microsoft object that follows the OLE (Object Linking and Embedding) criteria. Embedded objects no longer reference the host document, and any changes to the host (server) file will not be shown in the target (client) object.

Equation—A mathematical relation used to define dimensional relationships between feature or sketch dimensions.

"D5@Sketch3" = "D4@Sketch3"

Exploded assembly—Displays an assembly in a disassembled (exploded) state. Exploded assemblies can be used as an assembly or customer service aid.

Extrude—To project a profile along a straight line.

Face—A contiguous surface, planar or nonplanar, on a feature or part.

Feature—A solid object element used to create a solid model (i.e., boss or hole).

FeatureManager™—A graphical interface for displaying information on parts, drawings, and assemblies.

Fillet/round—A rounded corner that blends together two or more model edges.

Geometric relations—A set of rules added to sketch geometry to control the behavior of sketch entities (same as a constraint).

.015

Geometric tolerance—A set of standard symbols used to specify geometric characteristics and other dimensional requirements.

Grid—A pattern used by the system to aid the user in constructing geometry and dimensioning. The grid can provide a graphical display, as well as optionally allow the user to snap to grid points.

Helix—A curved circular path defined by pitch, rotation, and height (i.e., spring or thread).

.625 **Horizontal dimension**— The distance horizontally between two selected points or objects.

Icon—Graphical user interface button used to perform functions and commands.

IGES—A data interchange format used to transfer information between different CAD systems.

Inferencing—Intelligent cursor and constraint feature for sketching. Geometric constraints are automatically added by the system. The cursor graphics update to display the current condition.

Interference detection— An assembly function used to determine interference between assembly components.

Layout—A 2D representation of a part or assembly,

used to convey dimensions and details about a model.

Leader—A line, usually ending in an arrowhead, used to point to an object.

Leader Anchor

Leader anchor—The point at the end of a leader arrow that anchors its position. This point can be anchored to a face or edge.

Library feature—A part feature (or features) that can be reused for part creation.

Line—A straight sketch segment.

Pattern features

Linear pattern—Creates a copy of features in flat plane. Linear patterns can be defined in two directions at one time.

Linked OLE object—A Microsoft object that follows the OLE (Object Linking and Embedding) criteria. Linked objects reference the host document, and any changes to the host (server) file will be shown in the target (client) object.

Linked value—Dimensions that form an equality (i.e., D1 = D2 = D3). Modifying one dimension changes all linked dimensions.

Loft Profiles

Loft—A feature that uses multiple profiles to define a solid feature.

Macro—A program that records selections, menu

picks, and keyboard strokes for later playback.

Mass properties—Display the volume, surface area, centroid, and inertia tensor for a part or assembly.

Mate—Similar to a geometric constraint, a relation between entities, usually surfaces, between parts within an assembly.

Model dimensions—The dimensions used to drive the size of feature geometry and to show distances in drawings.

Mold cavity—The hollowed-out area of a block used to create molded parts.

Named view—A defined view using a view orientation and zoom state. These can be system default or user-defined views.

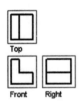

Neutral draft plane—The plane used to define the face pivot location for draft angles.

Normal—A vector perpendicular to a surface, planar or nonplanar, at any point on that surface.

Offset edge—A sketch entity at a given distance from an existing model edge that references that edge.

Ordinate dimension—Dimension in a drawing shown from a common reference point.

Parametric—Dimensions drive the creation of model geometry. Changes to dimension parameters change model geometry.

Part—A single, contiguous solid model.

Part configurations—A subset of features in a part that can be used to define an alternative or simplified part.

Parting line—The edge that defines the mating surfaces between the top and bottom halves of a mold.

Pattern—A part feature copied in a linear or circular fashion.

Plane—Planar entity used for sketching, as well as geometric and dimensional reference.

Point—A reference location defined by a single point entity.

Projection view—A view orthographically projected from an existing view.

Properties—Attributes of an object, such as entities, features, and dimensions.

Pull-down menu—A menu that appears when a title (or menu heading) is selected from the menu bar.

Rebuild—Regenerates a part, drawing, or assembly and incorporates any changes to dimension parameters.

Rectangle—A sketch entity defined by two horizontal and two vertical lines.

Relative to model view—A view relative to planar surfaces on a part or assembly.

Reorder—To change the creation order of selected features. This will affect how a solid model or assembly is created.

Revolve—Creates a solid boss or cut from a closed profile rotated about a centerline.

Rollback—To go back to a specified point in the part creation process. Used to insert features at a specific point in the creation order.

Section view—A cutaway view of a part or assembly that shows interior detail.

SECTION A-A
Scale 1:1

Scope—Defines what parts a new assembly feature affects.

Shell—A feature that creates a hollow part with at least one surface open to the out-

side. Often used for plastic molded and cast parts.

Sheet metal—A thin-walled part that can be unfolded into a flat sheet.

Shrinkage—The percentage a part contracts due to cooling after the molding or casting process.

fig13_51.tif

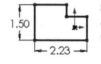

Sketch—A collection of 2D entities used to define features in a solid model.

Standard 3 Views—Three orthographically defined views: top, front, and right.

Stereolithography (STL)—A file format used to create rapid prototyping parts.

Suppress—To temporarily remove a feature or component from a graphics display and from memory. The features or components can be unsuppressed at any time.

Surface finish—A unit of measure that determines the roughness of a surface.

Surface finish symbol—A detailing symbol used to denote the operation, roughness, direction, and special requirements of a surface.

Sweep—Creates a feature by sweeping a closed profile along a trajectory.

Thin feature—A feature of constant wall thickness that can be used to create sheet-metal parts.

Tolerance—The amount of deviation allowable for a given feature, shown in a dimension.

Trim/extend—To shorten or lengthen a sketch entity.

Trimmed surface—A surface defined with a specific boundary used during IGES translation by solid modeling software.

Undo—Reverses previous operations to their original state.

Vertex—Corner or end point of an edge or sketch entity.

Vertical dimension—The vertical distance between two selected points or objects.

Weld bead—An assembly feature that represents the welded area between assembly components.

Weldment—An assembly of welded components.

Weld symbol—Detail symbol (or symbols) that defines a weldment.

Index

More OnWord Press Titles

Computing/Business

Lotus Notes for Web Workgroups
$34.95

Mapping with Microsoft Office
$29.95 Includes Disk

The Tightwad's Guide to Free Email and Other Cool Internet Stuff
$19.95

Geographic Information Systems (GIS)

GIS: A Visual Approach
$39.95

The GIS Book, 4E
$39.95

GIS Online: Information Retrieval, Mapping, and the Internet
$49.95

INSIDE MapInfo Professional
$49.95 Includes CD-ROM

Minding Your Business with MapInfo
$49.95

MapBasic Developer's Guide
$49.95 Includes Disk

Raster Imagery in Geographic Information Systems
$59.95 Includes color inserts

INSIDE ArcView GIS, 2E
$44.95 Includes CD-ROM

ArcView GIS Exercise Book, 2E
$49.95 Includes CD-ROM

ArcView GIS/Avenue Developer's Guide, 2E
$49.95 Includes Disk

ArcView GIS/Avenue Programmer's Reference, 2E
$49.95

ArcView GIS /Avenue Scripts: The Disk, 2E
Disk $99.00

ARC/INFO Quick Reference
$24.95

INSIDE ARC/INFO, Revised Edition
$59.95 Includes CD-ROM

Exploring Spatial Analysis in Geographic Information Systems
$49.95

Processing Digital Images in GIS: A Tutorial for ArcView and ARC/INFO
$49.95

Softdesk

INSIDE Softdesk Architectural
$49.95 Includes Disk

INSIDE Softdesk Civil
$49.95 Includes Disk

Softdesk Architecture 1 Certified Courseware
$34.95 Includes CD-ROM

Softdesk Civil 1 Certified Courseware
$34.95 Includes CD-ROM

Softdesk Architecture 2 Certified Courseware
$34.95 Includes CD-ROM

Softdesk Civil 2 Certified Courseware
$34.95 Includes CD-ROM

MicroStation

INSIDE MicroStation 95, 4E
$39.95 Includes Disk

MicroStation for AutoCAD Users, 2E
$34.95

MicroStation 95 Exercise Book
$39.95 Includes Disk
Optional Instructor's Guide $14.95

MicroStation Exercise Book 5.X
$34.95 Includes Disk
Optional Instructor's Guide $14.95

MicroStation 95 Quick Reference
$24.95

MicroStation Reference Guide 5.X
$18.95

MicroStation 95 Productivity Book
$49.95

101 MDL Commands (5.X and 95)
Executable Disk $101.00
Source Disks (6) $259.95

Adventures in MicroStation 3D
$49.95 Includes CD-ROM

CATIA

INSIDE CATIA
$80.00 Includes CD-ROM

CATIA Reference Guide
$49.95

Other CAD

Fallingwater in 3D Studio
$39.95 Includes Disk

SunSoft Solaris

Solaris 2.X for Managers and Administrators Guide, 2E
$34.95

SunSoft Solaris 2. User's Guide*
$29.95 Includes Disk

SunSoft Solaris 2. Quick Reference*
$18.95

*Five Steps to SunSoft Solaris 2.**
$24.95 Includes Disk

SunSoft Solaris 2. for Windows Users*
$24.95

Windows NT

Windows NT for the Technical Professional
$39.95

HP-UX

HP-UX User's Guide
$29.95

Five Steps to HP-UX
$24.95 Includes Disk

OnWord Press Distribution

OnWord Press books are available worldwide from OnWord Press and your local bookseller. For order information, terms, or listings of local booksellers carrying OnWord Press books, call toll-free 1-800-4-ONWORD (1-800-466-9673) or 505-474-5130; fax 505-474-5030; write to OnWord Press, 2530 Camino Entrada, Santa Fe, New Mexico 87505-4835, USA, or e-mail orders@hmp.com. OnWord Press is a division of High Mountain Press.

Comments and Corrections

Your comments can help us make better products. If you find an error, or have a comment or a query for the authors, please contact us at the address below, send e-mail to cleyba@hmp.com, or call us at 1-800-466-9673.

OnWord Press, 2530 Camino Entrada, Santa Fe, NM 87505-4835 USA

On the Internet: http://www.hmp.com

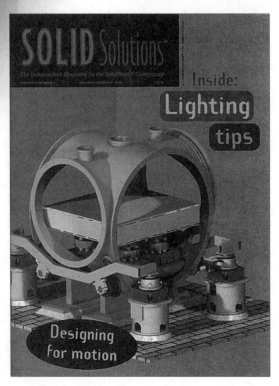